Genealogy
as Critique

Genealogy as Critique

Foucault and the Problems of Modernity

Colin Koopman

Indiana University Press

BLOOMINGTON AND INDIANAPOLIS

This book is a publication of

Indiana University Press
601 North Morton Street
Bloomington, Indiana 47404-3797 USA

iupress.indiana.edu

Telephone orders　800-842-6796
Fax orders　812-855-7931

Library of Congress Cataloging-in-Publication Data

Koopman, Colin.
    Genealogy as critique : Foucault and the problems of modernity / Colin Koopman.
        p. cm. — (American philosophy)
    Includes bibliographical references and index.
    ISBN 978-0-253-00619-6 (cloth : alk. paper) — ISBN 978-0-253-00621-9 (pbk. : alk.
paper) — ISBN 978-0-253-00623-3 (electronic book) 1. Foucault, Michel, 1926–1984. 2.
Genealogy (Philosophy) 3. Kant, Immanuel, 1724–1804. I. Title.
    B2430.F724K66 2013
    194—dc23

                                                                                    2012033557

1 2 3 4 5　18 17 16 15 14 13

"If Foucault is indeed perfectly at home in the philosophical tradition, it is within the *critical* tradition of Kant, and his project could be called the *Critical History of Thought*."

—Michel Foucault in "Foucault, Michel, 1926–" from 1984

"The notion common to all the work that I have done since *History of Madness* is that of problematization."

—Michel Foucault in "The Concern for Truth" from 1984

Contents

Acknowledgments ix

Introduction: What Genealogy Does 1

1. Critical Historiography: Politics, Philosophy & Problematization 24

2. Three Uses of Genealogy: Subversion, Vindication & Problematization 58

3. What Problematization Is: Contingency, Complexity & Critique 87

4. What Problematization Does: Aims, Sources & Implications 129

5. Foucault's Problematization of Modernity: The Reciprocal Incompatibility of Discipline and Liberation 154

6. Foucault's Reconstruction of Modern Moralities: An Ethics of Self-Transformation 182

7. Problematization plus Reconstruction: Genealogy, Pragmatism & Critical Theory 217

Notes *271*
Bibliography *311*
Index *341*

Acknowledgments

Viewed in one way, persons are bundles of debts and credits—who we are is a function of a complex assemblage of affordances offered to us by those who hold us in their various ways and who we, if we are fortunate, are able to hold for a time ourselves. The occasion of completing a book offers the opportunity to look at oneself according to this perspective. Seeing myself in this way, it is clear that the debts that I myself have incurred in the process of this endeavor are many. It is my hope, perhaps an overly ambitious one, that the publication of that for which I have indebted myself will repay in some small way those to whom I owe, with joy, so many thanks.

The material that went into this book has profited enormously from conversations, discussions, and exchanges with a great many persons. The entire manuscript, though in some cases a much earlier version, benefited from careful readings by Amy Allen, Barry Allen, David Couzens Hoy, Ladelle McWhorter, and anonymous press reviewers. Amy Allen and David Hoy were especially involved in many stages of the development of this book—I could not find a way to thank you both enough for your conversation, your stimulation, and your faith in this project. It helps immeasurably much to be able to rely on the credits extended by those to whose work one is directed.

That said, the argumentation and interpretation herein are addressed to many others as well. It is my fortune to be able to acknowledge many of those to whom this work is addressed for having read portions of the manuscript. Paul Rabinow has been particularly generous and characteristically provocative at almost every step—I have benefited immeasurably from both. Others who have been generous in discussing portions of the material herein deserve many thanks: Jim Clifford, Arnold Davidson, Penelope Deutscher, Christoph Durt, Jeff Edmonds, Dan Guevara, Ian Hacking, Lynn Huffer, Carly Lane, Jeremy Livingston, Tomas Matza, Edward McGushin, Paul Patton, Paul Roth, Jana Sawicki, Richard Shusterman, Hans Sluga, Brad Stone, John Stuhr, Ronald Sundstrom, Joseph Tanke, Dianna Taylor, Kevin Thompson, Zach VanderVeen, Christopher Voparil, and Rocío Zambrana. My thanks to you all, and most especially for the maintenance of your disagreements.

This book has been traveling along the West Coast with me for a few years now. Gratitude is therefore due to a not-small and still-growing list of colleagues, interlocutors, and philosophical friends in California and Oregon. While all of those named above have contributed directly to this work in some form, many others were participant with me in the conversations that made this manuscript the book that it now is.

This book began as part of my postdoctoral project at the University of California at Santa Cruz. I thank the Social Sciences and Humanities Research Council of Canada for providing the invaluable opportunity of that uninterrupted research time. I thank David Couzens Hoy for mentorship during my three years at UCSC. I also thank Paul Roth and Jocelyn Hoy for support in a variety of ways, both intellectual and practical, during my tenure at UCSC. Various other philosophical and institutional supports made this time both productive and enjoyable: thanks are due to Jim Clifford, Christoph Durt, Carla Freccero, Dan Guevara, Ian Hacking, Jake Metcalf, and Abe Stone. I would be remiss to leave unacknowledged the students from my Spring 2009 senior seminar on Foucault (in particular I thank Jesse Grove and Jimmy Hardwick); I cannot imagine a more generative seminar than this one, which came at just the right time in the final stages of revision of the first complete draft of this manuscript. Lastly, my most generative venue at UCSC was the "Foucault Across the Disciplines" reading group; among my steadiest collaborators there were Noriko Aso, Tomas Matza, and Daniel Narey.

During the tenure of my post-doc in Santa Cruz, I lived up the coast a little stretch in that romantic neverland called San Francisco. This afforded me ample time over at the University of California at Berkeley, where this book has benefited enormously from a great many conversations and philosophical friendships. I have already mentioned Paul Rabinow, whose example and insight continue to afford much instruction. I would also like to thank other members of the "Anthropology of the Contemporary Research Collaboratory" from whom I have learned immeasurably much about Foucault, social science, anthropology, the life sciences, emerging technologies, and much more: Gaymon Bennett, Stephen Collier, Jim

Faubion, Chris Kelty, Andrew Lakoff, Mary Murrell, Tom Schilling, Meg Stalcup, and Anthony Stavrianakis. My weekly visits also afforded opportunities for enriching conversations on matters related to this project with others over at Cal, including Mark Bevir, Martin Jay, Chris Tenove, and most especially Hans Sluga.

I finished the first versions of this manuscript down in Northern California, and then began the process of polishing it up after pushing northward to the University of Oregon. On my first day on campus a pair of bright graduate students approached me about my work on Foucault. That was the beginnings of the migration of the "Foucault Across the Disciplines" project up to Oregon, where it subsequently became the "Critical Genealogies Collaboratory." My sincere thanks to the steady participants in that group during my first two years in Oregon: Vernon Carter, Elena Clare Cuffari, George Fourlas, Greg Liggett, Katherine Logan, Ed Madison, Nicolae Morar, and Thomas Nail. My recent endeavors have been immeasurably enriched by my colleagues in Oregon. Mark Johnson and Scott Pratt have enriched my understandings of pragmatism (as well as the pragmatics of faculty life)—the material on pragmatism in the final chapter already bears the mark of our shared conversations on Dewey. A philosophical friendship around critical theory with Rocío Zambrana has been my immense good fortune, and the final chapter here bears, I should hope, its stamp—I already know that future work will show an even deeper impression. Thank you all.

Some of the material to follow has found its way into publication in other venues, though in almost every instance fairly significant revisions were involved. I acknowledge the following permissions to reprint. Slim portions of Chapter 1 were previously published in an expanded discussion of genealogy and archaeology in "Foucault's Historiographical Expansion: Adding Genealogy to Archaeology" in *Journal of the Philosophy of History* 2, no. 3 (Fall 2008). Portions of Chapter 2 previously appeared as "Two Uses of Genealogy: Michel Foucault and Bernard Williams" in Carlos Prado (ed.), *Foucault's Legacy* (Continuum Books, 2009), and are reprinted here with permission from the Continuum International Publishing Company. A few paragraphs from Chapter 3 formed the basis of "Historical Critique or Transcendental Critique in Foucault: Two Kantian Lineages" in *Foucault Studies*, no. 8 (Feb., 2010). Chapter 5 was previously published as "Revising Foucault: The History and Critique of Modernity" in *Philosophy & Social Criticism* 36, no. 5 (May, 2010) but is slightly revised here.

I thank Dee Mortensen, my editor at Indiana University Press, and also my series editor John J. Stuhr, for their quick faith in this project and their professionalism in seeing it through. I thank as well Wendy Lochner at Columbia University Press for ongoing advice and encouragement since the publication of my first book with that press.

While the portion of the book that I am responsible for is to be found between the covers, I am grateful for the invitation extended by the cover itself. Marcel Duchamp's *Network of Stoppages* is, in more ways than one, a symbol of what I understand genealogy to be about. Perhaps one day I can write about that at greater length than I have here. I am grateful to the Oregon Humanities Center and the College of Arts and Sciences at the University of Oregon for support with the cover art. I also thank Sarah Eileen Jacobi of Indiana University Press for her diligence in dealing with the details of rights and permissions, and many other details besides.

During the years that went into the work for this book, friends and family have helped me stay afloat through the turbulences of the work of life. My thanks to Aaron Poser, Tommy Thornhill, Bertie Pearson, and Seamus Campbell for stimulating me on so many matters involved in the background of this book—but also for their friendship, a word that means, of course, very much more than we are accustomed to acknowledging on a daily basis. My thanks to my mother, my father, and my grandmother for their steady voices. There are others of you whom I would like to thank—but some of you have gone, and though others of you remain, in various ways, I shall leave it to the pages that follow to body forth the blind impresses my words bear of you.

Church St. and 15th St.
San Francisco, California
June 2011

Genealogy
as Critique

Introduction

What Genealogy Does

What Do Genealogies Do?

Genealogies articulate problems. But not just any problems. Genealogies do not, for instance, take up those problems that come with supposed solutions readily apparent, or those problems that appear difficult to many but are simple for those few who are in the know. Genealogies are generally not targeted at problems that are themselves readily apparent to everyone or even just to everyone who ought to know them. Genealogies are concerned, rather, with submerged problems. The problems of genealogy are those problems found below the surfaces of our lives—the problems whose itches feel impenetrable, whose remedies are ever just beyond our grasp, and whose very articulations require a severe work of thought. These submerged problems are those that condition us without our fully understanding why or how. They are depth problems in that they are lodged deep inside of us all as the historical conditions of possibility of our present ways of doing, being, and thinking. Yet despite their depth, these problems are also right at the surface insofar as they condition us in our every action, our every quality, our every thought, our every sadness and smile.

Convicted concern with depth problems is characteristic of genealogy as a tradition in philosophy. A patient concern with what Michel Foucault called "problematizations" separates genealogists as philosopher-historians from both historians and philosophers. This is not to disparage history, nor philosophy, but only to distinguish them from genealogy, in which of course both of these figure quite prominently. What distinguishes the work of Foucault, Friedrich Nietzsche, Bernard Williams, and other may-be, would-be, and could-be genealogists is a rigorous focus, at once philosophical and historical, on the depth problems that swirl around the heart of who we are. Different genealogists address themselves to our different problematizations in different ways: some denounce them as deficiencies, others applaud them as achievements, and some remain content to illuminate difficulties we have always had some sense of but have not had a sense of how to articulate. The idea of bringing our submerged problems into view so as to do something with them is the thread that runs through all genealogies, though of course this characteristic commitment assumes greater self-consciousness in some genealogies than in others.

My aim here is to explicate genealogical methodology as it figures in the work of a range of thinkers who loosely (and only loosely) constitute a philosophical tradition. My central focus throughout much of the discussion will be on Foucault, but I shall also discuss genealogy as it figures in the work of Nietzsche, Williams, and others. My main claim in this book, following but also extending the work of Foucault, is that genealogy at its best involves a practice of critique in the form of the historical problematization of the present. This statement prompts more questions than it answers at the outset. What does a problematization look like? What is a problematization? How is a problematization different from the regular old problems that, as I said at the outset, are not the object of concern for genealogists? What is a problem that is simultaneously at the depths and all across the surface? Why is problematization privileged in an analysis of the present? Why even privilege the present as a site of inquiry? To begin working toward answers to these questions, it will help to start with a crisp image of genealogy in action.

Perhaps the most appealing image of genealogy is that featured in Foucault's 1976 book *The Will to Know*. This book was published as the first volume of a proposed series of investigations taking the title of *The History of Sexuality*. The French subtitle of the first volume in this series was *La Volonté de savoir*. The whole French title was uncomfortably translated into English as *The History of Sexuality, Volume 1: An Introduction*, uncomfortable because it dropped the French subtitle in its entirety, which should be rendered in English as *The Will to Know*. The publishing-house decision in which the subtitle was lost in (mis)translation was unfortunate in that it obscures what the book labors to make obvious: sexuality not only has a history, but historically emerged where we might least expect it. Sexuality, it is Foucault's argument, comes from a whole congeries of intersecting processes in which practices of knowing were just as important as strategies of power (both of which loom larger than the supposed mandates of our biology).

The Will to Know targets a problem that we take to be one of our most obvious obsessions, one of our most exhilarating engagements, and one of our most constant companions. That problem, or rather that constellation of problems, or better yet that problematization, is sexuality. What is my sexuality? How does it make me? How do I make my sexuality better? How do I gain access to my sex, get my sex, have my sex, make my sex? And how do I deny the sex that is not mine, that rightly should not be of me, and that expresses a sexuality that is not mine? And so on. These are questions all of us know so well to ask. And indeed we know not how to ask them except with fever and fervor—with that particular uptight delight that with us is almost unique to our sexuality. That sex should be so important to us, so crucial for who we are and so constitutive for what we do, suggests that sexuality functions as a great family of problems around which we elaborate ourselves, around which we accrete so many of those little things that comprise our selfhood. Foucault understood sexuality as a problem that is simultaneously submerged deep within us and also teeming and tingling at the very surface of our charged bodies. Foucault writes of this problematization: "In the space of a few centuries, a certain inclination has led us to direct the question of what we are, to sex. . . . Whenever it is a question of knowing who we are, it is this logic that henceforth serves as our master key. . . . Sex, the explanation for everything." Foucault's work on sexuality addressed itself to this great problem of who we are and who we can be. The question his genealogy asked was, "Why this great chase after the truth of sex, the truth in sex?" His genealogy, then, would take the form of "the history of a stubborn and relentless effort" whereby we have become "enthralled by sex."[1]

Sexuality is a great problem at the heart of who we are in the present. No one would deny this. But if others before Foucault had also asked this question, they had taught us to look for a single answer, a single key that would unravel in a splendid instant the knotted tangle of threads comprising our sexuality. The totalizing explanations of the nineteenth century (but, yes, they persist even today) had taught us to look for a golden thread amidst the many that form the knots of who we are. Foucault instead offered an approach that would seek to discern all of the various threads in their specificity so as to grasp the ways in which they had been woven together into a new singularity, or a singularly new problematization. He wrote directly against those other approaches: "There is no single, all-encompassing strategy, valid for all of society and uniformly bearing on all the manifestations of sex."[2] Where others had searched for a single, searing explanation, Foucault looked for a network of multiplicitous strategies. We are, Foucault says, "dealing less with *a* discourse on sex than with a multiplicity of discourses produced by a whole series of mechanisms operating in different institutions."[3]

The Will to Know attempted to capture the scintillating singularity that is sexuality in all of its massive multiplicity. It did so in part by outlining a series of future inquiries into that tangled problematization through which was formed, beginning in the eighteenth and nineteenth centuries and carrying through the twentieth century and now into our own times, the sexual problem at the heart of who we are. Among the multiplicity Foucault proposes to explore are the sciences of sexuality (including psychiatry, developmental psychology, pedagogy, demography, epidemiology), the medicalization of sexuality, the privileged place of the family in modern society, the pervasive strategy of confession inherited through religious sensibility, and the place of criminal justice and the law in securing society and disciplining deviance. This diversity, Foucault taught us, was knit together into that strange thing, simultaneously present and mysterious to us all, of modern sexuality. What is more plain to us and yet also more inscrutable to us than our sexuality?

Genealogy is designed to capture—that is to say, to articulate—such strange singularities. Of sexuality, Foucault claims that "It is the name that can be given to a historical construct [*dispositif*]: not a furtive reality that is difficult to grasp, but a great surface network in which the stimulation of bodies, the intensification of pleasures, the incitement to discourse, the formation of special knowledges, the strengthening of controls and resistances, are linked to one another, in accordance with a few major strategies of knowledge and power."[4] Genealogy articulates strange singularities by fashioning concepts that make visible linkages, assemblages, and networks, particularly with an eye to their overall coherence. The point, in part, is to help us see how that coherence was contingently composed, since a history of such a thing as sexuality surely shows us that any coherence sexuality may still have for us is not an inevitable imposition so much as something that we construct for, or deploy on, ourselves. In an interview given shortly after his book's publication, Foucault tells us that what his genealogical method reveals is "a thoroughly heterogeneous ensemble consisting of discourses, institutions, architectural forms, regulatory decisions, laws, administrative measures, scientific statements, philosophical, moral and philanthropic propositions."[5] Understanding how sexuality makes us who we are requires a methodology that exposes us and makes us answerable to all of this and much else besides. This methodological style, along with its advantages and its prospects, are my primary concern in this book.

What Is Genealogy?

This is a book about genealogy. A central aim of this book is to explicate genealogy in such a way as to show that it offers a valuable, effective, and uniquely important practice of philosophical-historical critique of the present. A motivating thought for this project is that a careful exploration of what genealogy involves can function to sponsor more effective uses of genealogical methodology when future philosopher-historians undertake critical inquiries in the shadows and under the guidance of existing genealogical critiques. If we philosopher-historians are going to produce genealogies by undertaking genealogical inquiries and launching genealogical critiques of our own, and more and more of us have been eager to do so in recent years, we need to be able to say something about what genealogy is, how genealogy functions, when genealogy does its work well, and why genealogy is distinct from other forms of philosophical and historical inquiry.

It is surprising how ill-equipped we are to answer these questions. It is surprising, in part, because over the past decade or so "genealogy" has turned into a somewhat trendy label in the academy. It sometimes seems as if anyone who does history and is not themself a historian is eager to describe their work as a "genealogy."[6] I have read many books and articles purporting to be genealogical in design. But few of them have said much, if anything at all, about what it means to be genealogical beyond offering a vague appeal to something called "history in philosophy," frequently combined with a reference or two to Foucault or Nietzsche. I have attended a host of conference presentations where speakers have claimed to offer a genealogy in the vein of Foucault, or Nietzsche, or both. But on many of these occasions, I was surprised by the way in which presenters who had in the course of their talks gracefully spoken of genealogy instantly stammered and stuttered when confronted by a deceptively simple question I now like to ask: "Could you tell me what a genealogy is as distinct from work that is just generally historical?" Too often these questions were answered with, again, vague appeals to something about how history shows us that taken necessities are really contingent. Such claims may be apt, but they do not claim enough to take us far in understanding what genealogies are.

Though genealogy is much in vogue today, it is widely misunderstood and malappropriated. This, of course, is the tendency of the trendy. We need not allow fashion to dictate our terms to us where rigor and creativity ought rather to provide our guidance. The widespread lack of self-consciousness about what makes a genealogy leads to too much work that is strictly anti-genealogical in design even if it is genealogical in label. Upon scrutiny it turns out that many of the histories that call themselves genealogies have very little to do with the methods, styles, and ideas at work in the philosophical tradition of genealogy as represented by Foucault, Nietzsche, Williams, and others who are, on any accounting, surely representative of genealogy. All of this may be fine, of course, because no one should get to own a word. But what is disconcerting is that the proliferation of genealogies too often discourages careful attention to the way in which the best genealogies are crafted with painstaking patience. For in these genealogies we find a method of severe thought that is both more rigorous and more creative than is typical of the myriad fashions in our midst.

There are, of course, prominent exceptions to my narrative. But they remain exceptions, and not the rule. I am grateful for the exceptions, as well as for the guidance they have afforded me in the course of my inquiries, and so I shall be eager to call attention to these exceptions in my discussions here. The majority of my own work on these matters is indebted to Foucault, and thus also to the work of a very small share of thinkers in whose work I find a critical redeployment of Foucault's genealogies.[7] Following this work on some, but only some, points, I understand genealogy as a singular effort to consider how philosophical critique can bring historical inquiry into its orbit.

I will say more about this in what follows, but one orienting feature of my approach is a commitment to the view that genealogy is primarily a methodological, or analytical, or diagnostic, toolkit. To frame this point it is helpful to make an initial distinction between critical *methods* (e.g., genealogy, archaeology, problematization) and critical *concepts* (e.g., discipline and biopower in Foucault or slave morality in Nietzsche) developed in the course of the deployment of those methods.[8] This distinction helps make visible that genealogy *as a method* is not so much about discipline or biopolitics as it is about a philosophico-historical inquiry into the conditions that make possible problems such as modern sexuality and modern punishment. There is, unfortunately, much work today that calls itself genealogical despite deploying methodological procedures that are better described in terms of what I like to call "biopower-hunting." The procedure of this work seems to be that of ferreting out the nefarious hidden workings of biopower (or disciplinary power, or slavish morality) in some context where its appearance was perhaps unexpected. Although such work bears obvious conceptual relations to Foucault's work, methodologically it is no closer to his genealogies than is old-fashioned ideological unmasking. The view I forward here is that the strengths of Foucault's concepts (discipline, biopower, self-care, etc.) depend in large part on his methodological ensemble (genealogy, archaeology, problematization, etc.). If we detach those concepts from the methods in which they function, they often lose their critical grip, and quite often they lose it rather quickly. By contrast, the methods, construed as analytical and diagnostic equipment, can be made to travel well without the concepts that specific inquiries have uncovered. This means that we can redeploy genealogical method to facilitate inquiries into the problematic aspects of our contemporary condition that Foucault himself could hardly have anticipated. It may be the case that discipline or biopower exerts its pressure in these contexts, too, but that is a question to be answered through genealogical inquiry rather than decided in advance as a merely conceptual matter.

Revising Genealogy and Revising Foucault

In this work I aim for severe and substantial revision of the tradition (genealogy) and figure (Foucault) that I take as my primary focus. It will be useful to make plain at the outset that many of the arguments, expositions, and provocations of this book are motivated by the thought that Foucaultian genealogy has been poorly understood in crucial ways by many if not most of its more zealous detractors and more dedicated defenders. This in turn has led to the malappropriations of genealogy through which the force of this tradition is evacuated of too much of its critical potency. All of this poses notable difficulties since both genealogy and Foucault have over the past few decades come to possess an influence in the contemporary intellectual landscape that is nothing short of enormous. This juxtaposition of influence and misinterpretation suggests that the time may now be ripe for a radical revision of received wisdom.

There are two primary ways in which I propose a revision to our understanding of Foucaultian genealogy. One concerns Foucault's relation to one of the centermost thinkers of our modernity, namely Immanuel Kant, in whom I discern an invaluable predecessor for Foucault's project of critique (but also Nietzsche's and probably also, in an indirect way, Williams's). A second way in which I develop my revision concerns Foucault's unique practice of Kantian critique, which he called *problematization* (and here I find an important distinction from both Nietzsche and Williams). Taking these two thoughts seriously enables a major reinterpretation of Foucault and the practice of genealogy.

To locate the importance of these interpretive shifts, and the philosophical adjustments they enable, it will help to briefly consider the context of the reception of Foucault in recent Anglophone academia and the locations that have been as-cribed to him on the familiar terrains of our contemporary intellectual landscapes. (In explicitly prioritizing Foucault's position in the Anglophone intellectual land-scape over his position in the Francophone world, I do not mean to suggest that the latter is unimportant, but rather that my own context for approaching Fou-cault is the uses to which his work is put in the circles I travel through.[9]) The story of Foucault's reception from across the channel and ocean is a complex and heterogeneous one. Simplifying somewhat, I discern two primary strands of reception in these Anglophone contexts: one is vastly more dominant than the other, and it is the minority strand of reception that I shall here seek to rejuvenate and extend.

The majority strand of reception reads Foucault's enormous interpretive ap-paratus through that loose amalgam of thought arising out of literary criticism and cultural studies that is often referred to today under the deceptively simple ban-ner of "theory." Thus it was that Foucault's thought migrated over the ocean and then throughout our vast interiors largely by way of a readership whose tuition has been in the disciplines of literary criticism and the various offshoots of critical and cultural studies it has vigorously produced in recent decades. This reception by way of literary and cultural studies has largely structured the ways in which Foucault has filtered into many of the other disciplines that are a little slower (but only a little) to take up work not originally published in English. Thus, to take my own disciplinary backyard of philosophy as an example, what is usually de-nounced or defended in Foucault by philosophers are not the fine-grained details of his inquiries nor even the methodological toolkit he used to undertake his re-search, but rather his "theories" of truth, power, modernity, and other venerable philosophical topics that most readers draw out of his portraits of prisons, asy-lums, and so on. The prevailing readings, pro and con, of Foucault amongst phi-losophers are in large part an effect of reading him as "doing theory" or "taking philosophical positions" rather than "undertaking inquiry." The usage of Foucault in other disciplines such as sociology, anthropology, and most obviously literary theory has quite often taken a similar course. Those employing him in these dis-ciplines almost always borrow from the part of his work that seems impressively "(high) theory" rather than the part that is "(modestly) empirical."

Consider now a different, and more minority, strand of reception that con-tinues to have an important presence in the way Foucault is often invoked today. This strand of reception can be discerned in certain corners of philosophy (namely, amongst philosophers of science using his work on knowledge formation, politi-cal philosophers using his work on power, and moral philosophers using his work on ancient ethics) and in the social sciences (most notably amongst small circles of anthropologists, sociologists, and historians). For this strand of reception, Foucault does not so much provide a warrant for certain theoretical positions as he provides equipment for certain practices of critical inquiry. This second strand is best seen through a pair of representatives. The more philosophical wing of this strand is ably represented in the work of Ian Hacking, who as early as the 1970s was already charting out the possibilities of a Foucault-influenced philosophy and history of science. A useful representative of the more social science–oriented wing of this strand is anthropologist Paul Rabinow, who spent much time with Foucault in his visits to Berkeley in the last years of his life and who co-authored with philosopher Hubert Dreyfus an invaluable early book on Foucault's place in contemporary thought. Both of these representatives use Foucault for both philosophical and social scientific purposes in their work, despite their sometimes leaning more toward one direction than the other.[10] In the interpretations and arguments that follow I shall be particularly eager to argue that this second strand of reception offers better means for interpreting and redeploying Foucault's work. Foucault, I argue, is a philosophical social scientist more so than a "theorist." Take, for a quick example, Foucault on power: perhaps most well known for his work on power, Foucault does not even have a "theory" of power but rather conducted rigorous inquiries, part philosophical and part social-scientific, into diverse and dynamic forms of power constitutive of who we are today. Frequently accused of having a wrongheaded theory of power, Foucault in fact made the point that power is not the kind of thing that is valuably theorized, if by that we mean creating conceptions of power without empirically inquiring into the actual functionings of power in carefully delineated contexts. The context of empirical-analytical inquiry was, for Foucault, the space where the work of thought is at its most urgent. As he stated: "[T]he analyses of these mechanisms of power . . . is not in any way a general theory of what power is. It is not a part or even the start of such a theory. The analysis simply involves investigating where and how, between whom, between what points, according to what processes, and with what effects, power is applied."[11] Not a theory of what power is, then, but an investigative inquiry into how power works.

Both of the two strands of reception I have named are probably better thought of as two massive cables themselves composed of a diversity of strands. With the metaphor adjusted, we can say that both of these cables remain enormously important to a diversity of fields of research today, but equally as important are the strong tensions between the two. Despite wide acknowledgment of the importance of the philosophical-historical-anthropological-sociological readings of Foucault, the

American embrace of Foucault is in large part premised on the terms offered by the amalgamated literary-cultural-theory strand of reception. This is even the case for most of the philosophers, sociologists, and anthropologists who mine Foucault for certain concepts and criticisms that more fully reflect the literary-cultural-theory framing of his thought. One central aim of this book is to correct the misplaced weight of emphasis that has accumulated over the years as a result of a one-sided reception of Foucault's accomplishments. Much of what follows can therefore be seen as an attempt to reread Foucault along those lines laid down early on by a small handful of interpreters-cum-users, carefully cultivated ever since by them and by others impressed by their work, and increasingly important today when our cultural moment calls not for some revolutionary promise implicit in postmodernism so much as the rigorous practice explicit in genealogical apparatuses for critique and inquiry. Explicating Foucault in this way helps situate his work as part of a loose tradition that should come to seem rather distant from that equally loose tradition involving the construction of "French Theory."

Many of the literary critics, cultural-studies scholars, and theorists who brought Foucault to the American academy did so by preparing his work as just one part of that broader program of French Theory that possessed for a while an enormous appeal for an ever-restless readership in the American academy. This unfortunately served to align the specific critical intervention of Foucault's work with the themes of a much broader postmodern assault whose principal protagonists are generally claimed to be (along with Foucault himself) Jean Baudrillard, Jean-François Lyotard, Jacques Lacan, and more recently Giorgio Agamben. The most common alignment in this vein, despite its implausibility at least as I read them both, is that of Foucault with Jacques Derrida. This is an alignment that Derrida himself has promoted, despite his prominent early criticisms of Foucault, when in his later work he referred to his own enterprise more than once as "deconstructive genealogy" despite the fact that nothing even resembling a genealogy is to be found in Derrida's rather speculative histories of ideas.[12] Commenting on these and other alignments, French intellectual historian François Cusset suggests that Foucault's reception on this side of the Atlantic "provided his American readers with a veritable *conspiracy theory*, in the name of which they scoured society to uncover its aggressors and victims." Cusset argues, rightly I think, that such an enterprise in unmasking "stands in direct opposition to Foucault's genealogical method" insofar as his work offers "an *analytics* of power, not an axiology of it."[13] When American readers interpret Foucault as a master of suspicion alongside the familiar heroes (most often cast as villains) of postmodernity, they should be seen as not so much focusing on Foucault himself as on that vast lobby of American

Foucaultianism that has come to define his work for readers on this side of the Atlantic. We are awash in interpretations of Foucault that purport to chart the dynamic career of a French philosopher but that much more realistically trace the contours of the late twentieth-century American academy's appropriation of almost every major Francophone philosopher. This filtering of Foucault not only distorts our image of his thought but—even worse—serves to appropriate it for intellectual pursuits that Foucault himself gave us good reason to be wary of.

The ease with which Foucault is so frequently categorized with the bellwethers of French Theory stands in striking contrast to the puzzlement that is often expressed at suggestions for reading Foucault alongside a quite different set of thinkers including, for instance, Thomas Kuhn, Willard Van Orman Quine, John Dewey, and even Richard Rorty and Jürgen Habermas. Foucault, we are told, is opposed on every important point to these supposedly stodgy sages—we were even told this by some of these sages themselves.

We have labored for too long under this supposed sagacity. I propose to read in Foucault a different series of conjunctures and connections. This requires returning to the second of my two strands of reception and restating the importance of Foucault in the terms offered by a small number of interlocutors and users of Foucault and the genealogical armamentarium to which he contributed his tools. This second strand of reception facilitates comparing Foucault with certain other twentieth-century philosophers who have sought to transform Kant's critical project on the basis of elements internal to that project. Like the Kantian pragmatists and Kantian critical theorists, Foucault always advocated patient and detailed inquiry concerning the most poignant cultural problems of the present. Foucault was not unlike Dewey or Habermas when he took up genealogy as a tool for inquiring into the historical conditions of the possibility of certain broad cultural formations that impact our ways of being in the present. Nor was he unlike them when he offered up his inquiries as providing the conceptual and practical materials we would need to conduct immanent critique for the purposes of transforming our cultural formations such that they might become less oppressive and more democratic.

My alternative to the postmodern amalgam that would adopt genealogy into its family circus is a plainer modern philosophical trio composed of genealogy, pragmatism, and critical theory. I previously argued for this combination from the perspective of pragmatism in my first book, *Pragmatism as Transition: Historicity and Hope in James, Dewey, and Rorty*.[14] The present book develops the same argument but with the different emphases required by taking the perspective of genealogy. The tradition of critical theory, while not the primary topic of either book, figures in both as a friendly ally for the pragmatists and genealogists alike. This triadic as-semblage is proposed on the basis of the ways in which these three philosophical traditions represent three potentially compatible ways of taking up the project of modern critical philosophy and transforming that project into forms that are suit-able for cultural critique into the twentieth, and we now also hope twenty-first, century. Foucault should be approached as someone who developed a rich set of analytic, diagnostic, and conceptual tools that can be taken up in the present for purposes of a critical inquiry into the present. This is exactly what Dewey (and others before and after him) did for pragmatism and also exactly what Habermas (and others before and after him) did for critical theory.

I thus implicitly adopt in this book a metaphilosophical orientation accord-ing to which we need not approach genealogy in search of a philosophical system or even a set of philosophical truths. There is no reason to think that Foucault got everything right. Not only would this be entirely unlikely; it is more importantly utterly needless. We can take from genealogy the richness of its best resources, take from other philosophical traditions their best resources, and leave behind those parts of past philosophies we find wanting. In this way I show how Foucault can be profitably read as equipping us with resources we can use to perform our own critical inquiries of our own present. Foucault helps us see our way to a prac-tice of philosophy as a critical inquiry into the complex and contingent formation of the present in which we find ourselves. Such a revision of philosophical prac-tice is crucial today. For if we are to reconstruct our present so that it may yield better futures, we first need a grip on the materials out of which our present has been constructed in the past. Perhaps this diagnostic grip is the greatest advantage of genealogical philosophy. That genealogy may fall short in other areas, including that of remedying for the future what has been diagnosed historically, need not be taken as a refutation of genealogy. For we can draw on multiple philosophical traditions to better perform our critical inquiries, and perhaps it is the case that pragmatism and critical theory can fill in for the purposes of forward-looking re-construction what genealogy leaves out. In doing so, we need not concern our-selves with supposed philosophical incompatibilities that are generated mostly as an effect of the old exegetical tendency of insisting that one philosophical figure or one philosophical tradition has got to get everything right.

In forwarding the above-sketched reinterpretation of Foucault against the grain of much of the scholarly (mis)reception, I am braced by two crucially impor-tant self-reflections offered by Foucault in the final year of his life. I take these self-reflections as epigrammatic for this book insofar as many of my arguments here can be seen as taking shape in the light they cast over the entirety of Foucault's corpus. I find it justifiable to cast the light of these self-reflections so widely because Foucault himself explicitly offered these self-reflections as comments upon the entire body of his philosophical-historical inquiries. These epigrams can be summarized in two slogans: Foucault as Kantian, and Genealogy as Problematization.

Foucault as Kantian

Here is my first epigram: "If Foucault is indeed perfectly at home in the philosophical tradition, it is within the *critical* tradition of Kant, and his project could be called the *Critical History of Thought*."[15] Now, reflect on this for a minute. We have here the claim that if Foucault is a philosopher at all, then he is a critical philosopher in the tradition of Kant. A remarkable claim: intriguing and provocative yet eminently plausible in its simplicity.

This is the first sentence from the second paragraph of Foucault's only explicitly autobiographical writing. He prepared this text with the aid of François Ewald, his then research assistant at the Collège de France, for publication in the *Dictionnaire des philosophes* published in 1984. Whatever we make of this self-reflection in terms of its self-reflective acuity, it clearly demonstrates that Foucault thought of himself as at least in some crucial respects a Kantian critical philosopher. Once we begin to take this claim seriously, it turns out to be entirely less surprising than it might appear at first glance. There is, in actual fact, only one figure in the history of thought who appears in all of Foucault's writings in each of his so-called periods of scholarship and who thus has unbroken central standing in Foucault's thought from the very beginning of his career right up to the tragic end of his life. That figure is Immanuel Kant.

Here is Foucault on Kant in a work that was among his earliest (his *thèse complémentaire*, written around 1960 as an introduction to his own translation of Kant's *Anthropology from a Pragmatic Point of View* into French): "In addition to its particular role as a 'propaedeutics' to philosophy, the *Critique* would have also played a constitutive part in the birth and the development of the concrete forms of human existence. Hence there would be a certain *critical* truth to man, a truth born of the critique of the conditions of truth."[16] Only a few years later we hear strong echoes of this Kantian theme in a book published at the height of Foucault's archaeological period, namely his 1966 *The Order of Things*: "We attempt to question afresh the limits of thought, and to renew contact in this way with the project for a general critique of reason."[17] In 1973, during those years in which he was working on his provocative genealogies of modernity and in which his references to Kant are at their most ambiguous, Foucault wrote: "I am convinced that there exist, if not exactly structures, then at least rules for the functioning of knowledge which have arisen in the course of history and within which can be located the various subjects."[18] A few years later, in 1978, Kant is again a very visible presence: "In his attempt to desubjugate the subject in the context of power and truth, as a prolegomena to the whole present and future *Aufklärung*, Kant set forth critique's primordial responsibility, to know knowledge."[19] And finally here is Foucault in 1984 during those final years when his references to Kant were frequent and unabashed: "The point, in brief, is to transform the critique conducted in the form of necessary limitation into a practical critique that takes the form of a possible crossing-over."[20]

Given the unshakeable fact of Foucault's unbroken interest in Kant's critical project, it is thoroughly surprising to note that many of his readers have by and large failed to take Foucault's claims to the Kantian legacy seriously.[21] Many commentators have gone to great lengths to show that Foucault must be read through or alongside some other towering figure from the history of philosophy. The most notable version of this story reads Foucault through Nietzsche—another story, one I find far less likely, reads a great deal of Heidegger in Foucault.[22] Another notable interpretive strategy involves focusing on a diverse set of more proximate influences—here emphasis is frequently laid upon the generation of French philosophers immediately preceding Foucault, such as George Canguilhem, Jean-Paul Sartre, Louis Althusser, and contemporaries of his own generation such as Gilles Deleuze or Paul Veyne. There is no need to deny that all of these thinkers, and many others too, equipped Foucault with key ideas that crucially informed much of his work. My claim is just that we ought to take seriously that it was Foucault's own view that Kant was certainly among those who most centrally informed multiple ranges of his philosophical and historical projects. Foucault's clear claims in his final years that his work is best understood as critical in the tradition of Kant can be given due weight without denying the copresence of other influential figures and traditions that Foucault also acknowledged. What has been denied, or at least overlooked, is Kant's influence on Foucault's thought. Whereas Nietzsche was undoubtedly important for Foucault, as was Deleuze, as were many others whose thought is frequently mined for explanations of Foucaultian themes, we should be prepared to not only acknowledge but also embrace the Kantian inflection of (almost) everything Foucault.

I should make plain that I persist in this interpretive strategy not out of fidelity to Foucault so much as out of interest in the philosophical and historical riches yielded by approaching his work as invested in a broadly Kantian project. Many, but of course not all, of Foucault's philosophical positions, methodological innovations, and historical inquiries are helpfully understood as internal transformations of the Kantian program of critique. Foucault's inquiries should be understood as investigations of the conditions of the possibility of the practices whose critique they perform. It is only in terms of Kant's critical project that the entirety of Foucault's work can be brought into focus as a transformative reworking of that project. The claim, of course, is not that Foucault is a Kantian through and through, by the book and to the letter. The claim, rather, is that Foucault's thought embodies a complex relation to Kant's thought, a relation that might be described as a transformative renewal of the Kantian critical project from within. That transformative renewal might be summarily described as follows: whereas Kant undertook a transcendental critique of the various employments of our reason, Foucault undertook a historical critique of the various deployments of our thought.

Kant described critique as a determination of the limits of our thought on the basis of an inquiry into the conditions of possibility of that thought itself. For Kant's project of an inquiry into the conditions of possibility of human thought *a priori*, critique had to be taken up as a transcendental project such that the regulative conditions of different employments of human reason form universal and necessary limits for that reason. Foucault was not interested in the transcendental conditions of possibility that were central for Kant's general inquiry into human thought *a priori*. Foucault was interested rather in the historical conditions of possibility that constrain singular forms of thought in the present. Foucault wrote in one of his final essays, an essay that is largely about Kant and titled after one of Kant's own essays, that "Criticism is no longer going to be practiced in the search for formal structures with universal value but, rather, as a historical investigation into the events that have led us to constitute ourselves and to recognize ourselves as subjects of what we are doing, thinking, saying."[23] Foucault shifted Kantian critique from the transcendental plane to the historical (that is, the archaeological and genealogical) field. This shift enabled Foucault to maintain important philosophical connections to Kant's project while at the same time transforming that project.

Critique connotes both decision and discrimination, at once crisis and cutting. Critique is etymologically linked to a confrontation with moments of crisis (which we today colloquially refer to as "critical moments") that call forth cleavages, cuts, or divisions in our thought (our colloquial expression here is "critical decision").[24] A critique is a practice of dividing, and as such carries with it enormous importance. Kant practiced critique so as to rigorously specify the divisions in our thought that he believed offered unsurpassable limits that thought cannot go beyond without generating paralogisms. Foucault practiced critique also for the purposes of rigorously specifying divisions that define the limits of our thought

But whereas for Kant transcendental critique would describe limits that we must not tread beyond, for Foucault genealogical and archaeological critique would describe our practices of division in such a way as to call forth experimentation on what we take to be the limits of our selves.

Foucault's theme of critique's transformative potential can be seen in a quick parade of quotations. The first is from his last essay on Kantian critique: "The critique of what we are is at one and the same time the historical analysis of the limits imposed on us and an experiment with the possibility of going beyond them."[25] Next is another often-quoted line: "Maybe the target nowadays is not to discover what we are but to refuse what we are."[26] Consider finally the following lines from an interview: "To do criticism is to make harder those acts which are now too easy. Understood in these terms, criticism (and radical criticism) is utterly indispensable for any transformation. . . . As soon as people begin to have trouble thinking things the way they have been thought, transformation becomes at the same time very urgent, very difficult, and entirely possible."[27] If Kantian critique is an inquiry into the ways we must be, Foucaultian critique is an inquiry that provokes us to transform ourselves into being otherwise. The crucial difference that separates these two conceptions of critique is that which divides philosophers of necessity from thinkers of contingency. The span between these two, and their attendant worldviews, measures the distance of the long nineteenth century that irrevocably separates Kant and Foucault. Once we passed through the evolutionisms and historicisms of that century, as well as the emergence of probability and statistics and their spawned ascendance of the order of information, there was much in the past that we could no longer go back to—the early modern idea of necessity stands out as one thing that was decisively lost. And yet despite the many rifts separating our age from that of Kant, the idea of critique was indeed carried over the divides, and triumphantly so, such that it remains with us today. We need our Kantian inheritance, but we need it differently than did Kant in his day. Although clearly not identical with Kant's transcendental critique of our various employments of reason, I thus take Foucault's critique, as Foucault himself did, to be born of the same spirit, attitude, or ethos that informed the core of Kant's philosophical inquiry.[28]

Genealogy as Critical Problematization

One advantage of rereading Foucault as a Kantian is that it enables us to approach his work through a fresh set of conceptual angles. Foucault is a Kantian in that his primary philosophical practice is that of critique in a technical sense that he inherited through Kant at the same time as he was transforming that inheritance. Foucault described that particular form of critique that informs his work as follows: "The notion common to all the work that I have done since *History of Madness* is that of problematization."[29] I take this as my second epigrammatic text. It suggests that the critical inquiries Foucault developed under the auspices of the analytic and diagnostic procedures of archaeology and genealogy are best seen as problematizations of our present. It is a primary aim of this book to show that what Foucault called problematization is a form of critique in Kant's sense but also a transformation of the practice of critique itself.

Foucault's transformative appropriation of Kant's critical project is best understood as deploying critical inquiry for the purposes of the problematization of our historical present. Kant's and Foucault's projects are both properly critical in that they are inquiries into the conditions of the possibility forming the limits of our human ways of being. Foucault explains in "The Subject and Power" that this is exactly the theme in Kant that he finds essential and that he sees as being carried forward in a certain philosophical tradition from Hegel to Nietzsche. He notes, first, that "Kant's question appears as an analysis of both us and our present." Foucault was well aware that there are other strains in Kant's philosophy that have been carried forward through certain dominant traditions in contemporary professional philosophy, noting dutifully that "The other aspect of 'universal philosophy' didn't disappear." But his primary point is that there is an additional strain in the Kantian tradition that is not reducible to, or rather reliant upon, its universalism. This second strain is rigorously focused on the singularity of the present and its limits. And it is this strain which Foucault finds important for us today: "But the task of philosophy as a critical analysis of our world is something that is more and more important. Maybe the most certain of all philosophical problems is the problem of the present time, and of what we are in this very moment."[30]   *↗ discursive introduction*

Foucault's project of critical inquiry is very much like Kant's in that both conceive the practice of critique as a prolegomenon to judgment. Neither Foucault nor Kant found judgment to be an unworthy exercise. Yet their primary concern was not to make judgments themselves (whether of an epistemic, moral, aesthetic, or teleological variety) so much as it was a form of critique that would describe the conditions of possibility (be they transcendental or genealogical) of our capacities for various forms of judgment. Recognizing this point goes a long way toward understanding Foucault's project as something other than a sophisticated expression of postmodern resentment issuing harsh judgments about various grand ideals constitutive of our modernity. Foucault in his historico-philosophical critiques did not issue judgments for or against the pantheon of glowing modern ideals, but rather elaborated the complex and contingent conditions of the emergence and stability of the practices in which these ideals found themselves expressed. In this way he provided us with many of the materials we would need to transform these practices, and their conceptual underpinnings, if we are to intervene into the locales where they operate. This explicates the sense in which Foucaultian critique is properly understood as an exercise in problematization. Foucault's involvement in the transformation of the present is valuable only to the extent that the present is problematic. But who ever thought that reason, illness, freedom, and power are unproblematic?

By reinterpreting Foucault's primary analytics of genealogy and archaeology in terms of his concept of problematization, as Foucault himself proposed near the end of his life, we can distinguish Foucaultian critique from other prominent engagements with history that have proceeded under the banner of archaeology and genealogy so as to arrive at a judgment. Specifically, I shall be arguing, we can distinguish Foucault's problematizating genealogy from the vindicatory genealogy of Bernard Williams (this is perhaps predictable) as well as from the subversive genealogy of Friedrich Nietzsche (certainly this thought is a bit more provocative). Whereas Williams and Nietzsche used genealogy to cast judgments on certain concepts (truthfulness and morality, for example) and the practices instantiating them, Foucault used genealogy to critically investigate the conditions of the possibility of the practical exercise of such concepts. The purpose of Foucault's unique conception of genealogy as problematization is to make manifest the constitutive and regulative conditions of the present as a material for thought and action that we would need to work on if we are to transform that present. If other genealogists have aimed at vindication or subversion of the problematizations at the heart of who we are, Foucault aims at a practice that would reveal our problematizations to facilitate their further transformation.

I wish, however, to note at the outset that my primary reason for engaging Williams and Nietzsche in what follows is not to encourage dismissal of their views. I hope rather to enter into conversation with two thinkers who I, perhaps idiosyncratically, cannot but take very seriously indeed. Recognizing the enormous value in the work of Nietzsche and Williams, there are indeed aspects of their genealogies that can and should inform and enrich our interpretation of Foucault's conception of genealogy. And regardless of scholarly compunction about Foucault, it needs be observed that genealogy, as something of a tradition in philosophy, is constituted as a tradition precisely insofar as there are productive internal disagreements. Traditions are always traditions of debate. One crucial item of debate amongst genealogists, then, concerns how to bring history to bear within the work of philosophical critique.

My broader reinterpretation of genealogy, especially Foucault's genealogy, as historicizing critique raises a crucial challenge. That challenge is to preserve a space for the core critical project of inquiring into conditions of possibility while at the same time bringing these conditions into focus by way of historical forms of critique that enable us to grasp their undeniable contingency and complexity. Can we preserve a place for the constraints of conditions of possibility in the field of historicity and temporality? A signal contribution of genealogical philosophy has been that of developing an array of affirmative answers to this question. At the heart of these answers is a vision of critique as an inquiry into those historical conditions of possibility that constrain us not with the iron fist of necessity but with the gentle yet persuasive arm of contingency. Genealogy explicates the contingency and complexity of our ongoing historical constitution. Genealogy also preserves a space for the potential universalizability of these conditions of possibility. An emphasis on contingency and complexity is compatible with an understanding of our practices as universalizable if we make a crucial but often neglected distinction between universalism as a static condition and universalization as a conditioned but conditioning process. Genealogy focuses on our constitutive constraints as temporal-historical processes of universalization that are contingent and complex all the way down. In this way genealogy ably inflects the practice of critique as an inquiry into conditions of possibility with a historicist rather than a transcendentalist sensibility.

This last point helps make plain the compatibility of genealogy, especially Foucault's Kantian genealogy, with those strains of Kantian-inspired critical theory and pragmatism already mentioned. For genealogists share with both pragmatists and critical theorists an invaluable but undervalued vision of philosophy as a tool for critical inquiry into the problems of present. In all three cases this stands in marked contrast to the exhausted image of philosophy as a tool for judgment, a weapon of truth, a sword of system. Thus I discern in genealogy, critical theory, and pragmatism the possibility for a renewal of critical inquiry in the present. This is much needed today.

The Plan of the Book

Foucault tells us that his work belongs in the critical tradition of Kant. He tells us that his work is offered in the mode of problematization. It has been nearly a quarter of a century since Foucault left us with these interpretations of his own work. What is to be gained by affirming these claims now? How might they enable us to pick up Foucault differently and put his work to use for different purposes? This book is, at least in part, a response to these and other questions concerning the potentialities of genealogy in the present. A brief overview of the arguments that follow in the sequel will be of use.

In Chapter 1 I begin by developing an account of problematization as the key to Foucault's historical-philosophical method. The central idea here is that of "the history of the present" as a critical practice of problematization that is simultaneously philosophical and political. I first use this idea to review the vexed question of the relation between archaeology and genealogy in Foucault. Rather than instituting a deep methodological break in Foucault's work, as is often argued, I show how genealogy is an expansion, not an abdication, of archaeology. I then use this idea to bring into initial focus the notion of problematization as a kind of master concept for Foucault's methodology. I conclude the chapter with a metaphorical image meant to facilitate a synoptic interpretation of Foucault's *oeuvre*, which it will be the task of later chapters to prove the worth of. In sum, my claim is that reading critical problematization as Foucault's central philosophical task enables us to assess the periodization of his work from a new perspective. This new assessment helps us see why there is just one Foucault (a problematizing Foucault) rather than, as the standard stories have it, three (on one read, an epistemic Foucault, a political Foucault, and an ethical Foucault, and on another read, an early, middle, and late Foucault).

If the first chapter addresses genealogy through a synoptic take on the figure of Foucault, then Chapter 2 addresses genealogy in more diversified fashion as a tradition of philosophical-historical thought. This chapter is largely a comparative effort of discriminating three different uses or modalities of genealogy. I distinguish Foucault's conception of genealogy as problematization from the subversive genealogy of Friedrich Nietzsche and the vindicatory genealogy of Bernard Williams. My preferred lens for elucidating this contrast is provided by the familiar criticism that genealogy commits the genetic fallacy in conflating genesis and justification. I suggest that although this criticism has some purchase on Nietzsche and Williams, it does not apply to Foucault because he did not undertake genealogies with the purpose of affirming or negating the practices whose emergence was the object of his study. If the logic of genealogy for Nietzsche and Williams is judgment, which operates with the logical categories of truth and falsity, then the logic of genealogy for Foucault (and some others) is problematization, describable by the logical categories of problematic indeterminacy and responsive determination.

In Chapter 3 I undertake a detailed explication of Foucaultian genealogy as problematization in terms of three core ideas: contingency, complexity, and critique. In practicing philosophy as critique, Foucault is one of Kant's most able inheritors in the twentieth century. Despite the similarities, however, I recognize that Foucault was not a Kantian all the way down. I argue for a distinction in Kant between critical conditions of possibility and transcendental conditions of possibility, where the latter are but one instance of the former. Foucaultian critique adheres to the former, namely critical inquiry into conditions of possibility, but does so by replacing transcendental method with a genealogical method of problematization. This is an idea that Nietzsche invented, though Foucault developed it well beyond anything Nietzsche had anticipated. What Foucault and Nietzsche do share is an understanding of genealogical critique as bringing into focus the contingency and complexity of the historical present. This chapter is an effort in characterizing that mode of critique, both by way of negative contrast to transcendental critique, and by way of positive portraiture drawing on metaphors and images supplied by a range of genealogists.

In Chapter 4 I further excavate some of the intellectual historical sources of Foucault's work. Having detailed Foucault's Kantian inheritances, I am concerned in this chapter with more proximate influences. These include Georges Canguilhem, Fernand Braudel, Louis Althusser, and most importantly Gilles Deleuze, whose work I regard as widely informing Foucault's conception of problematization. On the basis of the connections between Foucault and Deleuze I offer a picture of Foucaultian problematization as undertaken with an eye toward responsive reconstruction. Foucault did not problematize in order to subvert or to vindicate; nor did he problematize simply to demonstrate the lack of inevitability of our present ways. Foucault problematized in order to conceptualize and make intelligible that which contingently conditions our present. The crucial difference is between showing *that* the present is contingent and showing *how* the present is contingently made up. Foucault was always more invested in the latter project. A distinction between the *that* and the *how* of contingency helps us recognize that Foucaultian problematization specifically invites reconstruction: the work of problematization does not subvert, but rather sets problems that demand responses and resolutions. Here is how Foucault stated the point in a late interview: "Perhaps I should start by explaining what I intended to do in [*Discipline and Punish*]. I didn't aim to do a work of criticism, at least not directly, if what is meant by criticism in this case is denunciation of the negative aspects of the current penal system. . . . I attempted to define another problem. I wanted to uncover the system of thought, the form of rationality that, since the end of the eighteenth century, has supported the notion that prison is really the best means, or one of the most effective and rational means, of punishing offenses in a society. . . . In bringing out the system of rationality underlying punitive practices, I wanted to indicate what the postulates of thought were that needed to be reexamined if one intended to transform the penal system. . . . It's the same thing that I had tried to do with respect to the history of psychiatric institutions [in *History of Madness*]."[31] Foucault here clearly positions two of his major critiques of modernity not as attempts to denounce our present punitive and psychiatric assumptions, but rather as excavations of the conditions of possibility of the practices invoking these assumptions. Foucault's crucial point is that we would need to understand how these conditions of possibility were composed if we want to begin the difficult labor of transforming those practices, their assumptions, and the institutions, subjects, and objects they support.

The first four chapters, comprising roughly the first half of the book, offer a specification of the unique critical purchase of the genealogical tradition, particularly as exhibited in the genealogies of Foucault. In the final three chapters, comprising roughly the second half of the book, I employ this specification for the purposes of rereading Foucault's archaeologies and genealogies of modernity. Or, to state differently the relation between the two halves of the book, the first half is mostly an effort in a specification of genealogical methodology as exhibited by Foucault (but also others), whereas the second half is more an effort in specifying the conceptual products resultant from Foucault's deployment of that methodology in the context of a diagnosis of quintessentially modern practices. So, in the final chapters, I reconsider both Foucault's critique of modernity (in Chapter 5) in light of my understanding (developed in Chapter 3) of critique as problematization as well as Foucault's response to his problematization of modernity (in Chapter 6) in light of my claim (developed in Chapter 4) that problematization calls for reconstruction.

Chapter 5 is thus focused on Foucault's provocative problematizations of modernity. Foucault is best read as figuring modernity as a constellation of practices rather than as an epoch or an age. I focus specifically on Foucault's problematizations of the quintessentially modern practices that are the central foci in *Discipline and Punish* and *History of Madness*. Rereading these genealogies of modernity as problematizations of modern practices helps us see how Foucault's work serves to clarify and intensify certain philosophical difficulties that he is often wrongly criticized for not having solved. Foucault's aim was to emphasize how intractable many of our problems are, such that we might relieve ourselves of the pretense of possessing any straightforward solution. His work thus intensifies the extraordinarily thorny problems of the relations between structure and agency, discipline and liberation, and power and freedom. Facing up to the difficulties of the present, Foucault was arguing, requires a patient labor of responsively experimenting with the forms we find given to us in the present.

Chapter 6 takes as its focus Foucault's own somewhat incomplete response to his problematization of modernity as elaborated in varied writings from the last decade of his life. I show how much is to be gained by reinterpreting this late work as a responsive reconstruction of Foucault's problematization of the moralities attendant to modern disciplinary power and modern emancipatory freedom. At the key of this responsive reconstruction is an idea of an ethical orientation toward the transformation of our selves. Despite the provocations and promise of this orientation I argue that Foucault's ethical response was one that he nonetheless never fully developed. His ethics thus require some kind of supplementation or revision on a number of points. My point here is not that we should forget Foucault. Rather, we might allow ourselves to distinguish that in Foucault's ethics which we can take up and that which we should leave behind.

This opens up the perspective of the concluding Chapter 7, where I argue for bringing Foucaultian problematization into generative cross-use with certain other contemporary philosophical methods. These other methods aim more directly at ethical reconstruction and, as such, are in a better position than Foucault's self-transformational ethics to adequately respond to the critical problematizations of our modernity. I show that there is much to be gained from a combination of genealogy with the philosophical traditions of both pragmatism and critical theory insofar as all three operate according to the logic of problem-and-response (or, more technically, problematization-and-reconstruction). The final chapter thus aims at overcoming one of the most frustrating impasses in recent critical theory, namely that between Foucaultian genealogy and Habermasian critical theory—meanwhile, a Jamesian-Deweyan-Rortyan pragmatism, I argue, is especially well poised to help mediate this impasse. The central point in these conversations across traditions, which is also a central point for my reinterpretation of genealogy throughout the book, is the following: philosophy at its best, as a work in what I call *cultural critical philosophy*, is an attempt to develop and deploy a robust conception of critical inquiry as an immanent and reflexive engagement with the full complexity and contingency of the conditions of possibility for doing, being, and thinking in our cultural present.

1

Critical Historiography

Politics, Philosophy & Problematization

The History of the Present as Philosophical and Political

Genealogy articulates, or makes sayable and visible, that is conceptually available, the problematizations of our present. Genealogy thus involves the articulation of that which comprises a singular problematization out of a multiplicity of otherwise disentangled elements. This project in articulation facilitates a better understanding of those conditions of possibility that constrain and enable us today, right now, in our present. Genealogies are, in every prominent instance, addressed to today despite ostensibly being histories about the past. The present, or the difference that today makes with respect to who we are, is a key organizing idea for genealogy in the work of all genealogists. As such, genealogies function as critical histories of the present. Genealogies start with the present in order to trace the conditions of the emergence of the present in which we are present.

The use of history in order to reveal, but also to shake up, the present is made manifest in the work of the Friedrich Nietzsche, the thinker with whom the practice and concept of genealogy became prominent. Nietzsche was trained as a classical philologist and throughout his life consistently focused his work on an analysis of the past and especially of antiquity. So in what sense can Nietzsche's work, since it was work on the past, also be read as work on the present? Nietzsche's own explanation of this was that histories are invaluable for the present insofar as they are untimely within the present. In *On the Use and Abuse of History for Life,*

Nietzsche wrote, "I do not know what meaning classical philology would have for our age if not to have an untimely effect within it, that is, to act against the age and so have an effect on the age to the advantage, it is to be hoped, of a coming age."[1] This book was published as part of a series of four, the entire collection being titled *Untimely Meditations*. Indeed all of Nietzsche's genealogies can be seen as untimely in the sense that they work through the past of the present in order to redirect our present into some other possible future of the present. Nietzsche's thought is best seen as using history to intervene into the present.

Almost a century and a quarter after Nietzsche's *Untimely Meditations*, philosopher Bernard Williams published his *Truth and Truthfulness: An Essay in Genealogy*. Williams was there explicit about his debts to Nietzsche in crafting the philosophical-historical method he would use to address his central topics.[2] But what are the topics central to *Truth and Truthfulness*? Not truth as an ahistorical concept, though Williams does discuss that too.[3] But rather the value of our concepts of truth and truthfulness today, insofar as present-day culture finds itself committed to "two currents of ideas" that do not easily fit with one another, namely "the devotion to truthfulness and the suspicion directed to the idea of truth."[4] Williams is clear that his historical genealogy is about the compossibility of these two currents for us today: "My question is: how can we address this situation . . . I believe this to be a basic problem for present-day philosophy."[5] Williams's history of truth and truthfulness, then, is meant to illuminate a problem that is central for us today. It is not, by contrast, offered as a history of what certain concepts were taken to be in the past without respect to how those past iterations can be traced forward to today.

A similar view is adopted by another contemporary philosopher whose work combines a background in analytic philosophy and a deployment of historical genealogy. Ian Hacking makes use of genealogy in much of his work, even though he often presents it under other labels, such as "historical ontology." Whatever its label, Hacking's histories are clearly presented as histories of the present: "At its boldest, historical ontology would show how to understand, act out, and resolve present problems, even when in so doing it generated new ones." Of course, historical ontology need not be so bold: "At its more modest it is conceptual analysis, analyzing *our* concepts. . . . [B]ecause the concepts have their being in historical sites. . . . This dedication to analysis makes use of the past, but it is not history."[6] Hacking offers these descriptions in a paragraph that begins as a comment on Foucault. Williams seems to have learned his genealogy mostly from Nietzsche, and Hacking his mostly from Foucault. Both ably appropriate their predecessor's methodology for their own purposes, but there remains in each ample traces of that which preceded them. These remnant traces are worth bearing in mind when, in the next chapter, I typologically discriminate different uses of genealogy. For this chapter, however, my purpose is association and drawing together what is common among these and other thinkers for whom genealogy is a philosophical history of the present.

The most important contributor to the shared tradition of genealogy is, on my account, Michel Foucault. Foucault too was explicit that his histories were intended as histories of the present: these are histories that afford an intervention into the present leading to a possible redirection toward another future. In one of his earliest formulations of his idea of "the history of the present," given in a 1969 radio interview, Foucault stated, "To diagnose the present is to say what the present is, and how our present is absolutely different from all that is not it, that is to say, from our past. Perhaps this is the task for philosophy now."[7] It was precisely in this sense that he explicitly offered his 1975 book on modern punishment, *Discipline and Punish,* as an intervention into the present: "I would like to write the history of this prison . . . Why? Simply because I am interested in the past? No, if one means by that writing a history of the past in terms of the present. Yes, if one means writing the history of the present."[8] A few years later Foucault further clarified the intent of that book: "What I wanted to write was a history book that would make the present situation comprehensible and, possibly, lead to action. If you like, I tried to write a 'treatise of intelligibility' about the penitentiary situation, I wanted to make it intelligible and, therefore, criticizable."[9] In speaking directly to the present in this way, Foucault's genealogy locates itself at the intersection of reflection and intervention, or of what can safely be referred to as philosophy and politics. This specific relation was crucial for Foucault throughout his career, and increasingly so in his late work, for instance in his 1983 Collège de France course lectures, where we find him eagerly exploring "the necessary, indispensable, resistant, and stubborn relation of philosophical discourse or the philosophical life to political practice."[10]

Locating genealogy at the intersection of philosophy and politics enables us to see this tradition as making a contribution in the form of a political philosophy, a public philosophy, or what I elsewhere call a "cultural critical philosophy."[11] Characteristic of this form of philosophical practice is a reflection on conditions of possibility of contemporary cultural, social, political, and ethical problems. Cultural critique for the genealogist does not, or at least need not, take the form of taking a position or assuming a side in present debates. Rather it takes the form, at least primarily, of articulating the conditions of possibility of the fraught debates in which we find ourselves enmeshed. Cultural critical philosophy in genealogy takes the form of the articulation and intensification of the problematizations central to our fragile cultural formations. It will be a primary task of this chapter, as well as those that follow, to describe in detail this practice of cultural critical philosophy as made manifest in the genealogical tradition. I should, however, note at the outset that I shall not be here engaging in that practice of cultural critique, except by way of commentary on Foucault and others. This is not because I find the practice secondary in relation to clarifying the methodological issues I here take as primary. Rather it is because my hope is that methodological clarification can in some way assist practices of cultural critical philosophy already under way and already on exhibit. I do not, of course, hereby excuse myself from the practice of cultural critical philosophy. I only make plain to the reader that you will not find that practice herein, at least not in any sustained form that might count as an exhibit, an example, or an expression of philosophy as cultural critique.

Though all genealogists offer histories of the present, it was Foucault who fashioned that term, and it is also in his work that we find the most prominent statements among genealogists of such histories as forming at a hinge between philosophy and politics.[12] One such locale, particularly convenient for the connections it draws among political-philosophical reflection and the historical present that is the object of that reflection, is Foucault's 1983 Collège de France course lectures, titled *The Government of Self and Others,* quoted just above. The lecture series opens on January 5 with methodological considerations in which Foucault tells his audience that he proposes to practice "a critical thought which takes the form of an ontology of ourselves, of present reality."[13] As the lectures proceed, Foucault is increasingly clear that thought can reflexively direct itself at its own present by way of assuming a fragile position between philosophy and politics. The decisive moment in the lectures occurs on February 23 when Foucault asks: "The question I would like to pose . . . is this: must philosophy's need to confront politics, must philosophy's need to seek its reality in the confrontation with politics consist in formulating a philosophical discourse which is at the same time a discourse that prescribes political action, or is something else involved?"[14] The work of thought, Foucault continues, has too often assumed that philosophical reflection must stake out positions on the field of political reflection and that politics must seek its justifications in philosophy. Political philosophy, it is often assumed, must take the form of a systematic theorization of political concepts in such a way as to yield determinate answers to pressing political crises. Philosophy in this way can be applied to political debates on the ground just as partisans to those debates can repair to philosophy for a justification of the one correct position. This sort of metaphilosophical orientation is, I would argue, characteristic of the overwhelming majority of twentieth-century political and moral philosophy. For Foucault, the critical task involved in a history of the present is something quite different. There is, for him, something else involved in a practice of philosophy as cultural, political, and moral critique. Foucault's view is that "Philosophy and politics must exist in a relation, in a correlation; they must never coincide."[15] Philosophy should not tell politics what to do, nor should politics look to philosophy for its justification. Rather, philosophy must confront politics and find its reality for itself in that confrontation. Philosophy "does not tell the truth of political action. . . . it tells the truth in relation to political action."[16] Philosophy does not tell us which political conditions are the just or true ones, but rather it tells the truth about the very conditions of possibility of present political problems in the first place. Philosophy, in other words, challenges, confronts, or problematizes political life. Thus Foucault concludes in his final lecture, of March 9, that philosophy ought to assume for itself "a sort of restive and insistent exteriority towards politics."[17] Philosophy must remain exterior to politics so that it may, from a position that is very near, confront politics with the truth of itself.

The idea and practice of the history of the present should be located here, within the relation between a philosophy and a politics that are not reduced to identity. But this raises as many questions as it answers. Why did Foucault specify his work in terms of the historical present? Why should an inquiry that is avowedly historical in orientation have any important bearing on what he took the present to be? Why was the present so important for Foucault? One seemingly obvious answer to this final question would be to say that the present is where we always find ourselves. The present is important because it is only by being attentive to where we are that we can do anything to improve our situation. There is surely some truth in this answer, but it is too superficial to be of much use. Allow me to plumb a little deeper.

There are important philosophical issues relevant to these matters that can help us understand why Foucault's histories of the present would be motivated simultaneously by philosophical and political considerations. A more helpful answer to the question concerning the importance of the present can be developed by focusing on the way in which the question itself is posed. The question is not "Why did Foucault want to study the situations in which he found himself?" but rather "Why did Foucault want to study the present in which he found himself?" The question, in other words, should be posed as a question that is situated within a turn toward historicity and temporality as central to understanding who, where, and what we are. This suggests a more plausible answer to our question to the effect that Foucault was so concerned about the present precisely because he understood the present to be the site of the temporal and historical processes through and in which we constitute ourselves as subjects. To study the present situations in which we find ourselves requires that we study these situations as historically and temporally located amidst ongoing processes of change. The present is constituted by its historicity and temporality. A history of the present is requisite precisely because the present gains its coherence from the history out of which it has developed and on the basis of which it will flow into the future. As Foucault put it: "If history possesses a privilege, it would be, rather, insofar as it plays the role of an internal ethnology of our culture and our rationality."[18]

Thus, Foucault's understanding of the historicity and temporality of the constitution of knowledge, power, and ethics explains his patient focus on "the present" rather than on some other shadowy stand-in for "where one finds oneself," as exampled by more prominent, and often much darker, concepts for our condition, such as "the West," or "late Capitalism." An inquiry into the conditions of the possibility of the present enables us to understand who we are, where we have come from, and where we may go. The present is where we find ourselves as historically and temporally invested such that the present in which we are present is always conditioned by its own inertia. This inertia constitutes the crucial difference between being headed in one direction and being headed in the other, a difference that ahistorical inquiries cannot often discern. This difference, in its simultaneous political and philosophical perspectives, constitutes the precise object of focus in Foucaultian genealogy.

An understanding of the critical valence of genealogy as a historical practice sheds further light on a number of crucial methodological issues central to Foucault's project. The idea of the history of the present just elucidated helps us gain a proper grip, for instance, on the vexed relationship between the genealogical and archaeological methods as they are exhibited in Foucault's work. In the next section of this chapter, I therefore turn to matters rather erudite and scholarly in concern, my focus being the relation between Foucault's archaeological and genealogical methods. The point of this gray discussion is to gain a fuller sense of how Foucault's work is able to locate itself as a form of critique that is at once philosophical and political. I emphasize two key methodological moves: Foucault's idea of "power-knowledge" and his emphasis on temporal multiplicity. Foucault's conception of problematization, I then argue in the following section, provides a kind of master key for understanding Foucault's methodology. In the final section of the chapter, I leverage this interpretation of Foucault as a problematizer toward a synoptic reading of Foucault's work, showing how problematization is a critical focus throughout. This sets the stage for later chapters, where I explain in more detail both the methodological coherence of problematization as a critical practice and also how this notion enables us to reread the particulars of some of Foucault's major works.

Foucault's Expansion of Archaeology into Genealogy through Nietzsche and Kant

Issues concerning the relation between genealogical and archaeological methodologies are enormously complicated in the existing scholarship on Foucault.[19] Many commentators have misleadingly claimed that genealogy entails an abandonment or rejection of archaeology.[20] This seems justifiable insofar as Foucault's earlier works were explicitly offered under the banner of "archaeology" while many of his later works were explicitly placed under the different banner of "genealogy." The easiest way to make sense of this, then, was to interpret this methodological shift as a rejection of that which preceded the shift. Others have rightly suggested that the relationship is more complex, but even most of these have failed to focus their complementarity in the right kinds of ways.[21] My view, following on important points the lead of Paul Rabinow and Hubert Dreyfus in their excellent early book on Foucault, is that an inquiry into the history of the present requires philosophical and political resources not yielded by an archaeology taken by itself but that can be generated on the basis of an expansion of historical inquiry so as to deploy genealogy and archaeology alongside one another.[22] I take it that Rabinow and Dreyfus would agree with the precise and succinct formulation forwarded by Arnold Davidson: "genealogy does not so much displace archaeology as widen the kind of analysis to be pursued."[23] Following this thought, I hold that the transition involved here is best seen in terms of a methodological expansion rather than a philosophical division. Thus genealogy should not be seen as genealogy-instead-of-archaeology but rather as genealogy-plus-archaeology.

The twain political and philosophical requirements of the history of the present help us understand what genealogy adds to archaeology without thereby subtracting from it. I emphasize precisely the relation between philosophy *and* politics to make sense of Foucault's methodological shift. By contrast, those accounts that emphasize only political factors or only philosophical requirements remain incomplete. Those that emphasize only internal philosophical requirements fail to engage the fact that Foucault's genealogical work betrays a much fuller engagement with the cultural conditions in which he found himself. Those accounts emphasizing only external political motivations, such as Foucault's political involvements in Tunisia and Paris or his friendships with politicized intellectuals such as Deleuze and Sartre, fail to fully engage the labor of thought involved in Foucault's own self-transformations as a critical philosopher. The methodological expansion that took Foucault from archaeology to genealogy is one that both politicized his philosophical practice of history and philosophically strengthened his political histories.

Viewing genealogy as an expansion of archaeology enables us to refocus the issue of this methodological relation in terms of questions about exactly what sorts of historiographical elements are brought into focus by each contrasting methodology. What are the elements, lacking in archaeology-alone but present in genealogy-plus-archaeology, that enabled Foucault to embark on his philosophical studies of the history of the present? The answer I develop in this section emphasizes two interlaced methodological decisions: an analytic enabling *temporal multiplicity* so as to embrace both rupture and continuity in history, and an analytic for attending to the *relations between multiple vectors of practice* such as power and knowledge rather than any one of these vectors or dimensions on its own. Both of these elements can be looked at in terms of a genealogical expansion of archaeology: archaeology was informed by a singular conception of temporal discontinuity and a singular focus on the domain of knowledge such that genealogy expanded the view so as to wrestle with multiple temporalities and multiple vectors of practice. These two interrelated expansions enabled Foucault to eventually clarify a notion that had always been central to his work but that was not explicitly thematized until quite late in his career: *problematization*. The analytical idea of problematization enabled the late Foucault to crystallize what had remained only inchoately articulated in earlier works under such labels as "episteme" and "discursive formation." Though relatively inarticulate about this in the earlier work, Foucault throughout his career was concerned to expound the depth problems that condition our historical present. What changed, then, was not so much the critical intent of Foucault's patient research as the self-conscious clarity of that intent and the work of thought that would be required to achieve it. The best way of showing this is to focus on those methodological expansions just summarized.

Foucault's work during the late 1960s and early 1970s was characterized by explicit and severe methodological reflection on the uses of history and philosophy. This is no surprise from a retrospective viewpoint where we can see this period as the hinge between the high period of Foucault's reliance on archaeological method and the emergence of a genealogical approach on his writings. By the end of his grand methodological treatise, *The Archaeology of Knowledge* published in 1969, Foucault already seemed to be anticipating something broader than archaeology itself: "it may turn out that archaeology is the name given to a part of our contemporary theoretical conjuncture."[24] A part—but not all. This, as it happens, is exactly as it would turn out. Throughout Part IV of the book (with the empiricist title "Archaeological Description"), Foucault addresses over and over again, as if unsatisfied with his own answers, two key problems concerning historical continuity and the historical analysis of the episteme. Concerning the temporalities of history, Foucault notes that he will doubtless be criticized for a method "concerning itself primarily with the analysis of the discontinuous" and in response proffers an archaeological analytic of "transformations" as an alternative to the historiographical reliance on an unanalyzed concept of "change."[25] Concerning the archaeological concentration on knowledge rather than cultural or social practice more broadly construed, a methodological move signaled in the very title of the book, Foucault boldly claims that "any discursive practice may be defined by the knowledge that it forms" but then only a few pages later speculates about the possibility of "other archaeologies" beyond those focused purely on scientific knowing practices.[26] Notably, Foucault also explicitly addressed himself to both forms of methodological expansion in a number of writings that followed closely on the heels of the publication of that book.[27]

Before explicating these themes in detail, a few comments on the explicit intellectual antecedents of Foucault's methodological shift will help shed light on these matters. It is undeniable that Nietzsche is central to Foucault's writings during the period when he expanded archaeology into genealogy. In a 1983 interview, Foucault clarified his relation to Nietzsche as follows: "My relation to Nietzsche, or what I owe to Nietzsche, derives mostly from the texts of around 1880, where the question of truth, the history of truth and the will to truth were central to his work."[28] Foucault found through Nietzsche the means to formulate an inquiry into the history of the transformations of truth. But in noting Nietzsche's importance here, it is important to not overstate the influence of a single German. For why should one German be the explanans when two Germans would offer twice as much explanatory force? Alongside Nietzsche we should never forget Kant, for Foucault's confrontation with the present was a Kantian project as much as it was a Nietzschean one.[29] I have noted above that our situation is figured by Foucault as a present whose history can be subjected to a critique. Foucault made plain that Nietzsche offered one model for what critique in this form could look like: "Nietzsche discovered that philosophy's distinct activity consists in the work of a diagnosis of the present: What are we today? What is this 'today' in which we live?"[30] But also notable is that these are almost the exact terms that Foucault later used to describe that which he found most compelling in Kant: "He [Kant] is looking for a difference: What difference does today introduce with respect to yesterday? . . . It is in the reflection on 'today' as difference in history and as motive for a particular philosophical task that the novelty of this text [Kant's "What is Enlightenment?"] appears to me to lie."[31]

If Foucault was so eager to turn to Nietzsche in order to develop a genealogical critique of the present, he was motivated at least in part by Nietzsche's attempt to take seriously the possibility of any kind of critique of the present. Foucault's Nietzschean project of the history of the transformations of truth was undertaken on the basis of the problematizations that form the conditions of possibility of truth in history. Here lingers the deep and lasting influence of Kant over the entire tradition of genealogy. A core Kantian idea found throughout genealogy involves a critical interrogation of those depth conditions that make possible the various surface practices that are the object of critical inquiry. Thus Foucault in his archaeologies would study the depth knowledge (*savoir*) and depth power (*pouvoir*) that make possible the surface effects of knowledge (*connassiance*) and power (*puissance*). And thus Nietzsche would study the depth forces (e.g., the will to power and the will to truth) that condition possibilities of the surface effects of the various powers and truths (slave moralities and ascetic sciences) charted in his genealogies.

It is also sensible to infer that much of what Foucault inherited from Nietzsche as a critical historical method can be usefully seen as a Nietzschean inflection of an originally Kantian project. In his Preface to *On the Genealogy of Morals*, Nietzsche urged that "we need a *critique* of moral values, *the values of these values themselves must first be called in question*—and for that there is needed a knowledge of the conditions and circumstances in which they grew, under which they evolved and changed."[32] The call for a 'critique' by means of an inquiry into 'conditions' has undeniably Kantian resonances, even if for Nietzsche (as for Foucault) these conditions were historical 'circumstances' while for Kant they simply had to be transcendental 'categories.' Reading Nietzsche in a way that emphasizes his Kantianism provides a useful precedent for my reading of Foucault as developing a historical form of Kantian critique. Such a reading is supported by, among others, Foucault's interlocutor and friend Gilles Deleuze in his famous little book on Nietzsche.[33] Deleuze's 1962 book forwarded an interpretation of Nietzschean genealogy that exerted deep influence on the French thought of his generation.[34] At the heart of that interpretation is a view of Nietzsche as transformatively appropriating Kantian critique: "Nietzsche seems to have sought . . . a radical transformation of Kantianism, a re-invention of the critique which Kant betrayed at the same time as he conceived it . . . Nietzsche, in the *Genealogy of Morals*, wanted to rewrite the *Critique of Pure Reason.*"[35] Deleuze explains Nietzsche's genealogy as a form of critique that replaces transcendental investigation with immanent inquiry, thus more fully realizing Kant's own program of a critique of reason by itself.[36] Deleuze's strong redescription of Nietzsche as a Kantian clears sufficient space for the possibility that Foucault followed Deleuze in taking Nietzsche as a model for a transformed practice of Kantian critique that would emphasize inquiry into immanent rather than transcendental conditions of possibility. One view we might conclude with is that Nietzsche helped to provoke in Foucault the project of a historicized Kantianism, and then Foucault went on to develop this form of critique in a more rigorous fashion than can be found in Nietzsche.

For the purposes of the historicized practice of critique that Foucault built out of these Nietzschean and Kantian elements, it would be insufficient to study particular forms of stable knowledge or power found in the past. This, however, was the form that historical critique took in Foucault's earlier archaeological histories. Part of what provoked Foucault to expand his practice of historical critique was a sense that he needed, like Nietzsche, to engage the transformations that stable forms of knowledge and power are subject to when they are destabilized by one another. This led to a form of critical inquiry initially provoked by Nietzsche but quickly superseding German speculative genealogy. What Foucault developed beyond Nietzsche and Kant but with Nietzsche and Kant was a conception of archaeology-plus-genealogy that involved the scrutiny of practices traveling along *multiple vectors* in *multiple temporalities.* In the remainder of this section I discuss at a conceptual level the methodological expansion whereby Foucault opened up his inquiries to these two kinds of multiplicity. I shall also show how Foucault in *The Archaeology of Knowledge* already anticipated, in two key sections of Part IV of that book, the methodological hindrances that these multiplications enabled him to later resolve.

In describing genealogy as inquiring into practices along multiple vectors, I refer to the way genealogy focuses on neither power nor knowledge alone, but rather of the power-knowledge interplay. The interplay of the epistemic and the political in Foucault is a familiar story, but it is worth rehearsing if only to avoid the dangers of a cliché. It is often difficult to realize the immensity of a philosopher's ambitions retroactively after their efforts have been widely adopted. The works in which those ambitions are realized get cycled through round after round of critical review. Certain themes emerge in the literature. Interviewers focus on these topics. Anthologies get published. Gradually, everyone forgets that the philosopher had at some point struggled a great deal to initially elaborate some point that everyone now accepts as a matter of course. So it is with Foucault's idea of power-knowledge. This is an idea we should not take for granted.

While nearly everyone who reads Foucault admits that the power-knowledge relation was crucial for his work in the 1970s, what is too often passed over in silence is the amount of intellectual creativity involved in the development of a method for analyzing this relation. Foucault had to construct the power-knowledge relation as a coherent category for inquiry. The very idea of the entanglement of power and knowledge is, in a culture such as ours that is practically obsessed with neatly dividing off the factual from the normative, hardly evident. Rabinow and Dreyfus are therefore correct to highlight the power-knowledge relation as "the most radical dimension of Foucault's work."[37]

Foucault labored in his work leading up to and including *Discipline and Punish* to show that "We should admit . . . that power produces knowledge (and not simply by encouraging it because it serves power or by applying it because it is useful); that power and knowledge directly imply one another; that there is no power relation without the correlative constitution of a field of knowledge, nor any knowledge that does not presuppose and constitute at the same time power relations."[38] This coproductionist method played out in that book by tracing the problematization that funded the birth of the prison along vectors of both power and knowledge. These vectors, on Foucault's account, together traverse a multiplicity of practices, including ritualized temporal ordering in monasteries, spatial ordering as instantiated in military encampments, spatial partitioning techniques developed in architecture, mechanisms of narration and confession in religious practice, surveillance strategies originating in industrial and educational contexts as well as in military contexts to control against desertion, planning strategies perfected in urban regulations for controlling plague, medical techniques of individualization and practices of examination developed in clinical contexts, numerical technologies perfected by the rise of the statistical sciences, and religious themes of caring for a flock of wayward souls.[39]

It was in the process of the development of an analytical conception suitable to grasping such complexity that Foucault understood that he must abandon a narrow archaeological method in favor of the more complex mode of analysis we know as genealogy. In order to incorporate power into his analysis as a separate element not identical to knowledge and yet in constant interaction with it, Foucault had to widen the field of his analysis. In thus expanding his analytical focus, the older methodology of archaeology was reinscribed within the newer methodology of genealogy. What is important in the move to genealogy is a new form of critical inquiry that brings objects into focus through a new analytical lens that opens up said objects in the complexity of their coproduction. The concept of discipline exhibits the reciprocities and entanglements among knowledges and powers characteristic of genealogy. This coproductionist aspect of genealogy is valuable insofar as, in Barry Allen's helpful analysis, "[a]n appreciation of this new relationship between knowledge and power seems necessary for a sound grasp of present-day political reality."[40] But, we might ask, why? What is so important about the relation between power and knowledge for our historical present?

To better understand what motivates this shift in analytical procedure to the more complex objects of inquiry that travel along a plurality coproducing vectors, it will be helpful to first consider the reasons why archaeology alone, taken by itself, cannot muster the kind of critical inquiry facilitated by genealogy. This can be gleaned from a key section of *The Archaeology of Knowledge,* namely Part IV, Chapter 6, where Foucault is explicit that "in [archaeology], what one is trying to uncover are discursive practices in so far as they give rise to a corpus of knowledge, in so far as they assume the status and role of a science."[41] Foucault in this way makes good on the title of *The Archaeology of Knowledge* in the text itself. And yet although he seems to be exclusively concerned with an archaeology of knowledge in this claim, by the end of the section in which it appears Foucault indulges in one of those dreamy speculations, irresistible for we of a philosophical temperament, about the future uses of the research methodology he has just finished outlining: "I can readily imagine—subject to a great deal of further exploration and examination—archaeologies that might develop in different directions." Taking archaeology beyond the thus-far-explored domain of knowledge, Foucault suggests that he imagines writing archaeologies of "sexuality," "painting," and "political knowledge."[42] A little more than a year later in "The Order of Discourse," he again proposes archaeologies of power, sexuality, and psychology.[43] Foucault was perfectly consistent to insist upon the intelligibility of such anticipated projects. But the formulations he settled on in these methodological essays proved to be insufficient for the future research he proposed. When Foucault attempted to make good on these speculations in subsequent work, he did so by first turning his attention from an archaeology of scientific knowledge and toward an archaeology of political rationality. It quickly became apparent that in order to properly engage with this new domain of research he would have to make some major revisions to the archaeological methodology he had just completed. One revision that clearly stands out is a shift from the historical description of epistemes as deep discursive formations, which his archaeology models as isolated slices of time discontinuous from one to the next, to the historical explanation of depth complexes of power-knowledge, which genealogy describes in terms of historical transformations from past to present.

In order to understand why this revision was necessary for the historical-philosophical work Foucault envisioned for himself, it first needs to be understood exactly how Foucault thought power-knowledge should be studied. There are a number of common misunderstandings of Foucault on this point. Two in particular are worth addressing.

First, it is crucial to Foucault's view that power and knowledge are neither reducible to nor identical with one another, and yet neither are the two ever wholly separable. Foucault sought to study power in its relation to knowledge. As Foucault clearly stated, "studying their *relation* is precisely my problem." He explained why for the purposes of his work he was forced to reject the thesis that power and knowledge can be identified: "If they were identical, I would not have to study them and I would be spared a lot of fatigue as a result. The very fact that I pose the question of their relation proves clearly that I do not *identify* them."[44] The relation between knowledge and power is made visible at the conditioning level of depth *savoir* and depth *pouvoir*. As the value of this form of inquiry increasingly gripped Foucault, he thereby became increasingly clear about the status of his work: "New problems have appeared: no longer what are the limits of knowledge (or its foundations), but who are those who know? How is knowledge appropriated and distributed?"[45] There are myriad forms that power-knowledge relations have taken as exampled across much of Foucault's genealogical research: the entanglement of discipline as an exercise of power and a strategy of knowledge, the entrainment of statistical reason and state power in biopolitical equipment, the coalescence of individualizing knowledge and collective power in the early modern pastoral, or the entwinement of social knowledge and social control in the vast institutional apparatus of the police. All of these examples are drastically misunderstood if it is thought that Foucault's point was that power is reducible to knowledge or, even worse, that knowledge is reducible to power. The entire point of the coproduction idea is to open up a space for inquiry into the interactive relation between knowledge and power.

A second common misunderstanding concerns the idea that Foucault sought to elaborate a theory of power and a theory of knowledge. Contrary to this common assumption, it must be underscored that Foucault's point was never a philosophical one about the necessary relations between all forms of power and all forms of knowledge. Foucault sought to establish historical points concerning the relations that have contingently held between certain prominent forms of power and knowledge in our modernity. We can, for the purposes of historical critique, safely ignore questions about power in general or knowledge in general. Foucault was never attempting to write a general theory of Power nor a general theory of Knowledge, so much as he was describing specific powers and knowledges that condition our possibilities for action in the historical present. Foucault more than once described his work as effecting a methodological displacement that "consists in freeing oneself from any would-be general Theory of Power (with all capital letters)."[46] In this, Foucault's approach seems complementary to other empirically sensitive philosophical traditions. I am thinking in particular of the empirically trained work of the German critical theorists (think of all the empirical research projects especially characteristic of the original Frankfurt School) and the American pragmatists (think of the political theory of Dewey and Mead at the intersection of sociology and philosophy).

To summarize now the first crucial methodological shift involved in the expansion of archaeology into genealogy, this shift involves an analytical reorientation from a focus on an isolable depth episteme to a consideration of relations holding between two cross-invested vectors of depth knowledge-power. It is crucially important to note in this regard that other possible combinations of vectors of practice are quite possible—power and ethics, knowledge and ethics, all three taken at once, and of course combinations involving kinds of vectors that Foucault himself did not analyze, such as, say, aesthetics and power. In fact in the work of his final years, Foucault explicitly showed how genealogical method is extensible by using it for the purposes of analysis along three interleaved vectors of power, knowledge, and ethical self-relations. Throughout this late work, Foucault clearly stressed that none of these three forms is basic with respect to the other two. His emphasis remained on their coproduction. In his 1984 Collège de France lectures, published in English as *The Courage of Truth*, Foucault responded explicitly to those who had taken his previous analyses couched in terms of power and knowledge as in principle opposed to an analytical grasp of vectors of subjective self-formation (a much-circulated criticism of Foucault to which I will return in greater detail in Chapter 6): "What is involved, rather, is the analysis of complex relations between three distinct elements none of which can be reduced to or absorbed by the others, but whose relations are constitutive of each other. These three elements are: forms of knowledge . . . relations of power . . . and finally the modes of formation of the subject through practices of the self."[47] The crucial methodological point here is that genealogy involves an analysis of the interactions between, and thus the coproduction of, multiple vectors of activity. There is no upper (theoretical) limit to the number and kinds of vectors that might be subject to analysis, though there is a lower (theoretical) limit of at least two vectors such that the analysis can reveal the tensions and knots by virtue of which historical change can be grasped in its complexity.

This brings me to the second of the two methodological expansions and a consideration of how the coproductionist perspective of genealogy enabled Foucault to reconstruct his methodological uses of historicity and temporality. In his archaeological work Foucault had treated history as marked above all by discontinuity and rupture. *The Order of Things,* for instance, sought to register the differences between different epistemes (e.g., between the Renaissance episteme of resemblance and the Classical episteme of representation) but remained seemingly disinterested in charting the process whereby one episteme gradually gives way to another. Indeed through much of the text Foucault even seems opposed to the very idea of establishing historical lines of connection between the different epistemes his analysis uncovered. And yet in later work he forced himself to confront the reality of a history that undergoes transformations such that history can be studied as a process in which both continuity and discontinuity are essential in their temporalities. The juxtaposition of the torturer's spectacle and the prisoner's timetable at the outset of *Discipline and Punish* is featured as a bright historical rupture that the book itself then proceeds to analyze in terms of the process whereby the prison with its timetables would eventually be borne out of that very same world that was previously populated by the gallows.

A central concept for the more complex uses of historicity and temporality featured in genealogy is that of emergence. In a helpful characterization of genealogical and related modes of inquiry, Paul Rabinow describes his own genealogy-inspired anthropologies as follows: "The task is to invent concepts to make visible what is emerging."[48] If this is indeed the genealogical task, then we can think of genealogy as the articulation of concepts adequate to the emergent. Foucault's own first in-depth treatment of the concept of emergence can be found in his celebrated 1971 essay on historical method in Nietzsche.[49] He wrote there, "Emergence is the entry of forces; it is their eruption, the leap from the wings to center stage, each in its youthful strength." Emergence is conceptually central for any history written in terms of "substitutions, displacements, disguised conquests, and systematic reversals."[50] Herein we can discern an attempt to recover something like historical time without yielding to the suspect concepts of necessity and unity that Foucault had already thoroughly attacked, and with good reason.[51]

The historiographical category of emergence brings into focus the distance between the archaeology of rupture and the genealogy of transformation. If Foucault's genealogical work is oriented toward a study of the historical conditions that have enabled and disabled certain forms of power and knowledge, then it is fair to characterize this work as a study of the emergence of forms of power and knowledge. Archaeology, by contrast, is not a study of emergence but rather of existence. Archaeology asks about what has existed in the past, and without concern for how that which existed came into being. Genealogy asks how that which existed emerged into being in the first place. In this sense, genealogy is additive to, rather than substitutive for, archaeology. The genealogist studies the unstable emergence into being of the various forms of stabilized being that the archaeologist describes. Genealogy discerns transformations while archaeology discerns targets of transformations. Archaeology seems to be necessary but not sufficient for genealogy.

One way of understanding the increasing prominence of emergence in Foucault's genealogy is to think of it in terms of an engagement with historical processes of transition. If in his early work Foucault explicitly refused to engage historical change in resolutely focusing on the description of momentary slices of the archive, he later came to recognize that his critics were right to note that his tantalizing descriptions failed to capture the actual processes of historical change. But exactly what were these critics on to? The massive shifts registered in, for instance, *The Order of Things* are not registered as processes of change so much as events of discontinuity from which change itself is merely inferred. The effect of this procedure was to historiographically reduce dynamic change to an epiphenomenon of static moments at rest. Foucault's work thus seemed to freeze history—everyone in the archaeologies was made still, silent, and seemingly supine within the motionless episteme that had captured them. How, critics rightly wondered, would it ever happen that within such vast frozen epistemes there might occur the massive breaks and ruptures whose existence was so obviously demonstrated through these archaeologies? Facing such questions, Foucault could only make vague appeals to the thunder of events such as the French Revolution. These appeals served to confirm the suspicion that Foucault had no idea as to *why* so many people would risk their lives in a revolution and *how* that risk actually transformed the world in which it was ventured. Foucault's most influential critic of the tacit understanding of historical time operative in archaeology was Jean-Paul Sartre, whose memorable description precisely captures the difficulty: "Certainly Foucault's perspective remains historical. He distinguishes different periods, a before and an after. But he replaces the cinema with the magic lantern, movement by a succession of immobilities."[52] Sartre's worry was that history, when taken up through an archaeological analytic, is limp and unmoving, the dead frozen past dug up by careful excavation but incapable of living ever again. Influenced by Sartre's criticisms, a host of other French intellectuals critically responded to

Foucault.[53] In future decades, historians and political theorists in North America would echo many of the same criticisms.[54] Of further concern to Foucault himself was the political and social effect, or lack thereof, of his archaeological critiques, a concern that issued not in the least from his mutual engagements with Sartre in the turbid French political scene of the late 1960s.[55] Indeed if there is one thing that is clearly missing from archaeology, it is a clear sense of how archaeological inquiries might be deployed as critical contributions to the radical cultural ferment of the present in which he was immersed. Foucault's thought was ultimately an attempt to understand the world in which he found himself such that he might be able to provide tools that might help transform that world.

We find Foucault already wrestling with these problems in *The Archaeology of Knowledge*. The key section here is Part IV, Chapter 5, which Foucault opens by ap-ing Sartre's criticism of a few years prior: "Archaeology, however, seems to treat history only to freeze it." Foucault seems unsatisfied with his own response in admitting: "But there is nothing one can do about it." That, of course, is not entirely true, and a few pages later with a little more seriousness Foucault proposed an analytic of "transformations" in contrast to a reliance on an unanalyzable concept of historical "change."[56] As he proceeded in subsequent investigations, it became increasingly clear that he would need to retool methodologically to achieve a fuller engagement with transforming practices of power-knowledge. In order to analyze the "emergence" and "descent" of coproduced forms as proposed in "Nietzsche, Genealogy, History" he would have to expand the historiographical resources of archaeology.[57]

The historical transformations that Foucault came to analyze through the lenses of "emergence" and "descent" can be explained in terms of the first methodological shift registered above, namely the relations among two different vectors of analysis such as those formed at the twain of power-knowledge. On such a view the primary object of study is no longer either power or knowledge in isolation, but rather power-knowledge taken as an intersection. If the historiographical concept of a discursive formation was able to represent isolated scientific knowledge and presumably also isolated political knowledge as discrete historical slices in perfect repose, then the new historiographical concept of emergence reveals objects of analysis that are in continuous change precisely because coproduced complexes of power and knowledge are through and through historical. The historicity of these complexes is a function of the internal tension generated by the relations between elements of power and elements of knowledge. Pascal Michon helpfully notes of Foucault's genealogy, in a passage that seems as if intended as a response to Sartre's criticisms, "Through the historical study of the interplays of power-knowledge apparatus and of the succession of their conflicts, Foucault reintroduces movement in his descriptions, although without mobilizing a dialectical logic that would transform history into a process suited for the coming of the transcendence."[58] Foucault thereby reinvigorated the historical transformations ignored in archaeology without reviving the dialectics of transcendental subjectivity undone by archaeology.

But how does the coordination of two different vectors give rise to historical emergence if each vector by itself is insufficient for representing historical change? Change emerges at such sites of intersection precisely insofar as two vectors in interaction make possible the formation of tensions between the various elements that travel along each vector. These tensions provide impetus for change as each vector is resolved in order to accommodate the requirements imposed by the other vectors it intersects. As Foucault wrote, "Relations of power-knowledge are not static forms of distribution, they are 'matrices of transformations.'"[59] The twain of power and knowledge forms a matrix in which transformation becomes conceptualizable, that is, visible and sayable. The idea is that we can gain a sense of historical transition precisely by increasing the complexity of our objects of inquiry.

Is this really an appropriate way of recovering a sense of temporal and historical change? Did Foucault really need to shift to an analytical method privileging the relations between coproducing vectors rather than sticking to a method of serial multiple analyses of a single unified field? A single field taken by itself might very well lack any motivation to change once it establishes an internal coherence and stability. A body of knowledge, for example, may have little cause to innovate were it able to form a coherent set of assumptions and implications isolated from the impact of anything outside of that body of knowledge. It is only when that body of knowledge is forced to interact with external conditions such as social power (or economic forces or natural catastrophes or aesthetic experiences) that tensions might develop such that there will be sufficient motivation for revision in the body of knowledge. By shifting his interest to the interactivity between discrete vectors of power and knowledge, Foucault was able to develop an analytical perspective according to which these interactions already presume deep tensions that work to ceaselessly generate change. He was thus led away from a history of rupture and toward a history of continuity-with-discontinuity or repetition-and-difference: from solid being or empty nothing toward fluid becoming.

Foucault came to describe his new genealogical mode of research in terms that explicitly emphasized processes of transformation in place of factual discontinuities: "As you know, no one is more of a continuist than I am: to recognize a discontinuity is never anything more than to register a problem that needs to be solved." Reflecting back on *Discipline and Punish* a few years after its publication, he noted: "It was a matter not of digging down to a buried stratum of continuity, but of identifying the transformation that made this hurried transition possible."[60] We are a long way here from the archaeological resistance to continuity. Foucault's historiography came to look toward a temporality in which continuities and transitions, repetitions and differences, enabled one another. Dominick LaCapra helpfully summarizes the temporality at work in Foucault as "recurrence with change in contrast to either unbroken continuity or unproblematic epistemological breaks between periods."[61] Foucault's genealogy treats history as traveling along multiple temporalities: "History, then, is not a single time space: it is a multiplicity of time spans that entangle and envelop one another."[62] And again elsewhere: "several times, several durations, several speeds get entangled with one another, cross and form precisely events."[63] The genealogist recovers time's multiplicity through the lens of the contingent and complex intersections along multiple vectors of practice.

If all of this is right, then many of Foucault's commentators have been wrong to insist that genealogy furthers the historiographical retreat already under way in archaeology from historical time toward historical space. In one of the fullest treatments of Foucault's philosophy of history to date, Thomas Flynn interprets Foucault precisely along these spatializing lines by discerning in his work a "characteristically poststructuralist" approach that consists in the "emphasis on space over time both in the metaphors he employs and especially in the arguments he mounts."[64] Yet it is not at all clear that such an emphasis counts as "characteristically poststructuralist" or even as characteristic of Foucault. David Hoy convincingly argues that "despite Foucault's tendency to think about power in spatial pictures," his thought, just like that of another poststructuralist, namely Deleuze, "is in fact concerned with temporality throughout."[65] Genealogy does not aim to substitute space for time, but rather aims to substitute temporal complexity and contingency for historical unity and necessity. Foucault used genealogy to recover temporality rather than to reduce it.

The two methodological shifts I have traced are what enabled Foucault to bring into focus the sheer contingency of the processes by which we have constituted ourselves where his former work had only been able to treat the emergence of our processes of self-constitution as more or less arbitrary. This returns us, finally, to the crucial issue of the relation between philosophy and politics in Foucault's practice of critique. The difference between a genealogical history of contingency and an archaeological history of arbitrariness is, at least in part, the difference between a history oriented to the present and a history without any orientation at all. It is difficult to do anything about the present within which one defines oneself if one regards the history of the present as arbitrary. But if the history of the present is a story of unexpected contingencies, then we already have much material in hand for transforming that present in ways we had previously not yet dreamt of. The specific advantage of Foucault's form of critical inquiry is therefore not that it merely shows our practices of knowledge, power, and ethics to be contingent and hence capable of undergoing transformation, as many commentators have argued. The advantage is rather that genealogy shows the precise ways in which our knowledges, powers, and ethics have contingently formed. In so doing, genealogy provides us with a great deal of specific material we will need to make use of if we are to engage in the project of transforming the contingent forms of our subjectivation. Foucault's primary aim is not to demonstrate *that* our present is contingently formed but to show *how* we have contingently formed ourselves so as to make available the materials we would need to constitute ourselves otherwise. This crucial point of Foucault's philosophico-historical work has been so widely misunderstood that it is today commonplace that the central message of Foucault is *that* things could be otherwise than they are when indeed the real force of his thought is to show us *how* things might be transformed on the basis of the materials furnished by our contingently constructed present—this, as I argue at greater length in Chapter 4, is the difference between a quasi-transcendental approach to contingency and an empirical analytics of contingency.

Foucault's Critical Inquiry as Problematization

Foucault's shift from an archaeological inquiry into the past existence of an isolable episteme to an archaeological-and-genealogical inquiry into the emergence into being of related vectors of knowledge, power, and ethics opened up new possibilities for thought that had remained obscure in his earlier work. Foucault was able to now use genealogy-plus-archaeology as a practice of critical inquiry into the history of the present because of his crucial shift to a more expansive object of study than that sponsored by his earlier only-archaeological methodology. This involved a reciprocal elaboration of the study of both historical emergence and the relations between knowledge and power. This double expansion enabled him to overcome the philosophical and political limitations implicit in his earlier inquiries into temporally disconnected fragments of the archive and into deployments of either power or knowledge taken in isolation from one another. By analyzing practices in terms of the multiple interrelated vectors over which they range, Foucault could not help but realize that the historical events he was pre-viously content to regard as static were in fact undergoing constant change—and by treating historical events as subject to multiple kinds of transformation, Fou-cault could not but require himself to expand his focus so as to account for the interrelations amongst different vectors or trajectories of practice. If the object of archaeology was to present the particular series of truths that functioned to sus-tain any particular historically discrete form of knowledge or power, then the ob-ject of genealogy would be to present the way in which these series of truths were produced, sustained, and revised over the course of a particular historical period. It is in this sense that Foucault's interest shifted from a quaint Borgesian fascina-tion with the different shapes that truth can assume to a serious Kantian inquiry into the conditions of the possibility within which these shapes of truth emerge in their multiplicitous forms.

In this way, Foucault renewed the project of undertaking inquiries that func-tion to render intelligible and transformable the present situations in which he found himself. In this way, his work could begin to contribute to the forms of con-stitution of knowledge, power, and ethics that Foucault and his contemporaries were enacting. But how can an inquiry into emergent forms be used as a history of the present in these ways? To answer this question, we need to turn to another of Foucault's key ideas: problematization. Problematization thus functions as a kind of master key for explicating what Foucault used archaeology-plus-genealogy to do. A summary overview of my argument in this section can be put as follows: the idea of a history of the present offered Foucault a number of distinctive political-philosophical challenges to which he responded by developing a form of inquiry that would enable him to articulate the problematizations that are the conditions of possibility for the present.

By placing problematization at the center of Foucault's mature work, I pro-pose to take seriously the following claim, which he offered during an interview late in his life: "The notion common to all the work that I have done since *History of Madness* is that of problematization, though it must be said that I never isolated this notion sufficiently. . . . In *History of Madness* the question was how and why, at a given moment, madness was problematised through a certain institutional prac-tice and a certain apparatus of knowledge. Similarly, in *Discipline and Punish* I was trying to analyze the changes in the problematization of the relations between crime and punishment through penal practices and penitentiary institutions in the late eighteenth and early nineteenth centuries."[66] It is remarkable that, de-spite the enormous volume of critical literature on Foucault, very few commen-tators have taken seriously Foucault's claim that problematization forms a central theme for properly understanding all of his major works. For a number of years critics and commentators entirely ignored the presence of problematization as a distinct conception in Foucault's thought.[67] In more recent commentaries there has emerged a tendency toward a sort of grudging acknowledgment of problematization according to which this methodological strategy forms a kind of third axis for Foucaultian inquiry that follows up on the two separate axes of archaeology and genealogy.[68] But counter to this recent interpretation, I insist that we be clear that Foucault did not claim that "my work *now* is about problematization" when in fact he said "my work has *always* been about problematization." Problematization is not some third form of inquiry that one might take up alongside archaeology and genealogy—it is rather a methodological orientation which thoroughly inflects both.

Some might protest that Foucault's remark was rather self-serving such that it is really quite inappropriate to read his earlier works in terms of a concept that he did not explicitly elaborate until much later.[69] There is something to this criticism, but on the whole I find it too simplifying. Problematization indeed did not become an overt theme in Foucault's work until the late 1970s and early 1980s, and it was in 1978 at the earliest that the concept began to assume an explicit status in his theoretical repertoire.[70] But the concept (and the words "problématisation" and "problématique" themselves) can be found in an obviously inchoate usage in works of a much earlier date. We find them in the mid-1970s in *Discipline and Punish*, in the Collège de France course lectures later published under the title *Abnormal*, and in the short essay titled "The Politics of Health in the Eighteenth Century."[71] And going back even farther, one finds the concept anticipated in a surprising range of writings. In *The Order of Things* Foucault refers to "an archaeological analysis of knowledge itself" which explicates "the conditions that make a controversy or problem possible."[72] There are even a handful of passages in *History of Madness* in which Foucault appears to take up his core themes of madness and reason in terms of the problematization that motivated their segregation, though it should be noted for the sake of scholarly compunction that although the argument here relies on the notion of the emergence of "problems," it does not explicitly feature the term "problématisation" but rather only "problématique" and "problème."[73] Going back farther yet, the very first appearance of "problématique" in Foucault's work appears to be from his earliest publication, the 1954 introduction to Binswanger's *Dream and Existence*, though it is clear that the term here has a quite different sense than it would later assume when his more central focus would become "problématisation" as both verb and noun.[74]

In addition to textual evidence suggesting the importance of the concept of problematization throughout Foucault's writings, we can trace the circulation of the concept in Foucault's intellectual milieu at least as far back as the early 1960s. It was in the mid-to-late 1960s when Deleuze elaborated his own conception of problematization in a number of books with which Foucault would soon be intimately familiar.[75] It is not inconceivable that Foucault's thought was long invested by the notion of the "problematic" as that notion was featured in the earlier work of Deleuze and others including Canguilhem, Althusser, and even Heidegger. These considerations ought to enable us to at least take seriously Foucault's claim for the importance of problematization across his entire career. Remaining merely charitable to Foucault for the moment, I shall further discuss the claim in order to give it more weight in Chapter 4.

Taking Foucault's self-description seriously, then, I want to suggest that we regard genealogy as an analytic for orienting critical inquiries into the emergence of problematizations of practice constituted by the complex intersection of multiple vectors of practice. Such a form of inquiry is suitable for a history of the present because it enables an inquiry into the emergence of those problematizations within which we presently constitute ourselves. If this is right, then my account offers a more or less complete explanation of Foucault's shift from an archaeological analytic to a broader analytic that encompasses both genealogical histories of problematizations and archaeological excavations of historical problematizations. When he finally began to explicitly describe his own work as efforts concerned with problematization, Foucault described the relationship between archaeology and genealogy, as I have here, as compatible: "The archaeological dimensions of the analysis made it possible to examine the forms [of problematization] themselves; its genealogical dimension enabled me to analyze their formation out of the practices and the modifications undergone by the latter."[76] Archaeology describes the static forms of problematizations, whereas genealogy engages the contingent historical emergence of these problematizations in the context of complex practices. Archaeology lays bare a field of practices, while genealogy tracks the flow of these fields into the present practices that are their target. Archaeology analyzes logics of rules, and genealogy analyzes dynamics of strategies. These two modes of inquiry fit together quite nicely. And many of Foucault's own inquiries instantiate this nice fit.

Emphasizing problematization for understanding archaeology and genealogy suggests the need for a fuller explication of problematization itself. This is the work of the next three chapters. As a kind of preview, however, critique as problematization can be specified at a first pass as a form of critical inquiry with two core aspects: contingency and complexity. By focusing on the emergence of hybrid networks of problems, we can come to recognize our problems as contingent complexes rather than necessary givens. By clarifying and intensifying the conditions structuring these coproduced networks of problems and solutions, archaeology and genealogy enable us to adopt a more reflective relation to the situations in which we already find ourselves, whether consciously or not, enmeshed. In sum, problematization functions to open up our problems in their full contingency and complexity in a way that makes them available for critical investigation. This conception of problematization as both clarification and intensification exemplifies the general relation to the historical present that Foucault sought to elaborate in his mature work and that necessitated his shift from archaeology more narrowly conceived to a broader critical ensemble consisting of genealogy and archaeology together. If one objection to archaeology taken by itself was, as Rabinow and Dreyfus convincingly showed, a "qualified nihilism" about the present, then the advantage of archaeology-plus-genealogy is, as they put it, that Foucault is now "able to diagnose our problems because he shares them."[77]

To summarize the overall trajectory of the interpretation of Foucault's work offered thus far: the development of the genealogical form of critical inquiry is motivated by a need to write the history of the present in a way that answers to two related, but not coinciding, requirements stemming from philosophy and from politics. This is a function that archaeology on its own could not provide. The genealogical practice of critical inquiry that emerged to perform this service is one that emphasizes a study of the relations between power and knowledge as well as a study of temporal processes of emergence. These two aspects of inquiry can be brought together in terms of the clarification and intensification of problematizations. These three Foucaultian elements of power-knowledge, temporal emergence, and problematization constitute the core of his reconstruction of critique. Critique now becomes an inquiry into the conditions set by problematizations as they manifest in the contingent emergence of complex intersections of practices.

An Hourglass of Threads

To make sense of the complex relations composing the many aspects of a philosopher's work, it is often useful to package those many aspects together into simple images that offer memorable portraits of their relation to one another. Hence one of the most reliable tools of the philosopher: the chalkboard diagram. (Someone should, I think, put together a book of some of our diagrams with large high-quality images flanked by short little explanatory notes in the margins. Consider this an open proposal.)

In the case of important parts of Foucault's work, I often find it useful to coordinate their relation in terms of a diagrammatic image I like to call "the hourglass of threads."[78] Picture an hourglass horizontal on its side. In the two bulbs of the hourglass are not sand, nor powdered marble, nor mercury, but threads of multiple colors. The threads are thick enough so that they can be drawn through the thin neck of the hourglass only one at a time. In the left bulb of the hourglass, the threads are all tangled together in chaotic fashion: they look like they have come from an unkempt sewing box that would be a true chore to put back into disentangled order. Here it is difficult to pull out any single thread more than a little bit before one encounters a whole knot of threads that must be unraveled before any single strand can be further pulled free of the rest. In the neck of the hourglass, one can observe various individual threads as they are pulled through from the left bulb to the right: just one thread fits at a time such that they can pass through the neck not as a tangled lump of material but as singular strands, each displaying its unique color and texture. In the right bulb of the hourglass, one can observe the various threads as separated from one another in such a way as to make visible the relations that each thread holds with the others. The key to the image is this: the threads on the left are all tied together in a fashion that is difficult to discern, whereas the threads on the right are not unrelated or isolated, but rather coordinate with one another in some more coherent fashion, though certainly not a neat and tidy pattern.

This image can be used to represent two aspects of Foucault's work that are often difficult to make sense of. First, it conveys a convenient picture of the relation between Foucault's archaeological and genealogical methodologies. Second, if the horizontal axis on which the hourglass rests sideways is seen as a chronology of Foucault's publishing career, it conveys a picture of the various periods of Foucault's work and their relation to one another.

First, methodologically, we can see the left bulb as overflowing with the tangled threads of practices, institutions, ideas, and behaviors that as yet remain incomprehensible to the observer. The *left bulb* may be seen in terms of practices as they so often appear to themselves: unclarified, incomprehensible, and yet somehow functioning amidst the morass of multiplicities that make them up. The *neck* may be seen as a view of these practices as they are drawn up, or discerned, by an archaeological analytic. Archaeology neutralizes and isolates the various threads that remain confusedly tangled in the left bulb. Archaeology narrows our focus of vision such that we can get an intellectual grip on practical experience, and it does so by neutralizing part of that practical experience and allowing us to view it on its own in terms of the unity of a discursive formation. One can archaeologically isolate the thread of knowledge as found in a particular historically constrained set of practices (for instance, the conditions of representational science in the Classical Age as isolated by *The Order of Things*). Yet one can also archaeologically isolate all the other threads that may be constitutive of the practices in which we find ourselves: not just knowledge, but also those various other threads mentioned by Foucault at the end of *The Archaeology of Knowledge* as fields fertile for archaeological inquiry. We can, as Foucault insisted, perfectly well write not just archaeologies of knowledge, but also archaeologies of power, of sexuality, of aesthetics, and so on. The *right bulb* of the hourglass may then be seen in terms of these same practices as they are coordinated by a genealogical analytic. Genealogy takes as its material the neutralized singularities as they are drawn through the neck by archaeology. These singularized threads are then coordinated and related by a genealogy into a larger multi-threaded singularity. A genealogy lays hold of a multiplicity of disentangled threads and weaves them together in a coherent fashion such that we can discern their relations, complex and contingent as they are, between one another.

Two notes about the picture I have just offered are in order. It is important to note in the first place that the threads in both bulbs are the same stuff making up the very same practices. The left-side threads are the practices as they often appear to themselves without reflective orientation, while the right-side threads are the very same threads as they appear to the critical inquirer (who, of course, may also be a participant in the practices). Archaeology and genealogy thus help us get clear on the material that forms our practices. They do this not by abstracting from or radically altering these practices but rather by analytically drawing them up in a way that offers an opportunity to articulate practices. This articulation itself may, of course, facilitate transformative intervention into these practices. Insofar as they do facilitate this, they can be recognized as histories of the present that provide us with materials we might need to transform our futures.

It is secondly important to note that, according to my image, genealogy functions well only if it follows after an archaeological procedure of disentangling the various threads composing the practices in which we find ourselves. The implication, of course, is not that genealogy always requires archaeology. Rather, the implication is that the genealogical analytic of coordinating various threads in their relation to one another requires the work of another analytic that would provide genealogy with singular threads. The threads that are tangled in the left bulb must be isolated from one another, or neutralized, so that we may get a view of each thread on its own. Following the archaeological procedure of separating the various threads such that we do not find ourselves quickly stuck at a knot when we tug a little on any given thread, genealogy then conducts the operation of coordinating the various threads with one another. The point is not to reduce power or knowledge to one another. The point is to coordinate singular vectors of our practices in their relation to one another. Genealogy enables us to grasp the coherence of a complex welter of practical material that is contingently interrelated. It does so in a way that both encourages respect for the profound stability of this practical material as it functions and also enables acknowledgement of the sheer contingency of this stability. The worlds we have built for ourselves are always open to transformation. But that transformation will never be easy.

Turning now to a second application of the hourglass image, consider the periodization of Foucault's work. The usual periodization that divides Foucault's work into three sharply separated phases is rather misleading even if there is clearly some truth to the thought that Foucault was constantly innovating, continuously creating, and never immobile. The image of an hourglass of threads usefully represents the differences-within-continuities featured in the tripartite structure of Foucault's work, as the image helps us grasp how all of Foucault's work is devoted in different ways to the same critical imperative. Allow me to explain. Taking the hourglass on its side such that it horizontally charts the chronology of Foucault's published works suggests the following: the left bulb is descriptive of *History of Madness* and *The Birth of the Clinic*, the neck represents the high archaeological work of *The Order of Things* and much of *The Archaeology of Knowledge*, and the right bulb portrays the later enriched genealogical-plus-archaeological works from *Discipline and Punish* through all three volumes of *The History of Sexuality*.

We can interpret this image as follows. Foucault in his earliest works was proto-genealogical in his attempt to undertake an analysis of our practices in terms of the swarming multiplicity of practical material composing them. This was an admirable effort, but nobody reading these works, especially *History of Madness*, can admit to their being entirely successful. There are too many uncoordinated elements here, too many loose threads, and too many impenetrable knots. This is not to disparage the work but only to suggest that it announced a project that could not be completed within its pages. Foucault, I think, recognized that he had failed to fully unravel the tangled complexity he took as his object of inquiry. In the second phase of his work he therefore undertook to neutralize just a portion of those threads he had previously sought to inquire into. Thus *The Order of Things* is much more restricted in scope than *History of Madness*. The first dealt with psychiatry, reason, madness, and something called "unreason" in their composition by various threads including knowledge, power, and ethics. The second proposed to deal with the history of modern sciences by neutralizing just one of these threads, namely knowledge. In an interview, Foucault later explained: "*The Order of Things* is situated at a purely descriptive level that leaves entirely aside all analysis of the relations of power that underlie and make possible the appearance of a type of discourse. If I wrote this book, I wrote it after two others . . . precisely because in these first two books, in a manner a little confused and anarchical, I had tried to treat all the problems together."[79] The more humble approach of Foucault's archaeological period indeed yielded something grand and impressive: there is an almost inexhaustible fund of interesting things to say about the composition of the singular thread of knowledge in the history of the sciences. Foucault nonetheless felt restless with this approach, and rightly so. In the third phase of his work, represented by the right bulb of the hourglass, he began to attempt again an inquiry into practices in a fuller sense. He began to treat "all the problems" again, but now he no longer had to treat them "together" insofar as the advantage of an archaeological analytic would enable him to get the various threads into isolated views. The later work from *Discipline and Punish* forward could thus deal with the multiplicity of threads composing the materials of our practical realities, but in a way that would enable their coordination and relation as a complex material that has contingently coalesced in such a way as to form the conditioning limits of doing, thinking, and being in the present.

The hourglass image helps us see that Foucault's concern with the basic problems of modernity was central for all of his work. This reinterpretation, which recasts Foucault's work in light of the idea of problematization, helps us make sense of some of the most perplexing issues concerning the periodization of his major works. On my reading it follows that there was no big break in Foucault's career such that we might divide his work into two or three discontinuous phases of early, middle, and late thought. It is just as useful to focus on the fact of a continuity that runs throughout Foucault's work, all the way from *History of Madness* to *The Care of the Self*. This continuity can be seen in terms of Foucault's interest in, focus in terms of, and work on the basic problems faced by us moderns. These are the problems of the self-constitution of the various forms of knowledge, power, and ethics through which we form ourselves as subjects. In all of his major works, we witness Foucault eagerly exploring the processes of division through which we come to experience ourselves as knowing subjects, free subjects, and normed subjects.

Foucault struggled throughout his career to fashion a methodological analytic for articulating these processes of self-problematization. In *History of Madness*, his methodology remained more or less opaque. In *The Order of Things,* he described these processes in terms of the analytic category of "epistemes," whereas in *The Archaeology of Knowledge* he shifted terminology to that of "discursive formations." In *The Will to Know,* he employed, without all that much clarity, the category of "dispositif." And in his final work he made use of the category of "problematization," though as I showed earlier, this term appears in Foucault's work both earlier and with more frequency than one might expect. The methodologico-analytic challenge that all of these categories are working on can be put in terms of the following question: How can we come to understand heterogeneous collections of constitutive practices in terms of a singularity without invoking a transcendental category to do so? My argument in this book is that the concept of problematization provides us with a better grip on the full range of Foucault's methodology intent than do episteme, discursive formation, dispositif, and other such concepts, all of which I regard more or less as successive attempts to work out the kind of idea that achieves self-clarity with the concept of problematization. The concept of problematization is so appealing because it offers a way to unify the many methodological constructs haunting our reading of Foucault. Thus a guiding motivation for focusing on continuities in an interpretation of Foucault is that it facilitates a positive distillation of those methodological dimensions of Foucault's work that are superlative.

But of course calling attention to such continuity and unity in Foucault's work need not involve the effacement of lingering differences. There was, of course, a shift in Foucault's thought between the period in which he authored *The Order of Things* and *The Archaeology of Knowledge* and the period in which he authored *Discipline and Punish* and *The Will to Know.* I have detailed this shift already. My point now is that this shift should not be regarded as representative of a deep divide in Foucault's thought, as the common wisdom perpetrates. Foucault's move from a narrow just-archaeological form of inquiry to a more inclusive archaeological-plus-genealogical analytic was a major shift, but it should not lead us to the conclusion that his early and late books were about substantially different things or made use of incompatible methodologies. Carving up Foucault's thought into discontinuous periods effaces those precious points of correlation that run through all of his inquiries. I am not insisting that there are no differences across Foucault's career, but rather that the usual ways of understanding those differences are often misleading. My argument is that Foucault does not reject his previous self, as is commonly thought in terms of a genealogical rejection of archaeology or an ethical rejection of genealogy. Rather than rejecting his previous selves, Foucault elaborates a methodological perspective that, over the course of his career, gains increasing self-consciousness about the orientation, intention, and workings of a practice of critique that does justice to requirements of both philosophy and politics. To make all this more explicit, I can address in finer detail two misleading ways in which commentators divide Foucault's work against itself.

The first misleading tendency concerns the procedure of marking out a deep divide between the works of "the early Foucault" that supposedly share a methodological commonality and the genealogical investigations of "the later Foucault" from which they differ. This procedure lumps in *History of Madness* and *The Birth of the Clinic* with *The Order of Things* and *The Archaeology of Knowledge.* But, I contend, *History of Madness* and *The Birth of the Clinic* are much closer to *Discipline and Punish* than they are to *The Order of Things,* with respect to both methodology and theme. Arnold Davidson similarly situates the methodological trajectory of Foucault's *oeuvre:* "Both *Historie de la folie* and *Naissance de la clinique* were not only archeological, but genealogical *avant la lettre.*"[80] Rereading the recently translated full text of *History of Madness* (especially the now translated complete Part III), it is clear that this book was already broaching many of the thematic problems that Foucault would later take up in *Discipline and Punish* and *The Will to Know:* deviance, abnormality, the psyche, its training, and its transformation.[81] Understanding Foucault's genealogies of modernity written in the 1970s as of a piece with his histories of modern madness, psychiatry, and medicine published in the early 1960s helps us capture the continuities in Foucault's work that persisted across divides that, although real, do not involve philosophical incompatibilities. It is worth noting that Foucault himself suggested as much in a short autobiographical statement written near the end of his life.[82]

But how does my interpretation deal with the two works of Foucault's that appear purely archaeological in orientation, namely *The Order of Things* and *The Archaeology of Knowledge*? Foucault himself encourages us to see these books as explorations that are but partial attempts at carrying out his overall project as initially defined in *History of Madness* and later carried out more fully in *Discipline and Punish* and the *History of Sexuality* volumes. In many ways, these two middle books can be read as tracing a rather long tangential curve into a high archaeological methodology from which Foucault would eventually return to his genealogical analytic. This interpretation may seem odd. *The Order of Things* is, after all, the book that made Foucault famous. But, perhaps, this work should be read as offering a vivid display of the consequences of a young philosopher being derailed by the academic fashion of his day. Perhaps this book reveals a Foucault deeply caught up within Parisian poststructuralism. Fashion may have made Foucault famous. But it is notable that Foucault very quickly, and indeed quite explicitly in the preface to the English translation of that book, rejected the terms of his fame and declared almost immediately his exteriority to the terms on which he was being enthusiastically received. It was only after Foucault removed himself from the high fashion of Parisian intellectual circles (that is, after moving to Tunisia, taking up once again the work of Nietzsche, immersing himself for a time in Anglo-American philosophical work, and experiencing firsthand working practices of freedom in Tunis and Vincennes) that he could return from his partial archaeological analytic and his tangential nominalist orientation to his more central concerns with the problematizations of our diverse forms of modern experience. After Foucault's return to this problematization, he simply refused to hew to the approaches laid out in such enormous detail in *The Archaeology of Knowledge.* Consider in this light Foucault's strongly worded remarks about *The Order of Things* in a 1978 interview, when he described the book as a lightweight "kind of formal exercise." When pressed about this dismissive attitude by his flustered interviewer, Foucault went even further and claimed that "*The Order of Things* is not a book that's truly mine; it's a marginal book in terms of the sort of passion that runs through the others."[83] This is probably an overstatement, but it nonetheless usefully fits with my interpretation, especially if we note that Foucault never dismissed (at least in print) any of his other works.

A second misleading tendency characteristic of the usual periodization of Foucault's work involves a second supposed divide, this one between the first volume of *The History of Sexuality* and the work that would follow it. This break is supposed to mark two quite distinct phases in Foucault's thought: the power-Foucault and the ethics-Foucault. This interpretive strategy is much thornier for my purposes, and I shall continue to wrestle with it in later chapters. In short, what I will argue is that the genealogy of modernity laid out in *Discipline and Punish* and the first volume of *The History of Sexuality* stated a basic problematization that Foucault saw himself as responding to in later work such as *The Use of Pleasure* and *The Care of the Self.* The so-called "late work" is actually a direct response to the problems elaborated by the so-called "middle work" such that the ethical writings never abandon, not even for a moment, the terms of the problems to which they are offered as a response. There is, in other words, no discontinuity of principled opposition between these two phases of work. There is only the methodological transition (albeit not a smooth one) from the work of posing a difficult question to the effort at responding to that question. The shift in orientation involved here was nothing like an intellectual breach, but rather was a methodological change consisting in the subtle movement from the work of posing a problem toward the work of responding to a problem. Following up on his work on the problematizations of modernity, work that occupied him across the better part of two decades, the later work on ethics can be usefully read as responsive to the problems specified by the earlier inquiries. "In the face of normalization and against it, *Le Souci de soi*," observed Georges Canguilhem of Foucault's late work.[84] Many have argued, and I agree but with some important qualifications, that Foucault's ethical response remained incomplete at his life's end. Yet it was Foucault's thought that ethics would be an always-unfinished work that would be left to us to further for and by ourselves. This is to say that it would be a form of work that could never exhaust itself. Foucault never sought complete solutions, but rather rigorous problematizations that were to be followed up by self-transformative responses that could, by virtue of these problematizations, never be fully completed.

The reperiodization of Foucault's work I am proposing goes against much of the received wisdom in the existing scholarship, most notably the two accounts of division just discussed. That my approach diverges from a consensus should not speak against it, but it does suggest that my interpretation requires some amount of justification. The usual periodiziations of early, middle, and late work or knowledge-focused, power-focused, and ethics-focused work simply cannot capture the unifying subtleties of Foucault's many forms of thought. Foucault in all of his work is inquiring into the way in which we simultaneously constitute ourselves as subjects of knowledge, power, and ethics. His work can be seen as charting an overall trajectory of problematizations of the modern subject leading to responsive efforts to form ourselves otherwise.

Why is this work still valuable today? In short, because it involves a labor of thought that matters to us still. Who has not wandered, in moments of frightful solace, into the dark fear that only the thinnest border separates one from an irredeemable lapse into madness? Who has not dreamt of prisons, facing with real dread the possibility that one might one day have to find the courage for survival in some dark and lonely cell? Who has not conjectured that perhaps, after all, there is not so much that separates oneself from a criminal, a lunatic, a patient, or any other kind of "abnormal"? Who does not find it irresistibly attractive, both in one's brightest and in one's shallowest moments, to completely identify oneself with one's sexuality? These are not items of merely provincial concern that disturb certain philosophers, historians, and scandal-ready critics and readers. These are among the forms of experience, the knowledges and powers and ethics, through which we all daily constitute ourselves today. They are the forms in which we work on our selves. They are the conditions of possibility of who we

are and who we may yet become. Genealogy would promise to help us understand them, and hence our selves, better. And what of the new problematizations
we face today as the conditions of possibility for who we are? If Foucault himself
did not elaborate these, if he could not elaborate that which followed him, he did
however develop a methodological repertoire that should facilitate our gaining a
grip on who we have become in the time since.

2

Three Uses of Genealogy

Subversion, Vindication & Problematization

The Capaciousness of Genealogy as a Tradition

I have been describing genealogy as something of a philosophical tradition. But if genealogy is indeed a tradition, it is not clear that it is in the same way that, say, phenomenology, or critical theory, or pragmatism, or analytic philosophy constitute distinctive philosophical traditions. These traditions can be characterized by a continuity of intellectual work undertaken by a group of thinkers standing in various kinds of direct sociological relations to one another. Or they can be characterized in terms of shared philosophical commitments, such as the commitment to reflexive social critique in critical theory or the commitment to the priority of existence to essence in existentialism. And yet the traditions named above are instructive, for if we really want to specify why any of these four counts as a tradition, it turns out that shared philosophical commitments will not always do the work of helping us understand what makes a tradition. Internal disagreements are famous in pragmatism (Peirce versus James, Dewey versus Rorty) and in critical theory (Habermas versus Horkheimer and Adorno); it is not at all clear that we can find a commitment common to all of the major phenomenologists (Husserl, Heidegger, Merleau-Ponty, and what about Derrida?); and no one has yet achieved a satisfactory characterization of analytic philosophy that would capture every major figure who is undeniably analytic (Russell, Carnap, Quine, Davidson, Lewis, Kripke, and the list goes on).

Philosophical traditions are as much about shared debates as they are about shared beliefs, if not more so.[1] In the case of genealogy, at least, such a perspective seems entirely appropriate. Genealogy should be seen as a tradition not so much by virtue of a core set of shared philosophical commitments, but rather by virtue of a set of debates about the ways in which critical philosophy can bring history into its orbit in order to do the work that it has set for itself. Genealogy is best regarded as shorthand for a set of debates centered around a set of analytic and diagnostic procedures (or, to risk a fraught word already risked above, a methodology) for bringing philosophy and history together.

We ought to allow ourselves in this way to recognize the diversity, or rather the capaciousness, of genealogy. We also ought to encourage ourselves to specify the details of this diversity. That genealogy can take many forms does not mean it can take just any form—and so it is worth specifying and distinguishing the forms it has assumed. Edward Craig provides a nice starting point: "[Genealogies] can be subversive, or vindicatory, of the doctrines or practices whose origins (factual, imaginary, and conjectural) they claim to describe. They may at the same time be explanatory, accounting for the existence of whatever it is that they vindicate or subvert. In theory, at least, they may be merely explanatory, evaluatively neutral."[2] It is implicit in Craig's distinctions that a plurality of practices of critical inquiry rightfully passes under the name of genealogy. This pluralism, of course, is to be expected if we regard genealogy as a tradition of debate. A fuller comparative analysis of the plurality of critical uses to which genealogy has been put will enable us to better appreciate the specific diacritic of the different modalities of genealogy currently available. This chapter presents a non-exhaustive taxonomy of three different conceptions of genealogy: subversive, vindicatory, and problematizing. The first two forms, as the quote from Craig exhibits, are by far the more familiar to us today. But it is the third, more explanatory, use of genealogy I find the most interesting.

The best-known emblem of subversive genealogy is Friedrich Nietzsche's genealogy of morality, but we might also think of Charles Darwin's genealogy of *Homo sapiens* as another such emblem, and also of both of these as anticipated by David Hume's proto-genealogical account undermining standard accounts of the origin of religion.[3] These emblems help inform a good deal of rather misleadingly labeled work that today presents itself as genealogical merely by virtue of attempting to be subversive and a little historical at the same time. Emblems of my second category, vindicatory genealogy, include the work of new British genealogists such as Bernard Williams's genealogy of truth and truthfulness, Quentin Skinner's self-labeled genealogies of liberty and the modern state, and Craig's own genealogy of knowledge, all of which are perhaps informed to some extent by older British efforts in genealogy such as that offered in Thomas Hobbes's proto-genealogical account of the conditions of the possibility of the emergence of sovereign power.[4] Also worth mentioning in this connection are Barry Allen's genealogies of knowledge, art, and technology that, though not vindicatory in any straightforward sense, are presented as complex histories that are meant to capture what is of value in the contingent accomplishments we like to honor with grand labels like "knowledge" and "art."[5]

The third form of genealogy is much less familiar to us today. It is a form of genealogy that is neither for nor against the practices it inquires into, but is rather an attempt to clarify and intensify the difficulties that enable and disable those practices. Craig himself expresses skepticism about the very possibility of such a third form: "I doubt whether there can be such a thing as an intrinsically neutral genealogy, if that means one containing no feature that human beings could, even locally and temporarily, find to tell for or against the item whose history it purports to narrate."[6] Craig is right to suggest that the idea that any rigorous form of inquiry could be "neutral" is far from helpful. But he is mistaken if he means to suggest that genealogies cannot be put forward under a critical modality that aims to be neither for nor against. This is exactly the critical modality achieved in Foucault's practice of genealogy as problematization. Granted that no philosopher can be neutral about everything, there is still room for the philosopher to aim to remain neutral about some things. The mode of neutrality is the mode of doubt, indeterminacy, and vagueness. It is in this sense that genealogical problematization is neutral—it leaves us in doubt, with questions, and unprepared to pronounce a verdict.

To defend this view I want to contrast problematizational genealogy as it figures in Foucault's work from Nietzsche's subversive genealogy and Williams's vindicatory genealogy. My aims in this chapter can therefore be described as a kind of muddling-through of some of the thickets of the tradition of genealogy in order to discriminate three different taxa of historical inquiry while acknowledging that all of these different inquiries have enough in common that they can all rightly gather under the tent of genealogy.[7]

Let me begin then with some general commonalities. Williams defines genealogy as "a narrative that tries to explain a cultural phenomenon by describing a way in which it came about, or could have come about, or might be imagined to have come about."[8] Nietzsche never really offers definitions, but he does at least implicitly describe genealogy as a form of inquiry that should enable us "to know about the conditions and circumstances under which the values [of morality] grew up, developed and changed."[9] Foucault can agree with both of these conceptions of genealogical inquiry insofar as they are about inquiring into the conditions of emergence of practices.

Where Foucault departs from Nietzsche and Williams is in their ambition to use genealogy to obtain normative results. Nietzsche and Williams deployed genealogy as a practice of inquiry that can settle certain questions concerning the value of the practices inquired into. This is the ambition that Craig takes to be intrinsic to genealogy. Now, of course, Nietzsche and Williams deploy genealogy in two quite different senses insofar as the former used genealogy to undermine modern moral practices expressing a will to truth, while the latter sought to historically strengthen modern moral notions expressing the value of our practices of truthfulness. Despite these differences, Nietzsche and Williams diverge from Foucaultian genealogy in the very same way insofar as they both deploy genealogical histories to generate normative justifications. Foucault, by contrast, deployed genealogy in order to clarify and intensify problematizations. By thus differentiating these three uses of genealogy (and the two contrastive critical modalities they express) there arises an opportunity for reassessing the project of genealogy as critique. The point I am eager to make is that the kind of critical resources to which Foucault's genealogy is keyed are not the kind of traditional normative resources that fuel the projects of Williams, Nietzsche, and so much of modern "critical" thought.

There are, of course, other smaller differences separating Foucault on the one hand from Nietzsche and Williams on the other. I am not sure that these have much to do with the primary contrast between problematizing and normative genealogies that I am eager to draw. But at least one of these other differences is worth mentioning. Williams explicitly endorses the practice of "fictional" or "imaginary" genealogy.[10] Nietzsche, although he unambiguously denounces a certain "English hypothesis-mongering into the blue," clearly indulged in enormously bold speculations in the course of developing his genealogies.[11] This is in marked contrast from Foucault, who is the only one of these three philosophers to practice anything that might even be conceivably recognized by historians as connected to their craft. To the extent that Nietzsche and Williams did connect with history, they at best practiced an old-fashioned kind of history of ideas (which contrasts in many ways from more new-fashioned work in intellectual history), and without anything near the level of archival breadth and detail evident in Foucault's writings. Even when Nietzsche and Williams did look at practices, it was almost always in order to descry ideas postulated as representative of these practices. Nietzsche offers a genealogy of ideas of punishment and guilt, and of ascetic ideals, but he is not really concerned with the actual practical procedures through which those ideas are implemented. Williams presents a genealogy of ideas of truthfulness, but not the strategies and materials that let truthfulness live. These are not failings on their part—all I intend to reveal are differing objects of analytical focus. Foucault quite clearly analyzed ideas, mentalities, and theories, but his focus was always most centrally on what he called "problematizations and practices."[12] This difference between a speculative blue genealogy and a meticulous gray genealogy may be connected in important ways to the differences separating a normatively ambitious use of genealogy as vindication or subversion from a normatively modest use of genealogy as problematization. It may be easier to be ambitious about judging ideas when they are pried apart from the context of their practice, just as a more humble use of genealogy might be motivated by a cautious focus on actual practices.

The differentiation between normatively ambitious and normatively modest genealogy is worth making given the abundance of contemporary uses of genealogy that purport to be normatively robust.[13] It is also worth taking note of insofar as Foucault is usually taken as offering a warrant in his work for a normatively ambitious genealogy of subversion. As stated in the introduction to this book, I take this to be a misreading of Foucault. Foucault issues warnings, alerts us to dangers, and encourages a severe skepticism grounded in a rigorous empiricism. But skepticism need not always lead to pessimism and its attendants, namely the judgment of negation and the strategy of subversion. Foucault helps us learn the subtle difference between recognizing that something is dangerous and insisting that something is wrong. This subtle difference is, in part, the difference that history can make.

Genealogy and Genetic Reasoning

My argument makes use of a well-known criticism of genealogy: the charge that genealogy commits the genetic fallacy in conflating the past historical development of a practice with the present justification of that practice. Here is one contemporary and uncontroversial specification of the genetic fallacy: "any attempt to support or to discredit a belief, statement, position or argument based upon its causal or historical genesis, or more broadly, the way in which it was formed."[14] For example, a believer may form their religious convictions on the basis of a cult upbringing, but even if we find good evidence that the cult leader was a wacko, we do not yet have good evidence that the believer's convictions ought to be rejected in their entirety—some of the beliefs, indeed possibly all of the beliefs, might be valuable despite their lowly provenance. The fallacy is in the idea that the origin of a belief determines its justifiability. After all, fascists can still bake good cakes and, sometimes, even offer good arguments.

Genetic reasoning is, I believe, somewhat less fallacious than is commonly presupposed by philosophers who are not inclined to take history very seriously.[15] The impossibly strong claim that practices of logical justification are rightly conducted without the slightest concern for inquiry into the historical evolution of the objects of our judgment makes sense only by rigorously denying the counterclaim that justification itself is a temporal process that takes place both within and through time. This latter denial in turn makes sense only if one strongly affirms synchronic and therefore extremely rationalistic accounts of justification, knowledge, and truth.

But despite misgivings about the fallacious quality of genetic reasoning, it is not difficult to discern ways in which the charge of the genetic fallacy has at least some purchase on the ambitious normative uses to which some have put genealogy. For it is not at all clear that the historical development of our practices can be as strictly determinative of the current justifiability of these practices as some genealogists sometimes seem to claim. We are, however, right to insist that surely genealogy in at least some instances has at least some bearing on normative issues of justification. The last two claims, though seemingly inconsistent, can be easily reconciled as follows.

The charge that genealogies commit the genetic fallacy applies to strong claims that genealogy normatively bears on justification to such a degree that genealogy by itself can determine justifiability. A weaker claim for the mere relevance of genealogical histories to questions of normative assessment does not seem to involve fallacious genetic reasoning. In order to be precise here, it helps to discriminate amongst various ways in which genetic reasoning might be thought to be fallacious. The genetic fallacy is typically classed by theorists of argumentation as a "fallacy of relevance," which is to say that the fallacy involves using certain premises to support a conclusion to which those premises are irrelevant. Note that "relevance" here is more or less a technical term that should not be confused with more colloquial senses of this word. What the genetic fallacy asserts is that certain descriptive claims about the history and development of our beliefs are irrelevant in the context of arguments that determinatively ground normative conclusions. The genetic fallacy need not be taken as asserting that descriptive claims about the history and development of certain beliefs are always irrelevant to normative conclusion in every context. The genetic fallacy specifies the way that certain descriptive claims are sometimes irrelevant to certain normative claims forwarded as conclusions of something like a straightforward argument. The criticism of genealogy at issue therefore need not be taken as asserting the impossibly strong claim that genealogical descriptions are entirely irrelevant to the normative practices they are offered as descriptions of. One can, in other words, regard genetic reasoning as fallacious and still accept that genetic reasonings, including genealogy, are broadly relevant in less determinative senses to our projects of normative evaluation.

This distinction amongst varying strengths of genetic reasoning is perhaps a bit technical. But it is helpful insofar as it enables us to distinguish between certain deployments of genealogy. If critics typically object to the strong normative ambitions of genealogy as deployed in the context of arguments that are meant to seal the status of certain normative conclusions, then these critics need not be as disconcerted by more modest deployments of genealogy in the context of claims about possible inductive generalizations or abductive hypotheses. Genealogies, in other words, might still be taken to be broadly relevant to certain normative claims even if we accept that they cannot be determinatively relevant in our attempts to establish certain seemingly unassailable normative conclusions.

Returning to my three genealogists, my strategy will be to show that Williams and Nietzsche tended to deploy genealogy with high normative ambitions and in so doing flirted with the genetic fallacy in the stronger sense. Foucault, on the other hand, had more constrained ambitions in writing his genealogies and so avoided committing the genetic fallacy proper. In this way, Foucault was able to produce books that were broadly relevant to the subjects of those books (e.g., punishment, sexuality, madness) without engaging in fallacious denunciations or vindications of his subject matter. Foucault's genealogies thus provide us with resources we need for normative critique, but without risking the view adopted by Williams and Nietzsche to the effect that genealogy on its own can function as a tool of normative assessment. Nietzsche had attempted to show that the genealogy of the moral system of the will to truth can be used to subvert that morality and many of its central concepts, truth among them. Williams later attempted the similar project of showing how the genealogy of certain of our practices connected to the concept of truth can result in a vindication of truthfulness and its values against currently fashionable criticisms. These are ambitious projects. Whether or not one agrees that genetic reasoning is fallacious, the charge that genealogy commits the genetic fallacy serves to usefully focus our attention on the possibility that some have sought to use genealogy for ambitious purposes premised on an unsettling view of the relation between historical development and normative justification.

Bernard Williams: Genealogy as Vindication

In order to grasp the specific force of genealogy in Williams's work, it is important to understand the general project of which his genealogy is a part. Williams's *Truth and Truthfulness* is best read as a book that is trying to change the questions we ask of truth. Williams wants us to give up the project of trying to say what truth is, or at least he urges that there is precious little we can say of such matters, in order that we might opt instead for a very different inquiry into the value of truth: "I shall be concerned throughout with what may summarily be called 'the value of truth.'"[16] Williams has his own story about what motivates this shift from definition to value. In short, the need for such an inquiry is motivated by the recent culture wars over truth, which has resulted in confusion for both those who deny that truth has any value and those who insist that we can gain a solid understanding of truth. Williams thinks that the source of this mutual misunderstanding is rooted in the refusal to take seriously the question of the value of truth. We have been so busy arguing over what truth is and what it is not, that we have lost sight of Nietzsche's question: namely, why truth?[17]

There is, however, another way of understanding Williams's project that would more narrowly root his claims in the concerns of twentieth-century analytic epistemology. The present consensus holds that analytic theories of truth running from Tarski to Davidson teach us that there is very little to say about truth indeed. As Williams himself puts this point, "we should resist any demand for a *definition* of truth."[18] When asked the philosopher's question "what is truth?" we should simply point to Tarski's T-Sentences (*"P" is true if and only if P*) and insist on leaving it at that. This concept of truth has been variously described as leading to minimalist, deflationist, redundancy, or even scaled-down correspondence theories of truth. The point of most of these theories is to show that there is no epistemologically enlightening work to be done on truth. So we should move talk of truth over from the theory of knowledge to the theory of meaning and replace epistemology with semantics. Neither Tarski nor Davidson, as it happened, were looking for a theory of truth so much as they sought a semantic account of truth that could function as a stable element in a more general theory of meaning. That more general theory of meaning, exemplified in Davidson's truth-conditional semantics, would be aided by a primitive or minimal concept of truth.

Williams's achievement was to take on board these lessons of the twentieth-century linguistic philosophy of truth and yet still insist that we can do robust philosophical work on normative notions such as truth. Williams allows something like minimalism and deflationism to reign when we face the conceptual question of "what is truth?" but insists that we need something a great deal more robust if faced with the moral question of "why value truth?" Many proponents of minimalist theories of truth have taken the lesson of their theories to be that truth by itself is of precious little value since the real aim of belief is not truth so much as it is justification amongst our peers.[19] But, insists Williams, "Nothing ties minimalism to an instrumentalist view of the value of truth."[20]

It was Nietzsche who effectively enabled Williams to achieve this unique combination of minimalism and non-instrumentalism. Williams explains that his question about the value of truth is really Nietzsche's question: "The problems that concern this book [Truth and Truthfulness] were discovered, effectively, by Nietzsche."[21] It is rarely remarked that Williams had in fact long been concerned with Nietzsche's question. While he did not deal with this question in detail until the 2002 book, he registered his interest in the problem itself as early as 1981 in a little-read review essay in which he stated, first, that Nietzsche helps us bring into focus the particular "demands" of "truth and truthfulness" before going on to boast that "Nietzsche was the greatest moral philosopher of the past century."[22] This is no small compliment. Nietzsche scholar Maudemarie Clark notes that Williams personally conveyed to her that he had been planning a book on Nietzsche as early as the 1970s.[23] Given Nietzsche's long and strong influence on Williams's thought, one way of seeing the achievement of Williams's work on truth is to understand him as taking Nietzsche's question seriously without insisting that we need to give a robust metaphysical or epistemological account of truth to answer that question. Williams's achievement, in other words, has been to take Nietzsche's question seriously as a moral question. This enabled Williams to bring to life a whole new domain of questions and problems that can be used to generate philosophically interesting work on truth. Williams's deft combination of Nietzsche's provocative questioning with the rigorous skepticism of twentieth-century analytic epistemology allowed him to fashion an impressive combination of epistemological minimalism plus moral seriousness about truth.

It is through this combination of epistemological minimalism and moral robustness that Williams invokes his central distinction between truth and truthfulness. Truth, for Williams, is a minimal semantic concept about which we can say precious little. This concept has no history: truth is what truth is, not what truth does. Williams explains: "One thing I shall not consider, however, is the history of the concept of truth, because I do not believe that there is any such history."[24] There are, of course, histories of theories of truth. But the concept itself?

No history here. Once you get the concept right, you will see that a minimal and deflated concept of truth is the sort of thing that "is not culturally various, but always and everywhere the same."[25] Truthfulness, by contrast, is something whose history is rich and varied. There are all kinds of different odd ways of being truthful, of telling the truth, and of speaking truthfully. Different forms of truthfulness have a history, but truth itself does not. Truth remains a minimal notion about which we can say very little, while truthfulness reveals the moral richness of truth. One suspects that Williams could have just drawn this distinction as one between two aspects of truth: truth-metaphysical and truth-moral, such that truth-metaphysical has no history while truth-moral does. This is of course a cumbersome way of putting the point, even if it possesses the advantage of better revealing Williams's purposes. For the point of distinguishing truth from truthfulness is not to insist on a formal distinction so much as to bring into view a series of questions concerning the moral status of truth that have been occluded by more-classical questions concerning truth's metaphysical and epistemological bearings.

To inquire into the moral question concerning the value of truth, a question that "should be taken as shorthand for the value of various states and activities associated with the truth," Williams undertakes a series of genealogies of truthfulness.[26] These genealogies, says Williams, produce a "vindicatory" history in that they enable us to see "why truthfulness has an intrinsic value; why it can be seen as such with a good conscience; why a good conscience is a good thing with which to see it."[27] In Williams's hands, then, genealogy takes the form of an inquiry into various forms of truthfulness. Specifically, he offers rich and illustrative chapters on various episodes in the history of telling the truth about the past, about ourselves, and about our society—these include genealogies of historical truthfulness, romantic truthfulness, and liberal truthfulness.[28] These histories are meant to show how these various forms of truthfulness emerged in the past such that we can clearly see their value for us today.

As instructive and engaging as these genealogies are, they cannot by themselves answer questions that will motivate some critics to claim that Williams's argument involves fallacious genetic reasoning. The suspicion might run like this: "And so what if truthfulness has this history; that does not show that these practices of truthfulness actually ought to be vindicated by us in the present." I am not sure how Williams saw himself around such suspicions. While telling the truth about oneself in such-and-such a way may perfectly well have a history of a certain very inspiring kind, there will always be those among us who find these histories filled with dreadful details and would much rather go on telling little lies about whatever lies deep in their soul. It is not clear that we can use genealogy to show those who are dishonest that they are *wrong,* though we can of course use it to show them that they are not being *truthful.*

It may be in response to these concerns that Williams was led to retain a minimalist theory of truth according to which the concept of truth itself has no history even if the morality of truth does have a history. Perhaps Williams hoped he could use this ahistorical standard of truth in combination with his genealogical accounts of historical forms of truthfulness to vindicate truth as intrinsically valuable. It is not entirely clear how this combination might work in the way Williams seems to have intended, but it is clear both that Williams found it essential to retain a strong distinction between a historical truthfulness and an ahistorical truth and that he sought to somehow combine these two seemingly separate inquiries. It is worth noting that *Truth and Truthfulness* was not titled *Truth or Truthfulness,* even if many readers will find the proposed terms for this conjunction between ahistorical truth and historical truthfulness rather unclear. In his review of Williams's book, Richard Rorty expressed the puzzlement this point is sure to meet with: "I had trouble seeing the continuity between the first half and the second half of Williams's book; the connections between the more philosophical part and the more historical part are not perspicuous."[29] Clearly Williams took truth to be more than just truthfulness, and for him a moral philosophy of timeless truth is not exactly identical to a genealogical history of truthfulness. Yet just as clearly Williams took his genealogy of truthfulness to somehow vindicate the value of truth. Is this sloppy slippage or ingenious integration? I agree with Rorty's worries, but I want to give Williams's account as fair a reading as possible before saying why to find it misguided.

A great deal in Williams's account seems to turn on the particular kind of vindication for truth that he seems to have in mind. When Williams sets out to vindicate the value of truth, he sets out specifically to vindicate truth as "intrinsically" valuable.[30] It would not be enough for Williams to show that truth is instrumentally valuable. He has to show that truth, taken by itself, possesses a value that we should not let go of: "to the extent that we lose a sense of the value of truth, we shall certainly lose something and may well lose everything."[31] This point helps us grasp one rather important implication of Williams's insistence that the concept of truth itself has no history. If truth has no history, then it is at least minimally plausible for Williams to claim that truth is intrinsically valuable. But if truth has a history, then it would seem flatly incoherent to claim that truth itself is intrinsically valuable. Historically variable moralities of truthfulness might have a value, but whatever value they do have could not be anything but instrumental, precisely because they are historical. What such value might help us appreciate, however, is the greater intrinsic value of something that does not vary with history, namely the truth itself. Vindicating the value of truth, for Williams, therefore does not mean merely showing truth to be instrumentally valuable. This would amount to saying that we need truth if we are to be Historically accurate, and Romantically sincere, and tolerant Liberals. That sounds quite like Rorty's way of vindicating a thin concept of truth. But Williams always took great pains to distance himself from Rorty's approach. Williams wanted to vindicate truth by showing truth to be something worthy of "respect," and this means showing truth to be intrinsically valuable.[32]

There is a sensible presumption in Williams's approach to the effect that if something is intrinsically valuable, it cannot be subject to the contingencies of historical evolution. Williams reserves truth as something capable of possessing intrinsic value by insisting that the concept of truth has no history. This presumption might be seen as a response to a concern that has always pursued genealogy going back to its earliest emergence: including not only Nietzsche, but also Darwin, and perhaps even earlier to Hume. Consider Darwin's genealogy, which raises the following problem. If *Homo sapiens* is the contingent product of a long process of unplanned evolution, then we are not pristine in the timeless image of the Holy. If this is so, Darwin's critics worried, then humanity is stripped of its intrinsic dignity, goodness, and value. Whatever value we do have, we did not have to have it, but things just so happened to work out that way. Here, in germ, is the most momentous of clashes between necessity and contingency. And so with this, the nineteenth-century culture wars were under way. Similar battles were already brewing back in Hume's day, and for many of the same reasons, such that our contemporary debates about Truth might be seen as an analogue of older debates about Man, Reason, and Nature. But the most crucial clash emerged in the nineteenth century, well after Hume, in the wake of Darwin. The debate between William James and Charles Santiago Peirce over truth is a good exemplar. James thought of the value of truth as constructed by we humans, but no less worthy for our having constructed it. The achievement that we call truth is a grand achievement, and it is ours. By contrast, Peirce thought that in order to be really valuable, truth must stand on its own outside of the contingencies of human effort. Peirce wrote to James in 1902: "No doubt truth has to have defenders to uphold it. But truth creates its defenders and gives them strength."[33] One hundred years later, the more Jamesian Rorty encouraged us to think that if we take care of freedom we will be free enough to take care of truth, while the more Peircean Williams argued that taking care of freedom means taking care of truth first. James and Rorty found the Darwinian version of the message about truth an uplifting one because it suggests that our values are our achievements such that we can do what we need to in order to improve upon them. Peirce and Williams find parts of the message problematic because they believe that in order to be really valuable, valuable all by itself, truth must reside outside of history (be it at the end of inquiry or somewhere else altogether) as an impermeable reality whose value speaks for itself. But, importantly, Williams and Rorty both agreed that historical investigations of various forms of truthfulness are where all the most important work in a moral philosophy of truth will get done.

Williams's version of this idea is that such historical investigations help us approach truth itself and whatever intrinsic value we may be able to glimpse. This is because genealogical inquiries can help us understand the specific historical content that fills out an otherwise empty ahistorical concept of truth. As he writes in "Philosophy as a Humanistic Discipline": "[I]n many cases the content of our concepts is a contingent historical phenomenon . . . The forms of these dispositions and of the motivations they embody are culturally and historically various."[34] Williams's view seems to be that we can use philosophical reflection to discern "the necessary, structural features" of truth, but that "philosophy needs to make room for history" when we turn toward "specific cultural determinations" of truthfulness.[35] These are the two halves of Williams's enterprise between which Rorty can find no clear connection. The vague answer that Williams seems to offer to the challenges posed by critics like Rorty seems to be that philosophical reflection provides us with a minimal outline of an ahistorical concept of truth such that genealogical reflection can then go on to provide us with the historical details that fill in this thin concept with rather much thicker content: "General reflection can show that something has to support the disposition. . . . But what particular range of values in a given cultural situation will perform this role is a matter of real history."[36] It is in this sense that Williams's project on the whole is meant to offer a vindication (a real vindication, not just an ethnocentric paean) of truth as intrinsically valuable. While we could perhaps do without this or that particular form of truthfulness, genealogy is supposed to show us that the collective effect of all of these forms of truthfulness is to impress upon us that surely we could not do without any kind of truthfulness at all. Even if we could get by without telling the truth about the past or telling the truth about ourselves, we would still need some forms of truthfulness in our lives. It is in this sense that an ahistorical concept of truth is intrinsically valuable even if the contingent determinations informing this necessary value will shift according to the historical exigencies of the different practices of truthfulness that impress us around here and just now.

We should not buy Williams's story about intrinsic value and a concept of truth that is beyond history.[37] Williams's work is an ingenious, but ultimately unsuccessful, attempt to get a great deal of normative mileage out of a method of inquiry that is better reserved for elucidation, explication, and intensification. As an attempt of this sort, Williams is indeed instructive, as is Nietzsche. Like Williams, Nietzsche thought that he could use genealogy to seal some fairly controversial conclusions about modern morality. Williams vindicated—Nietzsche subverted. But no matter what one wants to prove about the situations in which one finds oneself, one should not use genealogy to try to *prove* anything about the present, other than that the present need not be the way that it is. Nietzsche, undoubtedly, tried to use genealogy for more than it could really do. Williams was either trying for too much or for too little, and it is never really clear which.[38]

In one sense, it seems fairly clear that Williams was trying to press more out of genealogy than is really there. This is unfortunate because it amounts to the abuse of a tool in such a way that can only lead to the tool being degraded rather than being taken up by others and put to use for the purposes for which it is best suited. Williams's genealogies of the moralities of truthfulness are rich, impressive, and learned. But his attempted vindication of truth is puzzling. Williams himself surely must have realized the obvious danger involved in using genealogy to vindicate anything. Aware of his proximity to the genetic fallacy, it seems as if Williams backed into a non-genealogical account of truth as an ahistorical concept. This certainly helps along his vindicatory story about truth, but only by ceding the territory of genealogy. That which does the vindicating in Williams's account may not be genealogy after all, but rather some non-historical philosophical reflection on truth as timeless. All the real normative mileage is being run not by the genealogical components in Williams's work but by the philosophical components that stipulate a formal theory of truth and then, through armchair reflection rather than empirical genealogy, attempt to show how this formal concept is intrinsically valuable. The central part of Williams's normative argument is thus located in the first, more philosophical, half of the book, in which he offers armchair musings on why a very minimal concept of truth may be taken to be intrinsically valuable to any form of human social life.[39] Williams calls this an "imaginary genealogy," and it is meant to provide the essential outline of a story about the value of truth that a real "historical genealogy" then comes along to fill out in the second, more historical, part of the book. But it is not clear why this armchair reflection is a genealogy at all. It seems more in keeping with the traditional analytical philosophical technique of a thought experiment. As for the real historical genealogies, these show us at best why truth might have been taken to be valuable at some point in our history, but they could not be used to show that truth is intrinsically valuable, nor could they be used to show that truth has no history. Williams's vindicatory story is, almost by definition it seems, not genealogical in design. Now, that may be to the advantage or disadvantage of genealogy, but it would surely be a disadvantage to pretend that the vindicatory thought experiments are genealogical when, truthfully, they are not.

In another sense, however, perhaps Williams was trying for too little. Digging further into his account suggests that the notion of intrinsic value has a fairly special sense in Williams's work. Williams asserts that "it is in fact a sufficient condition for something (for instance, trustworthiness) to have an intrinsic value that, first, it is necessary (or nearly necessary) for basic human purposes and needs that human beings should treat it as an intrinsic good; and, second, they can coherently treat it as an intrinsic good."[40] On this conception, truth can be intrinsically valuable if it turns out that it is necessary that we take it as such and we can in fact coherently take it as such. If this is the case, says Williams, "we shall have constructed an intrinsic good."[41] So it turns out that the concept of intrinsically valuable is compatible with genealogy after all insofar as we can offer a genealogy that shows how it came to be that we constructed a value in such a way that we have to take it as intrinsic (whether or not there are any such values is, of course, a matter for debate). If this is all Williams meant to show in vindicating the intrinsic value of truth, I freely admit that he in no way abused genealogy to generate objectionably strong normative conclusions. In this case, though, it is not clear why Williams needed to hold onto the view that the concept of truth has no history. For if we can construct intrinsic values, surely we can construct those of our concepts that are intrinsically valuable. Perhaps it is necessary that we not take ourselves to be constructing that which we take to be intrinsically valuable, but one point of genealogy would surely be to illuminate such processes wherever they take place. In this case, the genealogy of the value of truthfulness need not entangle itself at all with an ahistoricist minimalist theory of truth. It therefore remains unclear why, if Williams's ambitions are really of this less strenuous though perhaps more appropriately genealogical variety, he should insist that there is no history to a concept of truth construed in terms of a minimalist theory. Barry Allen, reviewing Williams, writes: "When it becomes clear that belief in truth's intrinsic value comes down to this ethical stance, having nothing to do with 'inherent natures,' one should have no qualms about Williams's use of the concept. The interest of his argument lies not in the audacity of its conclusion but in Williams's Nietzschean transposition of philosophy's concept of truth from the metaphysics of realism to the genealogy of values."[42] A similar thought is also urged by Ian

Hacking, who in his review of Williams writes, with deceptively simple verve, that "It is better to play down the 'intrinsic.'"[43] These read to me as suggestions that Williams has really drifted quite near to the views of Richard Rorty, as Hilary Putnam has argued.[44] In his own review of Williams, Rorty doubts that Williams can make his notion of intrinsic value respectable without "first of all taking a lot of Platonic-looking baggage on board" in such a way that "he can no longer hope for Nietzsche's approval."[45] What Williams really wants is Nietzsche's approval, and he also really doesn't want Plato's baggage anyway—to satisfy both of these desiderata he may have found himself defending positions that are quite difficult to distinguish from Rorty's neopragmatism. For if Williams plays down the intrinsic as per Hacking such that it becomes not much more than an ethical stance as per Allen, then it is no longer clear that Williams is among those who agree with Peirce that truth has a power all its own that we humans can profitably chain ourselves to.[46] Thus it begins to seem more and more as if Williams is among those who agree with James that truth has to have its defenders and that it may as well be us who take care of the truth. This kind of view would certainly incline Williams to a normatively less ambitious conception of genealogy. In that case, genealogy can certainly still be used do a great deal, though we should not count legitimation and vindication as among its best potential uses.

Insofar as Williams explicitly oriented his conception of genealogy toward normatively ambitious purposes, he failed to fully claim the senses in which his genealogies might be useful for quite other purposes. The best parts of Williams's book consist of learned intellectual histories of different practices of truth-telling. But if we are interested in theoretically exploring the ways in which genealogical inquiry can be used to explicate our historical condition and the problematizations constitutive of that condition, we would do well to turn away from Williams to some other genealogist whose work offers an explicit engagement with such theoretical explorations. For this we need Foucault.

Friedrich Nietzsche: Genealogy as Subversion

According to many of the standard criticisms of Friedrich Nietzsche, his work offers a straightforward normative assault on modern religion and modern science under the unified banner of the modern morality that sustains them both. Criticisms of Nietzsche on this score have persisted for well over a century. Their most recent form includes scathing critiques of Nietzsche as the inaugural symbol of a practice of thought generally referred to by celebrants and detractors alike as postmodernism. According to these critiques, Nietzsche's project is best characterized as, borrowing one of his own most overblown phrases, a "campaign against morality."[47] According to interpretations of Nietzsche that lend a great deal of interpretive weight to passages with this ring, Nietzsche's genealogy of modern morality is meant to make undeniably plain the slavish roots of modern moral practices such that only the most ardent disciples would be able to perpetuate their praise of our morality.

On this standard reading, Nietzsche not merely accidentally commits, but rather positively flaunts, the genetic fallacy in his writings. On such a reading, Nietzsche is a less complex genealogist than Williams in that he does not even bother trying to avoid the genetic fallacy. Take Nietzsche's critique of the morality embodied in what he eventually came to call the will to truth. In *Human, All Too Human,* Nietzsche had already registered a damaging blow against truth itself: "There is no pre-established harmony between the furthering of truth and the good of humanity."[48] Nietzsche labeled this a "Fundamental Insight." The insight must have come as a blow to even Nietzsche himself, for he spent much of the rest of his career tracking its implications. Here is Nietzsche a few years later in *The Gay Science:* "This unconditional will to truth—what is it? . . . 'Will to truth' does *not* mean 'I do not want to let myself be deceived' but—there is no alternative— 'I will not deceive, not even myself'; *and with that we stand on moral ground.*"[49] Much of Nietzsche's mature work was an inquiry into the conditions of this morality of the will to truth. It is crucial to note that both Williams and Foucault established their connection to Nietzsche precisely on this terrain of a genealogical inquiry into what we can today call "Nietzsche's question": "what is the value of truth?"[50] As for Nietzsche himself, his most rigorous attempt to pose this question was in *On the Genealogy of Morals,* which concludes as follows: "What sense would *our* whole being have if not for the fact that in us that will to truth becomes conscious of itself as a *problem?* . . . Because this will to truth from now on is growing conscious of itself, morality from now on is dying."[51] Nietzsche's conclusion in this book seems to be that as the moral will to truth grows increasingly conscious of itself through its self-expression in asceticism, bad conscience, and ressentiment, it must ultimately give way to a future that Nietzsche only vaguely invokes in terms of an Overman that is beyond the old slavish morality of truth and its attendant system of good and evil.

No one need deny that it is quite an easy task to amass from Nietzsche's writings an impressive apparatus of evidence suggesting that his primary intellectual task as a genealogist was to, as Alasdair MacIntyre puts it, "exhibit the historical genesis of the psychological deformation involved in the morality of the late nineteenth century," or to, as Jürgen Habermas states it, "explode the framework of

Occidental rationalism."[52] It will be useful to begin with MacIntyre's critical interpretation of Nietzsche in that he accepts many points of interpretation urged by Nietzsche's best defenders and yet is still convincing in his criticisms of even this version of Nietzsche's views. MacIntyre is an able proxy for standard criticisms of Nietzsche, but he is also more sympathetic than the usual critics, some of whom have called Nietzsche an "immoralist" or even a "moral terrorist."[53] After using MacIntyre's work to frame the debate, I shall then go on to engage Nietzsche's best defenders. There are many impressive new lines of Nietzsche interpretation from which to choose; I will take the two that I have found to be the most convincing. One is the best representative of the new "French Nietzscheans": Gilles Deleuze's 1962 book, *Nietzsche and Philosophy.* The other I take to be a strong representative of the American "New Nietzsche" scholarship: Alexander Nehemas's 1985 book, *Nietzsche: Life as Literature.* Central to both of these books is a picture of Nietzsche as an affirmative and creative thinker. This picture is offered as a preferable alternative to the old interpretation of Nietzsche as a dyspeptic denouncer. There is much to be impressed with in the philosophical picture informing this interpretation, but in the end I agree with MacIntyre and others that it is impossible to abstract the dourness out of Nietzsche in favor of an exclusive emphasis on his creative side. Even in the readings of Deleuze and Nehemas, it turns out that Nietzsche is never all that far from the genealogical subversion located by MacIntyre. Nietzsche's deployment of genealogy therefore remains, in the final analysis, in the service of delegitimation. Nietzsche was a debunker who used genealogy as a form of historical subversion—in other words, he drew normative conclusions about the present on the basis of genetic assertions about the history of the present.

MacIntyre's criticism of Nietzsche's genealogy assumes a subtle critical stance according to which Nietzsche is read as engaging in a complex procedure of "subverting" the system of modern morality. MacIntyre refuses to read Nietzsche as giving old-fashioned arguments against modern morality, if only because on such a reading Nietzsche clearly fails. MacIntyre's more-complex reading suggests that the genealogical subversion of modern morality is to be particularly understood as a subversion of the morality of truth and truthfulness. Nietzsche, then, does not fail to live up to the argumentative rigor presupposed by the morality of the will to truth so much as he encourages us to abandon this moral stance altogether. MacIntyre observes that "Nietzsche did not advance a new theory against older theories; he proposed an abandonment of theory."[54] The genealogical project is thus one of "dismissing any notion of *the* truth and correspondingly any conception of *what is* as such and timelessly as contrasted with what seems to be the case from a variety of different perspectives."[55] In offering such an interpretation MacIntyre generously concedes many, though not all, of the crucial points of Nietzsche scholarship sought after by recent defenders of a new Nietzsche interpretation, including Deleuze and Nehamas.

But unlike those who proffer the new Nietzsche and prefer it to the standard Nietzsche, MacIntyre finds the genealogical subversive attack on modern morality unjustified no matter how nuanced it may be. This is not because Nietzsche failed to live up to the rigorous academic standards of truth to which all serious scholarship should be subjected. It is because Nietzsche could not but help himself to some of these standards at least some of the time. As MacIntyre puts it, "the intelligibility of genealogy requires beliefs and allegiances of a kind precluded by the genealogical stance."[56] Genealogy, says MacIntyre, fails by its own lights. The genealogical subversion depends on making an exception of the relation between genealogy and the tradition that it subverts. As MacIntyre argues, "The genealogist has up till now characteristically been one who writes *against,* who exposes, who subverts, who interrupts and disrupts. But what has in consequence very rarely, if at all, attracted explicit genealogical scrutiny is the extent to which the genealogical stance is dependent for its concepts and its modes of argument, for its theses and its style, upon a set of contrasts between it and that which it aspires to overcome—the extent, that is, to which it is inherently derivative from and even parasitic upon its antagonisms and those towards whom they are directed."[57] To be against the tradition, genealogy must posit itself in relation to the tradition. Doing so requires simultaneously acknowledging the presence of the tradition and disowning the presence of genealogy within that tradition. This acknowledgment constitutes the historicist benefit of genealogy, while this disavowal constitutes its ahistoricist error. We ought to recognize with the genealogical historicist that genealogy can never fully escape the very perspective that it seeks to subvert. Genealogy, if it is anything at all, is inextricably tied to the modern will to truth that it seeks to overcome. The crux of MacIntyre's criticism could be put as follows: Nietzsche does not simply abandon the modern morality of truth but also urges that it is a good thing to abandon it, and insofar as he does not simply avoid this morality but also tries to subvert it, Nietzsche finds himself all tangled up in the very modernity whose subversion is his goal.

I find MacIntyre's critique of Nietzsche convincing in the main, but allow me to move along now to defenses of Nietzsche. Consider first Deleuze. The central point of Deleuze's book on Nietzsche is to offer an explication of a philosophy that proceeds not by way of a dialectical negation of contradictions but by way of a creative affirmation of differences. This involves a Nietzschean practice of philosophy no longer heaped by the negativity of refusal that is so characteristic of modern critical thought. Deleuze wants to free us to take up a practice of philosophy emboldened by its own joyous affirmations. The problem with this view is that it cannot escape the fact that one tradition's positivity is another's negativity. In affirming what we do, we deny what others affirm. We may want to escape from the responsibility implied therein, but it proves inescapable.

A main reason why Deleuze's book was so important, as both a landmark for Nietzsche interpretation and a landmark for the beginnings of poststructuralist philosophy in France, was its forceful break from dialectics. Deleuze states "the resolutely anti-dialectical character of Nietzsche's philosophy" that is important primarily in terms of the substitution of affirmation for negation.[58] For Deleuze the dialectic is defined by three ideas: the power of the negative in the experience of contradiction, the valorization of suffering, and the idea of the positive as a mere residue of the negative.[59] Dialectical thought attempts to negate difference, perhaps by instantiating higher unities in which lower contradictions can be resolved. Genealogical thought, according to Deleuze's Nietzsche, is by contrast an affirmation of difference, perspective, and plurality. If Nietzsche has been read primarily as a subversive thinker who is out to undermine modern morality, it is only because modern morality is itself a negative force incapable of affirming difference. It is therefore modern morality that is intolerant and negative. Nietzsche, in rejecting modern morality, is merely reasserting the possibility of a freer and more positive moral culture. To dismiss his hopes as subversive and debunking is precisely to ignore the content of those hopes. Nietzsche was neither nihilist nor negator, Deleuze claims, because "Nietzsche presents the aim of his philosophy as the freeing of thought from nihilism and its various forms. . . . A thought which finally expels the whole of the negative."[60]

Taken at a superficial level, Deleuze's argument fails insofar as he seems to be saying that the negation of negation is not itself a negation. That is a difficult line to take—in logic, two negations may equal an affirmation, but in practice the remnant of the negative can never be expelled. But we should take Deleuze's argument at a deeper level, where it involves not the rejection of negation so much as the positive elaboration of an alternative that differs from negation. On this reading Nietzsche does not reject negation so much as he overcomes it. Deleuze insists after all that "Negation is *opposed* to affirmation but affirmation *differs* from negation."[61] At this deeper level, however, Deleuze's argument faces the difficult burden of trying to explain how, in the flow of history, differentiation can avoid negation. Differentiation may not carry with it a psychological attitude of negation, but it certainly carries with it the historical force of the possibility of negation. Deleuze's point, presumably, is not merely psychological. Nietzsche's work on modern morality, modern science, and modern truth was not just an attempt to dig underneath to a psychological attitude, even if it is that too. It was an attempt to dig underneath our practices to a broader cultural flow and a greater historical tendency. The question we must ask, therefore, concerns the modality of relation between the historical tradition of which Nietzsche writes the genealogy and the inaugural conception that Nietzsche sketches as its alternative. Might Nietzsche's bold sketch of a different future serve to negate, reject, or refuse the present whose past he is considering?

One of Nietzsche's largest targets was the ascetic will to truth for which he sought an alternative in his development of a more artistic form of will. Deleuze sketches the relation between these two different "wills" as follows: "we want another ideal in another place, another way of knowing, another concept of truth, that is to say a truth which is not presupposed in a will to truth but which presupposes a *completely different will*."[62] In elaborating the Overman as differentiated from the dialectic figures of the Scientist, the Christian, and the Socratic, it is clear that Nietzsche was seeking to motivate the development of a new kind of culture and a new era in history. This culture and history of the Overman would break from the dialectical, scientific, and religious culture and history preceding it. It seems undeniable that this shift implicates itself in a historical negation. It is a turning toward one tradition and culture, indeed, but it is at the same time a turning away from another tradition and culture. Whenever the stakes are this high, affirmation carries negation at its rear. Deleuze writes that for Nietzsche, "Philosophy has an essential relation to time: it is always against its time, critique of the present world."[63] Nietzsche was against his time and his present, even if he was so only in the service of some envisaged future. My point is not that opposition to one's own present is a bad thing. I am rather concerned to point out that there is no small modicum of normative evaluation implicit in such a stance. It seems rather irresponsible to insist that there is not normativity, but only affirmative creativity, here.

Deleuze may be right that Nietzsche's dismissal of modern morality is rooted in an active and affirmative stance, not a reactive and negative one, but Nietzsche's philosophy is no less subversive in effect because of it. Nietzsche's emphasis on active and affirmative morality sounds quite like the morality of the aristocrat who dismisses the views of his inferiors as only so much vulgar opinion. The aristocrat does not even want to compete with the slave, or as Deleuze puts it, "Nietzsche says of himself that he is much too well bred to struggle."[64] Deleuze points out that this dismissive attitude is rooted in an active praise of one's own noble values rather than a reactive opposition to the other's slavish values. Deleuze says that Nietzsche's central point is that "we cannot think of affirmation as 'being opposed' to negation."[65] But whether we call it opposition or differentiation, the Nietzschean project historically subverts that which it philosophically overcomes. This subversion cannot but be normative. Nietzsche may not want to appear negative, but how are the Christians, democrats, women, and any others whom he ceaselessly makes fun of supposed to take his assumed air of effortless superiority? It is irresponsible to not own up to the normative opportunity costs of whatever we affirm. Nietzsche cannot just leave modern morality behind by insisting that we must differentiate ourselves from the reactive negativity of the modern moralists. However affirmative he may want to be, his genealogy is still an attempt to show how everything began to go wrong with modern morality in its reactive and negative origins. In this subversive move Nietzsche remains all too normative, even if he will not acknowledge his own normativity. The problem, then, is just that the historical fact of reactive origins is not by itself enough to deliver the normative conclusion that modern morality should be overcome.

The criticism of Deleuze's Nietzsche I have been sketching was urged against the whole of French Nietzscheanism by Vincent Descombes in an influential article calling for the close of a style of critique characteristic of a whole ensemble of French thinkers in the 1960s and '70s. Descombes noted the tendency amongst the French Nietzscheans to conflate history and philosophy. This, he pointed out, invites the dangers of conflating acceptance and justification, which I have been summarizing under the heading of the genetic fallacy: "If a distinction is to be maintained between history of ideas and philosophy, it is so that we can make a distinction between an argument's success and its content." When this distinction is dropped, we lose an important political and cultural distinction between the moralities of "instituted bodies" and of "individuals." Descombes was explicit that his criticisms were intended against a wide swath of contemporary French theory, but he was particularly critical of the implications of Deleuzeian Nietzscheanism: "In Deleuze, the opposition is between the moral, therefore responsible, man and the superior individual liberated from morality and therefore irresponsible." The supposedly superior individual liberated from responsibility is taken by Deleuze to be autonomous. But, Descombes pointed out, Deleuze fails to seriously engage the implication that such an irresponsible autonomy will be directed not toward ruling over oneself by means of imposing limits on the self, but instead toward ruling over others according to a superior nature. Thus, concluded Descombes, "The philosophy that chooses to understand autonomy as irresponsibility ends up in an apology of tyranny." There is, in other words, a real lack of positivity in the appropriation of a philosopher whose central project always remained that of denunciation: "The Nietzscheans introduce no new principle within the philosophical order. Their vigor is, if we may say so, ad hominem, purely dialectical.

And we know that ad hominem reasoning is logically valid but incapable of establishing a conclusion."[66] A project of positivity that refuses to be positive about
the present winds itself toward its strange fate of becoming a project that cannot
escape its own thoroughgoing negativity. That, in the end, is the difficulty with
Nietzsche. In seriously posing the question of the value of truth, Nietzsche never
took seriously enough the possibility that truth, and especially our forms of truthfulness, might be somehow essential to any creation, affirmation, and positivity
that we can muster.

The French Nietzscheanism of Deleuze and others (including Kofman and
Blondel)[67] offers one way of attempting to rescue Nietzsche from these negative
conclusions that have always hounded Nietzsche and his self-appointed progeny.
If French Nietzscheanism seems to fail in this project, there are still other interpretations of Nietzsche as an affirmative thinker to which the Nietzschean might repair. Most notable are the recent New Nietzsche interpretations from the past few
decades emerging in North American scholarship. Though much of the American New Nietzsche borrows its inspirations from the French New Nietzsche, there
are a number of important differences. So as to give Nietzsche as fair and wide
a reading as possible, I turn now to Nehemas's New Nietzsche to consider a second strategy for taking up Nietzsche as an affirmative thinker who may not after
all be representative of, as one critic of the French Nietzscheans recently put it,
"a repetitive style of delegitimation increasingly divorced from political and social
concerns."[68]

Nehemas explicitly considers the question of whether Nietzsche falls into the
genetic fallacy in his call for a revaluation of our present values. He concludes that
Nietzsche does not confuse origin with value because his argument is "more subtle
and more complicated" than this simple criticism would have it.[69] Nietzsche may
have encouraged historical awareness and reflectiveness, but he did not countenance appealing to history as a means of subverting the present whose history we
might consider. So says Nehemas. As did Deleuze, Nehemas defends Nietzsche primarily by way of an appeal to his affirmativity. It is above all Nietzsche's dedication to the positive creation of a new style of life, a life as literature in Nehemas's
well-chosen phrase, that enables him to develop alternatives to modern morality
without debunking that morality as incoherent, mistaken, or historically base.

Nehemas, also like Deleuze, considers Nietzsche's attack on the ascetic ideal
of truth summarized in the potent idea of the will to truth. Nehemas concedes
that "Nietzsche denounces the ascetic ideal, but . . . does not offer to replace it
with a positive morality of his own." Instead of replacing it with a positive morality, which could only but subvert its aims in expressing another form of the will
to truth, Nietzsche replaces asceticism with aestheticism. As for the ascetic ideal

itself, and Nietzsche's genealogical interrogation of it in the *Genealogy of Morals*, Nehemas describes Nietzsche as waging "a war against" these ideals with weapons of erudition and scholarship: "to show them for what they really are is sufficient to turn people away from them." Nehemas's Nietzsche is clearly more of a subversive figure than Deleuze's. But the essential point here too is not so much Nietzsche's campaign against morality as it is Nietzsche's attempt to develop an alternative to this morality that would not turn itself into just one more instance of that morality. Nehemas notes the difficulties implicated in this "effort to reveal the inner contradictions and deceptions of asceticism, and yet not produce a view that itself unwittingly repeats the same contradictions and deceptions."[70] This alternative is at the core of the more positive, more affirmative, and more joyous new Nietzsche.

The central problem facing Nietzsche's bid for affirmation without negation is a historical problem. If we situate ourselves historically, it proves enormously difficult to understand how one might favor one ideal without disfavoring another. As one's favored ideal gains momentum and perhaps even a following, those other, less-favored ideals lose their adherents and come to seem outmoded and inappropriate. This may not amount to psychological opposition, but it certainly looks like practical negation. It is in this sense that Nietzsche was against his own time. Nehemas articulates the difficulties Nietzsche faced in attempting to assume his particular mode of untimeliness: "Nietzsche's problem is that he wants to attack the tradition to which he belongs and also escape it. An explicit attack . . . would perpetuate that tradition. A complete escape from it directly into art . . . would simply change the subject but leave that tradition intact."[71] Nietzsche's response to this difficulty, says Nehemas, was to turn his life into literature, thus escaping the tradition in a way that exposes its deficiencies.[72] Nietzsche does not describe a morality that is an alternative to the tradition, nor does he offer a counter-ethics that would undermine the tradition, but rather he seeks to embody a form of living that would be an alternative to the asceticism he regarded as the general atmosphere of his times. Despite Nehemas's interpretive skill in showing that Nietzsche never needed to offer an argument against modern morality that might implicate him in suspicious genetic reasoning, it remains unclear at the end how Nietzsche's individualistic immoralist avoids the dangers of denouncing the modern ethos from which he departs. Departures do not always entail denunciations, but they do at least suggest them. And Nietzsche hardly kept quiet about his reasons for wanting to go his own way.

Having canvassed two readings of Nietzsche proposed by three commentators, I want to now attempt to split the difference between the anti-Nietzsche and pro-Nietzsche readings, but by locating the difference as one between Nietzschean history (about which I remain tepid) and Nietzschean morality (which I leave here an entirely open question). Although I agree with MacIntyre's critical assessments of Nietzsche, it seems to me hardly profitable to dispense with all of Nietzsche. To retain the best parts, however, we need not go all the way with Deleuze, Nehemas, and other celebrants. A way to split the difference is to make a distinction between Nietzsche's affirmative intentions for the future and his subversive consequences for the past. One can be an affirmative thinker with respect to whatever new future practice one is attempting to elaborate, but the effect of this with respect to extant practice is going to implicate negation even where no negativity is intended. With this distinction in view, I can more finely specify the sense in which I agree with MacIntyre while also not disagreeing with Deleuze and Nehemas.

Quite simply put, insofar as Nietzsche explicitly frames his genealogies as concerned with historical forms, one cannot help but witness the negativity at work. For instance, a reading of his *Genealogy of Morals* as a history of modern moral institutions cannot but reveal a subversive text. But in those moments (most of them can only be found in his other books) where Nietzsche was able to let go of the philological imperatives of his early training, and the awkward attempts at historical scholarship it continued to inspire in his writings, we can discern an affirmative thinker for whom negativity is but a mere aftereffect. This, I take it, is precisely Deleuze's point, and probably Nehemas's too. Thus, I agree with Deleuze and Nehemas that Nietzsche *as artist* is a positive thinker. And yet I also agree with MacIntyre that Nietzsche *as historian, as genealogist,* cannot but be a subverter. Now, what this indicates for present purposes at least, is simply that Nietzsche is an unsteady guide to historical genealogy. This leaves open the possibility that Nietzsche might be a steady guide, or at least a steady interlocutor, in other respects (though I want to be clear that this is a question I have not here explored).

What I am suggesting, in short, is that we allow ourselves the freedom to parse or divide Nietzsche, and possibly against his own self-interpretations. We should distinguish Nietzsche the genealogist, whom many cannot help but read as a terrorist of our recent moral past, from Nietzsche the artist, who continues to offer for many an inspiring vision for the moral near future. Nietzsche's artistry does not depend on his flailing attempts at subversion. I want to suggest that we can rather easily make the sort of distinction I am urging by continuing to accept the sort of platitudinous liberal tolerance we all already know so well. This is the sort of liberal vision sketched by, for example, Richard Rorty in his *Contingency, Irony, and Solidarity.*[73] Rorty was thinking of creative geniuses just like Nietzsche in attempting to show in that book why liberal culture ought to both tolerate these isolatoes and at the same time insulate them and the general public from one another.[74] Rorty recognized that even if Nietzsche did not want it, his firebrand ideas would in effect involve an opposition to much of what passes as customary in our culture. As hard as he may have *tried* to become a purely affirmative thinker, Nietzsche could never escape having the *effect* of being a seriously negative figure against his liberal culture. Rorty thought that the best response to these dangers was liberal tolerance as expressed in the separation between public and private. A key to understanding the workability of that distinction is to regard the private as concerned with protecting iconoclastic intentions and the public as concerned with controlling the damage of the effects those intentions sometimes have. Some may have serious doubts about that quintessentially liberal response, but it does at least have the benefit of acknowledging both that even the happiest souls amongst us are quite capable of a baleful even if unintentional destructiveness and that we should not prevent the sickest souls in our midst from trying to work out their weirdest ideas simply because they seem weird or sick to us. With respect to Nietzsche, what this liberal compromise amounts to is the following suggestion: it would be imprudent to ignore Nietzsche's impudence even if it was not of his intention.

Nietzsche's impudence seems to impugn his use of genealogy as a mode of historical critique, even if it leaves intact the potentiality of an inspiring form of moral artistry. For present purposes, then, the upshot is just that we ought to look elsewhere if we want to make use of genealogy as a serious and studied methodology for inquiry into our present, and public, patterns of conduct. What Nietzsche lacks, but what I below show Foucault provides, is the elaboration of methodological equipment through which genealogical inquiry can be seen as proceeding without the motor of dialectical contradiction. Nietzsche saw his way past the negativity of contradiction in his moral artistry, but his historical writings unfortunately remain pervaded by a kind of negative remnant. For overcoming contradiction as a historical category, the crucial idea is that of genealogical problematization. This idea is fully explicit in Foucault but at best implicit in Nietzsche.

In Preview of Genealogy as Problematization

Having characterized two prominent but deficient uses of genealogy, I shall now go on to show how Foucault facilitates avoiding the failings to which these competing conceptions are subject. In contrast to the foregoing pictures of genealogy as vindication and subversion, I shall offer a detailed portrait of how Foucault deployed genealogy in the service of what he called "problematization." But before moving on to Foucault it is worth observing that he is not the only historian-philosopher who has effectively navigated between the all-too-common errors of subversion and vindication. Foucault by no means holds exclusive license to the forms of inquiry exhibited in his work. As a methodological analytic, genealogy makes itself available for future use and reuse. So before discussing Foucaultian genealogy as problematization over the course of Chapters 3 and 4, I would like to first preview genealogy as it is featured in the work of other contemporary critical inquirers who equally well refuse the enticing gambits of subversion and vindication.

Most notable among this work for my purposes are exemplars of critical inquiry exhibited in that strand of scholarship (noted in the Introduction) that rigorously employs Foucaultian analytics and diagnostics for the purposes of careful historical, anthropological, sociological, and philosophical inquiry. My representative Foucaultians for these purposes are Ian Hacking and Paul Rabinow, though certainly I have also learned much from work by Arnold Davidson, Ladelle McWhorter, and others.[75] Though I take most of my leads from the work of these four practitioner-theorists of Foucaultian critical inquiry, there is today a burgeoning literature in which Foucaultian analytics are put to productive use for critical purposes that move us beyond familiar attempts at subversion and vindication. This literature is of course not of uniformly good quality, and much of it fails to explicitly thematize the methodological decisions made in the deployment of Foucaultian analytics—yet many of these works nevertheless offer valuable starting points for critical inquiry.[76] For the sake of space, I shall offer a quick and simplified presentation of some of what I take to be the best of a sprawling literature. And I shall do so somewhat arbitrarily: by simply focusing on that work from which I have personally learned the most. Thus I begin with Hacking's work, which I shall describe as an effort in critical problematization, and then move from there to a brief consideration of two instructive kinds of uses of methodological problematization as expressed in the work of Hacking and Rabinow.

Hacking's philosophical histories have charted a number of remarkably different, though of course not entirely different, areas of study. One major area concerns the stabilization of the sciences of probability and statistics.[77] A second major field to which he has devoted much work deals with the emergence of certain categorizations of modern mental illness and psychology.[78] In other works Hacking charts yet other seas, and seemingly more expansive ones. He has written studies of the genesis of forms of self-classification (or "kinds of persons") that represent a broader genus of which the study of certain mentally ill kinds of persons is just one species.[79] There are also studies of the emergence of styles of scientific thinking that offer a broader genus of which the study of statistical thinking is just one species.[80] This is not the space for me to recount, or even to summarize, the details of these diverse histories. My purpose is to summarize the methodologies, in part archaeological and genealogical, that have contributed to the production of these histories.

In a collection of methodological reflections published under the Foucaultian title *Historical Ontology,* Hacking clarifies that his work is chiefly about how new forms of being come into being: "Historical ontology is about the ways in which the possibilities for choice, and for being, arise in history."[81] This is a good Kantian project, and one that is also notably suited up for those of us living on the other side of the nineteenth century from Kant himself. Like Kant, we want to inquire into conditions of possibility, but unlike Kant, we want our critiques to be sufficiently historical in their orientation. The label "historical ontology" captures this with effective simplicity. The objects of Hacking's inquiries are nearly always the emergence of certain practical formations that inform our present. These are, in other words, histories of our present written in a way that calls attention to conditioning problematizations. Hacking notes, "The application [of my work] is to our present pressing problems. The history is history of the present, how our present conceptions were made, how the conditions for their formation constrain our present ways of thinking."[82] For Hacking, an inquiry into the conditions of the possibility of the present looks more like a critique in Kant's special sense of that word than like those all-too-familiar vindications and subversions of the present that we find more common amongst contemporary critical inquirers. Paul Rabinow and Nikolas Rose capture this point well in a co-authored contribution to the study of emerging sciences and politics of life: "If we are in an emergent moment of vital politics, celebration and denunciation are insufficient as analytical approaches."[83] This is precisely as it is for Hacking, and also as it was for Foucault, and before all of them this is how it was for Kant, despite the dour countenance that we often associate with his name.

There are at least two ways of developing this project of a critical interrogation of the limits of the present without descending to celebration or denunciation. We can look to Hacking for an example of one way, and to Rabinow for the other. Hacking tends to interrogate philosophical issues associated with the practices he inquires into—his genealogies help us take up a different relation to certain pressing philosophical issues. For example, a history of scientific styles of thinking sheds light on long-running debates in the philosophy of science, and a history of the tradition of natural kinds helps resolve burning debates amongst philosophers over kinds terms and the various-isms (nominalism, universalism, conceptualism) in which they have become embroiled.[84] A different, but comple-mentary, model is featured in Rabinow's work. Rabinow, particularly in his an-thropologies of contemporary biosciences, is clearly committed to interrogating our practices themselves in a way that might open them up for future transfor-mation.[85] In this work, Foucaultian analytics are deployed in such a way as to en-able us to take up a different relation to certain pressing practical matters. These matters are not always straightforwardly philosophical in orientation, though they do of course have philosophical implications. In short, Hacking often ap-pears most interested in these philosophical implications of genealogical problema-tization, whereas Rabinow appears most interested in the possibilities for practical transformation that such problematizations enable. The work of both expresses both kinds of interest, so my claim is just about where the emphasis stands out the most.

Now, this comparative interpretation may seem too predictable in its appar-ent reproduction of Hacking's and Rabinow's respective disciplinary abodes in philosophy and the social sciences. But this prediction would be misleading in-sofar as what is most powerful about the work of both (and indeed what is most powerful in Foucault's work as well) is that they effectively break out of their re-spective disciplinary blocks in order to develop forms of critical inquiry that simul-taneously speak to philosophical and social scientific modalities, methods, concep-tualizations, and conclusions. There are no important incompatibilities separating these two deployments of problematization. Hacking has most frequently taken up archaeology and genealogy for a history of present practices that would reveal something about our philosophical sensibilities. Rabinow has most frequently taken up the same for the quite different purposes of an inquiry into the present and contemporary significance of our practices themselves.

I discern a happy complementarity in these two uses of Foucaultian criti-cal history. Both are valuable ways of working within the innovative critical style of problematization unleashed by Foucault. To that style, and its description, I now turn.

3

What Problematization Is

Contingency, Complexity & Critique

Genealogy and Normativity

Genealogy in the forms of both Nietzsche's subversion and Williams's vindication is susceptible to the charge that it commits the genetic fallacy. Though Nietzsche and Williams use genealogy in almost opposite senses, their respective uses commit this fallacy for the same underlying reason. Both attempt to deploy historical inquiry into the (actual or hypothetical) emergence of present practices in order to establish a normative evaluation of these practices. Nietzsche aimed to critically debunk, while Williams aimed to critically legitimate. But the form of error is the same in both cases insofar as both use history to evaluate the present. If pressed, I would happily admit that such reasoning is not as obviously fallacious as many critics have argued. But it is also not as obviously sound as many prominent genealogists, including Williams and Nietzsche, would have us suppose.

We should count Foucault among those who are suspicious of straightforward genetic argumentation of this sort. Foucault deployed genealogy but not as a tool for debunking power or anything else. Foucault recognized that no matter how base and despicable the emergence of certain of our practices has been, we can neither reject nor legitimate these practices on the basis of the terms of their emergence alone. Foucault's use of genealogy is accordingly misrepresented where it is assimilated to the normative use of genealogy as subversion, an interpretation that is unfortunately all too common in the postmodern aftermath of the bomb that was Nietzsche. If I am correct about this, then it is also relatively safe to infer that Foucault's use of genealogy should not be assimilated to the normative use of genealogy featured in Williams's vindicatory genealogies.

It should be noted that Foucault has been amply, severely, and repeatedly criticized precisely along these lines, including by a number of prominent pragmatists and critical theorists. Perhaps one of the most cogent arguments to the effect that Foucault commits the genetic fallacy is Nancy Fraser's. Fraser's criticisms of Foucault are based on an interpretation of Foucault's use of genealogy according to which the genealogist deploys carefully developed empirical insights in combination with some minimal set of other relevant considerations so as to establish the normative conclusion that certain of our practices are unjust, oppressive, or in some other way bad. Foucault is supposed to commit the genetic fallacy insofar as he uses empirical insights to establish normative conclusions. But, argues Fraser, this procedure yields normative confusions rather than normative conclusions.[1]

It is important to be precise about the force of Fraser's criticism here. The claim is that Foucault cannot derive the normative yield from his genealogies that he wishes to. This is not the same as the claim that Foucault's genealogies are value-laden despite a claim to being value-free. Nobody, Foucault included, ever thought of genealogical method as value-free. For instance, there are values already implicit in Foucault's decision to focus on, say, the prison and the hospital rather than say, the university and the factory, or his methodological restriction of his analysis to the West rather than the Rest—clearly there is a normative load structuring genealogy (as is the case of any effort in social science) from the outset. Fraser's argument, then, must rest on the supposition that Foucault's project is not only normatively loaded but also normatively ambitious. I take it that Fraser would accept that it is possible for a philosophical project to be laden with norms and not for that reason alone normatively ambitious. So I take it that her claim is that Foucault's project is normatively ambitious by design, but unjustifiably so, since genealogy as history cannot produce the normative payoff it seeks.

My response to Fraser's criticisms is to show that Foucault did not use genealogy to normatively evaluate the present practices whose histories he was writing. He rather used genealogy to clarify and intensify the dangers of the present whose histories he studied. Foucault himself often described his work as discerning dangers rather than demonstrating defects: "How can we exist as rational beings, fortunately committed to practicing a rationality that is unfortunately crisscrossed by intrinsic dangers? . . . If intellectuals in general are to have a function, if critical thought itself has a function—and, even more specifically, if philosophy has a function within critical thought—it is precisely to accept this sort of spiral, this sort of revolving door of rationality that refers us to its necessity, its indispensability, and, at the same time, to its intrinsic dangers."[2] Describing the dangers of rationality, I shall argue, is not to the same as assessing rationality as dangerously defective.

The point that Foucaultian genealogy was not designed as a normative exercise in subversion has always been a source of confusion for his American audience. Foucault's texts, entrenched as they are in a style that sometimes seems sinister, indeed lend themselves to misinterpretation on this point. But Foucault was unambiguous about this on at least one occasion, namely in a group interview at Berkeley where Foucault was quizzed by Paul Rabinow, Martin Jay, Leo Lowenthal, Charles Taylor, and Richard Rorty. One of these interlocutors (who remains unspecified in the transcript) asked Foucault about his own work vis-à-vis Habermas's critique of Nietzsche's tendency to conflate genesis and validity in his genealogies—the questioner congenially offered Foucault the option that his work is just "the story of genesis" without a correlative validity claim. Foucault's response (which, along with the question, unfortunately did not make it into the published version of this interview) was unequivocal: "Yes. I think there is no relation between genesis and validity. The problem is: how could it be valid, at a certain moment, in a certain context."[3] Here we have an unmistakable denial of a view that has been too often attributed to Foucault and for which he has received much too much bad press.

That this remark remained unpublished (and that Foucault did not often bother to make this point clearer in his published writings) has made it easier for most of Foucault's readers to attribute to him the normatively ambitious claim that genealogies show their object to be unjust, or bad, or at least obnoxious. But if Foucault was truthful in this group interview, then it should follow that for him discipline and biopolitics were not at all the kind of thing that one should be for or against. Indeed, later in the very same interview (this portion did make it into the published version), Foucault was asked the following question: "But aren't there relations of discipline which are not necessarily relations of domination?" Foucault's reply: "Of course, there are consensual disciplines."[4] A few years previous, also at Berkeley, another interlocutor had given Foucault the opportunity to clarify his view on these matters. Foucault was asked if he thought it "repressive" or somehow bad to discipline children so that, for example, they do not scribble on walls. His response was again unequivocal: "There's no reason why this manner of guiding the behavior of others should not ultimately have results that are positive, valuable, interesting, and so on. If I had a kid, I assure you he would not write on the walls—or if he did, it would be against my will. The very idea!" Foucault's response to his Berkeley interviewers (many of whom would have been well aware of the kinds of criticisms urged against Foucault by Fraser, Habermas, and other contemporary critical theorists) suggests that his aim was never to show that discipline and biopolitics were a bad thing. Under a close examination, Foucault's work does not bear this reading. The point of Foucault's genealogies was to show that discipline, biopolitics, and other stable features of our modernity are problematic in that they demand our serious attention: "This is a domain of very complex relations, which demand infinite reflection."[5] To deliver a normative judgment on discipline would be to deliver it from the domain of the problematic by rendering it determinate. Thought could then, and would then, move on to something new. Discipline would no longer be an object of our thought, perplexity, and curiosity. That was not Foucault's aim.

To summarize, my defense of Foucault against Fraser's charge that he commits the genetic fallacy involves provisional acceptance of Fraser's first premise—that genetic reasoning is fallacious—and denial of Fraser's second premise, which asserts that Foucault's genealogies exemplify genetic reasoning of precisely this objectionable kind.[6] What this means is that Foucault did not use genealogy to establish any normative conclusions about the practices he was investigating. Yet it is precisely this attempt to establish normative conclusions on the basis of descriptive claims about the historical evolution of practices that critics such as Fraser find objectionable in genetic reasoning. The objection to this sort of reasoning seems fairly sound so far as it goes. That said, the seeming soundness of the critique of genetic reasoning should not prevent us from acknowledging prominent exceptions to the rule, nor should it prevent us from inquiring into the assumption that our discourse expresses forms of reasoning whose validity is established outside of the ambit of their own evolution.

Though my response thus far addresses Fraser's criticism, it is worth noting another critique, also issued from within the tradition of pragmatist critical theory, that cuts much deeper against Foucault. Jürgen Habermas argued against Foucault that a value-laden method is always already normatively ambitious, albeit in unconscious or, as he put it, "crypto-normative" fashion. Habermas denies the possibility that value-laden social science can avoid harboring within its conclusions certain values as the specific point of those conclusions. "*This* grounding of a second-order value-freeness is already by no means value-free," insisted Habermas.[7] Of course, Habermas is right that value-laden social science (in other words, all social science) always loads norms in at the front end such that they are an unavoidable remainder at the end of inquiry. But I do not see why this compels us to read Foucault's genealogies as cryptically harboring norms. The presence of an unavoidable normative remainder does not prevent value-laden social science from reflexively accounting for the norms it cannot avoid assuming at the outset—Foucault offers, after all, a model of reflexive social critique. Nor need this unavoidable normative reminder constitute the specific diacritic of a genealogy even if it is present therein—the force of Foucault is not to assert a normative judgment so much as to provoke a critical questioning.

Many devotees of Foucaultian genealogy are likely to find my defense to have ceded well too much ground to the criticisms of critical theory. Am I not retreating, in the end, to exactly their view, namely that Foucault's projects are structured by normative confusions? Not quite. For I am not conceding the claim that Foucault's genealogy is objectionable due to its being normatively confused. Foucault's genealogies, as I see it, were just not as normatively ambitious as Fraser asserted, nor need they be read as unconsciously normatively ambitious as Habermas insisted. Therefore, Foucault does not commit the genetic fallacy because his work is not normative in the sense specified by that fallacy, or at least it is not normative in this sense in those aspects where he is engaged in genealogical problematization.[8]

But, devotees may further respond, my rereading of the upshot of genealogy makes it seem as if I am depriving genealogy of its critical edge. To head off this potential misinterpretation, I would like to issue two important observations at this juncture. The first is that my defense of Foucault does not require us to regard genealogical diagnosis as incompatible with normative evaluation. The second is that this defense also does not require us to regard Foucault's genealogies as critically ineffective even if they are not normatively robust. Allow me to explicate both at greater length.

In the first place, it is important to observe that Foucault's genealogies are in no ways incompatible with certain forms of positive normative theory. This does not mean, of course, that genealogy by itself need offer a normative apparatus. It only means that the apparatus for critical inquiry constituted by genealogy is wholly consistent with certain normative conceptions that are not themselves genealogical. Take, for example, core democratic values like equality and liberty. Certain (though of course not all) conceptualizations of equality and liberty are fine and good as normative tools, but these are also tools that we should not hope to excavate from Foucault's genealogies even if we wanted to. Normative evaluation was just not Foucault's project, even if his project is in the end amenable to such normativity and is indeed an attempt to provoke the progressive reconstruction of our best values. Todd May offers a useful discussion of the compatibility of genealogical critique and democratic normativity in his proposal for a combination of Foucault's critical conception of genealogy and Rancière's po-litical conception of equality. May does not attempt to deduce norms of equality from Foucault's project but rather proposes such norms as a "precise complement to Foucault's project." May holds, I think rightly, that "we can construct a positive normative conception of political action that does not violate the lessons of Fou-cault's studies."[9] I turn in the final chapter of this book to Habermas and Dewey, in whom I find more useful resources than in Rancière for this project. But the guid-ing idea is the same regardless of to whom we turn. There is nothing in Foucault's work that prevents us from taking a stand. Perhaps the best indicator of this is that there was nothing in Foucault's work that prevented him from taking a stand on a number of localized political struggles that he found crucial in his own time.

It is important to observe in the second place that there is nothing about my defense of Foucault against Fraser's charge that prevents us from regarding Fou-cault's work as critically effective even if it is not itself normatively robust. The point of Foucault's genealogies, as I see it, is to critically establish the problema-ticity of certain of our present practices by way of an inquiry into the history of our present. We can show that practices are problematic, dangerous, fraught, and in need of additional attention without making any normative claims about these practices. Foucault was not attempting to show that discipline is a bad thing or a good thing. Nor was he attempting to show that its core strategies of normali-zation, surveillance, and examination are bad things. He was only trying to help us understand some of the precise ways in which the general problematization in which these strategies were inscribed is fraught with dangers. Descriptions of problems need not imply normative evaluations, particularly in cases, like those Foucault worked on, where the problematic dangers stand in need of descriptive articulation. It is crucial to bear in mind that before Foucault wrote his genealogies we could not even get the dangers into view, let alone set about the project of do-ing something about them. Foucault conceptualized the dangers of discipline and more, where previously we did not have concepts available that would enable us to handle these problems. Such genealogical articulations of the concepts that en-able us to grasp the problems of our present provide us with some of the tools we would need to set about the project of normatively reconstructing our present. It is in this sense that genealogy can be critically effective without implicating any specific normative intent. Genealogy can as such effectively function as one part of a broader apparatus of critical inquiry alongside other critical elements featured in neighboring traditions, including those once seen as rivals, such as pragmatism and critical theory.

Genealogy as problematization aims to provide us with materials that we will need if we are to engage in the difficult practice of reworking ourselves. These materials for self-transformation, according to Foucault, are what a genealogy seeks to recover in locating the precise practices and procedures that have contributed to our current forms of constituting ourselves. The ultimate goal of genealogy as such is an explication and conceptualization of a complex set of practices that have contingently coalesced. This can be described as an analytical and diagnostic project. The genealogist analyzes and diagnoses practices in a way that reveals the problematizations enabling them. These problematizations condition our possibilities for acting, thinking, and being in the present. Jana Sawicki makes this point well: "Foucault was not rejecting modernity or identity *tout court*. He was inquiring instead into the historical limits of our understandings and experiences of madness, criminality, and sexuality."[10] Foucault sought conditions of possibility rather than a position from which to condemn or congratulate.

The coherence of this conception of critical practice without the high normative ambitions of vindication or denunciation is not immediately obvious. Perhaps, critics will object, Foucault is not normative in the way featured in Nietzsche and Williams but, the objection will go, so much the worse for Foucault. What is the value of critique if it cannot tell us what we should do?

Critique Neither For Nor Against

Foucault was well aware of the problems facing any normative use of genealogy. This was made especially evident when he came in his later years to explicitly and frequently describe his own historical research through the concept of problematization. In Foucault's hands, genealogy was part of a local critique of some of our moral practices, the effect of which was to problematize these practices in a way that opened them up for future transformation.

In reinterpreting genealogy and archaeology as problematization, I am taking seriously Foucault's claims for the importance of problematization for all of his work: "What I tried to do from the beginning was to analyze the process of 'problematization'—which means: how and why certain things (behavior, phenomena, processes) became a *problem*. . . . I am studying the 'problematization' of madness, crime, or sexuality."[11] Foucault used genealogy to clarify the way in which our practices of sexuality or punishment depend on and reproduce certain problematizations at the heart of persisting conceptions of power and freedom. Modern punishment and sexuality do not demonstrate that these conceptions are wrong (incoherent or unjust). They show instead that for us moderns, power and freedom have precisely become the problematic field on which we are most earnestly focused. Power as discipline and freedom as liberation are not delegitimized by Foucault. They are shown to be the most critical problematic over which we moderns find ourselves constantly obsessing. Foucault's use of genealogy as a means of clarifying and intensifying this problematization is not incompatible with attempts to destabilize practices of discipline and liberation. My point is only that genealogical problematization by itself neither legitimates nor delegitimates.

In an interview with Paul Rabinow and Hubert Dreyfus given in Berkeley in 1983, Foucault was asked if his histories of ancient thought were intended to revive a golden age of ethics that might be a plausible substitute for our current moral practices. Foucault's emphatic response apparently demanded an exclamatory emphasis when transcribed into a written text: "No!" Foucault then used this question as an opportunity to specify the way in which he saw his historical research functioning: "I would like to do the genealogy of problems, of *problématiques*. My point is not that everything is bad, but that everything is dangerous, which is not exactly the same as bad. If everything is dangerous, then we always have something to do."[12] Todd May glosses Foucault's conception with the useful descriptor of "fraught." It is not that certain of our practices are incoherent or inadequate, it is that they are fraught: "Instead of prohibitions there are dangers. Instead of obligations there are opportunities. Instead of allowances there are multiple ways these dangers and opportunities can be navigated."[13] Other commentators have similarly noted that the aim of Foucault's genealogies is to "open up" difficulties in the forms of "problems" or "slippages" upon which we can now work.[14] A conception of genealogy as opening up problematizations and showing how practices elaborated upon them are fraught fits well with the following description Foucault offered of himself: "I am trying to analyze the way institutions, practices, habits, and behavior become a problem . . . The history of thought is the analysis of the way an unproblematic field of experience, or a set of practices, which were accepted without question, which were familiar and 'silent,' out of discussion, becomes a problem, raises discussion and debate, incites new reactions, and induces a crisis in the previously silent behavior, habits, practices, and institutions."[15]

Foucault was always more interested in posing challenging questions than in sketching convincing solutions. Showing a practice to be good or bad is ultimately a way of solving problems rather than provoking them. This explains why Foucault vigilantly avoided what he called the "blackmail" of being "for" or "against" the central features of our modernity.[16] Foucault was often quite clear about this point in reflections on his own analytic and diagnostic methods. Sometimes he merely mentioned this point casually in the context of other discussions: "[W]hat I have been trying to do this evening is not to solve a problem but to suggest a way to approach a problem."[17] At other times, most often in interviews, he was careful to establish this point in a more rigorous fashion. In the lengthy interview with Trombadori: "My role is to raise questions in an effective, genuine way, and to raise them with the greatest possible rigor, with the maximum complexity and difficulty so that a solution doesn't spring from the head of some reformist intellectual or suddenly appear in the head of a party's political bureau. The problems I try to pose—those tangled things that crime, madness, and sex are, and that concern every life—cannot easily be resolved."[18] In another interview with Rabinow: "My attitude isn't a result of the form of critique that claims to be a methodical examination in order to reject all possible solutions except for the one valid one. It is more on the order of 'problematization'—which is to say, the development of a domain of acts, practices, and thoughts that seem to me to pose problems for politics."[19] Lastly, consider this line from the essay on methodology published as the introduction to the second volume of *The History of Sexuality:* "The proper task of a history of thought is: to define the conditions in which human beings 'problematize' what they are, what they do, and the world in which they live."[20]

These many methodological reflections on problematization suggest that the point of Foucault's genealogies was to neither subvert nor vindicate existing practices, beliefs, and conceptions. Rather, it was to critically show the way in which certain practices, beliefs, and conceptions have become problematic in the history of thought due to the contingent intersection of a complex set of enabling and disabling conditions. To say that practices are problematic is not to insist that they are wrong. It is to insist that they constitute a field in which we find that we must continue to work. Foucault is saying, for example, that we must concern ourselves with the problematic relations between modern power and modern freedom— for example, between the powers that we at times unthinkingly use to regulate sexual practices and the freedoms we attribute to certain supposedly liberating sexual practices. Genealogy taken in this sense is an initiating, rather than a concluding, phase of thought. Genealogy is not judgment, but critique. It brings into focus the problems to which further critical work must develop responses.

At this point the objections of Fraser and Habermas may seem to return with force. If genealogy presents problems on which we *must* work, what is the force of the "must" here? If the point of Foucaultian genealogy is to conceptualize crucial "problems" we face such that we will be moved to transform ourselves, then does it not carry an implicit and contentious normative load in its diagnosis? What is a "problem" but some definite wrong or error, be it potential or actual? In short, is it not the case that normative judgment is inevitably entrained by problematization? What, then, is the big difference between a problem and a wrong?

Foucault never denounced discipline. Nor need we. You, like me, already endorse its strategies, including normalization and surveillance, in some parts of your life. Despite occasional irritations, you want everyone to drive on the right side of the road. And even if you are someone who does not like the police, you surely would not complain about some organization dedicated to surveilling drivers to ensure that nobody drove on the other side. Few think that mandatory examinations for driving licenses are a bad idea, including even those who are hateful of the bureaucratic apparatus entrained by these examinations. These are trivial examples, but they point to the positive effects of discipline that Foucault too acknowledged. And yet no one would deny that disciplines and their strategies bear enormous dangers within. Here is my point: discipline is not bad, though it can be put to bad uses. The problem is not discipline. The problem is that we disciplinarians know not what to do when discipline goes bad. This problem is not trivial for us today amidst the swarming of the disciplines. The dangers of the disciplines are daily manifest in our prisons, our hospitals, our schools, our courtrooms, our bedrooms, our shopping malls, and our workplaces—they even manifest right at the heart of who we are in our very conceptions of our body and mind.

Our problem is that when we find discipline going wrong, we often oppose it with practices of freedom as liberation or emancipation. But, Foucault insisted, the ideals of freedom with which we tend to work are often complicit with, rather than effective against, discipline. Liberation, once effective against repressive power, is rarely able to out us from the grip of discipline. This complicity runs in both directions. When we find freedom too free, too out of control, we try to cage it with our fine-tuned disciplinary apparatus. But the too-frequent result is blowback, or freedom flaunting itself in the face of discipline. That liberation and discipline are ineffective against the abuses of each other is an effect of the rigorous division (which I call the purification) of freedom and power charted by Foucault's histories of modernity. This purification goes to the heart of Foucault's problematizations of modernity. I shall describe in detail this entwinement of discipline and liberation in Chapter 5, where I reinterpret *Discipline and Punish* along these lines—for now I can only issue a promissory note. But if I can redeem this promissory note later, then I am justified now in claiming that Foucaultian problematization does not rely on an implicit normative mechanism to do its work. There is nothing wrong with discipline itself. But we do have a problem. When discipline goes wrong, as it often does, we often respond in ways that only reinforce discipline. This problem speaks more to the conditions of possibility for being, acting, and thinking in the present than it does to any normative judgment of what we are, do, or think.

I conclude that genealogy is coherently neither for nor against, which is to say that genealogy is coherent in its aim to be critical without being judgmental. My view that Foucault's practice of problematization is usefully contrasted to vindication and denunciation in terms of critical outcome can be connected to the idea that problematization is also usefully contrasted to certain typical historiographical methods in terms of critical procedure. The historiographical commitment undertaken by genealogy as problematization is to problems and responses as the units of historical narrative and explanation. This means that the genealogist will seek to narrate and explain historical processes by reference to the problems that motivate certain processes and the specific practices that develop in response to these problems. This can be contrasted to more common historiographical commitments to familiar themes of economy, territory, spirit, rationality, and ideology.

With this conclusion in hand, I want to offer a comment on the methodology by virtue of which Foucault was to effect the historiographical shift to history as problematization. One useful emblem for this can be drawn from a moment in his 1978 course lectures where he is reflecting on the methodological shift implicit in genealogy: "The point of view adopted in all these studies involved the attempt to free relations of power from the institution, in order to analyze them from the point of view of technologies; to distinguish them also from the function, so as to take them up within a strategic analysis; and to detach them from the privilege of the object, so as to resituate them within the perspective of the constitution of fields, domains, and objects of knowledge."[21] Throughout his course that year, Foucault made increasingly explicit reference to a conception that he would later come to explicitly thematize under the title of problematization. Foucault carefully explained that he was looking to move beyond a mode of historical explanation that would situate practices in relation to institutions, or functions, or established objects. He insisted that institutions, functions, and objects must themselves be explained, and in terms of the problematizations that enable them. Foucault referred to his earlier work on the problem of disciplinary power as a possible explanation of modern punishment practices. His point here is that punishment should not be explained on the basis of penal institutions, punitive functions, and objective analyses of prisons, courts, and hospitals. All of these are important, of course, but they themselves must be situated in relation to the more general problematization of discipline that enabled them. A problematization is a base out of which we elaborate the institutions, functions, and objects constitutive of our practices. To understand our practices and the strategies and techniques composing them, we must understand the problematizations to which they are a response. What Foucault is bringing into focus in his studies of discipline, security, and governmentality is not a new institution, function, or object, but rather "the emergence of a completely different problem" that enables the responsive development of emergent institutions, functions, and objects.[22]

Genealogy thus functions as a history of the present on the basis of the emergence of the problematizations that have enabled the development of present practices in response to these problematizations. Foucault, as a genealogist, both clarified these problematizations and problematized their continuing stability. Near the end of his life he described his work concerning prisons (both the philosophico-historical researches and the practical work with the prison reform movement and the Groupe d'Information sur les Prisons) as "an enterprise of 'problematisation,' an effort to render problematic and doubtful the evidences, practices, rules, institutions and habits that had been sedimented for decades and decades. . . . This problem cannot be solved by a few theoretical proposals. It requires many debates, many experiments, many hesitations, attempts, and reconsiderations."[23] To the extent that they are oriented by this more general procedure of problematization, genealogies and archaeologies aim to provide us with some of the tools we will need if we are to transform the possibilities of our present.

Analyzing Problematizations as Contingent and Complex

It will be useful at this point to engage in a rather precise specification of the uses that problematization is put to in Foucault's work, and hence in our work following his.[24] The cost of rigor is often dryness, so I will be as brief as possible in offering the fine-grained specifications that follow. This dry exercise is valuable, because clarifying the multiplicitous qualities of problematization enables us to better understand the different kinds of work that Foucault expected from his genealogies as well as the different kinds of work that we ourselves may reasonably expect of genealogy in redeploying it.

As I understand it, problematization can function along two dimensions. Each of these dimensions can be inflected with two senses.

With respect to its dual-dimensionality, problematization was for Foucault both an act of critical inquiry (expressed in the verb form as "to problematize") and a nominal object of inquiry (expressed in the noun form as "a problematization").

Foucault shuttled back and forth between deploying problematization along these two different dimensions such that his work itself is best seen as a dual deployment of problematization along both. Sometimes he claimed that he was writing the history of problematizations as objects of inquiry. Other times he described his work as if his histories were themselves acts of problematization. It helps to keep these two dimensions separate, and one way of doing so is to invent some nomenclature for this purpose. I refer to nominal problematizations with usage such as "the x problematization" and to active problematizations with terms such as "the problematization of x." For example, I speak of "the disciplinary problematization" as an object of inquiry and "the problematization of sovereignty" as one of the active effects of such inquiries into the emergence of post-sovereign forms of power.

Instead of presenting us with an impossible methodological incoherence, the nominal and verbal dimensions of problematization serve to reinforce one another even amidst the tensions they produce. Foucault as philosopher took already-existing problematizations (in a nominal sense) as his objects of inquiry while at the same time positioning his inquiries in such a way as to intensify these already-existing objects, thus further problematizing (in a verbal sense) the practices that have been elaborated on their basis. It is therefore not entirely misleading to regard problematization as a species of that wider genus of "history" that operates in light of a similar tension between an object of inquiry (history as the past) and a study of this object (the discipline of history).[25]

This dual-aspect or dual-dimension character of problematization helps us recognize how Foucault can be seen as offering existing problematizations a greater degree of self-consciousness than what they might be able to muster on their own. The role of the critical inquirer on this view is therefore not to produce a problematization that does not already have some basis in practice but rather to contribute to the ongoing reproduction of problematizations already under way. The critical inquirer observes practical problematizations that are already extant and seeks to fashion a methodological apparatus that would enable us to draw up, organize, and engage these problematizations. In this sense, critical inquiry aims to invest practice with theory and also to invest practice into theory. This relation between theoretical inquiry and practical object of inquiry is in no way manifestly contradictory, but it is also not obviously coherent. The tense relationship between philosophical clarification and practical development is never an easy one, and if it is always rife with tensions, it is primarily the job of the inquirer to ensure that these tensions do not undermine the otherwise productive aspects of the relationship. It is in this sense that problematization can be grasped as riding along a dynamic tension that gives rise to the generative work of thought itself. In other words, the tension between historical problematizations as practical objects of inquiry and historical problematization as a theoretical act of inquiry is precisely what enables Foucaultian problematization to intervene in the way it does.[26]

Now, in both their nominal and verbal (or objective and inquiring) dimensions, problematizations have two senses. First, consider the nominal dimension of problematization as an object of inquiry. Problematizations refer negatively to ways in which emergent practices render problematic certain other conceptions that are no longer capable of effectively performing the work they once achieved. This is the sense in which an emergent practice makes problematic certain other practices that it will eventually displace or force to alter themselves. Problematizations in their nominal dimension also refer positively to the ways in which the deficient status of these older practices themselves pose a problem to be solved or a question to be answered. In this sense, problematizations act positively as a basis for more work to be done. They describe a deficient situation in such a way as to establish a basis for repairing the situation according to the constraints already operative in the situation. Nominal problematizations function as bases that simultaneously disable (negatively) and enable (positively) the elaboration of certain practices.

Consider now the active dimension of problematization as a practice of inquiry, where we can also distinguish two senses of the term. In one sense, problematization is simply a descriptive study whose aim is to clarify certain past problematizations that have enabled the development of present practices. But in another sense, problematization is a critical tool that can be used to intensify our concern with those problematizations that continue to inform our present ways of constituting ourselves. The practice of inquiry as problematization thus has both what I will call a clarifying and an intensifying sense. As Foucault often practiced it, genealogy as problematization worked in both ways at once.

To summarize the two pairs of discriminations just made: I distinguish two senses each of two dimensions of problematization as this cluster functioned in Foucault's work. The two dimensions of problematization are as verbal use or activity (the problematization of x) and as nominal object or thing (the x problematization). In each of these dimensions we can further distinguish two aspects or senses of problematization. In the dimension of problematization as an activity of inquiry, problematization functions both to descriptively clarify extant problems and to normatively intensify the force we feel in confronting these problems. In the dimension of problematization as an object of inquiry, problematizations both render certain old practices problematic and act as the problematic bases out of which new practices can develop.

This rather fine-grained analytic description of problematization can be used to help bring into focus a crucial element of genealogy by virtue of which genealogy is properly historical. That genealogy is historical cannot be explained by reference to the idea that it studies the past or even the origins of the present. The historicity implicit in genealogy should be understood in terms of its concern with processes of emergence. A genealogical view presents practices (which are complex compositions of techniques, beliefs, styles, powers, knowledges, and ethics) as emerging in and through problematizations and the reconstructive responses provoked by these problematizations. In their nominal dimension, problematizations function to render problematic certain old practices at the same time that they establish a basis for the elaboration of certain new practices. Problematizations as such act as a kind of hinge by way of which we transition out of old practices and into new ones. They function as the basis on which both old practices recede and new practices emerge. A historiographical focus on problems does not mean, of course, that problematizations are explanatorily ultimate entities. It only means that for the purposes of a genealogy, we treat problematizations as that by virtue of which we are able to understand the emergence and recession of present practices.

Foucault's genealogical problematizations are able to function as an account of emergence just insofar as Foucault expanded his historiographical repertoire from an archaeological analysis of one vector of history, such as knowledge or power, to a genealogical inquiry into the multiple relations of two or more vectors, such as the multiple relations between strategies of knowledge and techniques of power. On the basis of such relations, tensions and difficulties arise in practices. These tensions and difficulties function like micro-problematizations that over time may become macro-problematizations or problematizations proper— that is, large networks of problems on the basis of which certain older practices are rendered ineffective and certain new practices are rendered more viable. For example, the biopolitical problematization that functioned as the basis for the emergence of a whole raft of modern practices is in part provoked by the tensions between regimes of power in which security and other militaristic means were operative and between regimes of knowledge such as probabilistic sciences that could be adjusted to and combined with these requirements for security in such a way as to establish a fairly coherent problematization according to which populations, for instance, became a basis for both the development of a vast number of quintessentially modern practices and for the increasing ineffectiveness of older pre-biopolitical practices concerned not with population but with, say, rituals of blood and magic. Once power and knowledge come together in biopolitics, it becomes increasingly difficult to disentangle the two and to facilitate the development of either in isolation from the other. Witness the decline of powers that do not know but only act, and the decline of knowledges that only know but are yet impotent.

Problematizations can be analyzed and diagnosed by inquiring into the multiple practices that are both conditioned by and manifestations of these problematizations. Foucault referred to his work as an inquiry into "the *problematizations* through which being offers itself to be, necessarily, thought—and the *practices* on the basis of which these problematizations are formed."[27] Practices can be understood as both complex constituents of a problematization and as themselves conditioned by complex assemblages. The precise point of focus of a genealogy is thus neither behaviors nor mentalities nor meanings nor structures, but practices and the problematizations they form in their multiplicity.

To summarize, genealogists study the way in which problematizations contingently emerge from the intersection of a complex set of practices to form the conditions of possibility of future practice. This summary is probably too laborious to be easily remembered. But the takeaway point is simple enough: genealogy emphasizes complexity and contingency in critical history.

As concerns complexity, it is useful to generalize Nikolas Rose's observation about a field of inquiry that forms just one aspect of Foucault's work: "governmentality is to be analyzed in terms of . . . the complex assemblage of diverse forces (legal, architectural, professional, administrative, financial, judgmental), techniques (notation, computation, calculation, examination, evaluation), devices (surveys and charts, systems of training, building forms) that promise to regulate decisions and actions of individuals, groups, organizations in relation to authoritative criteria."[28] Rose concisely indicates the sheer diversity of that which contingently intersects to form the problematization of governmentality. A genealogy is suited to study the broad array of practices that intersect wherever innovative forms emerge as general problematizations conditioning subsequent practices.

As concerns the contingency of these intersections, consider again Rose: "links between the political apparatus and the activities of governing are less stable and durable than often suggested: they are tenuous, reversible, heterogeneous, dependent upon a range of 'relatively autonomous' knowledges, knowledgeable persons and technical possibilities."[29] This suggests that genealogy proceeds with the assumption that there is no reason why any problematization had formed the way that it did. The emergence of a problematization is simply too complex to be ascribed to any one explanatory factor that would fully determine it. Genealogy in this way refuses appeals to some ultimate level as explanatory such that the emergence of a problematization can be regarded as having the force of necessity. There is nothing ultimate: no destiny, no teleological rationality, no class, no economy, no idea, and no thing dictates that reality had to be this way rather than another. Certain practices could have never come into existence such that certain problematizations would have never emerged. But when a complex set of elements coalesces to form a problematization, each of these elements is henceforth marked by the contribution it makes, and the problematization itself is informed by each of the elements.

Herein we find an invaluable philosophical contribution: recognition that that which is conditioned can condition its own conditions. Only one who does not take history seriously will find this paradoxical. No doubt, many will. In the remainder of this chapter I shall try to alleviate some of the familiar yet strange worries that we tend to have when confronted by the idea of conditioned conditioners.

Composing Problematizations out of Practices

One way of grasping the centrality of the related themes of complexity and contingency for Foucault's genealogy is in terms of the relationship between problematizations as manifold objects of inquiry and the diversity of elements composing them. There are many possible metaphors for this relation: Foucault often wrote of problematizations as composed of a diversity of practices, but he also sometimes talked about technologies as compositions of techniques; Hacking writes of niches as composed by numerous vectors; Rabinow develops metaphors of pathways and equipment to capture the diverse elements composing more general norms and forms; Rose similarly writes of pathways; others, including DeLanda, have followed Deleuze in focusing inquiry around a conception of assemblages.[30] The account I offer here of complex problematizations (or niches) as formed by the assembly (or intersection) of simpler yet still complex practices (or vectors of practice) is my own gloss on genealogical critique. This gloss is drawn up using terms supplied by others, but it cannot be found as such in the work of any of those from whom I draw.

A helpful image for bringing my preferred metaphor into preliminary focus is offered by Marcel Duchamp's 1914 painting *Network of Stoppages*. The painting shows in its foreground a series of vivid lines, suggestive of a network, set against a mostly brown background, suggestive of crinkled brown grocery-bag paper. There are nine lines (or vectors) in total, arranged in three sets of three, intersecting at a multiplicity of nodes (or niches). The image recalls commonplace senses of both genealogical lineage and historical timelines. Lingering in this commonplace, the painting's lines can be seen as representative of the vector metaphor for practices, and the nodes as representative of the niche metaphor for problematizations. Duchamp's painting, as an image, thus offers a helpful, if a bit simplistic, icon of genealogy. It is, as it were, genealogy on-the-go. You can carry the image around with you and draw it on any chalkboard or scrap of paper at hand. But the painting is not just an icon of genealogy. Felicitously, the painting itself also offers an instructive index of genealogical contingency and complexity. For the painting directly refers to Duchamp's earlier 1913 wood box sculpture titled *Three Standard Stoppages*. According to Duchamp, this earlier piece was produced by holding three lengths of string, each one meter long, above a canvas, and letting them drop from a height of exactly one meter. Each string thus settled on the canvas with a different curvature. The lengths were then used to cut three wood slats on one edge, with the result being three meter-length wood measures, none of which were identical because of the different curvatures. This earlier sculpture was used the next year as the basis for the arrangement of lines, in three sets of three, in *Network of Stoppages*. But the history of Duchamp's meter stoppages does not end there. One great theme of almost all of Duchamp's work is reperformance. In his major work of 1915–23, the *Bride Stripped Bare by Her Bachelors, Even* (a.k.a. *The Large Glass*), the stoppages reappear again in a work composed of a multiplicity of elements, all of which reproduce earlier paintings and sculptures. His later mixed-media pieces *Green Box* of 1934 and *Box in a Valise* of 1935–41 then packaged together miniatures of many of his works, including miniatures of *The Large Glass* and *Standard Stoppages,* into convenient portable boxes. The reproduction, resetting, and remixing of the stoppages across a diversity of work shows just how fecund can be an instantiation of the process of reperforming the standard meter. Within these works are tales with plenty to tell of contingency and complexity.

With this preliminary image in view, allow me to now turn back to the metaphors. A crucial point of Hacking's idea of vectors and niches is that they are meant to describe the complex combination of otherwise differently situated practices that are themselves complex. Hacking explicitly notes that one point of these metaphors is that they help emphasize "the complexity—and sheer size—of the manifold of elements" that enables new kinds of practices. One crucial methodological heuristic for which these metaphors are designed concerns "the importance of not focusing on just one thing, not just discourse, not just power, not just suffering, not just biology, when one speaks of a niche." Inquiry requires a method that enables us to bring into focus the multiplicity of vectors composing niches, or in other words, "the concatenation of an extraordinarily large number of diverse types of elements which for a moment provide a stable home" for certain kinds of practices.[31] Hacking's metaphors help us see how problematizations, which he called for a time "niches," are contingently formed out of complex combinations of practices that travel along a multiplicity of vectors.

It is not difficult to find similar language in Foucault. There are even a few instances where Foucault himself explicitly employed the "vector" metaphor.[32] The resonance is not only terminological. Consider the following "purely methodological comment" offered by Foucault amidst one of his course lectures to the effect that the forms of intelligibility he describes are established by "showing phenomena of coagulation, support, reciprocal reinforcement, cohesion, and integration . . . the bundle of processes and the network of relations."[33] Or consider the following formulation offered by Foucault, where he practically defines genealogy in precisely such terms, writing of it as "something that attempts to restore the conditions for the appearance of a singularity born out of multiple determining elements of which it is not the product, but rather the effect."[34]

The point that I take as crucial is the idea of the contingent intersection of a complex array of practical activities that form a kind of basis for both the elaboration of newer practices and the destabilization of older practices. That basis is a "problematization," and it is formed by intersecting "practices" that function as "vectors" or "pathways" along which "problematizations" propagate. When practices intersect (collide with, borrow from, build on top of, or merge into one another), they tend to produce tensions in a way that is often productive insofar as these tensions give rise to problematizations that operate as both obstacles to certain older forms of practice and bases for the elaboration of newer forms of practice. A problematization is formed by a multiplicity of intersecting practices such that whatever is at the intersection gradually achieves a degree of density or gravity by which it comes to constitute the conditions of the possibility of further practices, including future iterations of the very practices composing the problematization. The same practice can both in its earlier iterations feed into the emergence of a problematization and in its later iterations come to be conditioned by a problematization insofar as the practice might come to be intelligible only within that problematization.

Reading *Discipline and Punish* through this lens of problematizations-and-practices yields the following interpretation. Foucault's book describes the problematization of modern discipline and surveillance as formed out of the intersection of a diversity of practices of power and knowledge. These practices include those of jurisprudence, punishment, education and apprenticeship, social control, hygiene, sickness, clinical medicine, mental health, and a remarkable variety of other humble activities also invested for one reason or another in the emerging shapes of discipline and surveillance. These diverse practices of power and knowledge increasingly intersected so as to reinforce one another over the course of the nineteenth century. This is particularly evident at the site of punitive practice, the gradual consolidation of which around technologies of imprisonment is Foucault's object of explanation here. As all of these practical vectors increasingly coagulated, there slowly congealed the singularity of discipline. At a certain point this singularity passed through a certain threshold of density and entanglement that evidences the emergence of a problematization that could be leveraged as a basis for drawing in other practices of power and knowledge in other sites. The steady elaboration of further practices upon the basis of this problematization served to further reinforce the problematization itself. What Foucault offered in this book is thus best seen as an account of the emergence of a problematization out of the intersection of a rather humble procession of vectors of practices. These vectors are at once particular (located in the specificity of certain sites) and universalizable (forming strategies that reach beyond the limitations of their particular site of emergence). The problematizations they form are likewise particular (as based in certain practices) and universalizable (as basis for their own generalization into other practices). In this way genealogy captures that temporal process through which problematizations humbly emerge and yet over time come to occupy tremendous importance.

Allow me to offer yet another example drawn from my own ongoing, still very much tentative, work toward a genealogy of liberalism in America. Twentieth-century American liberalism emerged from, say, 1851–1923 across an array of sites including but not limited to the transition from federalism to nationalism, the transition from proprietary to corporate capitalism, the emergence and consolidation of scientific methods harnessing tools of probability, the complex racism of Reconstruction and Jim Crow, an increasing participation in colonial and imperial domination overseas, and the increasing dissemination of unifying venues of publicity such as broadcast media (Hearst's newspapers, commercial radio) and new forms of commons (Olmsted's public parks). These and other sites were witness to the elaboration of practices of power, knowledge, and ethics that intersected in such a way as to constitute a new problematization for liberal culture. The still-emerging complex of twenty-first-century American liberalism that has been developing from, say, 1929 to the present is conditioned by a related but not structurally isomorphic array of sites, including the advent of transnational global markets, the crystallization of consumerism at the heart of corporate capitalism, the politicization of a welter of categories of identity and affiliation, the birth of network-based communicative media, the emergence of big-money science, and the increasing use of disaggregated publics sponsored by all of these. These sites also yielded newer strategies that contributed to the formation of a quite different liberal problematization that may one day come to contest the very meaning of liberalism itself.

One useful way of studying the emergence of problematizations is to explore the vectors composing a given problematization such that we can grasp the diversity of ways in which the core problematization gets taken up and worked over. Inquiring into these different vectors requires both detailed empirical investigation of particulars and broader theoretical conceptualization of universalizable strategies. This yields a picture of broad cross-vector problematizations (such as liberalism or discipline) as emerging in specific sites (such as the newspaper or the prison) and at the same time enabling strategies (such as information centralization or normalization) that reach well beyond those sites.

Genealogy tracks complex histories of alliance, support, and reinforcement that facilitate the production of spaces of practical possibility. The point is not to discern how the intentions of those in the past effectively gave rise to the present, but rather to understand how various independently existing vectors of practice managed to contingently intersect in the past so as to give rise to the present. Rose usefully refers to "assemblages which may have a rationality" but one not derived from "a coherence of origin or singular essence."[35] Consider the role of monastic rituals of time in Foucault's genealogies of modern discipline. Foucault's point was obviously not that monks developed timetables with an eye toward eventually overturning sovereign power. His aim was to show how monks developed ritualized habits that existed for centuries in a relatively isolated fashion before they were hooked up in a relatively short span of time with certain other practices in a way that proved mutually reinforcing for both. The monastic rituals formed alliances of support with other practices such as merchant capitalism and wage manufacturing in a way that was certainly not inevitable—and yet there was no looking back from the first moment this alliance was formed. Foucault writes in one of his course lectures that his work aims to "replace a genetic analysis through filiation with a genealogical analysis . . . which reconstructs a whole network of alliances, communications, and points of support."[36] Foucaultian genealogies are not like Lamarckian family trees, which would show how the efforts of one generation pay off for those in the next generation. They are more like

Darwinian species trees, which would trace lines of alliance, colonization, conquest, and spandrel mutations to show the way in which the present is conditioned by a history that is complex and contingent.

Genealogy conceived in this way is capable of effectively avoiding a classical difficulty facing many other analytic and diagnostic methodologies. Genealogy proceeds without relying on ultimate units of explanation whether these units are conceived at the micro-level or the macro-level. The various vectors composing problematizations are themselves complex assemblages, just as the problematizations they form are complex assemblages. While monastic timetable rituals are merely one element in a broader assemblage forming the problematization of discipline, this vector is itself an assemblage that could be genealogically decomposed into its own constituent vectors. While discipline is already a complex problematization, over time it has proven itself quite capable of synthesizing with other elements such that in some contexts it is but one vector in an even broader assemblage. The point is that there is no analytically most simple unit of analysis or synthetically most complete unit of analysis—there are only heuristic exercises in decomposition and composition undertaken for the sake of elucidating the historical emergence of whatever practices constitute the objects of inquiry. We stop decomposing or composing when we want or need to rather than out of deference to the overwhelming force of some ultimate micro-or macro-reality itself. Genealogy in this way operates at the level of a singularity that at once speaks to particularizability and universalizability.[37]

Now, my aim is not to encumber would-be and once-were genealogists with an elaborate armamentarium. My hope is rather to show that genealogy is a mode of inquiry into problematizations and vectors that enables historians, anthropologists, sociologists, and philosophers to bring their material into focus through the lenses of contingencies and complexities without sacrificing the idea that this material can be described in terms of the tight constraint attributed to conditions of possibility. The upshot of my attempt to satisfy this desideratum can be stated as follows: genealogy tracks the complex interaction of different practical vectors in their contingent intersection with one another so as to form problematizations. The units of analytical significance for the genealogist are neither micro-(smallest) nor macro-(biggest) realities, but are rather practices (smaller) and problematizations (bigger). Genealogy enables us to investigate the conditions of the possibility of the present without referring these conditions to either a pure realm of the transcendental or a pure realm of the empirical.

The classical difficulty that genealogy thus overcomes is that of a certain crucial dilemma in the Kantian philosophy that has always hampered the project of critique. Foucault is thus a Kantian in one sense (he is a critical philosopher) but not a Kantian in another sense (he is not himself entangled in the thorns of transcendental philosophy). I would like to now turn to this fragile relation between Kant and Foucault, in part to address interpretive difficulties in the Foucault literature and in part to further clarify certain philosophical difficulties raised by the very idea of conditioned conditioners.

Kant and Foucault

Ian Hacking notes, with his characteristically effective simplicity, that "Foucault was a remarkably able Kantian."[38] One way of making sense of this claim is to regard Foucault as taking up Kant's project of critique in such a way as to transform that project. In this view Foucault was a Kantian in that his work, in Amy Allen's apt description, "constitutes a critique of critique itself, a continuation-through-transformation of that project."[39] A reading of Foucault as a Kantian need not dampen genealogy's radicalism by using it to recuperate old-fashioned philosophies of scientific understanding and moral freedom. Foucault remained a Kantian without even so much as flirting with deontological morality and transcendental idealism.[40]

In 1983 Foucault explicitly located his debt to Kant in terms of critical philosophy—but not in terms of a critical reconstruction of knowledge and morality—in describing his work as embodying critique in the form of the "problematization of an actuality and the philosopher's questioning of this actuality to which he belongs and in relation to which he has to position himself."[41] In that same year Foucault opened his Collège de France course lectures with an inviting discussion of Kant involving a distinction between the major critical apparatus (i.e., the three Critiques) and the critical interrogation of his present embodied in Kant's writings on his historical present (i.e., the writings usually described as political and historical). The former, Foucault says, acts as "the analytic of truth," whereas the latter involves "an ontology of the present, of present reality, an ontology of modernity, an ontology of ourselves." This leaves us with a crucial decision: "We have to opt either for a critical philosophy that appears as an analytical philosophy of truth in general, or for a critical thought that takes the form of an ontology of ourselves, of present reality."[42] This distinction, crucial for Foucault's appropriation of Kant, can be read as parsing transcendental critique and historical critique.

Hacking excellently illustrates the critical thrust of Foucaultian problematization by borrowing this latter idea of a "historical ontology" of ourselves.[43] Hacking describes his own version of historical ontology as inquiring into the historical conditions of possibility of certain of our practices, subjectivities, and other ways of being: "Historical ontology is not so much about the formation of character as about the space of possibilities for character formation that surround a person."[44] Such spaces of possibility form what Foucault called the problematizations within which our practices develop. Hacking's formulation in terms of inquiries into the possibilities conditioning our practices offers a useful warrant for connecting Foucaultian problematization to Kantian critique. Hacking offers in this connection a useful remark for grasping the specific quality of Foucault's Kantian inheritance: "Where Kant had found the conditions of possible experience in the structure of the human mind, Foucault does it with historical, and hence transient, conditions for possible discourse."[45]

If Hacking is correct, then Foucault's Kantianism does not assume the form of "transcendental history" or "transcendental as historical" method, as has been suggested by a phalanx of recent commentators including Béatrice Han-Pile, Andrew Cutrofello, Kevin Thompson, and Johanna Oksala.[46] These commentators are right in aiming to correct the common error of denying Foucault his Kantian inheritance. But in order to call attention to his Kantian inheritance they have thought it necessary to reread genealogy and archaeology through the lens of phenomenology, with its emphasis on the interlacing of the historical and the transcendental. I aim for a more direct relationship between Kantian and Foucaultian critique. Critical investigations of limiting conditions of possibility are central to Foucault's work. They take the form for him of historical ontology and epistemology rather than transcendental ontology and epistemology. The view I propose is that Foucault's work offers a form of critique in which transcendental inquiry is replaced by (or perhaps supplemented by) historical inquiry but is decidedly not combined with it in a way that would suggest an amalgamated historical-transcendental critique as is found in the many forms of phenomenology descending from Edmund Husserl.[47] Paul Veyne notes, rightly, "To Kant's and Husserl's notion of a transcendental origin of thought, Foucault was to oppose an empirical and contextual one."[48] Veyne, like Hacking, rightly emphasizes Foucault's empiricism. Yes, Foucault's *empiricism*.

I find the transcendental interpretation of Foucault's critical history impossibly difficult to square with such of Foucault's claims as this: "In all of my work I strive instead to avoid any reference to this transcendental as a condition for the possibility for any knowledge. . . . I try to historicize to the utmost to leave as little space as possible to the transcendental."[49] This remark, offered during the intellectually turbulent years in which Foucault was expanding his methodological toolkit to involve genealogy alongside archaeology, serves as a severe caution to those who see Foucault as striving for something like transcendental critique in his work. There are countless such remarks in Foucault's writings from those years; many of them are peppered throughout *The Archaeology of Knowledge* in thinly veiled quips where he appears to be carefully charting his distance from a phenomenology of the transcendental subject: "the essential task was to free the history of thought from its subjection to transcendence . . . its aim is to free history from the grip of phenomenology."[50] But my evidence for my interpretation is not just textual. I think there are also good philosophical reasons to reject, as did Foucault himself, a conflation of the critical and the transcendental.

My interpretation depends philosophically on a crucial distinction between two ideas at the heart of Kant's project: critique and transcendentality. This distinction can be approximately located through Foucault's texts, but it is better to just pose it directly.[51] I understand critique, in Kant's sense, to refer to an inquiry into the limits of a certain form of rationality on the basis of exploring the conditions of the possibility of that form of rationality. In the *Critique of Pure Reason*, Kant defined critique as an "estimation" of the "sources and limits" of reason.[52] In *Critique of Judgment*, critique is similarly defined as "inquiry" into "possibility and bounds" of reason.[53] Kant's project of critique is usually understood as an inquiry into certain structuring conditions or, in the terminology I prefer, conditions of possibility. Critique explicates conditions that make possible. Critique in this most general sense can be, and should be, distinguished from its more specific forms, including the more specific forms of transcendental critique and historical critique.

Kant explained in the first *Critique* that his critical project would proceed transcendentally, by which he meant that it would concern itself with "the mode of our knowledge of objects insofar as this mode of knowledge is to be possible *a priori*."[54] In the third *Critique*, he similarly told us that "A transcendental principle is one by means of which is represented, *a priori*, the universal condition under which alone things can be in general objects of our cognition."[55] Transcendental critique for Kant specified the limits of our synthetic *a priori* cognition of objects. Insofar as Kant is working with a generous conception of objectivity (such that this category includes any object of cognition whatsoever), the project of transcendental critique would seem to offer a prolegomenon to any future inquiry, be it metaphysical inquiry or scientific inquiry or anthropological inquiry. Underlying Kant's project, then, is the view that we can ascertain the conditions of the possibility of cognition *qua* cognition only through an investigation of the universal and necessary conditions that are transcendental to, rather than immanent within, the various forms that cognition might take in relation to its various objects (for example, as cognition of the objects of the scientific understanding or the objects of moral reasoning). Transcendental critique would be preparatory for the proper deployment of these separate forms of cognition. Kant liked to call this proper deployment, in a phrase that Foucault surely picked up on, the "discipline" of reason.[56]

Foucault, though following Kant down the path of critique, did not find much use for Kant's bold philosophical direction of transcendental inquiry and the disciplines of reason it entails. For Foucault, as he claims in his 1984 essay "What is Enlightenment?" titled after an essay of the same name written by Kant 200 years previous, "criticism is not transcendental, and its goal is not that of making a metaphysics possible: it is genealogical in its design and archaeological in its method."[57] Foucault thought we could locate the conditions of possibility of our present ways of thinking, doing, and being through historical investigations that would describe the problematizations that provide a basis for the elaboration of our thought, action, and existence. That this was his approach is borne out in much of his work. In *The Archaeology of Knowledge*, Foucault describes his research as "an enterprise by which one tries to throw off the last anthropological constraints" such that it can "reveal how these constraints could come about."[58] In *The Order of Things*, he states that "what I am attempting to bring to light is the epistemological field, the *episteme* in which knowledge . . . grounds its positivity and thereby manifests a history which is not that of its growing perfection, but rather that of its conditions of possibility."[59] In his prefatory description of *The Birth of the Clinic*, Foucault is clear that his work there is critical in a specifically historical sense in describing it as "a project that is deliberately both historical and critical, in that it is concerned—outside all prescriptive intent—with determining the conditions of possibility of medical experience in modern times."[60] Later, in *The Birth of Biopolitics* (his 1979 Collège de France course), Foucault explains that "the critique I propose consists in determining what conditions and with what effects a veridiction is exercised. . . . the problem is to bring to light the conditions that had to be met for it to be possible to hold a discourse."[61] And I have already discussed Foucault's very late self-descriptions in terms of a critical-historical ontology of the present.

The object of Foucault's histories is to discern the conditions of possibility— not of any object of thought whatsoever, but rather of distinctive objects whose possibility for our ways of thinking and doing are constitutive of our historical present. My way of putting this is to say that Foucault practiced critique but not transcendental critique. This suggests that Foucault's practice of critique is compatible with the Kantian project at the same time that it is not identical to it. This raises a crucial philosophical question for our times, a question initiated by Kant and asked again by Foucault: What is critique?

Critique in its most general sense is a procedure for explicating the conceptual conditions that make experiences, thoughts, and activities possible. Critique need not show us that we must have certain kinds of experience, nor need it show us the conditions under which certain kinds of experience are inevitable. Given a certain activity of experience, critique aims to elucidate the conditions that make that experience possible at all. Foucault follows in Kant's critical footsteps at least insofar as he explicates our present practices on the basis of the conditions of their possibility. This is precisely what separates Foucault and Kant from classical empiricists whose explications only consider conditions of actuality. Foucault and Kant are well beyond the minimal (some would say naïve) empiricism that inquires into conditions of actuality, that is merely causal conditions or mere conditions of connection. Behind whatever it is that makes the stuff of our practices actual, there are background conditions that make these very actualities possible. Sometimes we may want to know why a prison was built, by whom, for what purposes, and with what rationale. Other times we may want to know how it came to be that it ever became possible to build such a thing as a prison. The classical empiricist asks "why this prison?" while the critical empiricist asks "how this prison?"—two very different, yet not incompatible, questions. But Foucault does diverge from Kant in suggesting that conditions of possibility are themselves the products of actualities. Actualities, rather than transcendentalities, are what make other actualities possible at all. It's all made up of the same kind of stuff—and the point is that some of this stuff historically conditions some other of this stuff.

For both Kant and Foucault, the critique of ourselves reveals conditions that we have constructed. This is not to deny differences. In Kant's first *Critique*, the conceptual bounds of the present are conditions of cognition of objects in general, whereas in Foucault's work the critical thrust shifts such that conceptual bounds are conditions of certain kinds of practical singularities. In Kant's case we epistemologically construct these conditions as the necessary limits of certain forms of cognition that we make use of. In Foucault's case, we historically construct these conditions as the contingent limits of our present forms of practice. We need not assert any incompatibilities between these two versions of constructivism even if they do not entail one another. Notably, we can also leave open the question of whether historicist constructivisms should replace or merely supplement transcendental constructivisms. One enticing possibility follows the thought that the Kantian project of the critique of experience of objects in general would open up the possibility of the Foucaultian project of the critique of experiencing different forms of objects such that the two forms of critique might mutually enrich one another. Whether or not this dual approach would pan out, all I need for my present purposes is a distinction between different conceptions of constructivist critique that enables us to recognize Foucault as a critical philosopher but not for that very reason a transcendental idealist.[62]

This distinction between critique in general and transcendental critique more specifically raises the question of whether the center of Kant's own system should be located in the project of a critical inquiry into constitutive conditions of possibility as such or in the quite different project of a transcendental critique such that conditions of possibility must explicate the universal and necessary conditions of synthetic *a priori* cognition of objects. I shall adduce three reasons in favor of the former interpretation: one involving an examination of Kant's own work, another focusing on Foucault's interpretation of Kant, and a third resting on a spate of recent interpretations put forward in contemporary Kant scholarship.

My interpretation is recommended in the first place by a look at Kant's own work. It is notable and yet rarely noted that Kant was a methodological pluralist who never explicitly ruled out the viability of projects of critique that would not proceed on his own preferred transcendental level. Even if we consider just the purely transcendental approach taken by Kant in the first two *Critiques,* there is remarkable methodological and philosophical variation in what is meant by "critique." Critique, Kant recognized, faces different obstacles when deployed in different domains. Kant gives us every reason to think that radically different domains of inquiry might require radically different deployments of critique. We should note well those passages in which Kant is rather explicit about this, for instance when he says in the *Groundwork* that "all morals, which require anthropology in order to be applied to humans, must be entirely expounded at first independently of anthropology as pure philosophy."[63] Kant's point here is not that we can ignore anthropological critique altogether, but only that we must not mix together anthropological critique oriented toward application with philosophical critique providing a much more basic (or pure) orientation. What this suggests is the possibility of reasonably taking a more expansive view of Kant's critical enterprises. We find the best confirmation for this expansion of the critical horizon in Kant's late writings, where critique is used in a quite different way than that featured in the first two *Critiques* but yet still complementary with the earlier work. Kant's later publications, most notably his *Anthropology from a Pragmatic Point of View* and *The Contest of Faculties,* offer an extension of his critical project rather than an abandonment of it.[64] In this late work there is no stringent requirement that critique reveal universal and necessary conditions of possibility of cognition by way of transcendental procedures—there is instead a series of rigorous attempts to use critique to reveal the conditions of possibility structuring some of the general tendencies of human history and political possibility. Focusing on the continuities across Kant's writings enables us to affirm the breadth of his conception of critique: critical investigations of conditions of possibility can sometimes take a transcendental form and at other times an anthropological, or possibly even a historical form. Both kinds of usage are critical and, as such, can be compatible with one another. Kant may have insisted on necessity with all the honest purity of a Pietist heart. But there are more than a few aspects of his work that evidence an acknowledgment of conditioned contingencies that themselves condition. Philosophers, unfortunately, have for too long failed to acknowledge the fact that Kant was like Hume in that he also wrote extensively in history and anthropology. We need not make anything more of this than a mere grudging concession, but nor should we make anything less of it by insisting that it was not there. In carving out a small space for contingency in Kant's writings, we need not insist that the Foucaultian appropriation of Kantian critique under the sign of contingency is to be recommended on grounds that Kant himself would have appreciated it. Here is an obvious option to which I return at the end of this section: what Kant could not bring himself to wholly embrace back then, we Kantians can celebrate with a good conscience today.

Consider now, as a second reason in favor of my conception of critique without transcendence, Foucault's interpretation of Kant.[65] The subject of Foucault's *thèse complémentaire* was the relation between critique and anthropology in Kant's late work just mentioned. Foucault's primary aim in that early text is precisely the possibility of forms of critical inquiry that would not be transcendental in orientation and yet may in their criticality offer yet another perspective complementary to the transcendental. Foucault, anticipating much that would become central for his later work, wrote there of "the *necessity* of critical thinking and the *possibility* of anthropology."[66] Whether or not Kant himself understood philosophy in such capacious terms, Foucault was clearly interested in using Kant to move his own thought in such a direction right from the beginning of his career. The movement is one in which critique is itself extended beyond the transcendental plane to a plane whose terms are thoroughly invested in historicity. Foucault situates it as follows: "What the *Critique* presents as determination in the relationship between passivity and spontaneity, in the *Anthropology* is described as a temporal dispersion that will never end and has never begun. . . . The originary is not the *really* primitive, it is the *truly* temporal."[67] Foucault's early text, as halting and stammering

as it sometimes is, offers a warrant for rereading Kant as primarily a critical philosopher and only secondarily a transcendental idealist. Whether or not we affirm
Foucault's interpretation in the end, much of my point here is that it is plausible
to see Foucault's own work as issuing from within the very terms of his interpretation of Kant. Thus Foucault historicized and temporalized Kant, maintaining a
connection to the project of critique without indebting itself to a system of transcendental idealism.

For the purposes of an interpretation of the primary impetus of Kant's own
philosophical project, it is also advisable to consider the better authority (better
than mine and perhaps also than Foucault's) of contemporary Kant commentators working in both the analytic and continental traditions in philosophy. Relying
on other commentators is hardly historiographically sound, but appealing to them
to show that one's own interpretation already has at least some standing in the
literature is quite prudent. This strategy of an argument beginning with (though
not ending at) authority raises the importance in these matters of addressing background metaphilosophical questions concerning historiographical methodology
that weigh upon the kind of interpretive exercises I am engaged in.[68]

It is worth pointing out, even if only initially, that Foucault's particular style
of claim to a Kantian inheritance can seem quite natural to anyone who takes seriously Habermas's claim to a form of Kantianism that is de-transcendentalized but
also critical.[69] In fact, as I discuss in later chapters, the inflection of critique yielded
in Foucault's work sits remarkably well with the compatible but nonidentical inflection of critique yielded most clearly in Habermas's later work. But allow me
to consider in a little more detail certain analytic and continental interpretations
of Kant not from within the broad orbit of critical theory. P.F. Strawson, in his influential 1966 book *The Bounds of Sense,* offers a reading of Kant that I find congenial to my proposed interpretation. The first section of Strawson's book presents
a general overview of his full argument, and it concludes as follows: "The set of
ideas, or schemes of thought, employed by human beings reflect, of course, their
nature, their needs and their situation. They are not static schemes, but allow of
that indefinite refinement, correction, and extension which accompany the advance of science and the development of social forms." Strawson notes that our
dynamic conceptual conditions of possibility may all be variations on "a certain
fundamental general framework of ideas" which Kant helps us explicate. But he is
also eager to point out that this unvarying "general basis" does not block the road
to our "adapting" our conceptual conditions to changing circumstances.[70] Strawson's Kant, at least so far, looks very friendly to my Foucault. Perhaps a transcendental critique can reveal a general conceptual basis of experience, but this can

and ought to be filled out by more focused critical investigations that would reveal the dynamic variations this basis undergoes as situations and needs transform. More recently, Tom Rockmore offers a reading of post-Kantian philosophy
as a series of attempts to "transform Kant's question of the conditions of the possibility of knowledge whatsoever into the very different questions of how finite
human beings in fact arrive at knowledge" such that post-Kantian philosophers
have all worked to develop "an increasingly anthropological concept of the cognitive subject as already in the world."[71] We might see Foucault as waiting at the
end of this road of critique's detranscendentalization.

Even if the thorny matters of Kant scholarship in which I have now unadvis-
edly implicated myself were to get definitively settled (which is highly unlikely
given the centrality of Kant-debating to contemporary professional philosophy),
there would still remain other issues concerning the philosophical status of my interpretation of Foucault's Kantianism. I take it that these are the issues that truly
interest critics such as Beatrice Han-Pile when she argues that Foucault's thought
was always haunted by a certain phenomenological strain of thinking initiated
by Kant's meticulous purification of the empirical and the transcendental. Han-
Pile develops her argument by reworking some of the now standard criticisms to
the effect that Foucault was never able to fully answer the deep Kantian question
of how we might investigate the conditions of the possibility of our experience
of objects in a way that does not render these conditions both determining and
determined by confusing "the constituting (truth as a set of rules) and the constituted (truth as a commodity)."[72] The standard philosophical position here defended by Han-Pile is that conditions of experience or practice cannot also themselves be conditioned. Kant is commonly thought to have opened up a supposedly
deep philosophical question in formulating this position. This deep question was
then taken up after him by the great lineage of "H" philosophers: Hegel, Husserl,
Heidegger. Foucault, we are now told, was himself also climbing this ladder of H's
stacked upon one another. Han-Pile argues that Foucault is obliged by this general
Kantian problematic in which he was embroiled to provide the "theoretical foundation which [genealogy] needs philosophically."[73] It is not clear, however, that
Foucault must provide such theoretical foundations for the purposes of producing
his archaeological and genealogical problematizations. For if Foucault himself is
not in the first place philosophically invested in the Kantian diremption between
the empirical and the transcendental, then it is not clear that he must give a reply
to the particular philosophical difficulties that arise on the basis of that diremption. Foucault took from Kant only the notion of a critical investigation of limiting
conditions of possibility and not also the further philosophical distinction between

those conditions as transcendental and that which they condition as empirical. For Foucault conditions of possibility are made of the very same stuff as the actualities they condition, even if the conditioning material is not always visible from within the conditioned material. The Foucaultian response to Kantian rationalism is a more thorough empiricism: the conditioned is always already immanent to that which conditions.

The philosophical contribution here is the idea that the conditions of possibility structuring the present are themselves parts of the history of that present. Possibilities for thinking and doing in the present are conditioned by what has been thought and done in the past. Foucault's claim was not that our actual present is conditioned by the past, but rather that the whole range of possibilities surrounding our present is thus conditioned. This particular insight may not answer the particular philosophical perplexities that puzzled Kant, Hegel, Husserl, and Heidegger. Yet this insight can nevertheless function as a philosophically legitimate basis for inquiry if it remains appropriate to the objects of inquiry it is designed to study. So it might be possible that Foucault's critical project remains in keeping with Kant's critical project to the extent that Kant can be read as a methodological pluralist who accepted that there are a number of viable forms of critical philosophy. Indeed, as I have been keen to point out, Kant nowhere denies the possibility of non-transcendental inquiries into the conditions of possibility of certain kinds of judgments. He only insists that the form of our critique must be appropriate to the judgments whose conditions we seek to ascertain. Foucault similarly did not deny that transcendental critique might be possible, but rather just insisted that he himself was not practicing critique in that form.

This returns us to one of the ways in which I have been attempting to distinguish transcendental critique from historical critique: namely, in terms of the objects of inquiry to which these different forms of critique are appropriate. Kant was concerned with investigating the conditions of possibility of our synthetic *a priori* cognition of objects. Foucault by contrast sought to inquire into the conditions of possibility of objective practices whose stability is clearly contingent and yet remarkably widespread. Kant was correct to insist that synthetic *a priori* cognition can only be properly accounted for by means of a transcendental form of critique—for only transcendental critique can yield the unshakeable necessity and uncontainable universality appropriate to the way in which judgments revealing this form of cognition are conditioned.[74] But this does not rule out the possibility that other kinds of practices can be accounted for in terms of a historical critique—for a historical critique can produce as its yield a sense of the full weight of the inertia that tends to accompany the contingencies that condition our practices.

It is helpful to note that in following Foucault down this path we can leave open the question of whether certain borderline cases are better approached by way of a transcendental or genealogical critique. For example, whereas cognition in general clearly demands transcendental critique and the relative specificity of late modern political experience clearly demands genealogical critique, we need not issue judgment on what sort of critique would be most appropriate to fuzzier cases such as our cognition of geometrical objects. I only want here to establish a distinction between transcendentality and genealogy as two planes of critique. To establish this I need not decide in advance where to classify all possible objects of cognition, experience, and practice. We rather should, I think, leave this question open and let the transcendental and genealogical critics wrestle over these various objects in the particular. Let the philosophers and historians of mathematics hold their debates over the proper status of triangles and tangents. My point is just that there is room enough for both these philosophers and these historians especially as concerns objects of practical inquiry whose classification is not nearly so fuzzy.

In leaving these questions open, it helps to recognize how truly open they are by noting that Foucault allowed room for a conception of universalizability within the terms established by his focus on contingency and complexity. The concept of universality yielded by universalism may be too entangled with simplification and necessity for Foucault's purposes. But this leaves open the possibility of an idea of processes of universalizability consistent with contingency. It was one of Foucault's best insights to develop analytic and diagnostic orientations that simultaneously faced both of these directions. According to such an account, universality in the sense of processes of universalizability turns out to be nothing more surprising, but also nothing less remarkable, than the way in which some objects and concepts proliferate across just about any context and get packaged into portable forms that can be transported just about anywhere. Think of the way that a standard of measurement *qua* standard rather than a *qua* mathematical object can be carried just about anywhere. Think of standard units of measure (e.g., the meter, the volt, the kilogram) or standard digital communications protocols (e.g., the Internet protocols IP, TCP, UDP). If something as quotidian as standards of measurement and communication can be regarded as universalizable without requiring an overarching transcendental story to explain their gradual proliferation across the planet, then something as complex as modern sexuality or modern punishment may be universalizable in just the same way, with requisite accounting for complexity. How did we get, in less than a century, from the spectacle of torture to the ubiquity of imprisonment? How, in so short a time, did the prison, which was once unheard of, become the only viable option for punishment in our society?

The story of these standardizations is very much at the heart of Foucault's gene-alogy of discipline. Genealogical problematization can thus be understood as a critical inquiry into the conditions of the possibility of the proliferation of practices and problematizations. The idea, useful for such critical inquiries, of a distinction between the classical universality of universalism and the reconstructed univer-sality of universalizability is one I will return to in the final chapter.

But why does Foucault's idea that historicity can yield the force of real con-straint seem so incoherent to so many of his critics?[75] Such questions help locate the rift between Kant at the beginning of the nineteenth century and Foucault at the end of the twentieth. Kant's view was that transcendental conditions must constrain judgments with the force of necessity, or else they cannot count as con-ditions of possibility at all. But this is an unfortunate stipulation that has not sur-vived the intervening philosophical sea change of two centuries. My view is not that Kant's insistence on transcendental critique as revealing the necessary condi-tions of cognition is philosophically mistaken. It is rather that it is difficult to see that it is not an outworn curiosity. Of far more interest for us today are critiques of practical conditions that constrain us not with the force of unshakeable neces-sity but with the weight of a contingency that bears down upon us in a way that allows uncomfortably little space for transformation. There are no deep difficul-ties with the idea that certain of our ways are limited by conditions that are them-selves the products of long historical processes that will surely unravel in some future time just as they crystallized in some past time. Foucault shifted the terms of Kantian critique from a project concerned with necessary conditions of possi-bility (giving rise to transcendental critique) to one concerned with the conditions of the possibility of the remarkable stability of contingent practical assemblages (giving rise to archaeological and genealogical critique). Between the two sit all of the tendencies of nineteenth-and twentieth-century culture that speak in favor of contingency and against necessity. Filter Kant through Darwin and you are bound to get something quite like Nietzsche, and then after him another very much like Foucault. At our end of this massive shift in intellectual sensibility we can begin to discern in Foucault a continuation-through-transformation of Kantian critique according to which there exist historical constraints on our ways of thinking and being that are no less constraining for the fact that they are the contingent accu-mulations of historical sequence rather than necessary issuances of Nature, God, Destiny, Reality, Reason, Whatever.

But wasn't the evisceration of necessity from philosophy precisely what Kant was battling against with his critical system?[76] Those enticed by this criticism will make much of the fact that Kant insisted on "the lawfulness of the contingent" in the *Critique of Judgment* and that in the *Groundwork* he set forth as "an essential principle of all use of our reason" that it must "push its knowledge to a consciousness of its necessity."[77] These critics will point out that Kant hardly tolerated contingency in insisting upon its conformity to lawfulness, for this only turns contingency into yet another instance of celebrated necessity. These critics are right that Kant would have shuddered at some of the philosophical underpinnings of Foucault's investigations. Where Foucault happily discerns contingency, Kant vigilantly insists on necessity. Contingency was reviled by Kant, who never tired of insisting that the only things of philosophical interest were those that are what they are because necessity made them so. Foucault sensibly balked at this, feeling free to regard the seeming need for necessity as an optional preference. Kant surely would have rejected Foucault's thought that conditioned contingencies can themselves become conditions of possibility worthy of serious philosophical study. But for those of us on the other side of the nineteenth century, we need not find this thought repulsive. Why can we not say that Kant's great construction—critique—has burst the contexts for which it was conceived? It now has a life all its own well beyond what Kant ever could have imagined. This is a familiar story in the history of philosophy, which like any history is one of unplanned appropriations, revisions, and reversals. The deployment of critique beyond the cages to which Kant sought to confine it can be confidently embraced by us today. Now that contingency has replaced necessity as the sign of contemporary thought, we ought to feel free to appropriate critique under this new star. Kant may have hated contingency, but in a strange twist of fate we who today love contingency can also love critique. Here is a good rule when wrestling with giants like Kant: take from them what you can use and feel no guilt in dropping the rest if you see the possibility of coherence where they insisted upon contradiction.[78] Employing this rule with Kant, I arrive at the following idea: against the classical view that conditions of possibility can bear no malleability, we can accept non-transcendental genealogy as a coherent deployment of critique that shows how and why we face certain constraints in our present that we can hardly see our way out of, even if these constraints are constituted by nothing greater than the contingencies of the history of our present.

Varieties of Historical Critique

That contingent and complex problematizations can indeed function as constraining conditions of possibility is illustrated not only in Foucault's work but also in the work of a wide range of other historicists and genealogical philosophers in recent decades. To further illustrate the transformation of critical philosophy proposed by later genealogy, I would like to briefly feature related ideas from these other philosophers.

Consider first the range of work described under the broad rubric of "historical epistemology." That term was originally Gaston Bachelards's and then it was Georges Canguilhem's—both were influential on Foucault's maturation as a philosopher-historian. Paul Rabinow summarizes historical epistemology as a practice of inquiry according to which, "Epistemology is a rigorous description of the process by which truth is elaborated, not a list of final results."[79] Though Canguilhem and Bachelard are clearly important for my discussion, there is a different lineage of historical epistemology in recent work by Lorraine Daston, Peter Galison, Mary Poovey, Arnold Davidson, and others.[80] (The conceptual connections between the "classical" historical epistemology and the "new" historical epistemology remain rather opaque, although there do seem to be important overlaps deserving further study.[81]) Historical epistemology, like Hacking's Foucaultian historical ontology, is about ways in which possibilities for knowing and being emerge. It is about the changing bounds of who we are and what we do: the emergent possibilities that form the limits of our present. These limits are fraught with tensions that practically guarantee that our future will be different from our present. The historicizing move common to all these meta-epistemologists and meta-ontologists is described by Daston and Galison in their jointly authored *Objectivity*, which offers a history of objectivity itself. How is such a history possible? The authors tell us that "Sequence weaves history into the warp and woof of the present: not just a past process reaching its present state of rest—how things came to be as they are—but also as the source of tensions that keep the present in motion."[82] Objectivity is undoubtedly one of the most fraught ideas in our present. History helps us see why this is so.

Another vein of critical inquiry that I find illuminating for exploring Foucaultian inquiry can be located in the work of Rabinow, which excellently exemplifies how both contingency and complexity can inform critique. Rabinow's recent work under the banner of "the anthropology of the contemporary" focuses attention on those difficult-to-attend-to "heterogeneous zones" where all manner of different actors, institutions, and practices come together. The complexity of the heterogeneous problematizations on which this work focuses is described in general terms as an inquiry into "how a contingently assembled practice emerged, composed of distinctive *subjects,* the *site* in which they worked, and the *object* they invented."[83] An anthropology of the contemporary helps us grasp the tangled present in all of its contingency and complexity, however beautiful or ugly it may be. Through this we can learn about the conditions that make possible who we are, what we do, and how we think today. Preceding more recent anthropologies of the contemporary such as that developed in his *French DNA*, Rabinow's earlier work remained closer to Foucault in constructing his inquiries under the guidance of genealogy. These "histories of the present," for instance in his *French Modern*, were about "the emergence of certain practices of reason" that can be analyzed "as a set of practices bearing complex relations with a congeries of symbols."[84] Rabinow later described this in terms of "a genealogy of a number of the elements that had been gradually assembled (over the course of two centuries) and stabilized for a time."[85] Through both his histories of the present and his anthropologies of the contemporary, Rabinow conducts inquiries that show us the complexity and contingency of processes of emergence. The cumulative effect of these helps us realize that there are many modes of inquiry that we can follow outward from Foucault in seeking to understand who we have become and who we may yet be.

Another prominent vein of thought that helps explicate the way contingency and complexity inform our understanding of conditions of possibility is featured in the work of the French philosopher-turned-sociologist Pierre Bourdieu. Like others who early felt the impact of Canguilhem, Bourdieu took it as his goal to explain how something so seemingly meager as the historical accumulation of everyday practice can turn into something so severe as limiting conditions on our practices we cannot cross beyond. Bourdieu's signature concept of *habitus* is remarkably resonant with Foucault's signature concept of problematization.[86] Bourdieu's *habitus* connotes a practical logic formed by "a system of practically integrated generative principles that function in the most diverse fields of practice." He is clear about the historicity of *habitus:* "The *habitus,* a product of history, produces all individual and collective practices—more history—in accordance with the schemes generated by history."[87] It is not my intention here to delve into the intricacies of Bourdieu's practice theory. But note how his conceptualization of *habitus* raises an issue that was also decisive for Foucault—how can a mere product of history generate dispositions and strategies that serve to constrain action across a diversity of fields of practice? There is no easy answer to this difficult question, and it is one of the central tasks of Bourdieu's rich body of work to develop a response. Here, in capsule, is the reply his work offers: "It is in history, and in history alone, that we must seek the principle of the relative independence of reason from the history of which it is the product."[88] In short, historical practice is capable of producing logics of practice that function to constrain practice itself or, the limiting conditions of possibility of present practice are products of historical practice itself.

The foregoing discussions indicate that there are a great many philosophical-historical-anthropological-sociological veins of thought that might be used to illuminate Foucaultian genealogy as a critical project (certainly many more than I have here surveyed). Ian Hacking's work is closest to my own favored range of focus.[89] But there is no reason to downplay the significance of other work just canvassed. I attend more often to Hacking's histories not because I find him somehow more essentially Foucaultian than any of the others I have referenced, but rather because his work better fits my particular purposes in explicating the rigors of Foucaultian thought in Kantian terms. In Hacking's work the historicization of traditional philosophical categories is meant to reveal how historical and hence variable practices can give rise to very formidable constraints that might seem to deserve the Kantian label of conditions of possibility. Hacking, like Foucault, has been unafraid to describe his work as "a continuation of Kant's project."[90] For this reason both theorists merit our attention today in an era in which Kant has been so widely dismissed by those who emphasize the contingent, the complex, and other aspects of a more humble conception of critique.

In his work on styles of scientific thinking, to take but one example, Hacking describes styles as specifying the conditions under which scientific reason stabilizes so as to enable possible fields of investigation.[91] Different styles of thinking form different spaces of possibility for the formulation, authentication, and revision of scientific truthfulness. Styles condition thought so that we might produce statements that are true-or-false. Outside of, or apart from, these styles, there simply is no truth to aim at, no way of telling the truth because no way of telling true from false. On this account, reasoning and truthfulness replace invariant categories of reason and truth in such a way as to enable us to inquire into different forms that reasoning and truthfulness might take. Styles of scientific reasoning constitute historical conditions of possibility for achieving truthfulness in the sciences. Styles of reasoning are thus limiting conditions that enable and disable various empirical judgments, and yet they are not therefore transcendental because we can definitively show that they arise within history. Despite the fragility implied in their contingency and complexity, they nonetheless form very real constraints on practice.

Hacking boldly claims that styles of reasoning are self-authenticating.[92] This does not mean they are relativistic, but precisely the reverse: they establish the conditions for the possibility of objectivity and method in the sciences. I see this as a version of the provocative Foucaultian claim that the conditions of the possibility of the present can be both historically generated and objectively constraining. One way of understanding Hacking's views on these matters is to see him as attempting to account for the successes of science in terms less puffed-up than usual realist and antirealist accounts. To avoid these views, Hacking offers a conception according to which the successful vindication or authentication of a style reasoning can be accounted for in terms of nothing less than the whole historical development of that style itself. Anyone who knows his work will know that Hacking is a careful historian: also an erudite, encyclopedic, and exhilarating historian. In discussing the stabilizing techniques that enable the self-vindication of a style of reasoning, Hacking notes in dutiful detail the various component vectors that intersect in such a way as to contingently form that complex style. He says, "I am at pains to list these because it is so easy to slip back into the old ways and suppose that there are just a few kinds of things, theory, data, or whatever. My taxonomy is among other things a demonstration of the 'motley of experimental science,' which at the same time strives for some breadth of vision and does not merely meander from fascinating case to fascinating case."[93] The idea is that a historical account of the emergence of styles of reasoning can help us understand how these styles can be self-vindicating in a way that refuses to refer the success of these sciences to ponderous macro-level claims about Reason and to tedious micro-level specifications of case after case. The success of science, on this view, is referred to nothing less than the whole of scientific practice itself—and this whole ensemble is to be accounted for in terms that throw into relief both its broadest contours and its most motley conjunctures. The point, I take it, is that stabilized scientific success is an extraordinarily complex and contingent sort of thing. We do ourselves a disservice if we attempt to reductively explain away scientific stability and success in terms of macro- or micro-processes that boil off complexity and contingency. As I read him, Hacking is employing a certain historical account of scientific self-vindication in such a way as to describe the historical conditions of possibility of this success without reference to the pure realm of the transcendental or the pure realm of the empirical.

This approach of building explanatory accounts out of material that is neither audaciously transcendental nor merely empirical unites Hacking's historical ontology with the other veins of inquiry I mentioned previously. Historical epistemologists Daston and Galison describe their historiographical method for discerning the emergence of scientific objectivity over the nineteenth and twentieth centuries: "We reject the metaphorical (and metaphysical) reflex that, without further justification, prefers excavation to enlargement as a privileged method of understanding; instead, we suggest that in some cases an exploration of relationships that all lie on the same level, a widening of the angle of vision, can be more enlightening. . . . we are within the realm of history, not necessity."[94] This difficult labor of conceptualizing a conditioning that remains on the same level as its conditioned explanandum provides a crucial link between historical ontologists like Hacking, historical epistemologists like Daston and Galison, anthropologists of the contemporary like Rabinow, historical sociologists like Bourdieu, and the work of genealogy and archaeology developed by Michel Foucault.

Numerous philosophers have explored this difficult relation between conditioning and conditioned. Perhaps the most notable in connection with Foucault is that of Gilles Deleuze, whose thought on these matters is often figured in terms of a philosophy of immanence. Deleuze and Guattari's discussion of the plane of immanence in *What Is Philosophy?* sheds much light on these matters. In that discussion, we are told that "concepts" function as that which both conditions and is conditioned, insofar as they are assembled on a "plane" of immanence: "Concepts pave, occupy, or populate the plane bit by bit, whereas the plane itself is the indivisible milieu in which concepts are distributed without breaking up its continuity or integrity . . . The only regions of the plane are concepts themselves, but the plane is all that holds them together."[95] For Deleuze and Guattari, concepts and planes are not identical with one another, but there is a relation of immanence such that conditioning planes are themselves composed of the very concepts they condition. This suggests a philosophical temper involving an empiricist methodology, in connection with the empiricisms of genealogy, historical epistemology, and the anthropology of the contemporary. Deleuze and Guattari would refer to this as a "radical empiricism" and Deleuze himself would write of it as a "transcendental empiricism."[96] Deleuze's conception of an immanent relation between condition and conditioned, which thus radicalizes empiricism itself, is one that many readers of Deleuze have struggled to make sense of.[97]

But rather than veer into the fascinating and dense subtleties of hyper-abstract Deleuzeian metaphors, I prefer to stay closer to the ground, for the time being at least, by visiting a more concrete metaphor that I find powerfully evocative of the idea at work in all of the philosophers and historians just named. The metaphor was offered by Paul Veyne, who, it is worth pointing out, is impressively confident in offering in his 2008 book an interpretation of Foucault as "an empiricist and a philosopher of understanding."[98] In his 1978 tribute to Foucault titled "Foucault Revolutionizes History," Veyne offers a concise and forceful image of Foucault's empiricist conception of conditioned conditioners. Veyne's image is of Foucault as empiricist, picking away at a massive flotilla of ice so as to reveal the submerged base of the iceberg whose tip is our more-or-less conscious conceptions of our present practices. This image indelibly imprints a crucial point: "the concealed base of an iceberg is not some agency that is different in nature from the exposed tip; it is made of ice, like the rest."[99] It's all made up of the same stuff, all of which is on the same level—the explanans is the same material as its explanandum—it's all just so much ice.

Veyne's crucial point is that Foucault's histories describe the submerged conditions of possibility of our exposed practices on the tip of the iceberg, but without figuring these submerged conditions as a secret motor of history. The difference between the exposed and the submerged in Foucault is not the metaphysical difference between appearance and reality, nor is it the Kantian difference between universally necessary transcendental determinants and locally contingent empirical determinations. It is the difference between the massive inertia of historical accumulation formed in the past (depth *savoir* and *pouvoir*) and our present practices that are now forming on the basis of that accumulation (surface *connaissance* and *puissance*). Foucault did follow Kant at least far enough to insist that we must be eager to capture this difference so as to move beyond a naïve empiricism according to which all of the material shaping our practices is already exposed within those practices. To put the point in terms of Veyne's metaphor, the rejected empiricist view would be that the iceberg in its entirety merely floats on the surface of the salted sea without any conditioning whatsoever from submerged conditions unavailable to plain sight. Foucault's point is like Kant's point in that he is eager to insist that there is a massive conditioning process going on beneath the surface of the water, where another set of dynamics is continually generating constraints and opportunities for the practices up above. Whereas Kant regards those submerged dynamics as unknowable noumena whose transcendental conditions for cognition we can nonetheless somehow discern, Foucault regards them as made up of the very same stuff of practice that they constrain but not for that reason immediately discernible from within our standard modes of practice.

Veyne claims that his metaphor is meant in part to help us understand that "Foucault's importance is precisely that he is not 'doing' Marx or Freud."[100] Unlike the old masters of suspicion, Foucault does not take as his object of critique "some mysterious agency, some substratum of history, some hidden engine" because he is instead focused on "what people do."[101] If Freud and Marx sought to reveal the necessary psychological or material conditions of reality, conditions that could function as a secret motor of history in precisely the way that Kant's categories could function as an invariant structure of thought, then Foucault sought to explicate the contingent historical conditions of the present. Foucault's historical conditions are no less constraining than are various classical formulations of transcendental conditions, and yet they do not stand on a whole new level of reality than does the conditioned.

Foucault's insight, as Veyne pointed out, is that the conditions and the conditioned are made of the same stuff—it is all just so much more ice. Nothing less than the whole historical floating mass of ice itself conditions our present, and without any hidden motor propelling the whole thing along its course. The crucial point, for Veyne, is that "the driving force behind the kaleidoscope is not reason, desire, or consciousness."[102] The driving force, rather, is the whole complex and contingent ensemble of practice itself: in short, the full problematization. Genealogical inquiries reveal the submerged conditions constitutive of our present. And what they so often reveal is that what remains below the surface possesses such a tremendous inertia that its trajectory of motion is virtually unchangeable no matter what we try to do up above.

Foucaultian critique thus adds to Kantian critique a rigorous appreciation of the complexity and contingency of the conditions of possibility out of which our present practices are composed. The core themes of contingency and complexity mark the singular contribution of Foucault's genealogical project to the broader critical apparatus initially formulated by Kant. On this interpretation of Foucault's Kantianism, how might we understand critique? Perhaps as follows: "A critique is not a matter of saying that things are not right as they are. It is a matter of pointing out on what kinds of assumptions, what kinds of familiar, unchallenged, unconsidered modes of thought the practices we accept rest."[103] This is Foucault's description of critique, but it could just as well have been Kant's, at least in a certain mood, though perhaps a mood that Kant did not often find himself in. There are, to be sure, at least two radically different ways of operationalizing critique understood in this way. But whether we operationalize it in terms of transcendental inquiry into invariant categories or historical-anthropological inquiry into problematizations, the underlying impetus remains the same. This is why, for both Kant and Foucault, "Our age is, in especial degree, the age of critique, and to critique everything must submit."[104]

4

What Problematization Does

Aims, Sources & Implications

The Point of Genealogy

What should a genealogy aim to accomplish? There is a standard answer to this question that circulates almost silently throughout contemporary theory: genealogy denaturalizes, destabilizes, and renders (historically) contingent that which was assumed to be (metaphysically) necessary. This is the standard coin of the theory realm—it is backed up by more than just the frequency with which it is credited, for behind it is the truth that this is exactly what Foucault, Nietzsche, Williams, and just about every other genealogist told us to take from their work. The problem with this coin is not that it is counterfeit, but rather that it is not worth nearly as much as is commonly supposed. For, I shall argue in this chapter, there is a deeper lesson we ought to learn from genealogy. Whereas I offered a methodological specification of genealogical problematization in the previous chapter, in this chapter I turn to a consideration of the point of this methodology as specified.

According to the argument I shall be making, the point of a genealogy is not just to denaturalize—though certainly it is that, too. The more important point of a genealogy is to show *how* that which is so easily taken as natural was composed into the natural-seeming thing that it is. It is so natural for us to take our sexuality as biological destiny. Foucault's point is not just *that* sexuality is more than biology, more than nature, and so not as necessary as it had once seemed. Foucault's point is in part that, to be sure, but it is also to help us see how sexuality came to be composed as the seeming destiny that we take it to be. Consider two questions. Is our sexuality a necessary fact about who we are, or a contingent construction? A genealogy helps answer this first question, but so too does much else. Now shift to the second question. How was our sexuality contingently constructed? To answer this second question, we need something quite like genealogy, namely something involving an empirical inquiry into the history of sexuality.

Getting clear on the distinction between the *fact that* our practices are contingent and the *history of how* these same practices were contingently composed goes a long way toward recognizing the broader import of genealogy. For if genealogy helps us see *how* our present was made, it also thereby equips us with some of the tools we would need for beginning the labor of remaking our future differently. Merely knowing that some construction contingently came into being does not equip us with much if our goal is to remake that construction. It provides us, perhaps, with a little confidence, or at least a solace that the work we want to do is possible—that we will not be bumping our heads against cognitive, biological, or metaphysical necessity. But the comforts of possibility are not quite the tools of actuality. To make those constructions different, to make ourselves otherwise, we need to know, amongst other things, how it was that we made ourselves into who we are. To put this point in another idiom that I shall be eager to develop in this and later chapters: pragmatic reconstruction requires a genealogical problematization that would equip the work of reconstruction with a sense of how the problematization that is being reworked was itself constructed.

To make my way toward this point, I begin this chapter by tracing some of the intellectual antecedents of Foucault's conception of genealogy in the context of his French philosophical milieu. This will provide, especially by way of Foucault's intellectual interactions with his erstwhile interlocutor and friend Gilles Deleuze, a useful lens for seeing the details of how problematization links up with reconstruction.

Sources of Foucaultian Historiography

In considering the intellectual historical filiations informing all of the central elements composing Foucault's conception of genealogical critique as I have explicated them (practical multiplicity at the intersection of power and knowledge, temporal multiplicity in the combination of continuity and discontinuity, and above all problematization), one approach would involve granting analytic priority to Foucault's intellectual milieu. Concerning each of these elements of power/

knowledge, emergence, and problematization, it must be emphasized that Foucault of course did not simply assemble his intellectual toolkit by taking these concepts, techniques, and strategies unaltered from the various sources motivating his own approach. Rather, he appropriated the work of others in his intellectual milieu in ways that transformed the constituent elements that would compose genealogy. This appropriative transformation was facilitated, at least in part, by Foucault's intimacy with the living reality of the ideas he would transform.

Concerning Foucault's methodological expansion to a multiple-vector analysis situated at the intersections of various vectors of experience such as power and knowledge, we can discern a quite general precursor to this idea in the atmosphere of Friedrich Nietzsche. A more local and precise inspiration was, however, that of Georges Canguilhem, who writes, "In order to study the particular aspect of the history of science defined above, one must look not only at a number of different sciences bearing no intrinsic relation to one another but also at 'nonscience,' that is, at ideology and political and social praxis."[1] While Canguilhem did not develop his histories of science situated at the intersection of knowledge and "nonscience" to anywhere near the precision that Foucault later achieved, we can nonetheless find in Canguilhem a sensitivity to the relations between multiple kinds of experience or multiple vectors of practice, which Foucault would hone to a degree unparalleled by any other historian of the twentieth century preceding him. Another possible line of influence here, noted by Arnold Davidson, were Foucault's engagements with analytic philosophy, particularly a pragmatized version of analytic philosophy under the influence of Ludwig Wittgenstein.[2]

Canguilhem, along with Bachelard, was also influential on Foucault's early historiography insofar as his method there was primarily an attempt to trace epistemic ruptures or breaks. But, as I described in the first chapter, Foucault's conceptualization of temporality underwent a methodological expansion as he added genealogy to archaeology in his historiographical repertoire. The result was a conception of history that emphasized temporal multiplicity above any single temporally unifying category. No longer was Foucault interested in charting either continuity or discontinuity. Foucault was now writing histories that could take account of the multiplicity of time spans that measure the relations between our past and our present. This was by no means a departure from Canguilhem, but there is enough of a difference to suggest that we should look for sources of this aspect of Foucault's thought elsewhere. Once again the general atmospheric influence of Nietzsche would be important here. But we can also look to more local and direct motives for this methodological expansion in Foucault's relation to the work of the famous French Annales school of historians, most importantly

Fernand Braudel. Braudel's influence on historical thought was felt everywhere, and deeply so, during the decades in which Foucault was writing. So it is not extraordinary to conjecture that he may have provided a useful precedent for Foucault's temporal expansion from the single archaeological temporality of rupture to the multiple genealogical temporalities of shift, evolution, continuity, event, and problem. Braudel wrote in 1958 that "From the recent experiments and efforts of history, an increasingly clear idea has emerged—whether consciously or not, whether accepted or not—of the multiplicity of time and of the exceptional value of the long time span."[3] In his intellectual history of the new French historiography, François Dosse describes this Braudelian theme of "pluralizing time" as follows: "Time was decomposed into several different rhythms that would break the unity of the duration . . . One could then distinguish different levels of time and the distances between them."[4] Braudel himself emphasized that "these different time spans which we can discern are all interdependent: it is not so much time which is the creation of our own minds, as the way in which we break it up."[5] Now my point is not that Foucault's expansion from a single archaeological temporality to multiple genealogical temporalities is a direct inspiration from the work of Braudel and his Annales collaborators, for certain important differences remain.[6] Foucault's methodological expansion can, however, be seen as informed by the work of Braudel such that a fuller understanding of Braudel would profitably inform our understanding of Foucault.

Finally, as for Foucault's concept of problematization, which I am arguing functions as a kind of master concept that ties together the other core conceptual elements of his mature genealogical critique, we can trace multiple paths of influence leading from Deleuze, Canguilhem, Althusser, Dumézil, and Braudel. More distantly we can detect the influence of Nietzsche to no small extent. Perhaps even Heidegger's thought may have acted as a potential source here in the centrality assumed by the concept of questioning in his work.[7] But the direct influences seem more pertinent, and so it is worth noting that the French intellectual scene in the 1960s vibrated with any number of different versions of a concept meant to point out the constitutive nature of problems. The influential Annales school has been characterized as enacting a problem-based methodology, as evidenced in Jacques Le Goff's succinct definition: "New history is history-through-problems."[8] Even more proximate to Foucault, Althusser offered perhaps the most influential such notion with his concept of a "problématiques," which he worked out over the course of the 1960s. In explicating his conception, Althusser referred back to earlier works by Canguilhem and Bachelard and even on occasion to Foucault's *History of Madness*.[9] Following this initial lead, we can trace historiographical problematization to Canguilhem's 1943 doctoral thesis (republished in book form in 1966), where he advocated "yielding to a demand of philosophical thought to re-open rather than close problems."[10]

Despite the tremendous importance of all of these thinkers to the formation of Foucault's thought, I believe that the most influential source for Foucault's concept of problematization was Deleuze's work of the late 1960s. We can profitably read Deleuze's work on problematization as having partially motivated and enabled Foucault's expansion of critical inquiry to include genealogy alongside archaeology. One might say that Deleuze's concept of problematization forms the problematization for Foucault's conceptualization of problematization. A more tempered claim would be that Deleuze invented a clever concept that Foucault immediately found useful and subsequently appropriated for his own purposes.

Deleuzian Problematization

Although it is difficult to deny the importance of Deleuze's work for Foucault's conception of philosophy as the work of problematization, this is a connection that has not been emphasized enough in existing accounts of the Foucault-Deleuze relationship.[11] Drawing a connection between Deleuze and Foucault in terms of problematization helps explicate the often-quoted remark, made by Deleuze in the context of a conversation with Foucault, that theory functions as a toolkit, or a pragmatic device.[12] This connection also helps explicate the conception of problematization that I am forwarding as the heart of Foucault's critical methodology.

Though the critical literature on Deleuze can hardly be said to have achieved many important points of consensus, a number of commentators have been quick to acknowledge the importance in Deleuze's thought of what DeLanda calls "problematic epistemology" and what Rajchman describes as a form of thinking that consists of "making visible problems for which there exists no program, no plan."[13] In Deleuze's thought, the very practice of philosophy itself can be expressed in terms of this work of problematization. Deleuze is well known for the view he developed with Guattari in *What Is Philosophy?*, according to which, "philosophy is the art of forming, inventing, and fabricating concepts." Often not acknowledged, however, is their related claim that "concepts are only created as a function of problems" such that "concepts are connected to problems without which they would have no meaning and which can themselves only be isolated or understood as their solution emerges."[14] For Deleuze, the primary task of philosophy is the cultivation of problems such that philosophy can then go about the task of creating concepts. Why problematization as primary to conceptualization? Because concepts without problems would be empty. Concepts ought to be relevant, and what they ought to be relevant to are the problems we have shown ourselves to be facing.

This emphasis on the priority of problematization runs throughout Deleuze's work. Here it is in *Difference and Repetition:* "The virtual possesses the reality of a task to be performed or a problem to be solved: it is the problem which orientates, conditions and engenders solutions, but these do not resemble the conditions of the problem. Bergson . . ."[15] And indeed it is to Deleuze's work on Bergson that we should first turn if we want to understand his distinctive way of developing his conception of problematization. It might be first noted in passing, however, that it may have been Deleuze's engagement with Kant that first oriented him toward the conception of problematization that he would begin to develop more fully only later on in his engagement with Bergson. Deleuze's most ambitious work on the concept of problematization is to be found in his two major works of the late 1960s, *Difference and Repetition* (1968) and *The Logic of Sense* (1969). In both of these works, problematization is linked primarily to Kant and only derivatively to Bergson. But if we turn back to Deleuze's earlier books on each of these philosophers, we find that his book on Bergson (1966) is engaged with the concept of the problem throughout while his book on Kant (1963) only refers to this concept in passing.[16] I will begin with Deleuze's work on Bergson before moving on to his elaboration of problematization proper in his two major works of the late sixties.

Deleuze uses Bergson to develop and explicate a conception of philosophy as a work that begins in problematization. Deleuze interprets Bergsonism in terms of three acts, or rules, and it is the first one that concerns us here insofar as it holds that the work of philosophy shall be problematization: "We are wrong to believe that the true and the false can only be brought to bear on solutions, that they only begin with solutions . . . True freedom lies in a power to decide, to constitute problems themselves."[17] Deleuze almost makes it sound as if it were obvious that philosophy ought to concern itself with the freedom of constituting problems. It is therefore helpful to remember that this is in fact quite a radical departure from the received wisdom throughout the history of philosophy.

Problematization, in this view, does not come easy. There are, after all, true and false problems. The "first rule" of Bergson's philosophy according to Deleuze is: "Apply the test of true and false to problems themselves."[18] This implies the crucial refusal to divide problems according to the soluble and the insoluble. Deleuze's claim is that we should not reject a problem as false simply because we regard it as insoluble. Indeed, insoluble problems might be precisely what philosophy should seek to develop so as to provoke the work of difficult thought. And yet there are still false problems: "The very notion of the false problem indeed implies that we have to struggle not against simple mistakes (false solutions), but against something more profound: an illusion that carries us along, or in which we are immersed, inseparable from our condition."[19] What is to be rejected are not insoluble problems, but rather problems whose only possible solutions carry us along paths of thought that leave us unable to deal with the conditions that we impose on ourselves by taking up these problems.

In Deleuze's distinction between simple mistakes and false problems, one can already hear the vibrations that would later come to full resonance in the work of Foucault. But to hear in Foucault an echo of Deleuze, we must be careful to take both at their word. The false problems or illusions in which we find ourselves ensnared are not the simple false solutions of ideology that could be unveiled by clever philosophical investigation. Breaking free of false problems requires not that we contradict or oppose them, but that we produce in their place a new problematization. This conception of transformation by way of creative differentiation suggests how Deleuze, with Foucault close behind him, inaugurated the great break from thought in the form of negative opposition or what is commonly known as "dialectics."

While Deleuze's concept of problematization has resonances across many registers, there are at least two central aspects of this concept that seem to have had an impact on Foucault's subsequent attempts to read himself through (an appropriated form of) this concept: problematizations are both objective and generative. These constitute quite a departure from the traditional philosophical conceptions of problems, doubts, errors, and perplexities.

Deleuze regarded problems as not merely subjective illusions capable of being exposed, refuted, or dissipated—his view was that problems are objective realities independent of mere mistakes in thinking.[20] He wrote in *The Logic of Sense* that "[t]he problematic is both an objective category of knowledge and a perfectly objective kind of being."[21] And in *Difference and Repetition,* he similarly claimed that "'Problematic' does not mean only a particularly important species of subjective acts, but a dimension of objectivity as such which is occupied by these acts."[22] Deleuze's view was that problems are crystallized in objects as bases for the elaboration of thought. This runs counter to the traditional philosophical conception of problems as subjective failures marking a lack, need, omission, or sin. I take Deleuze's primary point to be that problems are not simply illusions that rationality must overcome, but are better thought of in terms of constitutive conditions of rational practice. Deleuze's view was that we can study problematizations in terms of the objective realities that they condition and that therefore manifest them. Problems are thus neither "ready-made" simples nor obvious "givens" but are rather "multiplicities or complexes of relations and corresponding singularities."[23] Since they are not ready-made givens, problems themselves are the result and object of inquiry. This conception of problematizations has clear resonances with Foucault's descriptions of his own work as an inquiry into problematizations that are funded by and in turn reinvest in our concrete practices: "It was a matter of analyzing . . . the *problematizations* through which being offers itself to be, necessarily, thought—and the *practices* on the basis of which these problematizations are formed."[24]

A second central aspect of problematization as conceptualized by Deleuze concerns the way in which problems are generative for thought rather than oppositional to it. Deleuze refers in *Difference and Repetition* to "the intrinsic genetic power" of problems and writes of problems as "the differential elements in thought" and "the genetic elements in the true."[25] And in *The Logic of Sense* he asserts that "the problem itself is the reality of the genetic element."[26] This conception counters the traditional view of problems as a lack of thought with a view of problems instead as a propulsion for thought. This enabled Deleuze to reconceptualize the form of thought that problematics generate as non-dialectical (or at least as not dialectical in its traditional sense of a logic of contradiction). Thought as generated by problems is no longer "a simple confrontation between opposing, contrary or contradictory, propositions."[27] It is rather a more creative act that engenders transformation by means of responsiveness to objective problems that prove more resilient and thus more generative than subjective doubts.[28]

I am suggesting that we understand Deleuze's concept of problematization as an important source not only of Foucault's concept of the same, but also of Foucault's entire genealogical and archaeological ensemble insofar as Foucault himself was, as I have been arguing, right to suggest that this complex ensemble should be understood as an effort in problematization. One potential problem with my attempt to establish such an intellectual historical relation between these two thinkers concerns the apparently dissonant chronology of Deleuze's conceptualization of problematization in the late 1960s and Foucault's seemingly deferred deployment of this concept much later, as early as the late 1970s but certainly no later than the early 1980s. If Foucault really took up his concept of problematization on the basis of Deleuze's work, why did he wait so long to take it up? Although we can find traces of this concept in Foucault's earlier work going back even before Deleuze's publications, Foucault appears to not have seriously elaborated this concept with rigor until the late 1970s (as discussed in Chapter 1).

I think that the best way of responding to this difficulty has already been offered by Foucault himself. Foucault in his final years described the core trajectory
of all of his work in terms of the concept of problematization such that something
like problematization would have been central to his thought right from the beginning, in the early 1960s. His encounter with Deleuze in the mid-1960s provided an intellectual inspiration in the form of a detailed explication of the concept of problematization, a concept that offered a way of bringing into focus a core
feature of what he had thus far been aiming at. But only in later years did Foucault finally begin to explicitly thematize this conceptualization, and when he
did so he returned to the terms of Deleuze's concept though he would also freely
transform it.

One piece of evidence in favor of this intellectual historical postulation is
Foucault's own discussion of Deleuze's concept of problematization from 1970. In
his long review of *The Logic of Sense* and *Difference and Repetition,* published under
the title "Theatrum Philosophicum," Foucault brings problematization into vivid
focus. He writes, "The freeing of difference requires thought without contradiction, without dialectics, without negation; thought that accepts divergence; affirmative thought whose instrument is disjunction; thought of the multiple." Foucault then goes on, employing yet more Deleuzian vocabulary, to a description of
problematization. "What is the answer to the question? The problem. How is the
problem resolved? By displacing the question." By the end of the paragraph, Foucault has established the crucial point of Deleuzian philosophy: "We must think
problematically rather than question and answer dialectically."[29] To situate problematic thought as a productive alternative to negative dialectical thought in this
way is no small matter in the context of French theory in the 1960s. If Deleuze
was regarded by many of the leading French intellectuals of his generation as the
inaugurating figure of poststructuralism and postphenomenology, then it is because he, in his little book on Nietzsche in 1962, was able to sketch for French philosophy an alternative to the Hegelian dialectical logic that had dominated French
thought ever since the close of the Second World War (though it must be emphasized that the then dominant paradigm represents only one possible reading of the
sense of Hegel).[30] In urging that we must "think problematically" rather than "question and answer dialectically," Foucault explicitly names his entire generation's
debt to Deleuze. And the name he gave to it was "problematization." Years later
Deleuze himself would acknowledge the importance of the concept of problematization for Foucault's historical-philosophical project: "One thing haunts Foucault—
thought. . . . To think means to experiment and to problematize."[31] I agree with

Deleuze here if he indeed meant to suggest that experimentation and problematization together form the motor of nearly every aspect of Foucault's work.

Having now traced important lines of connection between Foucault and Deleuze with respect to philosophical problematization,[32] let me briefly feature how Foucault's use of problematization departs in certain significant ways from Deleuze's use of the same.[33] Deleuze was a source for Foucault's conception of problematization, but this does not mean that Foucault's practice of problematization through genealogy is thoroughly Deleuzian, nor that Deleuze was a model genealogist. The difference between Deleuze and Foucault can be thought of in terms of the gap between transcendental empiricism in Deleuze's case and a more radically skeptical empiricism in Foucault's. It took Foucault to develop Deleuze's rather philosophical and abstract conception of the work of thought as problematization into a more focused concrete series of practical inquiries which would take the shape of problematizations. Deleuze was always more interested in a philosophical conception of problematization according to which the philosopher develops new problems that virtually enable the formation of new concepts in response. Foucault was interested in this, to be sure, but he himself was always more interested in a genealogical practice according to which the thinker would examine past problematizations so as to clarify and intensify our ways of constituting ourselves in the present. Foucault's work was always balanced by the enormous counterweight of historical empiricities insofar as the present that the genealogist problematizes is a present that has contingently formed in response to past problematizations on which the genealogist must work to focus our attention. The empiricities that figure in some of Deleuze's works always assumed a rather virtual and abstracted quality. Now, both of these approaches have much to recommend them—what I want to point out is that Deleuze is easily read as abstract and imaginative, whereas Foucault is easily read as empirical and focused. This is a difference of degree, rather than of kind, and it is a difference rather than an incompatibility—but it is nonetheless a real difference. For while it is quite easy for the Deleuzian to dream themselves into some labyrinthine possible world of problems, the rigorous Foucaultian is unlikely to ever stray far from the actual historical present where real problems are operative, meaningful, and in need of careful critical investigation.

Despite these differences, the underlying commonalities are of much greater moment. For both Foucault and Deleuze, problematization as a methodological orientation might be wielded as one element of a critical repertoire compatible with a reconstructive orientation for inquiry. In other words, for both Foucault and Deleuze, the work of problematization was meant to invite the work of responsive melioration. Both were also admirably skeptical about the price at which many solutions are purchased, and this explains why both devoted so much labor to explicating the enormous complexity of the problematizations we face. Foucault and Deleuze, in other words, did not simply work to develop problems to which they hoped we would be able to offer simple solutions in a way that would enable the predictable intensification of existing capacities. Rather, they worked long and hard to develop, clarify, and intensify problems that are in many ways constitutive of our present ways of living. These problematizations were meant, for both, to provoke the work of solvent thought. But, again for both, solvent thought works within the space of the problematizations rather than as solutions that enable us to simply overcome problems.

Here is how Deleuze put the point in a 1990 interview where he contrasted history (Foucault's preferred modality of problematization) to experimentation (which Foucault often took up as a model for reconstructive problem solving): "History is not experimental, it is just the set of more or less negative preconditions that make it possible to experiment with something beyond history. Without history the experimentation would remain indeterminate, lacking any initial conditions, but experimentation is not historical. . . . Becoming is not part of history; history designates only the collection of conditions, however recent, that need to be overcome in order 'to become,' that is, to create something new."[34] It is clear that for Deleuze there is a productive interplay between historical conditions and experimental reconditioning. This same interplay also proved invaluable for Foucault. In a 1986 interview about Foucault, Deleuze had urged that for Foucault history is "the set of conditions that make it possible to experiment with something beyond history."[35] Contrary to a common mistaken assumption, Foucault did not aim only to historically problematize our present, for his aim was to problematize our present so as to reveal conditions we must work on to experimentally create an improved future. In a recent essay Paul Rabinow situates Foucault's work in the context of the contrast offered by Deleuze. Rabinow distinguishes "the critical task of the *thinker:* to seize the event in its becoming" from "the work of the *historian*" as being "to insist on the importance of historical elements as conditioning whatever takes place."[36] I am urging that this twofold task of historical problematization and critical anticipation is the frame through which we should view Foucault's (as well as Deleuze's) philosophic labors.

Foucault and Deleuze thus stand together as two relatively pragmatist problematizers against a backdrop of hyper-problematizing postmodernists for whom

pragmatic problem solving holds little or no appeal. This is why Foucault and Deleuze could never be easily understood through the frame of what was called
"postmodernism." For they are, after all, quite able moderns whose thought bears
comparison to other post-Kantian philosophical lineages including pragmatism
and critical theory. It is thus particularly unfortunate that it has especially been
critical theorists and pragmatists who are responsible for the erroneous reception of Foucault as a postmodern who keeps company with the anti-Kantians. As
against this reception, my way of contrasting Foucault with the postmoderns and
aligning him with the moderns rests on a crucial but thus far largely overlooked
point about Foucault's claim for the contingency of the present.

Foucaultian Problematization toward Reconstruction

Genealogy as problematization does not function to definitively establish the de-
ficiency of our present forms of life. This point is essential to both a proper understanding of how Foucault took genealogy to function and to a proper conceptualization of how we might today take up genealogy in the midst of our own ongoing
attempts at critical inquiry. Contrary to the accusations of countless critics, it is
time to recognize that Foucault's genealogy enables rather than disables normative critique. This is so, however, not because genealogy itself supplies us with
norms, but because genealogy can effectively be wielded as one part of a broader
critical ensemble that looks both backward into history and forward into futurity.

It is widely accepted that Foucault labored to explicate the contingency of the
present, but it is rarely affirmed that this work was philosophically oriented not
only to demonstrate *that* the present is contingent but also pragmatically oriented
to show *how* the present has been contingently constructed. The difference between the *that* and the *how* of contingency is of enormous importance, for it makes
all the difference between a genealogy that simply reveals our bottomless freedom
and a genealogy that gives us the material we need for working on our complexly
constituted selves. The sense in which Foucault uses genealogy to mount contingency thus has crucial consequences for the critical capacities of genealogy itself.

Most of Foucault's commentators have urged that the specific force of genealogies is to render contingent that which we formerly took to be necessary—
call this the *anti-inevitability thesis.* David Hoy argues that Foucault's genealogies
should be seen as suggesting that the "stultifying aspects of ourselves that we had
assumed to be universal and natural might in fact be arbitrary and contingent
features that could potentially be changed."[37] Jana Sawicki holds that "Foucault
brings to our attention historical transformations in practices of self-formation

in order to reveal their contingency and to free us for new possibilities of self-understanding, new modes of experience, new forms of subjectivity, authority, and political identity."[38] Paul Rabinow describes Foucault's work as an attempt to "cultivate an attention to the conditions under which things become 'evident,' ceasing to be objects of our attention and therefore seemingly fixed, necessary, and unchangeable."[39] Nikolas Rose writes that "in showing the contingency of the arrangements within which we are assembled, in denaturalizing them, in showing the role of thought in holding them together, they also show that thought has a part to play in contesting them."[40] Wendy Brown offers one of the strongest claims of this type in holding that "For Foucault, the project of making the present appear as something that might not be as it is constitutes *the* distinctive contribution of intellectual work to political life."[41] Judith Butler is equally assertive on this point when she describes the upshot of a genealogical account of gender as performance in terms of "the recognition of a radical contingency in the relation between sex and gender in the face of cultural configurations of causal unities that are regularly assumed to be natural and necessary."[42] These few quotations collect, from those I regard as among Foucault's very best readers (I could easily have filled pages with quotations from other commentators whose work I do not admire so much), a common but uncommonly questioned cliché in the literature.

There is of course much in Foucault that speaks to the anti-inevitability thesis. Foucault wrote of archaeology as enabling us to "tear away from [historical unities] their virtual self-evidence" and of genealogy as exposing "the secret that they have no essence or that their essence was fabricated in a piecemeal fashion."[43] Taking note of these and other claims by Foucault himself, I do not so much disagree with the scholarship I have cited as much as I worry about the cumulative effect of the scholarly tendency to locate the central point of genealogical critique in its capacity for undermining the sense of inevitability that so often accompanies our most deeply held ideas. My worry is that existing scholarship, even the best of it, underemphasizes precisely those aspects of genealogy that I find most crucial for deploying it as an effective critical apparatus.

For in my view, the point of Foucault's genealogy is not only to demonstrate that our present practices are contingent, but also to show how these practices contingently emerged. Contingency was for Foucault not a point of conclusion but a point of commencement: we do not demonstrate contingency as the result of our inquiry, but we use inquiry to investigate the specific events that have constituted the contingent form into which we are inquiring. By focusing on the specific ways in which our practices are contingent, and not merely the general fact of their contingency, genealogy invites specific strategies for either developing

alternative practices or improving existing practices. To see Foucault as otherwise insisting on contingency *per se* rather than on the specific shapes our contingencies have assumed might lead us to interpretations of his work that effectively
undercut the connection between genealogical problematization and other forms
of critical inquiry that aim at the reconstruction of problematic situations.

I can underscore this point with a brief consideration of Brown's and Butler's attributions of a considerable critical capacity to the mere recognition of the
fact of contingency. Brown claims that "The measure of genealogy's success is its
disruption of conventional accounts of ourselves."[44] This is in some senses obviously right, but my worry is that disruption is an extraordinarily ambiguous concept. Brown is right to claim that Foucault "sever[s] critique from prescription,"
but she is too hasty in associating the resultant form of critique with "temperament, desire, imagination, skill, and luck."[45] No doubt Foucault did not want to
exclude these factors from his critical project, and no doubt he aimed to explicitly invite them back into the critical work of thought, but nowhere does he indicate that he wants to exclude rationality, intelligence, and deliberation by identifying critique with non-purposive forces. Foucault did indeed opt for what Brown
helpfully describes as "a politics of projects and strategies rather than moral righ-
teousness," but Foucault knew well that imagination as much as reason can feed
the convictions of the righteous, and that a politics of luck as much as a politics of
will can lead down the hopeless path of destructive moralizing.[46] Similar difficulties plague Butler's attempt to mount a critical project on the basis of a mere "recognition of a radical contingency" where we had once assumed our practices to be
"natural and necessary."[47] Butler argues that such recognition can be motivated
by parody and result in laughter. But it is not clear that this is an effective strategy
for political self-transformation. Butler's *Gender Trouble* famously ends on an un-
easy seesaw between "a subversive laughter in the pastiche-effect of parodic practices" and a call for "locat[ing] strategies of subversive repetition."[48] Butler elides
the difference between these two on the basis of failing to distinguish the mere
recognition of the fact *that* our practices our contingent with the rigorous inquiry
needed to show *how* we have contingently constructed ourselves. It turns out that
we live in a world in which it is indeed quite easy to recognize the contingency of
the self. But it is quite another thing, and a very difficult one at that, to engage in
the loving labor of reworking the contingencies that we have become.

Recognizing that genealogy aims to reveal not only the fact of contingency
(*that* the present is always contingent) but also the composition of singular contingencies (*how* our present has been contingently made up) is the best way of
making sense of Foucault's commitment to a form of critical inquiry that is clearly

both philosophical and historical. A related aspect of Foucault's work that is too often overlooked concerns his dedication to rich descriptions of the various component practices that were contingently fused together in such a way as to form the basis for present problematizations and practices enabled by these problematizations. Foucault wrote very thick histories of the present, and in doing so sought to sacrifice none of the complexity of our contingent conditions of possibility. His aim in writing about prisons was not merely to mount a criticism of the prison system, though surely that was part of it. His aim is better described as providing practitioners, including prisoners, with the tools they might need to begin thinking about ways in which the prison system is problematic and hence capable of improvement. These tools, as Foucault saw it, were the stuff of empirical accounts of the emergence of prisons. Foucault's inquiries provide some of the materials people will need to remake themselves. These materials are nothing other than the historical accumulation of the diverse practices, strategies, and tactics that form the problematizations in which they continue to operate. By showing *how* the present is contingently constructed, Foucault delivered precisely those materials they would need to reform and improve their present. This suggests, of course, an interpretation of Foucault as a radical reformist rather than a revolutionary whose radicalism is merely oppositional. According to such an interpretation, problematization does not so much disrupt or denounce the present, as it opens up the present as a problem so that we may engage in the difficult work of learning how to form ourselves otherwise.

Here is where I locate the greatest advantage of Foucault's genealogical problematization over other forms of argument displayed by other historically attuned thinkers through whom Foucault is too often interpreted. Foucault was not particularly interested in a general project of unmasking the present that would prove the contingency of that which we had taken to be necessary. Foucault was rather involved in investigating the particular forms that contingently make us up. The most crucial difference separating critical problematization from critical denunciation is that the former invites the work of a pragmatic response to the specific contingencies that form us. Problematization opens up problems and asks questions in the mode of critical interrogation, whereas denunciation tends to make assertions in the mode of determinate judgment. Foucault's histories need to be read as if they were written with a question mark, not an exclamation mark, appended at the end. Foucault provokes curiosity and scrutiny, not castigation and scorn. But by emphasizing *that* our practices are contingent while ignoring exactly *how* our practices have been contingently constructed, we lead ourselves toward the attitude of denunciation. To dissociate Foucault from this attitude, I need to emphasize that his work was both a demonstration of our contingency and a description of the details of our contingency. While these two implications of genealogy are indeed analytically separable, they always appear intertwined in the context of Foucault's work. In his histories, the critical force of philosophically demonstrating that a practice is contingent always relies upon and feeds back into the critical force of historically showing how practices are contingently constituted. Those suspicious of where I put the emphasis might reply that it is, in any event, always the case that the use of genealogy to demonstrate the fact of contingency relies on the use of genealogy to narrate the particular details of some contingent emergence. That may be so. But my point is one that concerns what we should take away from these genealogies. It is, in short, a point about emphasis. If you want your audience to take home the idea that some seemingly natural practice is optional, you could appeal to genealogy, but you could also appeal to deconstruction, psychoanalysis, or any number of other philosophical methodologies. If, by contrast, you want your audience to go home with an understanding of how some practice contingently came to appear natural such that they might begin the difficult labor of reworking those contingent materials, then genealogy uniquely will serve. It is in this sense that the genealogical prioritization of *how* contingencies are composed differentiates Foucault from supposedly subversive postmodernists who relentlessly show us *that* every last blessed thing is contingent.

Another way of understanding my distinction between *the fact that* some practice is contingent and *the history of how* some practice was contingently constructed is in terms of the relationship between contingency and stability. According to one usual story, necessity connotes stability, while contingency connotes instability.[49] Foucault is anything but the usual story. One thing that makes his work so provocative and appealing is his attribution of stability and contingency to the selfsame objects of his historical inquiries—or to put it differently, his employment of stability and contingency in the selfsame analytic for historical inquiry. Foucault's objects of inquiry are often remarkably stable structures such as disciplinary power and their corollary institutions such as prisons. Unlike those who take this stability as flowing from some necessity (which the traditional historian would prove by way of a causal explanation referring to, say, economic necessity or social efficiency or the interests of those wielding repressive power), Foucault shows how high degrees of stability sometimes flow from the contingent coalescence of congeries of chancy occurrences. The fact that these very stable structures and institutions emerged contingently does little to unseat or disrupt them, however. They are, after all, remarkably stable. And that, after all, is part of Foucault's point. This is why Foucault is not content to merely make a philosophical or onto-logical point but rather pushes himself to combine philosophy and ontology with history. Because these stabilities are conditioned by a massive historical inertia, we cannot easily transform them. If we do want to initiate a transformative re-sponse to the problematizations that these stable structures and institutions form, then one thing we would require is a historical inquiry that places at our disposal an understanding of the materials that conditioned the emergence of these stabili-ties. A historical understanding of these conditions equips us with a reflexive rela-tionship to the contingencies that make us who we are such that we can begin the long and hard labor of transforming those remarkably stable structures to which we find ourselves subjected.

Despite the disagreement I have been airing, my interpretation of Foucault's practice of genealogy as problematization is in keeping with the best aspects of the interpretations forwarded by Hoy, Sawicki, Rabinow, Rose, Brown, Butler, and others whose claims I have been criticizing. And indeed in more recent work, some of these commentators have articulated positions that trend closer to my own. Rabinow is perhaps most visible on this shift in having recently written that "Foucault's task consisted not only of making what was self-evident contingent, but in analysing how it had been linked in complex ways with 'multiple historical processes, many of them recent'."[50] Such statements of revision duly noted, my worry is best phrased as follows: most readers of Foucault (including, of course, myself) have on occasion overemphasized the idea that the point of a genealogy is to demonstrate the mere fact that our practices are contingent. The cumulative effect of all this overemphasis in the literature is the cliché of anti-inevitability that every college student in the humanities hears of when they learn about ge-nealogy. The anti-inevitability thesis is the *lingua franca* when it comes to articu-lating the point of a genealogy. This is misleading at best, and counterproductive at worst.

The difference between emphasizing the fact that a practice is contingent and emphasizing the story of how it contingently developed is a difference we should insist upon. This is because Foucault rightly understood that this difference can help equip us with a philosophical methodology that can be applied not only to the natural sciences but also to the tangled realms of the human sciences. The work of many Foucaultians has been in large part an effort to destabilize the seem-ing naturalness of certain concepts central to our natural sciences, for instance, concepts of sexuality invoked by biology. Genealogy has been used to show quite effectively that some of our usually taken-for-granted ways of thinking about

things are contingent products of messy history. Consider now that using genealogy to make a similar point about some overtly political formation, such as liberal democracy or its attendant fulcrum of a distinction between public and private spheres, would not be nearly so interesting. Almost everyone already admits
that our political forms, even our best ones, are constructions of our doing. We
take pride in our having made such wonderful things. To use genealogy to show
that these constructions are contingent would be greeted as redundant. Here is
where the emphasis on the specific ways in which these contingencies were constructed becomes important. My broader aim in reconstructing Foucault's philosophical analytics and diagnostics is to use genealogy to inquire into the materials of which our political present is composed such that we might begin to more
effectively recompose that present where it has been rendered problematic. For
the purposes of reconstruction we need to know not only *that* our political life is
a contingency but also *how* it was contingently made into what it is. In Chapters
5 and 6, I produce an extended case of this by offering a rereading of Foucault's
problematizations of, and reconstructive responses to, the political and ethical
constructions of our modernity.

My larger point is that Foucault's problematizations specifically invite the
work of reconstruction. That genealogical problematization was in fact understood
by Foucault himself to open up a space into which alternative forms of thought
and practice might develop as responses was made especially clear in a late interview Foucault gave to Rabinow. Asked by Rabinow about his concept of problematization, Foucault stressed the relation between his histories of problematization and the work of thought. He explained that "for a domain of action, a
behavior, to enter the field of thought, it is necessary for a certain number of factors to have made it uncertain, to have made it lose its familiarity, or to have
provoked a number of difficulties around it."[51] Problematization, Foucault explained, is that which enables us to submit our practices and ourselves to the field
of thought. It is clear as the interview goes on that Foucault regards the work of
thought as a valuable instrument. He explains that thought is "freedom in relation
to what one does" and is "what allows one to step back from this way of acting or
reacting, to present it to oneself as an object of thought and to question it as to its
meaning, its condition, and its goals."[52] Foucault summarizes his position just a
little further into the interview: "This development of a given into a question, this
transformation of a group of obstacles and difficulties into problems to which the
diverse solutions will attempt to produce a response, this is what constitutes the
point of problematization and the specific work of thought."[53] Since this interview
with Foucault, Rabinow the interviewer has gleaned a similar understanding of

how backward-looking problematizations invite us to forward-looking anticipations. He writes in his later work: "What forms are emerging? What practices are embedding and embodying them? What shape are the political struggles taking? What spaces of ethics is present? It is in the muffled movement and experimentation in and around these poorly articulated issues, rather than in the noisier scraps about beliefs and values, that a future is taking shape."[54] Like Foucault in former decades, Rabinow is today one of our most able problematizers, and also like Foucault before him, he takes problematization as a way of provoking a greater attention to what plagues us in the present.

What all this suggests is that genealogical histories of the present (and similar modes of inquiry such as Rabinow's anthropologies of the contemporary) can be coupled with something like pragmatist critical theory, where the latter supply problem-solving thought and the former supply a field of problems that require our patient attention. I find this interpretation the best way to make sense of Foucault's claims in "What is Enlightenment?" on behalf of a "historico-practical test of the limits we may go beyond." At the very end of this essay, Foucault describes a dual-aspect characterization of an ethos of critical activity that would be "at one and the same time the historical analysis of the limits imposed on us and an experiment with the possibility of going beyond them."[55] These two aspects can be construed as oriented toward problematization on the one hand and problem resolving on the other. If this interpretation is suitable, then I believe genealogy can be seen as one crucial aspect of a broader apparatus of critical inquiry whose primary functions are that of genealogical problematization and pragmatist reconstruction. On this interpretation we need not claim for genealogy the status of an entire philosophical system that can be used to perform all of our critical tasks. We can more modestly claim the value of genealogy as just one methodological part of a fuller ensemble of critical methodologies.

This points to what I regard as the most effective way of responding to the familiar criticisms, discussed in the previous two chapters, of Foucault as normatively deficient.[56] We can concede the claims that Foucault's work is defective in some respects (normative reconstruction) while acknowledging its decisive advantages in other respects (critical problematization). The problem, it turns out, is not so much with the criticism as it is with those who have taken the concern it expresses as enabling a general rejection of Foucault's work. Remember my rule from the discussion of Kant in the previous chapter: we should feel free to take what we need from our predecessors and discard the rest.

In an instructive essay that goes a long way toward a rapprochement between genealogists and critical theorists, Raymond Geuss correctly notes that Foucault's genealogical critique should be understood as "a way of problematising something" by asking "how has a specific historical process led human beings to develop and embody this sort of identity?"[57] Geuss explicitly contrasts this Foucaultian form of critique to those rather quite different forms of critique that are aimed at repudiation or subversion. I find it important to continue to emphasize such contrasts given the continued reception of Foucault as primarily a subversive intellectual.[58] Contrary to this reception, the real value of genealogy, in the view I share with Geuss, is not a delegitimation or legitimation of this or that form of subjectivation. It is rather the reflexive problematization of the various factors contributing to some crucial way in which we constitute and condition ourselves. Genealogy offers precise problematizations that pave the way for the precise responses we may yet, with honest hope, develop. Far from ruling out agency and the constructive development of alternative forms of power and freedom, as so many detractors have insisted, Foucault's genealogy can be fruitfully seen as an orientation for inquiry that serves to motivate constructive theoretical and practical work. We should not be fooled into thinking that this will be an easy task, and Foucault himself insisted it would not be. For the problems that we today face as our most important challenges are, as Foucault has convincingly shown, very deep and very wide indeed.

The Relation between Politics and Ethics in Foucault

Interpreting Foucault's historical analytics of archaeology and genealogy through the lens of problematization enables us to clarify an important issue that has proven insurmountable in the literature on Foucault up until now. This is the issue of the relation between Foucault's so-called "middle" work on power and his so-called "late" work on ethics. While there is clearly some sort of shift between Foucault's earlier histories of disciplinary and biopolitical power on the one hand and his later studies of ancient ethical practice on the other, commentators have obsessed over whether this shift constitutes a conceptual break such that Foucault's earlier work had invalidated many of the concepts explicitly featured in the later work. The most familiar form of this worry is that Foucault's genealogies of modern power entail a principled rejection of concepts of freedom, subjectivity, and ethical agency, whereas his later work on ancient ethics explicitly revives and perhaps even relies on these very same concepts. There is, some critics have supposed, a principled contradiction between these two supposedly separate phases of Foucault's thought. A number of Foucault's readers have come to his defense by urging that Foucault's work on discipline and biopower never invalidated the concepts that his later work takes up. Foucault never denied our capacity for free-dom, they suggest, he only resituated it.

Commentators on both sides have inappropriately framed the issue. The re-lations amongst the many aspects of Foucault's work from the 1970s and 1980s is indeed a difficult one, and there is no easy solution, but I think much ground can be gained by reframing the terms in which we approach these works. We should not see the genealogies of modern power as philosophically invalidating certain concepts later featured in the histories of ancient ethics. We should rather under-stand the genealogies of modern power as problematizing certain concepts so as to invite precisely the sort of reconstructive response that Foucault undertook in his later work on ancient ethics. This enables us to effectively reply to Foucault's most hostile critics.

A more usual strategy for defending Foucault against these criticisms, but one I find misguided, relies on an overemphasis on the importance of the notion of governmentality for Foucault's work on the whole. This defense comes from a group of devoted Foucault scholars who have generated over the past few decades a growing cottage industry commonly referred to as "governmentality studies." Although the governmentality scholarship has generated an enormous amount of very useful critical work, it has done so on the basis of an interpretation of Fou-cault that overstates the case for the importance of the idea of governmentality in his work. According to this interpretation, Foucault's work on governmental-ity in the late 1970s provides the conceptual bridge from his work on power in the middle 1970s to his work on ethics in the early 1980s. Thomas Lemke offers a representative statement of the usual claim for the enormous importance of the concept of governmentality in Foucault's critical project. Lemke boldly asserts that "governmentality is the missing link" between the two sets of genealogies of political rationality and genealogies of ethical subjectivity found in Foucault's work after *Discipline and Punish*.[59] Foucault's work on governmentality certainly appears between his research on modern politics and ancient ethics, but it does not function there as a link or hinge that would provide a stable frame of refer-ence in terms of which the political and ethical work can be situated. In my view, the hinge is not to be found in Foucault's concept of governmentality, but rather in terms of Foucault's varying methodological approach in this period.

In much of his work between 1977 and 1981, Foucault was able to concep-tualize the core problematizations he had traced in *Discipline and Punish* and *The Will to Know* as well as the inchoate responses to these problems that he would later trace in *The Care of the Self* and *The Use of Pleasure*. But Foucault did not in these years establish governmentality as an overarching frame through which we should read both his diagrams of modern disciplinary power and his research toward a new transformative ethics. Foucault rather took up the concept of governmentality in a way that enabled him to re-elaborate the problematization defined in his earlier books such that he could then go on in some of his later work to begin sketching a response to this problematization. The writings on governmentality form, to be sure, a missing part of the long genealogy of the development of an ancient ethics of self-care into the late modern politics of self-discipline by way of and as inflected through processes of religious interiorization, communal pastoralization, and governmental repoliticization.[60]

If this interpretive sequencing stands up to scrutiny, then governmentality is by no means the master heading under which to file all the key forms of subjectivation-power-knowledge with which Foucault was concerned. A better interpretation involves seeing those portions of Foucault's long genealogies which remain largely unavailable and to which the governmentality writings make just one contribution as fleshing out in greater detail the problematization of modern powers and freedoms already undertaken in earlier work. This further problematization reveals some of the vectors formative of our modernity that Foucault seemed to think might serve as possible points of a transformative counter-elaboration of ourselves. If it would turn out that early Greek self-care is indeed one small part of later European formation of self-discipline, then Foucault discerned in self-care a possibility for an alternative ethics that seemed however to have disappeared long ago, somewhere between the Greek and the Roman ages.

The interpretation I am offering has generally not been pursued in the existing literature. But it does possess the very nice advantage of having been anticipated by two interlocutors of Foucault's whose importance for his thinking I have emphasized above: Deleuze and Canguilhem. Deleuze describes the relation of Foucault's final works to his earlier projects as follows: "It's nothing to do with him repudiating his earlier work. It's all his earlier work, rather, that pushes him into this new confrontation."[61] Canguilhem offered an assessment of Foucault's work that is even more to my purposes here: "In the face of normalization and against it, *Le Souci de soi*."[62] To the extent that Foucault developed his own positive ethics, then, this would be an ethics in response to the specific problems of modern morality to which Foucault's problematizations of modern power and freedom had pushed him. The genealogy of modern power and freedom provided Foucault with a problematization, or problem, to which his later genealogy-cum-archaeology of ancient ethics should be seen as an inchoate response.

This helps us recognize that an expansive reading of the concept of governmentality (or of anything else) does not function as a substantive conceptual hinge that enabled Foucault to simultaneously inquire into power and ethics. The continuity of focus in Foucault's work is in fact better realized in terms of a connection between two methodologies or modalities of inquiry deployed by Foucault: problematization and reconstruction. Whereas governmentality fills in a supposed substantive gap between conceptualizations of political and ethical life as well as partially filling in an evident historical gap between ancient self-care and modern self-discipline, there is no giant breach separating the methodological analytics of problematization and reconstruction insofar as they are but two faces of the same coinage. *Discipline and Punish* and *The Will to Know* (and the lectures and writings of those years immediately following their publication) articulate a problematization of modern powers and freedoms. *The Use of Pleasure* and *The Care of the Self* (and even more the lectures and writings of the years immediately preceding their publication) articulate nascent ethical responses to this problematization. Over the course of the next two chapters I will further explicate this reading.

Before doing so, I want to draw out just a few further consequences of this reinterpretation. The governmentality scholars are overstating things quite a bit when they emphasize that "the problematics of government [are] the greater context of [Foucault's] work."[63] The "greater context" of Foucault's work, to the extent that such a metaphor is even useful, should be looked at in terms of the analytic and diagnostic method of problematization by virtue of which Foucault detailed the core problems of modern power and freedom such that he could then begin elaborating a series of possible practical responses to this problematization. So it is not governmentality that forges a connection between Foucault's work on power and on ethics, but rather the fact that the work on power clarified a problematization such that the work on ethics could elaborate a response to these difficult problems. Foucault would never have been so brazen as to believe that the whole of our modern experience can be summarized in a single concept—in place of that mode of totalization, he adopted instead a more patient practice of inquiring into the problematizations and reconstructions by virtue of which we have become and may yet become otherwise.

My proposed interpretation does, however, raise a further question that I ought to be able to address: How, then, should we interpret Foucault's work in the late 1970s, especially insofar as governmentality is a key concept featured in that work? My view is that Foucault's work in these years evidences the beginnings of a crucial distinction between two competing conceptualizations of freedom. In these years we sometimes find Foucault continuing to describe freedom as something he obviously finds quite dangerous—this is the familiar but caricatured Foucaultian conception of freedom as the merely co-opted and co-opting twin of modern disciplinary and biopolitical power. This is the sense of freedom that is often taken up by those who have extended Foucault's work along the seam of governmentality that he was mining in his 1978 course lectures, as for instance when Nikolas Rose writes of "be[ing] governed through our freedom."[64] In other moments, however, it is clear that Foucault is striving to articulate a positive conception of freedom, and so he makes more hopeful remarks that have led many to believe that he went back on his earlier "rejection" of freedom. In these moments Foucault talks about freedom in terms of "resistance" and "experimentation" and "counter-conduct" in the sense later developed by, among others, David Hoy in his work on critical resistance in Foucault.[65] Both Rose and Hoy could cite on behalf of their opposing views a well-known cryptic line from Foucault's essay "The Subject and Power," portions of which were probably composed in 1978 though it was not published in full until 1982, as follows: "Power is exercised only over free subjects, and only insofar as they are 'free.'"[66] Depending on what one chooses to do with the scare quotes, Foucault can be read here as either defending a form of freedom harbored within every exercise of power or as noting the disturbing complicity of freedom with power. Scare quotes are like curtains that open or close for us a view of the scene that lies between—in this case we should ask if the curtains are indicative of the impending end of the story of an old form of freedom or the hopeful beginnings of a story of a newly found freedom.

We cannot resolve the dilemma inherent in this famous Foucault quotation. But let us not treat it as a riddle whose solution would unlock a profound mystery. Foucault's descriptions of freedom in 1978 were in actual fact extraordinarily ambiguous between two different readings. This ambiguity is probably best seen as a function of the fact that Foucault's thought was undergoing remarkable transformations in these years. As such, it is really not all that helpful to decide what Foucault's precise views about freedom were in the late 1970s and early 1980s. The important thing, rather, is to recognize the ambiguity of Foucault's thought and travel along the real splits in his conceptualization of different forms of freedom. We do not gain anything, and we lose much, if we artificially resolve this ambiguity.

We lose much if we do so because it is on the basis of the difference at the heart of this ambiguity that Foucault was able to go on in subsequent years to clarify a distinction between two forms of freedom. One is a concept of a problematic or dangerous practice of freedom as complicit with discipline and biopower featured in our most familiar and available forms of freedom understood in terms of liberation, emancipation, and autonomy. The other is a quite provocative concept of freedom as self-transformative resistance and experimentation that would come into increasing focus in Foucault's final writings. The ambiguity of Foucault's work on freedom in the late 1970s and early 1980s should be seen as evidence of a mighty struggle to develop this crucial distinction between two concepts of freedom. This distinction, which Foucault would come to work out only in subsequent years, has been ably captured by, among others, both Rose and Hoy.[67] Rose urges us to "distinguish freedom as a formula of resistance from freedom as a formula of power."[68] Hoy claims that "Foucault radicalizes tradition by way of his distinction between practices of freedom, which he favors, and practices of liberation, of which he is wary."[69] Thus both Rose and Hoy, as quoted earlier, in their opposed respective discussions of freedom as complicit with power and as resistance to power, are right. It all depends on what conception of freedom furnished by Foucault we are considering. Foucault, in the view I am endorsing, labored to explicate the possibilities harbored by a cloudy distinction that we would benefit by seeing better. Despite its being recognized by a small handful of commentators, many have failed to work with this distinction in their understanding of Foucault. My view is that it needs to be made more central in contemporary work on Foucault's analyses of powers, freedoms, and ethics. I thus turn in what follows to carefully explicating the difference herein. In Chapter 5, I consider freedom as liberation in its complicity with modern forms of power. In Chapter 6, I discuss freedom as self-transformation in the face of our modern ideals of discipline and liberation.

5

Foucault's Problematization of Modernity

The Reciprocal Incompatibility of Discipline and Liberation

Foucault's Histories of Modernity

Michel Foucault's works were transmitted from France to America through the filter of that American invention of "theory" that came to dominate much of the American intellectual scene in the 1970s and 1980s. I briefly discussed these terms of Foucault's American reception in the Introduction, where I noted one particularly significant effect of this historical accident of intellectual transmission, namely the way in which Foucault's reception through the powerful combination of literary criticism and cultural studies (i.e., the newly emerging constellation of "theory" and especially "French theory") worked to obfuscate potential linkages between genealogy and the thought of philosophers and social scientists working in the traditions of American pragmatism and Frankfurt School critical theory. The theory movement's interpretation of Foucault gradually grew to dominance in American intellectual discourse despite the better efforts of some of Foucault's best commentators, whose work, though clearly influential in bringing Foucault across the Atlantic, would later be engulfed in the fury of theory that then swept across the academy with still-lasting effects. And so it is today widely assumed, indeed often without even reflecting upon it, that American pragmatism and German critical theory are opposed on the most crucial points to the central themes of French Theory. What is contestable, even if not often contested, is the extent to which Foucault is properly articulated to that subversive postmodernism imported by those designing the new "theory" complex.

The time is now ripe for revising our received version of Foucault. We are today in an opportune position for reconsidering his thought without the obfuscations thrown up by the filters structuring much of the early reception of his work. Now that Foucault's works have been thoroughly saturated with commentary, we are freed from the task of exhaustive interpretation such that we may turn instead to the work of considered elucidation. Revising our vision of Foucault will enable us to assess anew his methodological relations to postmodernisms, pragmatisms, and critical theories. According to the reinterpretation of Foucaultian methodology I have offered in previous chapters, Foucault is best read as a critical inquirer in whose work is combined the theoretical ambition of the philosopher and the empirical rigor of the historical-anthropological social scientist. Foucault is not, or at least not primarily, a paradigm case of that subversive intellectual whose chosen disciplinary matrix in the contemporary American academy would be one of the manifold variations of "theory" on the scene. This is not to say that Foucault does not yield considerable resources for various aspects of literary and cultural studies, nor is it to say that those employing Foucault for these purposes are committing some sort of intellectual treason. All I aim to show is that Foucault's vitality for contemporary philosophy and social science has been greatly misestimated.

In what is perhaps one of the most delicious ironies of the story of Foucault's reception in America, the pernicious effects of the prevailing assessment of Foucault as a postmodern were fueled in large part by two of Foucault's most influential European interlocutors, namely Jürgen Habermas and Jacques Derrida. Both mounted severe criticisms of Foucault's work in terms that would further the prevailing perception of Foucault as a postmodern theorist whom Habermasians (i.e., critical theorists and many pragmatists) should rightly oppose and whom Derrideans (i.e., the "theory" crowd) should consider as at least a partial ally if not also a primary inspiration.

The critical salvoes of Habermas and Derrida have long served as two of the strongest anchors for our prevailing wisdom about Foucault. This wisdom, common to those both hostile and sympathetic to Foucault, holds that his work offers us a historical critique of modernity in which power and rationality are seen as excluding and subjugating freedom and madness. According to this view, Foucault not only laments the loss of madness and freedom essential to modernization, but he finds himself forced to admit that neither is any longer possible. Foucault is therefore often said to paradoxically claim that we are bound to be both rational and unfree. This familiar portrait of Foucault is at the heart of the widespread reading of him as a postmodern denouncer. I have argued that Foucault did not use his genealogical and archaeological methodologies to denounce modernity but to inquire into the constitutive problematizations that function as conditions of possibility constraining our present. Turning now to two of Foucault's books that have served most crucially for this interpretation, *History of Madness* and *Discipline and Punish*, I show in this chapter how Foucault's methodology enabled him to produce concepts of modernity that do not at all match the received views of his work as resolutely anti-modern.

Before turning to those concepts, a preliminary comment is requisite concerning what sort of thing they are conceptualizations of. What sort of object of inquiry is modernity? Foucault's studies of modernity are often read as epochal analyses of something we tend to want to call the modern age. But on my reading of Foucault, modernity is not, or at least not primarily, an epochal category. This is because Foucault's mode of analysis is not cast in terms of epochs. There is no modern period; there are rather only modern practices and modern problematizations instigating them. These practices and problematizations might, when scrutinized by an epochal analysis, turn out to be structurally dominant in a given epoch. But Foucault's point, I take it, is not to characterize an era so much as it is to delineate a set of practices that are at the core of what we take to be modernity, and hence of who we take ourselves to be. A more useful, but more cumbersome, term than "modernity" would simply be "practices of modernization." In this context it is worth quoting again the following claim of Foucault's on the use of history: "If history possesses a privilege, it would be, rather, insofar as it plays the role of an internal ethnology of our culture and our rationality."[1] The historical ethnologist does not aim to offer a totalizing account of an epoch (the modern age) but rather a detailed account of the complexity and contingency of a problematization and its practices that are remarkably widespread but not for that reason totalizing. The model is not epochal so much as it is ethnological, to use Foucault's term, or anthropological, to use the term I prefer.[2] This distinction helps explain Foucault's otherwise-puzzling remarks in "What is Enlightenment?" where he suggests that we come to terms with "modernity as an attitude rather than as a period of history" and as an "ethos" rather than an "era."[3]

Foucault saw modernity, understood as an assemblage of practices, as problematized by ineliminable tensions between constitutive couples: power and freedom, in one version of the story, and in another, reason and madness. Foucault learned to see that we moderns find ourselves increasingly unable to negotiate the tensions arising within such couples—and so it is that reason and madness as well as freedom and power are increasingly purified of one another in our modernity. In Foucault's reading, the problematization we moderns face, in short, is not that of the *exclusion* of madness or freedom by rationality or power (a problem that could very well be met by the liberation of each), but rather that of the *purification* of rationality and freedom such that they are unmixed with madness and power (a problem that must be met by what Foucault variously called transgression, experimentation, or better yet transformation).

My contrast between exclusion and purification will be central in the rereading that follows, so it will help to clarify up front the sense in which I am using these terms. Exclusion can be taken in the rather colloquial sense of banishment or expulsion, such that the exclusion of madness by reason amounts to the exile of madness wherever rationality reigns. Purification can be taken as describing a process in which two kinds of practices rigorously isolate themselves from one another, such that the purification of madness and reason amounts to the simultaneous production of both madness and reason in such a way that they cannot admit of admixture with one another. Purification is not a process of exclusion, but rather of inclusion through separation. We can schematize these relations as follows: a excludes b, while y and z are produced so as to purify themselves of one another; exclusion is a getting rid of b; purification is y and z preserving both themselves and one another by means of a rigorous separation. It also helpful to state, even if only in schematic form, a contrast concept for each: the exclusion of b by a is overcome by the liberation of b from a, while the purification of y and z is overcome by developing a more integral relation between y and z. I understand exclusion and purification as categorical generals that can be more precisely specified in context. For example, in the context of political theory, the category of exclusion can be characterized in terms of what Foucault called sovereign power, whereas the category of purification can be characterized in terms of Foucault's discussions of disciplinary power and biopower.

The Received Foucault: Modernity's Exclusions

Many of the widespread misrepresentations of Foucault's portraits of modernity are rooted in a body of theoretical work that has been subtly dominant in twentieth-century thought and that as a result has been imperceptibly applied to the work of Foucault too. I shall refer to this body of theoretical work by way of one of its paradigmatic instances, namely Max Weber's thesis that modernity is an age of relentless rationalization and bureaucratization.[4] At the outset of the twentieth century, Weber developed a profoundly influential argument to the effect that

modernity is characterized by the categorical differentiation of various rational-
ized value spheres (science, politics, aesthetics) such that the internal rationality
appropriate to each can function only by excluding from within its purview all
activity that cannot be operationalized according to this rationality. This portrait
of the modern exclusion of unreason by rationalization and bureaucratization has
often served as an anchor point for interpretations of Foucault, be they favorable
or not. But, I will argue here, Foucault cannot be understood as a sociologist of
modernity in terms of Weberian differentiation and is instead better read as a historian and an anthropologist of modernity working on a critique of its constitutive problematization.

It may seem surprising at first blush that two thinkers as disparate as Derrida
and Habermas expressed similar bad reactions in confronting the work of Foucault. But given the deep influence of the Weberian interpretation of modernity
as rationalizing bureaucratization, it really should come as no surprise. When one
goes looking for the Weberian interpretation of modernity, it begins to crop up
practically everywhere, including in the critical literature on Foucault's histories
of modernity. While some have explicitly attributed the Weberian thesis to Foucault, it is far more common that critics will implicitly impute it to him in offering interpretations of his work that they then cast doubt on for one reason or another.[5] It is not surprising that so many critics read Foucault through Weber, given
the pervasive influence of the latter. What is surprising, rather, is the extent to
which Foucault freed himself from this nearly pervasive interpretation of modernity. Foucault offered a new philosophical-historical interpretation of modernity
that simply left behind the familiar Weberian categories that have structured the
thought of so many who have confronted modernity as an object of thought.

The standard interpretation of Foucault upon which I want to cast doubt is
one that leaves him in that same difficult bind that Weber bequeathed. The bind is
captured in an image of modernity as increasingly swept up in an insidious form
of disciplinary rationality that leaves us with impossibly little wiggle room by
which we may come to free ourselves of our disciplinary constitution. On this interpretation, a stifled and disturbed Foucault offers us little better than, in Richard
Rorty's catchy phrase, "more and more sophisticated expressions of resentment."[6]
Even sympathetic commentators are beholden to such a view, as for instance
James Bernauer, when he claims that "confinements are the central experiences
that Foucault's work describes."[7] These familiar images commonly attributed to
Foucault are patterned, whether consciously or not, after Weber's famous asser-
tion of the "iron cage" of modern rationalization.[8]

Weber's poignant and influential image depicts modernity as a prison in which we are trapped. This image suggests that modernity works according to a logic of exclusion by which all that cannot be swept up into modernization is effectively excluded from modernity. Our iron cage forces us to modernize. Those who do not oblige are no longer trapped in the cage but are, even worse, excluded altogether. If Weber shows us that modernity is an iron cage, then Foucault is supposed to show us that modernity is something like an iron cave: not only are we imprisoned in a world of totalizing exclusions, but we cannot even see that we are imprisoned, let alone see our way out of the imprisonment. Despite superficial resemblances, Foucault's equally poignant images of modern prisons, asylums, and other such locales should not be portrayed in a Weberian light. For Foucault's argument was never that prisons were the originary site of modern discipline such that modernity is modeled on the prison. Foucault saw the prison as something more like a laboratory for certain prominent modern practices that would later proliferate throughout modernity. At the heart of this image is the prisoner, ever alternating between his rigid routine of self-discipline and his unguarded but impotent dream of self-liberation—the obedient prisoner dreams of an escape from confinement that would not be possible but never considers to question their own perfect obedience to the rules of the institution. The prison thus does not exclude the prisoner from a modernizing society so much as it produces the prisoner on the basis of the purifying mechanisms at the heart of modern society. Foucault's modern subjects are not excluded, confined, and resentful. They are too busy forming themselves through exercises that rigorously purify practices of power from practices of freedom.

One of the most provocative attempts to present Foucault in this sort of Weberian light is offered in Giorgio Agamben's efforts to appropriate and outflank Foucault's critical history of modernity in his *Homo Sacer*. Agamben explicitly aims to one-up Foucault when he insists that "The [concentration] camp—and not the prison—is the space that corresponds to this originary structure of the *nomos*."[9] But, against Agamben, it should be noted that Foucault never regarded the prison as originary for modern power and freedom. If one understands Foucault correctly, it becomes impossible to entertain fanciful ideas about singular institutions being "originary structures" for the totality of modern society. The subject of Foucault's history is certainly not the prison but rather that ever-expanding avalanche of practices of all variety that concatenated to form the problematization of disciplinary power. To take just one example, consider the emphasis on the influence of the military context for the emergence of discipline. "[B]ut there was also a military dream of society," insisted Foucault.[10] The discipline elaborated in this military version was leveraged into and reinforced by its rearticulation in punitive, economic, medical, and pedagogical contexts. The paradigm of the modern subject is thus not the prisoner excluded from society (and even less is it the camp victim so brutally extinguished). The paradigm modern subject is the perfectly well-disciplined soldier—and student, patient, prisoner, employee, too. Modern discipline is not a prison—rather, prison can exist only within modern discipline.

Agamben's attempted ahistorical ontologization of Foucault's concepts offers a useful stereotype for errors plaguing other more-careful interpretations of Foucault's work that run rampant in contemporary commentary. This generalized Weberian reading is clearly visible in many prominent commentaries on *History of Madness* and *Discipline and Punish*, all of which deserve our serious attention. I shall now consider each of these books in turn and air the familiar attacks, focusing on those by Derrida and Habermas, along the way.

In common accounts of *History of Madness*, Foucault is described as tracing the history of a Western rationality that would separate itself from its primary other, namely madness, so as to exclude it from modern culture. For example, in his otherwise excellent book on Foucault's archaeologies, Gary Gutting presents Foucault as charting the "suppression," "conceptual exclusion," and "condemnation" of madness by reason. According to this standard interpretation, Foucault near the end of the book issues a desperate cry on behalf of those banished madmen by lyrically invoking the names of Nietzsche and Artaud, Sade and Hölderlin. Gutting finds in these closing pages Foucault's "romantic desire to see madness as an infrarational source of fundamental truth."[11] The received wisdom on *History of Madness* is that it is a lamentation of modern reason's domination of madness, a domination that seems to leave us all, including Foucault himself, helplessly trapped in the iron cage of modern rationality.[12]

Having interpreted *History of Madness* in this way, a number of critics have rallied to the defense of the frenzied madness that Foucault supposedly found excluded by reason. We are not as trapped as Foucault suggests, the critics argued, because irrationality and its correlates were never totally excluded by reason and its correlates. One of Foucault's most provocative critics even went so far as to argue that madness had always remained lodged at the very heart of reason itself. Derrida used as an epigram for his enormously influential critical essay on Foucault the following line from Kierkegaard: "the instant of decision is madness." In the essay itself Derrida disparagingly referred to Foucault's book on reason and madness as a "Cartesian gesture for the twentieth century" because it unwittingly attempted to intern Cartesian reason itself, a claim clarified by Derrida's reference to Foucault's supposed "revolution against reason." Derrida's interpretation of Foucault turns on two claims. First is the claim that Foucault understands modern reason as attempting the internment of madness. Second is the claim that this internment is an impossible project that could never work. The two claims, taken together, assert that reason can never fully exclude madness and that Foucault had said that it could. Derrida wrote in his essay that philosophical reason itself is "the reassurance given against the anguish of being mad at the point of greatest proximity to madness." Derrida was thus able to insist on a point Foucault never would have entertained: "this crisis in which reason is madder than madness . . . and in which madness is more rational than reason . . . this crisis has always begun and is interminable."[13] As Foucault would put it in his rebuttal essay many years later, the picture offered by Derrida is one in which "philosophical discourse is finally excluded from excluding madness."[14] In conceptualizing the relation between rational philosophy and irrational madness in terms of a logic of exclusion, Derrida took himself to be rebutting Foucault. But this rebuttal depended on his first imputing to Foucault the view that modern philosophical rationality was an attempt to exclude madness. This was not, as I shall show below, Foucault's view.

Derrida went on to make an impressive career out of the style of argumentation he employed to make his case against Foucault. Much of his later work can be seen as variations on the theme that madness remains lodged within reason as its simultaneous condition of possibility and condition of impossibility. Derrida improvised on this point right up until his final years, when he surveyed his own long career of work as "keeping within reason, however mad it might appear."[15] A key idea running throughout all of Derrida's work is that Nonreason (writing, undecidability, madness, violence) unceasingly haunts Reason (speech, decidability, rationality, law). I would argue that all of Derrida's key terms (trace, differance, aporia) can be understood as attempts to state this unstatable nonmeaning at the heart of all meaning. The crux of deconstruction is thus not unfairly glossed in the following formula: the deconstruction of x reveals a y that is simultaneously the condition of the possibility of x and the condition of the impossibility of x. But let me turn now from Derrida back to Foucault.

It is notable that almost identical misinterpretations structured the reception of Foucault's image of modernity drawn up in his later *Discipline and Punish*. On the standard accounts of this work, Foucault was diagramming for us the workings of an insidious and unbeatable form of power that had over the course of the past few hundred years (the period of the modern era) come to structure modern society, modern knowledge, modern law, and even modern subjectivity itself. It is Foucault's point, commentator after commentator declared, that we cannot free ourselves from the exercise of modern discipline. The Panopticon, once thought to be a mere architectural innovation, turned out to be a diagram for the whole of modern society itself. We have so thoroughly internalized panopticism that we inhabit that mode of thinking nearly everywhere: we accept and embrace discipline in our factories, our workplaces, our schools, our hospitals, our clinics, our prisons, our sexuality, and above all in our innermost selves. According to this reading, Foucault is a deep pessimist about modernity. What his work shows is that we are swept up in a power that renders freedom totally impossible. This leaves him, and us, in an impossible bind. As Frank Lentricchia put this common criticism, Foucault "cannot explain why he himself is not a mindless zombie, how he himself can mount a criticism of the system."[16] Habermas famously urged this criticism in arguing that Foucault's "socialized individuals can only be perceived as exemplars, as standardized produces of some [discursive] formation—as individual copies that are mechanically punched out."[17]

Critics interpreting Foucault in this way were quick to castigate him for leaving us moderns in too submissive a posture. Freedom is surely not so caged up as Foucault tells us, they chirped. A freedom liberated from the grip of power is in fact the very essence of modernity, they barked. The crux of the standard criticism is that Foucault's interpretation of modernity under the sign of disciplinary power eviscerates from modernity the very premise of emancipation that is the condition of possibility of modern reflection at all. This leads Foucault into a performative contradiction—his diatribe takes place under the very conditions of modern freedom that it announces as impossible such that his critique invisibly performs precisely what it loudly insists cannot be done.[18]

Having reviewed some of the most damning criticisms of Foucault's genealogies of modernity, I want to call attention to a curious fact about these standard criticisms that has thus far escaped the notice of most contributors to these debates. Thinkers who usually see themselves as opposed to one another, for instance Derrida and Habermas, found themselves aligned against Foucault on the very same points and by deploying the very same sets of assumptions. It is remarkable that two thinkers as otherwise disparate as Derrida and Habermas would find common ground not only in disagreeing with Foucault but even more so in the terms in which they articulated that disagreement. The terms in common here are those involved in showing the way out of a strong form of the Weberian logic of exclusion that both critics attributed to Foucault. This shared interpretive apparatus suggests that it is perhaps Derrida and Habermas, but not Foucault, who understand modernity in terms of all the familiar Weberian oppositions. In other words, Derrida and Habermas impute to Foucault a Weberian perspective that I do not find in him: the view that the basic problems of modernity can be cast in terms of relations of exclusion and incorporation. When seen through the perspective of these terms, Foucault appears to argue that reason dominates madness by totally excluding it, and that power dominates freedom by totally incorporating it. Derrida sets out to rescue madness by showing how it is always already internal to reason. Habermas sets out to rescue freedom by showing how it must always already preserve its externality to power. These are, to be sure, two very different rescue operations. Derrida wants to show, against Foucault, that reason's separation from madness is impossible, whereas Habermas wants to show, against Foucault, that freedom's separation from power is necessary. Regardless of the viability and success of these two very interesting critical projects, my point here is just that both of these philosophers oppose Foucault by reading him through a logic that he himself could not have accepted. Derrida thinks Foucault's view is that the modern exclusion (of madness by reason) has already taken place. Habermas thinks Foucault's view is that modern exclusion (of power from freedom) was an impossible dream. But Foucault did not construe modernity in terms of the Weberian logic of exclusion. Derrida and Habermas may share enough common ground to be at odds with one another, but Foucault evades these interminable debates by redrawing the terrain on which the issues are located.[19]

Foucault thought it hopeless to think that we moderns should try to either liberate freedom from power (as Habermas would have it) or to locate madness within reason (as Derrida would).[20] For Foucault, both of these positions are rooted in a failure to perceive the problematization of our modernity. Madness and reason, like freedom and power, presuppose one another in modernity. They are, in Foucault's memorable phrase, "reciprocal and incompatible."

The Revised Foucault: Modernity's Reciprocal Incompatibles

Near the end of *History of Madness,* Foucault offers a striking characterization of the thesis of that book: "Man and madman . . . are joined by the impalpable link of a reciprocal and incompatible truth."[21] Throughout the book, Foucault invokes this idea in a number of ways, in describing a "movement of reciprocal reference," a "mutual process of redemption," and in analyzing the mutuality of "forms of liberation" and "structures of protection" that he provocatively calls "a double movement of liberation and enslavement."[22]

I find the idea of reciprocal incompatibility crucially useful for understanding the logic of the problematization of modernity diagnosed by Foucault. What this formulation suggests is an understanding of reason and madness or power and

freedom not on the model of exclusion, but on the model of what I will call purification or reciprocal incompatibility. Exclusion seeks to eliminate by means of
separation; purification seeks to preserve by means of separation. Exclusion is
the logic of war, where the enemy must be eliminated. Purification is the logic of
a modernity in which reason must preserve madness as its other, in which clinical medicine must isolate health from illness while at the same time requiring the
preservation of illness as the abnormal other against which normal health can
be recognized, and in which punishment must preserve criminality rather than
eliminate it in order to justify the continued need for the entire punitive apparatus. The proper response to exclusion would be that classic ideal of liberation from
domination or exile. The proper response to purification would be what Foucault variously called experimentation or transgression, or what he finally came to
write about in terms of self-transformation. Foucault has been read by critics and
disciples alike as sketching a modernity bent on exclusion, oppression, and domination to which liberation is the only possible (but hardly efficacious) response.
But Foucault is better read as sketching a modernity bent on purification, to which
transformation is the most effective reply.

Foucault's point is that the relations between pairs like madness and reason
or power and freedom constitute the very problematic of modernity itself. What
Foucault's historical problematizations demonstrate is that these relations are an
intractable problem for moderns such that they are constitutive of the modern
condition as such. To complain that Foucault failed to fully liberate either side of
these oppositional terms from the total repression of the other, then, is to miss the
point almost entirely. Foucault's point was that these terms are reciprocal but incompatible: they can neither be fully liberated from one another nor totally assimilated to one another. Reason or power could never fully dominate madness
or freedom—and at the very same time, these terms could never be fully detached
from one another. Assuming either a rational freedom purified of mad power or
a rational power at root identical with a mad freedom is precisely what would be
the most difficult thing for we moderns to do.

This can be clarified by focusing attention on what was for Foucault a crucial point: categories like madness and reason are not universal and invariant.[23]
Foucault did not theorize madness, reason, freedom, and power as totalizing con-
stants. Rather, he was concerned to describe the precise historical shapes assumed
in their specific, and variable, instantiations. Foucault described various powers,
but not power itself; he traced the shape of modern rationalities, but not the structure of universal reason itself; freedoms and madnesses, not Freedom, not Madness. As such, Foucault could not have been interested in liberating invariant ex-

periences of madness or freedom from their repression by unwavering rationality or power. What Foucault always insisted upon, rather, was that our problem today consists in bringing these reciprocal yet incompatible aspects of modernity into more explicit tension with one another. What he insisted upon with various key concepts such as transgression, experimentation, aesthetics of existence, bodies and pleasures, and self-creation was a form of critical practice in which we manifestly assumed the intertwinement of our power and our freedom as a basis for elaborating ourselves and our relations to one another. To expand upon the revised interpretation of Foucault, let me return again to *History of Madness* and *Discipline and Punish*.

I first want to note an underlying continuity of concern that explains my focus on these two books in particular (rather than, say, *The Will to Know* and *The Birth of the Clinic*). Both are centrally structured around related conceptualizations of the problematization of the modern subject. This continuity has recently been made manifest to the English audience with the translation of the full version of *History of Madness*. In the now fully translated Part III of that book, we find Foucault broaching many of the themes that would later be at the heart of *Discipline and Punish*. At one point he writes: "Surveillance and Judgement: a new type of personage was coming into being. . . . Something was born here, which was not repression but authority."[24] This is Foucault not in the middle 1970s but in the early 1960s. This line (there are many others) underscores the continuity of his career-long concern to develop a critical problematization of our modernity. With that, I turn to these two texts in sequence.

The Reciprocal Incompatibility of Madness and Reason

The reception of Foucault's *History of Madness* is a checkered affair. John Rajchman notes one troubling aspect of this reception: "[m]any had found in [Foucault's] early work a kind of romanticism about madness."[25] Rajchman and others, including Clare O'Farrell, have attempted to correct this perception by revisiting the passages at the end of *History of Madness* in order to propose an alternative interpretation. In this revised view, these passages witness not a celebration of a repressed madness that artists like Nietzsche or Goya could liberate, but rather the idea that, as O'Farrell puts it, "[t]he work of art can only resemble or produce an *effect* of madness, it is not the language of madness itself."[26] It is not that Nietzsche is for Foucault a forgotten madman, but rather that Nietzsche is capable of reinvigorating a forgotten dialogue between madness and reason. Foucault laments not Nietzsche the excluded madman, but the fact that Nietzsche, like any other modern, can no longer be "at the limits of reason and unreason" since that border limit is precisely what modern purification rejects.[27]

For Foucault, madness is not banished or excluded by reason—rather, madness and reason are simultaneously produced as incapable of interaction. Foucault's text does not witness reason's subjugation of madness so much as a more insidious purification of reason from madness. Foucault had indeed spoken of madness at one point in terms of "inaccessible primitive purity," but as Ian Hacking shows, this theme seems to have been later regarded as a mistake, or at least as a nonessential element for the central argument of the book.[28] For the central argument is not that some primitive reality of madness is held down by a subjugating reason, but rather that madness and reason in their modern form are simultaneously produced as incoherent with one another. Foucault is in fact quite clear on this point: "In the Renaissance, madness was present everywhere and mingled with every experience by its images or its dangers. During the classical period, it was also on view, but on the other side of bars . . . In comparison to the incessant dialogue between reason and madness that had marked the Renaissance, classical confinement had been a silencing."[29] Foucault thus notes that his study of madness and rationality aims to "go back toward the decision that simultaneously links and separates reason and madness; it must aim to uncover the perpetual exchange, the obscure common root, the original confrontation that gives meaning to the unity, as well as to the opposition, of sense and non-sense."[30] The aim, in other words, is to restore that broken interaction where madness and reason could converse.

That broken interaction is what Foucault's puzzling discussions of *déraison* (unreason) in the book are a reference to. Unreason is that lost space in which madness and reason would, or at least could, interact. One of the thresholds of modernity is the loss of that space. Hacking asserts that "The whole book is about the play back and forth between madness and unreason."[31] I agree, understanding this to mean the book is about the formation of the reciprocal incompatibility between reason and madness such that unreason is unmoored from where it once was and floats adrift in a modernity that would give it no home. When Foucault describes his book in the preface to its original 1961 publication as "the archaeology of that silence," he is describing his project as an excavation of the emergence of a hollow space of soundlessness where once there had been an effusive chatter of unreason.[32]

There is no question that *History of Madness* remains deeply ambiguous regarding the status of madness in modern culture. In the earlier chapters on the Classical Age, Foucault seems to be describing reason's separation from madness in the interests of exclusion such that he often seems to be just the kind of quasi-romantic emancipator of madness that most critics have taken him to be—here madness indeed appears to be an inaccessible primitive purity. But in later chapters on the Modern Age proper, Foucault inches page by page toward a description of reason's separation from madness as in the interests of a ritual purification of rationality that would not exclude madness but rather keep it separate as the necessary other of reason.[33] While the book on the whole provides ample evidence for both interpretations, it is worth taking seriously the periodization implicit in Foucault's argument. For if Foucault sees modernity as beginning with a blatant exclusion of madness by reason that later gave way to a subtler purification of madness and reason, then the upshot of his history would seem to be a claim for the purifying logic as a basic problem facing our historical present. Consider also the resonance of the periodization implicit in *Discipline and Punish* that shifts from the scene of blatant exclusion in the form of sovereignty's splendorous torture rituals to the subtle purification in the form of the new uptake of crime within disciplinary punishment. We can apply this later periodization to *History of Madness* and recognize that, after making heavy weather of "exclusion" in Chapter Two, Foucault explicitly insists throughout Chapter Three that "What is at stake here is not a negative gesture of exclusion, but of a whole ensemble of operations that slowly gave shape over a century and a half to a realm of experience where madness would recognize itself. . . . For confinement did not simply play the negative role of exclusion, but also had a positive organizing role. Its practices and regulations constituted a domain of experience that had unity, coherence, and function."[34] The overplayed theme of repressive exclusion names a reality, to be sure, but it is one that should be referred rather to the lens of productive purification. This, to reiterate, is exactly the argument Foucault would later make in *Discipline and Punish* and *The Will to Know:* disciplinary power and biopolitical power are more apt concepts than sovereign power for our quintessentially modern uses of power.

The artists and thinkers that Foucault invokes in the final pages of *History of Madness* should, accordingly, not be modeled as repressed geniuses liberating themselves from the chains of social constriction. Rather we should read Foucault's references to Van Gogh, Artaud, Nerval, Hölderlin, and Nietzsche on the model of unreason's attempt to open again that "incessant dialogue" between reason and madness. This is clarified in Foucault's discussion of Diderot's strange little book, *Rameau's Nephew,* in an often-unnoticed (in part because not included in the abridged English translation of *Madness and Civilization*) short section introducing Part III of *History of Madness.*[35] The important point for present purposes is that Rameau is figured by Foucault as one of the last specimens of the extinct spe-cies of unreason: "The last character in whom madness and unreason are united, Rameau's Nephew is also where the moment of separation is prefigured."[36] At the end of this short introductory section, Foucault laments that "For us, confronting unreason in all its doubtable unity has become impossible."[37] Rameau's Nephew is a better model than the Romantic image of the liberated genius for the thinkers of unreason Foucault invokes at the end of the text. This is a model, moreover, of the purification of reason and madness that would silence unreason without ex-cluding or banishing anything at all.

That Foucault in *History of Madness* was already on his way to a conception of modernity in terms of purification is confirmed in his next major statement on madness and reason, the 1963 essay "A Preface to Transgression." The Nietz-schean concept of transgression elaborated in this essay makes sense only against the background of an understanding of modernity as enacting the purification of reason and madness. Transgression, in other words, cannot be made sense of on the model of the exclusion of a subjugated madness by a sovereign reason. In this essay, Foucault invokes an exemplar for transgression in what he calls "the pos-sibility of the mad philosopher."[38] He is thinking of Nietzsche here, who is named throughout the rest of the essay, even though the piece is ostensibly devoted to Bataille. This is confirmed by the earlier appearance of the same term in *History of Madness* where Foucault had written of "the Nietzschean possibility of the mad philosopher."[39] Foucault's further musings on the mad philosopher nicely clarify his earlier claims from *History of Madness* insofar as a mad philosopher would be one who would seek to restore the broken dialogue between reason and madness, between the light of clarity and the frenzy of confusion, between what Nietzsche had thematized in *The Birth of Tragedy* under the headings Apollo and Dionysus. Nietzsche there wrote that "the intricate relation of the Apollonian and the Dio-nysian in tragedy may really be symbolized by a fraternal union of the two dei-ties: Dionysus speaks the language of Apollo; and Apollo, finally the language of Dionysus and so the highest goal of tragedy and of all art is attained."[40] Fou-cault's hero, following Nietzsche's insistence here and elsewhere on "reciprocal dependence," would be at once mad and philosophical, thereby transgressing the limit between reason and madness that forms a core problem of our modernity.[41] Such transgression, in any event, could make sense for Foucault only if he under-stood modernity in terms of a purification of reason and madness whereby a di-vide or limit was instituted between the two so as to preserve each in its purified form. Transgression would make no sense in a world of contradiction and exclu-sion according to which reason opposes madness. In that case, madness would be essentially foreign to modern culture itself. But Foucault does not mourn a banished madman so much as a rarely noticed silencing of the narrow border between reason and unreason in which all the mad philosophers raise their trembling voices.

The Reciprocal Incompatibility of Discipline and Liberation

There is an important symmetry between Foucault's earlier work on modern reason and his later work on modern power. In the earlier work Foucault had attempted to show that madness is neither subject to, nor can it be liberated from, reason. In later work he should be read as offering very much the same point about the relation between freedom and power. In some ways our modern ideal of freedom as liberation harbors all the same promises as does our ideal of an untamed madness. Foucault's point in his work on power and freedom was that positive transformation is to be sought elsewhere than in liberation, emancipation, autonomy, and other prevailing conceptions of freedom in modernity.[42] Foucault expressed frequent misgivings about modern freedom practices construed in these terms. But he did not thereby throw into doubt the very concept of freedom itself. His point, as I see it, was just that we too often assume forms of freedom that are anything but freeing in the contexts in which they are deployed.

Foucault's central point in *Discipline and Punish* was not that we are trapped in power, nor that we should be pessimistic about freedom, nor that modernity was a prison or any other kind of bad thing. Foucault, rather, sought to carefully elaborate the difficulty we moderns face in our task of simultaneously negotiating freedom and power. The complex idea Foucault was striving to articulate and that so many of his critics have misunderstood was that freedom and power can be neither dissociated nor assimilated. They must be deployed simultaneously so that we can work within the internal tensions of their relationships. But in purifying freedom and power, we moderns have too often understood our problematization to be either that of maintaining a rigorous separation of these two (the promodern attitude of Habermas) or that of showing them to have been unified all along (Derrida's anti-modern polemic). In contrast to these perspectives, Foucault explored complex series of interstitial relations between freedom and power.

This remains a point that Foucault's critics have found it enormously difficult to grasp. Béatrice Han-Pile, for example, ends her study of Foucault with the disappointing observation that Foucault is "very ambivalent" on the question of freedom insofar as he found himself over the course of his life "more and more torn between two irreconcilable extremes." She explicates these "two interpretations

of subjectivation" as follows: "On the one hand, the subject appears as autonomous, as the source of the problematizations of what he is and as a free actor in
the practices through which he transforms himself. On the other, he is shown by
the genealogical analyses to be inserted into a set of relations of power and practices that are subjecting to various degrees, and that define the very conditions of
possibility for the constitution of self." The upshot of the difference between these
two views is, says Han-Pile, a "fundamental ambivalence" in which it is "very difficult to say if, for [Foucault], the subject is constrained or constituted."[43] How remarkable to accuse Foucault of the very point he sought to establish. Foucault's
point was just that it is enormously difficult for us moderns to say whether we
are constraining or constituting ourselves. If this were easy, then things would
look very different than they do—the problems we now understand ourselves to
be facing would have vanished into the rarefied air of an antiquity. Critics such
as Han-Pile are effectively complaining that Foucault leaves us staring into the
vacuum of the very ambivalence on which he so patiently sought to focus our attention. But it is not Foucault who is ambivalent—it is the problematic of our modernity itself that is torn between two seemingly irreconcilable tendencies.

Foucault's claim is that modernity produces emancipatory freedom and disciplinary power as two reciprocal but incompatible aspects of our existence. Foucault's model is not one of the exclusion of opposites, but of the purification of
reciprocal incompatibles. Modern power-knowledge is described in *Discipline and
Punish* as functioning "according to a double mode; that of binary division and
branding . . . ; and that of coercive assignment, of differential distribution." Foucault situates his work in the book as tracing "[t]he constant division between
the normal and the abnormal."[44] The regime of discipline does not exclude the
criminal, the mad, and the free romantic, but rather preserves them by dividing
them off from the legal, the sane, and the docile. In his Collège de France course
lectures he was giving at the time *Discipline and Punish* was published, Foucault
explicitly described the changing face of power in the modern age as the passage
"from a technology of power that drives out, excludes, banishes, marginalizes,
and represses, to a fundamentally positive power that fashions, observes, knows,
and multiplies itself on the basis of its own effects."[45] Foucault's contrast here is
between division by way of repressive exclusion and division by way of purifying production. The formerly excluded 'other' is now included within the reach
of an assertive power that preserves the "abnormal" as the ever-present inverse of
the "normal." Foucault's point, put in general terms, is that freedom and power
now stand in a relationship of reciprocal incompatibility in which they both imply
one another and oppose one another such that neither is capable of overturning

the other. Foucault's point is thus that modern conceptions of freedom as liberation and modern conceptions of power as disciplinary are tied up with one another such that transforming one requires transforming the other. We think that
power operates on the sovereign model, so we practice freedom in terms of liberation. But in fact power more frequently operates on a more disciplinary model,
and where it does we lack the concepts and practices of freedom that might effectively resist these forms of power. Lacking such practices of freedom, we ineffec-
tively deploy liberation against discipline, as if the problems of discipline involve
being excluded and subjugated by a sovereign.

Foucault recognized this general relation of the reciprocal incompatibility
of modern power and freedom as functioning in a rather wide variety of contexts. In some instances he argued that autonomous individuality is one of the
intended effects of disciplinary power, rather than a predisciplinary capacity for
freedom that might seek its revenge on power.[46] In other work he held that "opposing the individual and his interests" to disciplinary power is to be avoided because modern "political rationality" effects "both individualization and totalization," such that a defensible form of freedom "can come only from attacking not
just one of these two effects but political rationality's very roots."[47] The more general point was most fully developed in the context of Foucault's genealogies of disciplinary power and liberationist freedom. A central thesis of *Discipline and Punish*
was that freedom as liberation and power as discipline both require one another
and require their separation from one another. Discipline can neither banish nor
incorporate liberation, because power must preserve freedom as its purified other,
at least for the moderns. Liberation for Foucault is therefore not a mere illusive effect of discipline, but is something real that discipline, in doing its work, both pu-
rifies itself of and preserves.

Foucault forcefully states in *Discipline and Punish* that "The 'Enlightenment,'
which discovered the liberties, also invented the disciplines."[48] This discovery, this
invention: they were forged in the same crucible. The precise relay between liberation and discipline instantiates Foucault's more general point about modern
forms of freedom and power: complex practices of autonomy-freedom-liberation
and complex practices of discipline-security-biopower emerge in tandem as effectively purified of one another.

Understanding Foucault's problematization of modern hybrids of power and
freedom in terms of a logic of purification brings the advantage of helping us recognize that his late work on ethics never sought to rehabilitate a liberating form of
freedom as a site of resistance to an increasingly irresistible disciplinary complex of
power and knowledge. To long for emancipatory practices of freedom as a counter

to repressive powers would be to entirely miss the crux of the problems we face, as Foucault saw things. The problems we now face, according to Foucault's elaboration, is that there is infrequently a pure freedom to be emancipated just as there is infrequently a pure power to dominate it. Modernity produces emancipatory freedom and disciplinary power as two reciprocal but incompatible aspects of our political existence. It is not that modern power eliminates freedom, just as it is not that modern rationality eliminates madness. It is rather that power and freedom are simultaneously produced so as to render emancipatory freedom ineffective against disciplinary power. And yet freedom in modernity is often understood in romantic terms of total autonomy opposed to the total dependency induced by the utilitarian efficiency of disciplinary power. But, it is Foucault's point, just as madness finds itself in no position to question reason in the modern age, freedom on the modern model of liberation finds itself hardly equipped to oppose power on the model of discipline. The problem is not that discipline is bad, but rather that we have little idea what to do when discipline is put to bad uses.

Foucault therefore held that freedom must be sought elsewhere than in the romantic ideal of freedom as autonomy with its paradigmatic association with events of liberation and emancipation. This point is important because it enables us to recognize that Foucault was indeed a friend of freedom even if he was not impressed by the familiar modern ideals of freedom. The crucial thing about those ideals is that they offer an image of freedom purified from power. But in actual fact liberationist freedom and disciplinary power constantly invoke one another in their operation. So Foucault's point was that we must learn to understand how freedom works through, not merely against, power. This means trading in the model of freedom as liberation for a more transformational model of freedom. David Hoy notes this point well in his discussion of Foucault's work on freedom as resistance: "Resistance is never simply to constraint in general, because one is always constrained by something or other. There is no originary freedom with absolutely no constraints."[49] Just as Foucault's concept of transgression would seek to restore a broken dialogue between madness and rationality, his concept of transformative resistance envisions a multiplicity of interactions between freedom and power. Transformative freedom envisions a practice in which freedom and power are no longer purified of one another and is thus a vision of a practice that, strictly speaking, is neither disciplinarian nor liberationist. As such, it requires neither the metaphysical voluntarism nor the metaphysical determinism that so many of Foucault's early critics have imputed to him.

Of all of those working in the wake of Foucault, none have developed these points as fully as Judith Butler. Butler situates her own work within the trajectory of Foucault's cautions about our ready embrace of liberatory models of freedom: "I follow Foucault to a certain degree here in wondering whether *liberation* as a term promises us a radical freedom from constraint that in the end is impossible and that will just redeliver us to new constraints and plunge us into forms of political cynicism."[50] While other critics have complained for more than two decades now that Foucault leaves us staring into a vacuum, namely the hollow vacuum of our ambiguous selves, Butler helps us see how Foucault's project is to fix our attention on our own dangerous ambivalences about freedom and power or agency and structure. It was not Foucault's project to resolve those ambivalences, but rather to clarify the extent to which they constitute problematizations in which we moderns find ourselves always situated. Butler, following Foucault, writes, "My purpose is neither to enumerate nor to resolve the contemporary instances of this debate [over subjection and subjectivity]. Rather, I propose to take account of how a paradox recurrently structures the debate, leading it almost always to culminate in displays of ambivalence."[51] Through this procedure Butler is able to effectively deploy the Foucaultian theme of the reciprocal incompatibility that holds between heteronormative strategies of discipline and biopower on the one hand and dreams of liberation and autonomy on the other. In this vein Butler offers a most helpful description of Foucault's practice of critique: "To be critical of an authority that poses as absolute requires a critical practice that has self-transformation at its core."[52] In a discussion of practices of resistance in one of his course lectures, Foucault offered a formulation that offers much credit to Butler's interpretation and usage of his work: "there is no first or final point of resistance to political power other than in the relationship one has to oneself."[53] So, as Butler puts it, to enact freedom in the context of heteronormativity requires a "critical subversion" not already co-opted by the lie of "liberation" complicit with heteronormative regulation itself.[54]

Does all this not suggest that Foucault really was an anti-modern insofar as he was dubious about the cherished modern models of freedom as liberation, emancipation, and autonomy? On the contrary, Foucault explicitly defended modern models of freedom, only not those models given over to the romantic dream of liberation and therefore also to its corollary model of disciplinary, biopolitical, and controlling power. It was never Foucault's point that we need regard modernity as a trap—his more modest point was simply that modern practices of an autonomous freedom totally liberated from power is but a corollary of modern practices of disciplinary power. Far from being anti-modern, as his accusers have claimed, the notion of freedom elaborated in Foucault's final work indeed resonates remarkably well with many quintessential modern freedom movements. It does not, of course, resonate with those paradigmatic freedom movements instantiated in glorious dreams of liberation, emancipation, and revolution. But there are nonetheless many modern practices of freedom that it does capture. Think not of rebels, but of silent inventors and steady experimentalists. In considering Foucaultian freedom in relation to sexuality, for example, do not think of the howl of a sexed body breaking free of its cages but rather of the whisper of a silent sexuality experimenting on itself with others. Think not of what is open and out in The Castro but rather of what goes down over on Folsom Street (where Foucault himself spent a good amount of his time in the San Francisco scene). Think not of the glory of the revolution rising up against the powers that dominate but rather of the steady resolve of those who reform themselves by living the "lives of infamous men."[55] Freedom, we may find, is most transformative when it is humble and hesitant, exploratory and experimental. Freedom, perhaps, is not always as obvious as we would have wanted. Experimental freedom perhaps does not make for good cinema on the blockbuster model. But it does make, and may make further, for good practices of freedom.

My point can be clarified with a distinction between freedom as a doctrinal right to private autonomy at the heart of liberation practices and freedom as a critical-experimental practice of self-transformation. It was only with a great effort that Foucault was able to arrive at this distinction: for it is one that is lost on most moderns. And indeed it must be admitted that even in much of Foucault's own late work, this distinction remains implicit at best and confused at worst. But there are a few instances where the distinction I want to emphasize rises up to the very surface of Foucault's thought; for example, at the very end of a lecture he gave at Berkeley in April 1983: "The problem, then, is not to liberate, is not to free, the self, but to consider how it could be possible to elaborate new types, new kinds of relationship to ourselves."[56] Or in an interview given in January 1984: "I have always been somewhat suspicious of the notion of liberation . . . I emphasize practices of freedom over processes of liberation . . . This ethical problem of the definition of practices of freedom, it seems to me, is much more important than the repetitive affirmation that sexuality or desire must be liberated."[57] What this distinction helps us realize is that Foucault did not find a positive conception of freedom in the idea of autonomy working against power to liberate itself, but rather in the idea of transformative freedom working through power to re-create itself. Freedom in Foucault's favored sense of self-transformation can and must work at those crucial interstices where modern liberationist freedom and modern disciplinary power interlock, interleave, and interdigitate.

Problematizations and Responses: Politics and Ethics in Foucault

Equipped with this distinction between liberationist freedom and transformative freedom, I am now prepared to add crucial detail to the interpretation I have been offering of the overall trajectory of the last ten years or so of Foucault's work. This will enable me to offer a fuller answer to some of the important interpretive questions I left hanging at the end of the previous chapter. Foucault's genealogies of modern culture increasingly came to emphasize the point that disciplinary power and emancipatory freedom were reciprocally but incompatibly implicated in the same modern practices, apparatuses, and problematizations. In considering this entwinement of liberation and discipline, Foucault often appeared unenthusiastic about freedom. But once Foucault finally got clear on this problem, he was able to turn his attention to offering a response to it. It was at this point that Foucault, rather unsurprisingly, began offering more positive conceptions of freedom. In this later work where Foucault finally begins to explore the value of freedom, it is not the freedom of autonomy, liberation, and emancipation that he holds in high esteem but the freedom of transformation, experimentation, and resistance. In reviewing Foucault's work during those years when he was actually developing this shift in modality from genealogical analyses of power and freedom to ethical responses in the form of experimental transformation, namely in his work in the years between 1977 and 1981, one easily recognizes a deep ambiguity insofar as at times Foucault is clearly unexcited about freedom and yet at other times clearly in favor of it.[58]

Persisting puzzlement over this ambiguity can be dissipated if we regard Foucault as in these years working out a delicate distinction between liberationist freedom and transformative freedom.[59] We can and should acknowledge that there are real difficulties in Foucault's work on the relationship between power and freedom in the period between about 1977 and about 1981. This is because Foucault in these years was in the process of working out a distinction between self-liberation and self-transformation—thus he was not already deploying a distinction of this sort in any straightforwardly clear fashion. When we find Foucault writing about freedom in these years, he is indeed often ambiguous. And there is no easy way for us to resolve these ambiguities. But what we can do is realize that in the years before this transitional period Foucault most often wrote of freedom in the sense of liberation with a cautioning tone, while in the years after this transitional period he tended more often to write in a positive tone about freedom in the sense of transformative resistance and experimentation. In the years

in between, we have access not to Foucault's decisive claims for or against freedom, but to thought in motion as he attempts to work out a way of distinguishing
what is fecund in freedom as self-transformation from what is bound to be disappointing in freedom as self-liberation.

This story about the development of Foucault's thinking on freedom could
be enriched a great deal by situating it biographically in the context of Foucault's
own philosophical life in Paris, Berkeley, and elsewhere in the late 1970s and
early 1980s. It is beyond my intention to undertake this biographical portrait here,
but a few preliminary observations might be helpful, drawn mostly from the work
of others.[60] The sort of story I would like to tell might enable us to see that Foucault's writings about the dangers of disciplinary power and liberationist freedom
can be understood in part as a function of his own personal frustrations within
the Parisian intellectual atmosphere. Paris in the 1970s was not perhaps the utopian world that many today dream about. It was not, at least, such a utopia for
Foucault. The visions of May 1968 were increasingly failing to fructify such that
it became a real worry that the widespread liberationist rhetoric of earlier years
had perhaps been misguided. Add to this an increasing frustration that Foucault
must have felt about the heteronormative hegemony of French sexual life. And
though Foucault himself was seemingly at the apex of French intellectual life at
the Collège de France, the wider environment of that intellectual milieu could
very easily have been felt as oppressive. As Foucault's fame rose, he was increasingly misunderstood, and increasingly criticized, and castigated (we intellectuals
all know how much we love to call each other names: we harbor in safety some of
the most sophisticated playground bullies the world has ever known). Then there
was also the concrete working conditions of the French library system, consoli-
dated in the single state institution of the Bibliothèque nationale de France, where
books were not available on the shelf for browsing (let alone available for digital
access from the café across the street) but could be read only upon request and
at the discretion and mood of the bureaucracy of reference librarians and pages.
Anyone who has spent time in an archive under the gaze of suspicious librarians
knows the chilling disciplinary effect of such working conditions (though I do not
intend to suggest here that all archival librarians I have worked with have shown
suspicion). What a drag it must have been to finish a history of discipline only to
find oneself working away at the heart of institutions that all too perfectly pose
discipline in their every maneuver. Perhaps it was in response to this that Foucault began searching for different venues and contexts for his research. This included, for instance, his seemingly inconsequential act of switching research libraries to the Bibliothèque du Saulchoir, run not by the French government but

by the Dominican order. Also meaningful may have been the momentous life changes involved in Foucault's increasingly frequent visits to California. Here he collaborated more closely with colleagues and graduate students in Berkeley than seemed possible in Paris at that time. He also seemed to enjoy the available pleasures yielded by transformative practices of sexual experimentation in San Francisco. Here Foucault was incited to begin thinking about how to live differently, how to take care of oneself otherwise, and how to practice the philosophical life without the constant accomplice of the problematic tendencies of discipline and liberation. Foucault's late work on ethics can perhaps be seen as consonant with his attempts to re-create himself amidst the fresh conditions he found in his new life. But until such a time as this sort of biographical picture can be filled in by more capable research than I am presently able to carry out, the story I am telling about the development of Foucault's thought between 1977 and 1981 must be defended on textual rather than biographical grounds. So let me turn now to that.

One obvious place to look for textual evidence for or against my interpretation is in Foucault's course lectures from this period. Consider for instance his discussion of "counter-conduct" in the 1978 course lectures, published now as *Security, Territory, Population*. Foucault there introduces "counter-conduct" as a name for something that he calls "resistance, refusal, or revolt."[61] His usage of these terms in other writings makes it amply clear that Foucault is at the very least interested in the positive potential of counter-conduct. Furthermore, he also refers here to ascetic practices in a way that directly anticipates his later work on an ethics of freedom. This counter-conduct is a form of freedom "in the sense of a struggle against the processes implemented for conducting others."[62] This counter-conduct is thus a potential form of transformative freedom. While everything he needed to develop a conception of freedom as transformation was here present, it is also quite clear that Foucault had not yet arrived at an adequate response to what he took to be his problem. Indeed it seems as if at times he does not yet have the problem in full view. But we can in this text at least glimpse the beginning of a response.

Foucault would turn in his next year's 1979 course lectures, published as *The Birth of Biopolitics*, toward an analysis of the neoliberal forms of governance developed by the German Ordo-liberals and American Chicago School economists of the Post-War period. Foucault in these lectures brings his prior problematizations of modernity up to the present: here we witness Foucault sorting through the political rationality of twentieth-century neoliberalism as manifested in policies implemented even right up through the early seventies. Foucault describes himself as charting the emergence of a newer problematization of power that is gradually transforming and modifying the problematization of discipline-and-liberation charted in Foucault's earlier work. Contrary to the worries of many and the interpretations of a few, Foucault does not here advocate neoliberalism as something like a preferable alternative to discipline, biopolitics, security, and all the rest so much as he excavates neoliberalism as a continuation of these earlier strategies on the basis of a reproblematization. Foucault explicitly describes liberalism as taking place in a milieu in which "the development, dramatic rise, and dissemination throughout society of these famous disciplinary techniques for taking charge of the behavior of individuals day by day and in its fine detail is exactly contemporaneous with the age of liberties."[63] Just as clearly as he is insisting upon a further development in neoliberalism that presses us beyond discipline and liberation, he is also just as clearly insisting on a connection between neoliberalism and what we tend to call liberalism, or what he had earlier called "the disciplines" and "the liberties." After charting in this way the further elaboration of this crucial modern problematization in the lectures of the early months of 1979, Foucault went on in subsequent years to more fully develop the notion of counterconduct and the non-emancipatory freedoms he had only briefly ventured into in 1978. This soon led him into a long and detailed exploration of ancient forms of freedom as self-transformation. He would, unfortunately, not live to finish that exploration.

Whereas the standard modern conception of freedom as liberation is reciprocally incompatible with disciplinary power, Foucault's conception of freedom as self-transformation offers resistance to, and revision of, both disciplinary power and emancipatory freedom. Distinguishing these two conceptions of freedom helps clarify a crucial point of Foucault's work. Difficult as it may seem, and it was precisely Foucault's point that it would be difficult, resistance to modern practices of power requires resistance to modern practices of freedom. A resistance to the twain of power and freedom suggests an integral connection between the two such that the transformation of either requires the transformation of both. Experimentally freeing ourselves of any particular powers circulating through us necessarily involves freeing ourselves of the freedoms through which we enable that circulation. But what form might such an experimental transformation of discipline-plus-liberation take?

Before answering this question in the next chapter, I want to first clarify the terms on which Foucault himself sought to pose the question. To do so I shall return to some of the central points I made in previous chapters concerning the method of critique as problematization.

Recall first that for Foucault a problematization is constituted at the intersection of a multiplicity of vectors of practices. In urging that a response to the modern problematization of freedom and power requires a transformation of both liberatory freedom and disciplinary power, Foucault is urging that we must reconstruct ourselves in light of the entirety of our problematization. It will not do to intensify our commitment to just one of these vectors. A genealogical perspective enables us to see how such an intensification only feeds additional energy back into the broader problematization of which it is a part. While discipline and liberation may appear opposed when we are caught up within them, it was Foucault's point that they are constitutive of the same problematization, so any apparent opposition experienced within our practices only betrays a deeper complicity at the level of the problematizations that form the conditions of possibility of those practices. Reconstructing our self-disciplining and self-liberating tendencies requires not that we oppose one of these tendencies (the good one) to the other (the bad one), but rather that we take up different relations to those aspects of ourselves through which we realize and perform our discipline and liberation.

Recall next that for Foucault a problematization is constituted through concrete practices in which more general tendencies get inscribed, leveraged, and amplified. The reconstruction and re-performance of ourselves that Foucault anticipated must therefore be articulated in terms of the specific practices through which we instantiate discipline and liberation. This helps explain why Foucault was always so diligent in his detailed inventories of the practical vectors through which we have formed ourselves. His ethnologies of modernity revealed specific sites, institutions, objects, subjects, and ideas that we must learn to reconstruct if we aim to transform ourselves. Any attempt to rework modern tendencies toward discipline and liberation must confront localized practices that function as vectors through which the broader problematization of discipline-and-liberation is instantiated. But at the same time it must be respected that these are but singular vectors through which that broader problematization is intensified. Confronting this problematization through these vectors thus requires reworking elements found within those vectors with an eye toward the broader problematization of which they are a part.

The interpretation of Foucault I am offering ultimately enables us to recognize a far greater continuity between Foucault's work on power and ethics than some critics have acknowledged.[64] My view is that the later work on ethics is best understood as a direct response to the earlier work on politics—it is an attempt to explore an alternative form of freedom to that conception of liberatory freedom complicit in the deadlock of disciplinary power. It would have made little sense for Foucault's late work on ethical practices of freedom to have aimed at an elaboration of modern practices of freedom as liberation since his middle work on power had highlighted this as part of the very problem of modernity. Foucault in his late work did not abandon his earlier theses about modern power in order to elaborate a theory of modern freedom that these theses had explicitly invalidated. Contrary to this critical misinterpretation, the middle work on power can be seen as providing the problematic context to which the late work on ethical freedom is offered as a response. Foucault's late work thus elaborates practices of freedom that respond to the deep problems set by our reciprocal but incompatible practices of modern disciplinary power and modern liberatory freedom.[65]

Understanding Foucault's late ethics as a responsive engagement with his middle work on forms of power-knowledge is facilitated by recognizing that Foucault was asking a very different kind of question than we are used to: What if our most dangerous problems are not those painfully obvious forms of subjection of which we are all quite aware, but rather those muddled forms of purification and reciprocal incompatibility that are so difficult to recognize in ourselves? If Foucault was working with a different interpretation of practices of modernity along such lines, then his famous doubts about certain modern forms of freedom make a great deal of sense. For if modernity presents us with the dangerous problem of reciprocal incompatibility, then liberation is a less helpful practice for responding to this danger than the ethical work of self-transformation. Foucault's work is distinctive in part because it offers a distinctive problematization of modernity that has been too readily dismissed by those who are eager to draw up the basic problems of our modernity through quite different diagnostic procedures. In many ways, Foucault's point was directed precisely against the overplayed Weberian theme of modernity as an age of exclusion for which a prison cage is our most apt metaphor.

Foucault countered this cliché by laboring to problematize our modernity such that we might work to reconstruct it. His late work on ethical self-transformation is a contribution to that reconstruction. Even if that reconstructive contribution remains underdeveloped, as I shall argue toward the end of the next chapter, this suffices to show that Foucault's project of a problematization of modernity is at a minimum compatible with the project of a reconstruction of modernity, including for instance such projects as initiated in other philosophical traditions whose representatives have for too long now taken Foucault as an opponent, most importantly for my purposes critical theory and pragmatism. Critics such as Habermas and Rorty have needlessly dismissed Foucault in large part because they have read him as proffering an especially dark version of Weberian modernization theory. Of course Foucault will appear normatively deficient if his diagnosis of modernity is cast in such terms. My claim in this chapter has been that this assessment is rooted in a mistaken interpretation of Foucault's narrative of modernity. Foucault offers a rich alternative to the Weberianisms that have dominated too much of critical theory and much of pragmatism too. This alternative diagnosis of our modernity is much more amenable to the reconstructive efforts of Habermasian critical theorists and Deweyan pragmatists than has typically been supposed. Foucault's diagnostic problematization of modernity can serve as a basis upon which we can more effectively deploy the reconstructive analytics at the center of critical theory and pragmatism. My proposal, then, is for a delegation of work—from Foucault we take a diagnostic problematization of modernity and only a very limited portion of his uncompleted reconstructive ethics, whereas from Habermas, Honneth, Rorty, and Dewey we take a set of reconstructive analytics in order to redeploy them on a quite different problematization of modernity that they themselves have given short shrift. Before sketching the terms of this combination-via-delegation in the final chapter, I need to first show in the next chapter why and where Foucault's reconstructive response to his problematization of modernity is in certain respects incomplete and thus in need of resources furnished by critical theory and pragmatism. This will put us in a position to see both that Foucault offers a better way of problematizing our modernity than do the critical theorists and pragmatists and that these other traditions inversely offer a better way of reconstructing our modern problematics than does Foucault.

6

Foucault's Reconstruction of Modern Moralities

An Ethics of Self-Transformation

Foucault's Responsive Ethics

In the later years of his foreshortened life, Foucault began to elaborate a conception of ethics that might have functioned as a serious alternative to the behemoth moral systems that have thoroughly dominated the ethical practices of our modernity. Foucault in this work was doing nothing less than challenging the past few centuries of modern moral philosophy and the dominant forms of moral practice that philosophy has aimed to systematize and sustain. As I have described Foucault's problematizations of modernity in *Discipline and Punish* and *History of Madness*, a core tension constitutive of our practices of modernity involves the problematization of the purification of power and freedom. It is from our perspective within this problematization that we find it incredibly difficult to determine if our actions are exercises of self-constraint (the exercise of power) or of self-constitution (the exercise of freedom). It is in response to this problematization that Foucault sought to elaborate the possibility for alternative ethical practices in which power and freedom would no longer be parceled out—for example, in their familiar forms of discipline and liberation—but would rather be integrated as a simultaneous practice of the co-transformation of powers and freedoms. In a summary account of his 1981 Collège de France lecture course titled "Subjectivity and Truth," Foucault offered this striking description of his future research plans: "The history of the 'care' and the 'techniques' of the self would thus be a way of doing the history of subjectivity; no longer, however, through the divisions between the mad and the non-mad, the sick and the non-sick, the delinquents and the non-delinquents . . . but, rather, through the putting in place, and transformations in our culture, of 'relations with oneself.'"[1] In the face of purification and against it, Foucault sought to elaborate an alternative ethics of the transformation of ourselves.

Foucault rejected the suggestion that an easy solution could be found here and that any easy determinations are to be had here. What he claimed was that the reciprocal incompatibility of discipline and liberation, despite its difficulty, is our task and our problem. Foucault's ethics, accordingly, is best read as a kind of prognostic response to the problems featured in his earlier diagnoses of the constitutive tensions of modernity. If Foucault's earlier works traced the formation of the modern moral subject, then his later works outlined possibilities for the self-transformation of that selfsame subject.

Though this way of reading Foucault's late works is nonstandard, it is also not without warrant. Near the end of Chapter 4 I cited two of Foucault's closest interlocutors, namely Gilles Deleuze and Georges Canguilhem, with claims to this effect.[2] Further recent scholarship has seen a growing chorus of voices now supporting this underappreciated interpretation of Foucault's ethical inquiries. John Rajchman writes, "The Foucauldian history of ethics is a history not of principles and their mode of legitimation, but of ways of replying to specific or individual problems."[3] Edward McGushin describes Foucault's late work in similar terms as a "response to a modern problematic of power and knowledge." McGushin distinguishes two "moments" in Foucault's work: "a diagnostic moment and an *etho-poetic* moment."[4] Adopting this terminology, we can say that the Foucaultian diagnostic with which I have thus far been concerned should be seen as preparing the ground for the Foucaultian etho-poetic in which is elaborated a response to the difficult problematizations of discipline and biopower rigorously diagnosed in earlier work. Most helpful for my purposes is a label proposed by Erinn Gilson, in discussion of both Foucault and Deleuze, of an "ethic of problem and response" or a "responsive ethics."[5]

In describing Foucault's ethics as responding to his earlier diagnostic problematizations, my claim is that his ethical work is not a principled conception of what *must* be right in a given situation but rather a melioristic conception of *how* to respond to the specific problematic situation in which we find ourselves. Ethics for Foucault was neither a systematic project nor an attempt to develop rules for moral judgment, but rather a form of practice for responding to the problematizations we find ourselves facing. This underscores, once again, that the logic of thought and practice for Foucault proceeds through the categories of the problematic and the responsive, rather than through such categories as position and negation.

It is worth being clear that bringing the responsive dimension of forms of ethical practice into focus need not involve denying that ethical work can also be focused along other dimensions. At least one other dimension traversed in Foucault's own late ethical writings is the diagnostic dimension, which for Foucault involves an archaeological-genealogical problematization of the conditions of modern subjectivity. In his course lectures in the early 1980s, Foucault further developed the genealogies of modernity central to his work in the mid-1970s by reaching back further in time well before the advent of moral modernity as we know it. In so doing, Foucault historically inquired into some of the oldest strands constituting the formation of our modern selves. One formulation of the sequence charted in this work is ethical in focus and moves from ancient self-care through self-knowledge and self-decipherment down to modern self-surveillance and finally self-discipline.[6] Another formulation of the sequence is more political in focus and involves what Foucault once described as a "genealogy of what could be called political discourse" that travels from the public orator and counselor in antiquity to the pastoral minister of early modernity to critical discourse in the Enlightenment and then to the more recent emergence of the figure of the revolutionary.[7]

Foucault's late writings thus make manifest both dimensions of critical inquiry I take to be at the heart of immanent social critique: that of the genealogical problematization of the present and that of the reconstructive response to this problematization. There is no contradiction in a philosopher working in both of these dimensions at once (though there is the evident danger of exhaustion in fighting on two fronts at once, and it is an indication of Foucault's remarkable intellectual virtue that he was able to do so). We can read Foucault's final writings as both problematizing our modernity and as proposing ways in which we might transform ourselves on the basis of this problematization. Unfortunately, the majority of Foucault's readers deny the coherence of this compossibility. To take just one example of this common refrain, Charles Scott has argued that Foucault was exclusively concerned with problematization: "our impulse to make ourselves better by applying the values of the discourse, our hope of improving the world by reading Foucault are the kinds of motivations that his work makes questionable."[8]

I propose a different way of cutting up the differences. I have argued in previous chapters that Foucault is an excellent guide to critical inquiry in the modality of problematization. I shall argue in this chapter that Foucault also provides us with some resources for critical inquiry in the modality of ethical response or moral reconstruction, although he does not give us everything we should require for such a project. To the extent that we can discern deficits in Foucault's responsive ethics, we can also hold that there is in Foucault's problematizational methodology no principled reason underlying these deficits and certainly no basis of opposition to a more complete ethics. The lacunae in Foucault's reconstructive moments are not an effect of his having harbored illegitimate crypto-normative ambitions or irrational anti-normative aspirations. Perhaps there is a much less grand explanation: maybe Foucault responded to his remarkably fecund problematizations with the labor of reconstructive thought and yet was not himself able to completely develop his responsive ethics. Would it really be all that surprising should it turn out that Foucault did not do everything we should want from philosophy and yet did not for that reason do nothing important for philosophy?

To bring the responsive or reconstructive dimension of Foucault's late ethical writings into proper focus, it will be useful to begin with a second discussion of Foucault's genealogical problematizations of modernity insofar as these can be read as specifically diagnosing modern morality. In the next section I delineate the particularly moral implications of Foucault's problematization of our modern reciprocally incompatible forms of power and freedom. Much of this work had already crystallized in Foucault's writings in the 1970s such that we can discern a problematization of modern morality in texts like *Discipline and Punish* and *The Will to Know*. Foucault's subsequent turn to ethics following the publication of these two volumes can be seen as a natural response to these earlier works. This later work is an explicit, albeit unfinished, attempt to develop an orientation through which we might effectively respond to the problems of modern morality brought into focused by the previous work.

Foucault on Two Modern Moral Systems

Discipline and Punish and *The Will to Know* are both explicitly addressed to our modern projects of power and knowledge. They are also about our modern projects in ethics. They serve well as remarkable genealogies of our most captivating visions of systems of modern morality. Foucault himself saw fit to describe *Discipline and Punish* as "a genealogy of modern morals" on the back cover of the book.[9]

The crux of modern ethical practice, as Foucault described it, was an attempt to disentangle, or more precisely to purify, power and freedom from one another.

Our modern ethics is problematized around attempts to establish this purifying relation. Consonant with this problematization, we moderns find ourselves choosing amongst various moral systems that embody this strict purification of power and freedom. Modern moralities thus tend to be expressions of either a disciplinary form of power purified of a strong sense of freedom or of a liberationist conception of freedom purified of a sense of the importance of power. The upshot of the system of modern morality as Foucault traced it in his work on modern power is that we find ourselves in a position where we can appeal to only one of two options: either to the strict utilitarian rationality of disciplinary efficiency (think Benthamite bureaucracy) or to an uncompromising ideal of liberatory freedom (think Kantian autonomy).

Foucault was, I think, clear that both of these options ought to be seen as dangerous, fraught, and problematic. Even if, as I have pointed out, Foucault did not take discipline to be necessarily a bad thing, he was quite rightly concerned about the tremendous dangers of disciplinary power, especially when exercised in disregard for its corollary forms of freedom. Perhaps less frequently noticed by many readers, yet certainly no less emphasized in Foucault's writings, were the dangers of a liberationist conception of freedom exercised in complete disregard for the powers circulating through it. Foucault made it clear that we should not draw from the lesson of the debilitating effects of discipline that we ought to liberate ourselves from some repressive power. Neither discipline disarticulated from freedom nor liberation opposed to power will do. Indeed, what is most problematic about modern morality is the diremption implicit in our reciprocally incompatible conceptions of power and freedom.

I would like to offer now a way of characterizing these two quintessentially modern moral options that helps bring into view some of their more debilitating aspects. Perhaps this characterization carries the cost of smoothing out some of the more fascinating subtleties of these two moral options. But we can always bring these back in later. I shall offer the labels of "fascist" and "freespirit" morality as summary headings for the two alternative moral systems generated by the modern purification of disciplinary power and emancipatory freedom. Foucault helps us see not that every moral agent in modernity has been either a fascist or a freespirit, but rather that the overwhelming tendency for us moderns has been to gravitate toward these two ways of constituting ourselves. We might think of fascist morality and freespirit morality as two ends of a spectrum at which power and freedom are fully disentangled from one another according to the great modern ideal of purification. It is perhaps rare for any of us to achieve, either alone or together, the zero degree of moral activity located at either pole. But the important point is that we so often spend so much of our lives trying to accomplish exactly this. We unceasingly strive to disarticulate our actions undertaken in freedom from the pernicious distortions of power and to disconnect our efficient deployment of power from the undisciplined dangers of absolute freedom.

The ideal of fascist morality is at the heart of the grandiose vision of the perfect disciplinarian. It is a morality of total vigilance and unbroken surveillance. It is a morality of austere control. Its paradigmatic realization in Foucault's writings is the utilitarian diagram of Jeremy Bentham's panopticonical socius. The design is not the historical fascism of Hitler and Mussolini, but the more quotidian fascism that all of us, even the most blessed, carry around inside of ourselves. The ideal of fascist morality was interrogated by Foucault in his preface to Deleuze and Guattari's *Anti-Oedipus* where Foucault offered their book the alternative title of *Introduction to the Non-Fascist Life*. He wrote there of "the fascism in us all, in our heads and in our everyday behavior, the fascism that causes us to love power, to desire the very thing that dominates and exploits us." Foucault's point was that the fascist moral system is so exceedingly quotidian that we can barely discern it in ourselves. It is the morality of the accountant and the quality engineer, the timecard and the human-resources file, the watchtower and the multiple-choice test. It is the morality of the terrible impositions inflicted by the clueless bureaucrat rehearsing the code in the face of our utter disbelief. It is the morality of the self that dreams of an absolute mastery, a dream that is entirely banal and yet in its central impulse is continuous with the totalizing fantasies of the historical fascisms that wrought havoc the world over in the middle of the twentieth century. Foucault provokes the dawning realization that the cold heart of the bureaucrat, the dossier, and the fascist is inside of us all. We should note well, then, that he enigmatically says of Deleuze and Guattari's work that this is "the first book of ethics to be written in France in quite a long time." He explains that the central ethical problem of the book, and so presumably also the central ethical problem of his own work, concerns the attempt to rid ourselves of the fascism that we use against ourselves, "the tracking down of all varieties of fascism."[10]

The ideal of freespirit morality is a perhaps enticing alternative to the control-freak morality of the fascist. The freespirit lets go of control, runs free of routine, takes leave of bureaucracy, and thereby proposes to escape all imposition. One might take Foucault's occasional positive references to experimentation with drugs and sex as embodying a freespirit morality. But that is not quite right. For Foucault was wary of "our present culture of the self" or what he once called "the

Californian cult of the self" in which "one is supposed to discover one's true self, to separate it from that which might obscure or alienate it, to decipher its truth."[11] This is obviously a caricature, but one gets the idea. Consider as an image for this morality Woody Allen's portrayal of the cheapness of the California cult in his film *Annie Hall*. Recall the scene of the Hollywood party set in some big South-lands mansion. The first thing we witness is a conversation between a small group of ultra-tan mid-executives who are trying to arrange a meeting ("all the good meetings are taken," one laments, but without even a shade of irony). The last thing we witness is a man on the phone in the hallway asking his guru for more and more spiritual advice ("I forgot my mantra," he pleads, but without even a trace of shame). These self-addicted Californians. Everything, including their skin, is baked into a luscious golden glow. Everything, including their selves, can be ordered through the phone, or now online, for a nominal charge. Woody Allen's character sarcastically whines about it all to his girlfriend, played by Diane Keaton, "And gradually you get old and die—you know it's important to make a little effort once in a while." Allen is offering a wisecrack, indeed a sophisticated one, against that morality of the liberated pure soul disentangled from all the little nooses of power. Nobody tries. Nobody is bothered. Nobody doubts or worries. Nobody feels any shame. Such empty dreams of liberated selfhood, Foucault argued, are all too intoxicating. In seeking to liberate ourselves, we lose a sense of who ourselves have been and, in so doing, we play ourselves right back into the very powers from which we thought we were being freed.

We puritanical moralists and poetic romantics. Who has not felt the pull of both of these moralities? Who is not, at some times even if not all the time, captivated by their allure? We each carry within us the grandiose plans of the fascist and the halcyon dreams of the freespirit. The energies of so much of our lives is compressed and compacted into the narrowed channels of these two morality systems: by day we discipline ourselves to work as hard as we can with maximal efficiency so that we may yet pull up to whatever misty dream is above us, and by night we indulge to enormous excess in whatever desires we can yet wrestle out of our otherwise languid souls. This critique is not meant as a denunciation of a culture we ought to detest, but rather as a problematization of a culture in which we are all implicated. To use myself as an example that may be familiar to some readers, I know all too well the enormous gravitational attraction of these two moralities: trained in all the rigorous disciplinary efficiency of the professionalized academy and yet also compelled by the shadowed streets of contemporary urban allure with its vague promise of an excessive sublimity. It is in response to the problematization that enables these moralities, in other words to all the dangers and tensions implicit in our modern moral problematization, that Foucault turned to less familiar ethical practices in hopes of elaborating an alternative.

Distinguishing Orientations and Commitments in Ethics

Foucault's final work should be interpreted as an attempt to develop a set of tools that would enable us to respond to this problematization of the modern dilemma of the alternative between fascist and freespirit moralities. Having problematized the ethical options available to moderns in such a way as to provoke the work of elaborating alternative forms of ethical living, Foucault went on to embark on the difficult labor of beginning to elaborate such alternatives himself. The turn to ancient Greek and Roman ethics, the amplified interest in a Kantian critical practice, and other characteristic aspects of Foucault's late work are best seen in this light of responsiveness. Foucault's ethical response specifically focuses on the imbrication of powers and freedoms as an alternative to the purifying moral systems of the disciplinarian fascist and the liberated freespirit. What was this alternative? How did it work? What does it look like?

We can do the best justice to Foucault's project, and also to our ethical selves today, if we approach his final writings in terms of a distinction not made available in those writings but that helps make sense of a good deal of them. We can distinguish between the *orientations* (or structural background, or formal conditions) in an ethics and the particular normative *commitments* (or contents, theses, positions, strategies, techniques, equipment, rules, and concepts) offered by an ethics. Ethical orientations help us recognize the conditions of possibility of ethical response in the present. Ethical commitments specify the conditioned practical matters of an ethics thus oriented.

My view is that the real value of philosophical work on ethics consists not in pronouncing verdicts (the claim of commitment) but in clarifying and conceptualizing extant possibilities for ethical living in the present (the work of orientation). We philosophers are in a better position to develop normative orientations than normative commitments or contents. Ethical commitments are perhaps not something that we should expect philosophers to prescribe but are rather something we should be expected to develop for ourselves in practice. Indeed, it is only within the specificity of actual practices that commitments come to have much of a value at all. Commitments as such are often tightly bound to the contexts in which they do their work. Orientations, by contrast, are usable across a remarkable variety of contexts. Orientations burst out of the specificity of the contexts of their deployment and attain a generality of normative authority across context.

To apply this distinction to Foucault's ethics, I shall be arguing that we can learn a great deal from the orientation of self-transformation that Foucault elaborated but that the positive commitments (to, e.g., bodies and pleasures, an aesthetics of existence, the philosophical way of life, parrhesia, etc.) he developed in the context of his transformatively oriented ethical work leave a little too much to be desired. Many have found Foucault wanting in his writings on ethics—and the story of the reticent reception of his ethics is now well known. My response to these lukewarm, indeed sometimes downright chilly, critics is to point out that their target has often been the normative commitments featured in Foucault's works. Their criticisms thus hit their mark, but only because they are aiming at the wrong target. They miss the best point of Foucault's final writings. The critics can be forgiven for focusing their attention on Foucault's commitments just insofar as many of his most ardent defenders have been the most vociferous to encourage such interpretations. The shift of interpretive weight I am proposing is thus a response not only to Foucault's harshest critics but also to some of his most devoted champions. Almost everyone has had their sights trained on Foucault's ethical commitments. This, I am urging, is the key meta-ethical mistake in understanding Foucault's ethics. We need to shift attention from commitment to orientation. I follow Paul Bové, who, in response to prominent critics of Foucault's ethics, diagnoses as an error "the reduction of Foucault's text, of his style and writing to 'position.'"[12] Bové's fine advice is to not look into Foucault to discern a set of normative judgments, but rather to look there to begin the practice of developing different modalities.

The crux of my approach is to load the normative weight of Foucault's work not on the content of specific ethical commitments featured in his work, but rather on the broader ethical orientation by virtue of which these specific contents gain any normative force they might possess. Thus it follows that, on my view, the specific normative commitments featured in Foucault's work are usable only so long as we can productively orient these contents as transformative practices that enable us to generate real normative validity. One happy consequence of this shift in interpretive load is that it opens up the possibility of richer continuities between Foucault's ethical orientation and the ethical orientations of other philosophers to whom Foucault is too often seen as opposed, namely philosophers in the traditions of critical theory and pragmatism. Affirming these sorts of continuities in turn enables us to shore up ethical resources for our own practices of critical inquiry where Foucault fails to supply everything we should want even if he does do much to point us down the directions in which other more normatively rich traditions have been traveling.

Foucault's Self-Transformative Ethical Orientation

I have been urging that Foucault's ethics is best seen as a responsive attempt to elaborate alternatives to modern moral systems within the genealogical frame of our modern moral problematization. A general way of stating this point is to say that the central theme that links nearly all of Foucault's diverse attempts to elaborate such an ethical response is that of ethics as a self-transformative process. This theme distinguishes Foucault's ethics from concepts of morality drawn up in terms of decisive adjudication. Foucault offered a number of ways of self-reflectively characterizing his ethical work. Many of these characterizations can be helpfully understood through my distinction between adjudication and transformation.

Perhaps the most prominent instance of this distinction in Foucault is found in his contrast between moral codes and ethical practices from the methodological "Introduction" to the second volume of *The History of Sexuality* project.[13] Moral codes are oriented toward the law-like adjudication of moral disputes, while ethical practices are oriented toward the transformative reconstruction of an ethically charged situation. Foucault used this distinction to elaborate an alternative to contemporary modes of ethical practice that are almost obsessive about the rules and codes guiding moral living. Anyone conversant with twentieth-century moral philosophy knows that the field is practically dominated by rather narrow debates between adherents of supposedly opposed utilitarian and deontological moral codes. These are debates over what Bernard Williams diagnosed as the peculiarities of our modern "morality system."[14] In recent years, an alternative approach has emerged within a strain of moral philosophy rooted in ancient practices of virtue ethics where codes often take a back seat to practices, techniques, strategies, and other elusive elements of phronesis. Foucault much preferred this alternate approach to the exclusive focus on the morality system. His distinction between ethical practices and moral codes helps motivate that alternative.

Another poignant expression of Foucault's conception of ethics as transformative rather than adjudicative is offered in one of his late lectures from 1983: "[O]ne does not have to take up a position or role towards oneself as that of a judge pronouncing a verdict. One can comport oneself towards oneself in the role of a technician, of a craftsman, of an artist, who from time to time stops working, examines what he is doing, reminds himself of the rules of his art, and compares these rules with what he has achieved thus far."[15] The distinction here is between judges who legislate over practices and engaged ethical practitioners who reflectively orient themselves to the process of transforming their ethical living.

Most of Foucault's sustained contributions to his project of refashioning ethics as transformative are to be found in his writings from the final year or two of his life. We can, however, locate evidence in prior pieces suggesting that Foucault began drifting in the direction of a transformative ethics even earlier. One instance is an articulation of this distinction in terms of differing conceptions of the Kantian project of critique from 1980: "In sum, it is a question of searching for another kind of critical philosophy. It would not be a critical philosophy that seeks to determine the conditions and the limits of our possible knowledge of the object, but a critical philosophy that seeks the conditions and the indefinite possibilities of transforming the subject, of transforming ourselves."[16] Another earlier elaboration of a self-transformative ethics was developed by Foucault in a short homage piece from 1979 in which he compares philosophy with journalism. It is clear in this piece that Foucault has not yet fully worked out the distinction between emancipatory and transformative freedom that I emphasized in the last chapter. Yet it is at the same time also clear that he has already begun thinking seriously about an ethics of transition insofar as he takes the occasion to praise the book that he is reviewing as a "treatise on movable thought." Foucault is glad to note that the book tracks "the imperceptible moments of modification" that are our best alternative at present to impossible revolutions and liberations. It is clear that Foucault himself would like to, as he says, "dive into that general mobility."[17] Foucault has, in this relatively early piece, already begun to reconceptualize ethics not as a compendium of commitments but rather as an orientation of modification, experimentation, and transformation of the self by and through the self.

Allow me the pleasure of just one more quotation from Foucault that can helpfully be read through this distinction between transformation and adjudication: "I can't help but dream about a kind of criticism that would try not to judge but to bring an oeuvre, a book, a sentence, an idea to life; it would light fires, watch the grass grow, listen to the wind, and catch the sea foam in the breeze and scatter it. It would multiply not judgments but signs of existence. . . . It would bear the lightning of possible storms."[18] Be not a judge, but rather something else, perhaps a poet.

In these various versions of the distinction between transformative and adjudicatory ethical orientations, we can discern a crucial break from the project of the modern morality system. Unlike much of modern moral thought, Foucault's late work does not revive a stable moralizing subject whose inner reality can be hermeneutically deciphered. This is why he does not in his late writings revive the very subject that he had previously problematized, as many of Foucault's critics have claimed was his impossible project. Rather, Foucault was attempting to elaborate a conception of the subject as a practice, site, and agent of self-transformation.

Some of Foucault's best commentators have captured well the crux of this idea. Frédéric Gros writes that for Foucault, "the subject is understood as transformable, modifiable." The central question that the transformable subject asks of itself, Gros suggests, is not "Who am I?" but rather "What am I making of my life?" This latter question "opens between the self and itself the distance, not of a secret, but of the unfinished work of life we must accomplish."[19] John Rajchman refers to Foucault's ethics as a "critical philosophy of freedom" and describes it as follows: "For Foucault, freedom was thus not a *state* one achieves, once and for all, but a condition of an 'undefined work' of thought, action, and self-invention . . . Freedom always remains still to be done, and we are never done with it."[20] James Faubion rather concisely and precisely names Foucault's work "an analytics of ethical change."[21] And Lynn Huffer suggests, in terms I obviously find very congenial, that "We might go so far as to call transformation the basic ethical principle in Foucault."[22] The point offered by all of these commentators, who indeed constitute minor voices in a major critical chorus that would have us believe that Foucault thought quite differently of ethics, is that the subject of ethics was for Foucault neither a substance nor a transcendental ego but rather a reflexive practice of transformation simultaneously working on its own exercises of power and freedom.

This interpretive nexus suggests a theme central to Foucault's conception of ethics, namely that of reflexive process, or self-change, or self-transformation. This involves the subject taking itself as an object of work. Practices of self-transformation thus take place at a hinge between which we are both subject and object. We find ourselves made as an object of work at the same time that we find ourselves capable as a subject reworking that object.

Self-transformative activity is the guiding orientation for the positive conception of freedom that Foucault began to work out in his final writings. Freedom, in this sense, is the conceptual center of Foucault's ethics. "Freedom is the ontological condition of ethics," Foucault once said in an interview.[23] Freedom, for Foucault, must remain undefined, in the sense that it must be something we work out for ourselves in practice. Behind all of the forms of ethical commitment discussed by Foucault in his writings (e.g., the care of the self, the aesthetics of existence, the philosophical way of life, philosophical truth-telling) is an orientation of self-transformative freedom as a necessarily unspecified (that is, until enacted in practice) condition of possibility of any ethics whatsoever. It is precisely this that Foucault offered in response to the modern problematization of the purification of disciplinary power and liberationist autonomy (and their attendant fascist and freespiritist moralities). "Freedom," Foucault once said, "is a *practice* . . . The freedom of men is never assured by the institutions and laws that are intended to guarantee them. This is why almost all of these laws and institutions are quite capable of being turned around. Not because they are ambiguous, but simply because 'freedom' is what must be exercised."[24]

As I understand his work, the ethics of freedom that Foucault began to work on in his final years was one in which freedom is not a state or a capacity, but is rather a practice of a process. If freedom were a state or capacity, then we could of course aim to guarantee freedom under the rubric of either an outcome or an opportunity. But, insisted Foucault, there is no external guarantee of freedom: "The guarantee of freedom is freedom."[25] We may find it appropriate and legitimate to guarantee certain outcomes or opportunities, but we should not attempt to guarantee freedom as a practice of transformation. The very project of trying to guarantee freedom is what leads to the modern moralities that Foucault found so problematic. The control-freak morality of the fascist insists on the rigorous training of our capacities of freedom to achieve whatever disciplinary purposes are at hand. The fancy-footed morality of the freespirit insists on an originary capacity of freedom that absolutely must remain unchained and untrained. To conceptualize freedom as a state or capacity is to crystallize it into a particular static *form*. In so doing freedom is disconnected from crucial dynamics of *trans*formation.

I turn now to two more detailed descriptions of the theme of self-transformative freedom featured in Foucault's late ethical writings. I shall focus on the self-transformative orientation as developed in Foucault's discussion of ethical experimentation in his late reflections on modernity (in his "What is Enlightenment?" essay) and in his discussion of a distinction between spirituality and philosophy in ancient ethics (in course lectures from the early 1980s). These two rereadings will help prepare the way to a more detailed analytical explication of the idea of ethics as self-transformation at the end of this section.

Foucault's late essay "What is Enlightenment?" is one of the most important of his late reflections on an alternative ethics. Insofar as this essay takes its bearings from Kant and Baudelaire, I read it as an attempt to establish a positive relationship to our disciplinary (in the figure of Kant) and romantic (in the figure of Baudelaire) inheritance but without fully investing ourselves in the moral systems countenanced by this dual inheritance. Paul Rabinow offers a perceptive comment that I find crucial for understanding Foucault's aim in this essay: "unlike Kant, Foucault does not accept social and political conformity as the trade-off for freedom of thought; equally, he refuses Baudelaire's restriction of a modern ethos to the arena of art." Divesting himself of Kantian discipline and Baudelairean liberation, Foucault attempts to articulate through the generous remainder between the two an ethics of what I am calling "transformation" or what Rabinow calls "transfiguration" when he notes that for Foucault, "The point of seizing hold of the present is to transfigure it."[26] Recall that transfiguration is urged by Foucault as an ethical orientation rather than as a positive moral content. Foucault is not arguing that transformation is a moral good so much as he is suggesting that ethical improvement requires a certain transformative orientation to oneself. This reflexive orientation is a condition for moving ourselves beyond the freespiritisms and fascisms so characteristic of our moral living today.

Foucault goes on in his essay to positively elaborate the "philosophical ethos" that would form "a permanent critique of our historical era." Positively, this ethos possesses three characteristics. First, it is critique as "a limit-attitude" that "takes the form of a possible crossing-over." Second, it is critique as "historico-critical attitude" that "must also be an experimental one." Third, it is a form of critique that is capable of resisting co-optation insofar as it is pertinent, coherent, and systematic. Leaving to the side the third characteristic (which seems to me to be an advance response to potential criticisms of relativism), it is clear from the first two characteristics that the proposed philosophical ethos is one that is invested in practices of transformation. Foucault is clear that he is not interested in a critique that determines once and for all the limits of thought. This would be a conception of critique as a static and universal project. Foucault instead is interested in a critique that "crosses over" extant limits and experimentally "tests" them for their capacities for change. As he sums it up in that essay, he is interested in "at one and the same time the historical analysis of the limits imposed on us and an experiment with the possibility of going beyond them."[27] Criticism on this description sounds like a search for the conditions of transformation. This fits with how Foucault described his practice of critique elsewhere: "Criticism—understood as analysis of the historical conditions that bear on the creation of links to truth, to rules, and to the self—does not mark out impassable boundaries or describe closed systems; it brings to light transformable singularities."[28] The first moment of critical problematization for Foucault always points to a second moment of experimental practices of testing the limits of the transformable singularities constraining us.

These and others of Foucault's remarks on modern critical-ethical practice resonate with his research on the ethical practices of antiquity he was conducting at the same time. It is unfortunate that Foucault did not live long enough to fully draw the connections between his two later projects of studying ancient ethical practices and developing a uniquely modern ethics of transformative critique, though there is some evidence that he was expressly hoping to do so.[29] Despite the absence of a fully overt connection, we can certainly discern in much of Foucault's writing on the ancients an interest in the possibility of an ethical orientation of transformation in their practice.

This helps situate the second of the two texts I want to examine, in which is featured an interesting contrast between spiritual conversion and philosophical knowledge. The text is Foucault's 1982 Collège de France course lectures published under the title *The Hermeneutics of the Subject* (this title can be misleading, because the lectures are really an attempt to discern an alternative to the modern morality of hermeneutically deciphering the self). These lectures both refine some of the themes Foucault would later publish as the final two volumes of *The History of Sexuality* at the same time that they offer much looser discussions of the import of these ethics as a whole vis-à-vis the alternative ethical modes of Platonism, Christianity, Kantianism, and Benthamism to which Foucault explicitly offered his own ethics of self-transformation as an alternative. They are both more detailed and less exact.

In these lectures, Foucault establishes an important distinction between practices of spirituality characteristic of certain strains of ethics in antiquity and practices of philosophy more characteristic of modern thought. This distinction helps brings into special focus the transformative quality of his ethics. Foucault develops this contrast primarily through two ways of conceiving our relation to truth. Philosophy is "the form of thought that asks, not of course what is true and what is false, but what determines that there is and can be truth and falsehood and whether or not we can separate the true and the false." Spirituality is "the search, practice, and experience through which the subject carries out the necessary transformations on himself in order to have access to the truth."[30] Foucault explained in response to an interviewer's later query about these notions: "By spirituality I mean . . . the subject's attainment of a certain mode of being and the transformations that the subject must carry out on itself to attain this mode of being."[31] Whereas in the mode of philosophy, the truth is something that is given to the subject who knows, in the mode of spirituality, the truth is an achievement and is never something to which the subject simply has access by default. A crucial implication of this distinction is that the philosophical subject has a relation to truth that need not involve a transformation of the subject whereas the spiritual subject can achieve truth only through a profound conversion, modification, or transformation of the self.

The basic problem taken up by the ethics of spirituality, according to Foucault, is this: "What is the price I have to pay for access to the truth? . . . What then is the work I must carry out on myself, what fashioning of myself must I undertake, what modification of being must I carry out to be able to have access to the truth?" In contrast, for the ethics of philosophy (paradigmatically represented by Descartes in Foucault's discussion), "the subject as such became capable of truth. . . . The subject, then, does not have to transform himself. The subject only has to be what he is for him to have access in knowledge to the truth that is open to him through his own structure as subject."[32] Philosophy is an inquiry into the conditions of the possibility of the fact that the subject as such, the universal subject, has access to the truth (whether or not in fact any particular subject at hand does access the truth). Philosophy thus asks how it is possible that we have access to truth at all. Spirituality, by contrast, asks what we have to do to ourselves in order to achieve access to this truth. The crucial point of the distinction is between a subject who already has access to the truth by virtue of simply being a subject and a subject who can gain access to the truth only by way of self-transformation.

One interesting point in Foucault's discussion is his passing reference to a handful of modern figures he regards as attempting to revive the ethics of spiritual transformation lost amidst the modern morality system. Among these figures are Nietzsche, of course, but also Montaigne, Goethe's Faust, Schopenhauer, and Stirner.[33] We might presumably add to this list those equally compelling images of spiritual self-transformation drawn up by those Renaissance thinkers who, according to the work of Stephen Greenblatt favorably cited by Foucault in his later work, articulated an ethics of self-fashioning within which, in Greenblatt's words, "to abandon self-fashioning is to abandon the craving for freedom."[34] Despite the fact that we could easily multiply the range of references, Foucault is surely right to note that spiritual self-transformation and self-fashioning remain rather peripheral to our modernity on the whole: "We may have to suspect that we find it impossible today to constitute an ethic of the self, even though it may be an urgent, fundamental, and politically indispensable task, if it is true after all that there is no first or final point of resistance to political power other than in the relationship one has to oneself."[35] It remains to be seen, of course, if practices of spiritualistic self-transformation can be taken up today in a viable way under modern conditions far removed from the ancient world. Foucault's work on the modern critical practice of philosophy outlined in "What is Enlightenment?" and other essays of that period constitute his fullest attempt to sketch these possibilities.

I have been arguing that a conception of ethics as self-transformative practice is the core of Foucault's ethical response to our modern moral problematization. My discussion of this theme thus far has mostly been an effort in quotation, so allow me to tie it up by offering a summary analytical explication of the concept of self-transformation. There are two essential ideas in the concept of self-transformation as I am using it to make sense of Foucault's ethics. These are the ideas of ethics as transformative activity and of ethics as reflexive process.

First, the idea of transformativity suggests that ethics is primarily about process and modification. Rather than thinking about ethics in terms of moralities through which we can be in the right or produce the good, we should think in terms of the process of adjustments that are required to turn ethically deficient situations into ones that are righted or bettered. The crucial thing about ethics in this view is not the rule that shows us what would be moral, but rather the processes of modification through which we come to realize whatever moral values we endorse. In thus emphasizing ethics as transformation, Foucault in many ways approximates the pragmatist ethics of thinkers such as William James and John Dewey, for whom ethics takes shape as reconstructions that bring betterment, improvement, or growth. I will say more about this approximation in the next chapter and also there link the idea, albeit indirectly, to the normative philosophy of Jürgen Habermas.

Second, the idea of reflexivity central to a self-transformative ethical orientation helps bring into focus the object of modification or transformation on Foucault's ethics. Standard moral theories focus on acts as the object of ethical adjudication. Foucault's ethics departs from act-centered moral theory in that his view is not about telling others how to act or who to be—it is about gaining a view on ourselves in such a way that we can come to modify ourselves. Foucault encourages us to focus on reflexive relations as the object of critical inquiry in ethics. This is similar, but not identical, to the focus on character at the heart of ancient ethics (at least Aristotle's and Plato's) as well as some minority strains of modern ethics (such as Hume's). Foucault's focus on reflexivity is distinctive here in that reflexive relations need not be construed individualistically, as many have worried about Foucault's ethics. While character, at least on most accounts, happens at the individual level, Foucault supplies a reflexive ethics that could be deployed at the level of social groups, communities, and other publics. While some selves might be individualized monads, most selves are associated with other selves, and it is precisely in these associations that ethical problems arise. Foucault's point is that ethically deficient situations require a reflexive relation whereby ethical agents find ways of modifying themselves. This reflexivity at the heart of Foucault's orientation of self-transformation is one of his best contributions to contemporary ethics. Where I discuss the value of an ethical perspective rooted in pragmatist critical theory in the next chapter, it should be kept in mind that Foucault's reflexive ethical orientation supplies a key ingredient often missing from those traditions, even if those traditions do supply a necessary normativity that is often missing from Foucault's work.

I shall conclude my discussion of Foucault's self-transformative ethics with a few examples of how we might play up this ethical orientation today. To do so I will draw on a spate of recent books that I take to be among the very best contributions to contemporary Foucaultian ethics. I will briefly bring into focus four works that elaborate a Foucaultian ethics in senses that can be read in terms of an orientation of self-transformation. Three of these works are contributions to feminist theory, two are written by anthropologists, two by philosophers, and all four elaborate a self-transformative ethics in a vein that can be fairly described as empirical. These works are James Faubion's *An Anthropology of Ethics*, Cressida Heyes's *Self-Transformations*, Saba Mahmood's *Politics of Piety*, and Ladelle McWhorter's *Bodies and Pleasures*.[36]

What distinguishes these works is that they tend toward reportages on ethical experiments in self-transformation, thereby offering welcome contrasts to that majority of work tending toward explications-cum-justifications of ethical commitments mined from Foucault. One distinguishing feature of these works is that they are all situated, or can be described as situated, at the intersection of philosophical theory and anthropological inquiry. They proceed by way of fieldwork, case study, and practical immersion as much as by way of conceptualization and argumentation. Heyes, in a book that skillfully charts ways in which discourses of normalization and transformation inhabit contemporary gender structures, helpfully captures the importance of situated inquiry for the broadly transformative orientation I envision: "[C]ase studies are so important within the kind of Foucaultian method I am developing here because they each happen at just such a point of rupture, crisis, or contradiction, and illustrate the workings of corporeal normalization at a level where transformative agency through local interventions is both possible and imaginable."[37] Mahmood, in a book locating the significance of Islamic Revival practices for contemporary feminist movements, similarly states: "Any discussion of the issue of transformation must begin with an analysis of the specific practices of subjectivation that make the subjects of a particular social imaginary possible. In the context of the mosque movement, this means closely analyzing the scaffolding of practices . . . that provided the necessary conditions for both their subordination and their agency."[38] Faubion, in a book that that theoretically engages Foucault's ethics in its first half so that it may open up in its second half to empirical fieldwork on ethics, describes his approach as follows: "[A] broader effort to develop a diagnostics and a theoretical model capable of a clear-sighted approach to and an elucidation of the consequences of what I will call . . . ethical 'complexity.'"[39]

One point of emphasizing an ethical orientation of self-transformation is to suggest that ethics is an ongoing project we must take up with and for ourselves amidst the present in which we find ourselves. This is a point ably captured in the work of Heyes, Mahmood, and Faubion in their radically different contexts of gendered North American bodily practices (weight-watching and working out), gendered Egyptian religious practices (prayer and piety), and anthropological-historical fieldwork that crosses from Waco to Lisbon (from a millenarian to a marquis). All three remain largely ambivalent about the normative thrust of their inquiries into ethical self-transformation. Their work is largely descriptive, or diagnostic, rather than prescriptive, or responsive. Mahmood is particularly explicit on this front: "Our analytical explorations should not be reduced to the requirements of political judgment."[40] So too is Faubion: "[M]y project here is not 'normative' . . . I neither begin nor conclude with some collection of judgment and conduct."[41] Such normative avoidance is valuable just insofar as moral judgments on specific ethical contents and commitments often obfuscate matters. Mahmood ably describes how a logic that affirms or negates norms can be a hindrance in situations where it would be better to "explode the category of norms into its constituent elements" by means of detailed empirical inquiry and rigorous conceptual analysis.[42]

Nevertheless, it remains crucially important to gain a normative grip on our contemporary practices insofar as where we lack such a grip we easily lose sight of why any practice whatsoever would be worth preserving, extending, and deepening. To gain this kind of normative grip in a way that does not violate the sensitivity to context exemplified by Heyes, Mahmood, and Faubion we need to develop new ways of posing questions about whether our ethical contents and commitments are effectively oriented as ethical self-transformations. This suggests that we need rigorous inquiry into the ethical modes of subjectivation that make possible the practices inhabiting the present. And if this inquiry is not to be merely diagnostic, then we also need to fashion forms of inquiry that enable us to attend to ways in which certain subjects have formed means of ethically responding to the problematizations at the heart of modern morality systems.

The need for such situated inquiries in a vein that is not merely diagnostic but also responsive is ably developed in McWhorter's first book (notably, her second book, *Racism and Sexual Oppression in Anglo-America: A Genealogy,* is exemplary of Foucaultian genealogical diagnosis as I have been describing it).[43] McWhorter plainly states the centrality of transformation for Foucault's ethics: "Foucault's work operates to transform various politically charged sites. . . . Instead of asking what kind of political stands Foucault takes and whether he is justified in taking them, I'm interested in asking what kind of political effects Foucault's texts have."[44] Work such as this is most stimulating where it involves developing detailed ethical responses to problematic situations in ways that are clearly oriented by the idea of ethical self-transformation. McWhorter's book performs precisely this in describing and developing the author's experimental ethical responses to the grip of heteronormativity and all the peril therein. These ethical responses are elaborated in situational and contextual fashion. As such, McWhorter's work provides a valuable set of signposts for future cross-disciplinary deployments of Foucault's thought.

Despite the enormous potentiality featured in these four texts (and there are others), I shall argue in the next section that it is not clear how the normative commitments that Foucault dug out of antiquity can be made suitable for modern moral living insofar as they form a kind of reliquary of curiosities that to us moderns look very curious indeed but also curiously lacking in currency. That said, my hope is that the largely negative claims of the next section not be seen as diminishing the positive claims of the present section. My argument concerns where, and how, to locate the best insights of Foucault's ethics. In this section I have shown how, under the sign of a general self-transformative ethical orientation, we can begin the critical labor of situated inquiries facilitating and fostering situated responses to the ethical problems of our own present. How can we undertake specific inquiries into responsive practices of ethical self-transformation in the present? How can we further develop the modalities and methodologies requisite for undertaking such inquiries? An elaboration of positive commitments oriented by an ethics of self-transformation must be an ongoing project requiring sensitivity to the welter of historical conditions imposed on our ethical present. Projects looking to leverage the lessons of self-transformation should take the form not of definitive treatises but of ongoing series of essays in the old sense of that word: this could include collaborative practical experiments, cross-disciplinary theoretical engagements, anthropological and historical forays, and all the work required to connect such essays to pressing practical and theoretical problems.[45]

In venturing these essays, we would do well to orient our study of self-transformation vis-à-vis the prevailing modes of moral practice against which Foucault positioned the ethics of self-transformation. For example, in order to perform an inquiry into contemporary practices of self-transformation considered in relation to Foucault's criticisms of the modern ethics of disciplinary power and liberatory freedom, we must also inquire into the way powers and freedoms are related to one another within contemporary practices of self-transformation. Are power and freedom regarded as internally related to and in tension with one another in self-transformation? Or are they seen as incompatible yet reciprocal? If they are in a relation of internal tension with one another, what are the specific forms that power and freedom assume in the ethics of transformation? It may be that these crucial questions can be positively answered only by detailed inquiries into actual experimental practices of an ethics of self-transformation. If so, then there are a multiplicity of field sites and objects of study amenable to such inquiries and, as such, a great deal of good work for us to do. The challenges therein are excellent excitations.

Foucault's Ethical Commitments

The particular historical and philosophical space that Foucault's ethics of self-transformation opens up can and ought to be distinguished from the substantive ethical commitments with which he filled in this space. Foucault's meticulous descriptions of the forms of self-transformation characterizing Ancient Greek and Roman ethical life catalog the sprawling museums of antiquity's ethics. In reading through this catalog I am reminded of a makeshift statuary I once saw in the yard behind one of Rome's countless museums: a number of marble statues had been placed in the back corner of an untended lawn with no obvious concern for their arrangement. It was clear that they had just been left outside, perhaps for lack of room on the museum floor and in the storage cellar; there they were exposed to a hot sun beating down upon them as the tall grasses crept up around their pedestals and then their ankles. It was not that anyone had decided that these statues were worthless, but somewhere along the way it had become clear that they did not fit inside with the rest, and so here they sat out in the yard until somebody could come up with a better idea of how they might be used here or there in a pinch. Yet there always remained the possibility that an entirely different kind of problem would one day emerge within the museum such that the statues may never be brought inside again, left to linger out in the grasses long enough that one day they might become marbled gravestones for themselves, a stony white face lifting out of the bush as a sign of its own gradual burial. This, of course, is probably the very condition in which the statues had been "rediscovered."

Before explaining why I am less confident about commitments than orientations when considering Foucault's ethics, I wish to enter the caveat that the doubts I will be expressing in this section should not be taken as symptoms of a profound pessimism. My point is not that the commitments featured in Foucault's ethics are in principle confused. My much humbler claim is only that these commitments remain, for now, underdeveloped both in Foucault's own writings and in much of the philosophical work that has been undertaken in his wake. This is why we should emphasize instead the self-transformative orientation, at least until the substantive commitments can be given more normative purchase. And even though a small yet growing minority of commentators has focused on the importance of self-transformative freedom for Foucault's ethical work, such as those quoted in the previous section, it yet remains the case that some particular Foucaultian commitment always seems to emerge as more central in almost every account of his ethics: self-care, bodies and pleasures, the aesthetics of existence, fearless truth-speaking, and the philosophical way of life are just a few of the most familiar focal points.[46]

With respect to these (and other) commitments featured in Foucault's work, I do not deny that there are cases in which they have been exceptionally developed in the course of exemplary ethical lives. To substantiate this point I should lay out all my cards and mention that I have in the context of my own ethical self-formation attempted to make use of some of the more fecund ethical commitments featured in Foucault's work, including practices of self-care as oriented by a transformative reflexivity and the idea of replacing psychological structures of desire with embodied practices of pleasure. But on the whole I find that these anecdotal deployments (both my own and those of others) have yet to yield a viable alternative to the much broader political-cultural problematizations we find ourselves facing today. I readily affirm the benefits (again, both in my own case and those of others) on the level of personal ethical practices. But I am less optimistic than many others about the possibilities for generalizing these smaller-scale ethical-moral projects to the level of the larger-scale political-cultural projects where I think the question of the ongoing value of any ethics ought to be considered.

A powerful counter-response to my caution about Foucault's ethics emerges at this point. For one may want to resist my separation of micro-personal ethics

from macro-political ethics. Indeed part of Foucault's point in elaborating the difficulties of discipline and liberation was that these two are almost always inseparable such that the transformation of our polities, cultures, societies, and communities always begins with the transformation of ourselves.[47] This thought is crucial
to the self-transformative orientation that I take to be Foucault's central contribution to contemporary ethical thought. This orientation would seem to suggest
that the appropriate level on which we ought to assess any given ethical commitment would be the smaller-scale level of personal ethical practice. This response
to my caution is welcome, but what still needs to be shown is how any given
ethical commitment exampled in any personal ethical practice can be generalized
beyond that instance, or to put it differently, can effectively transcend the context in which it is developed. Accordingly, one of the most promising paths forward for future work on the various ethical commitments featured in Foucault's
work would be to develop routes for generalization of local successes that have
been achieved with Foucaultian commitments. My cautions here should thus be
read, above all, as provocations (meant not only for others, of course, but perhaps
above all for myself).[48]

What I aim to provoke, then, is a fuller response to a question about what
might be thought of as ethical reactivation. The literature on Foucault's ethics
today is dominated by a diversity of attempts to describe, develop, and defend
certain of the specific commitments and strategies forwarded in Foucault's late
writings. With respect to each of these, commentators too often overlook the perplexing issue of just how we are to reactivate any ancient ethical practices in the
context of modern moral situations. Foucault's ethics, we might say, remained unfinished. To frame my caution here, it will help to situate the ethical commitments
Foucault proffers in his late writings on the ancients in terms of more general
problems that continue to dog the broader twentieth-century revival of ancient
virtue ethics. One characteristic feature of late twentieth-century moral theory
across philosophical traditions was a turn away from modern moral systems of
judgment in favor of a renewal of ethics as rooted in ancient conceptions of virtue
and character. This suggests the possibility of rich connections between Foucault's
work and, for example, the contemporary analytic virtue ethics of Martha Nussbaum, Alasdair MacIntyre, and Bernard Williams, as well as other work motivated
by the earlier criticisms of modern moralities offered by Elizabeth Anscombe and
Phillipa Foot in the middle of the twentieth century.[49] Possible connections between Foucault's ethics and the work of the other scholars of ancient moral philosophy poignantly brings to the surface the issue of whether the particular ethical
commitments explicated and investigated by Foucault can be brought into attun-

ement with the modern moral order. This crucial question has still not been satis-factorily answered by these other contemporary classicists. It remains a source of enduring criticism of their proposals.

This exact question remains very much unanswered in the work of Foucault as well. In all of these thinkers it is quite unclear how we might reactivate ancient ethical practices in the context of modern moral situations characterized as they are by tightly woven social interdependencies, continuous bureaucratic regular-ization, increasingly precise divisions of labor, the mass distribution of informa-tion, the fever we all feel for equality today, and other characteristically modern features that the Greeks and Romans did not confront. Foucault seems to supply us with accounts of ancient ethical commitments, practices, strategies, and styles that were elaborated on the basis of a vastly different problematization than what we face in modernity. It is not clear how we might span the gap between those ancient ethical problematizations and our modern ethical problematizations—as such, it is not clear how practices elaborated on the one side of that gap might be at all useful on the other side. Powers, freedoms, knowledges, and ethics today travel along radically different vectors than those that sustained them in former millennia.

But, it might be replied, perhaps the concept of revival serves up the wrong metaphor for understanding recent work in ancient ethics. Perhaps those contem-porary thinkers in question are not trying to carry over the divide certain mate-rials from the ancients that might be useful for us today. Perhaps they are better understood as excavating some of the ethical possibilities lodged in our ethics of today but deposited there long ago by the ancients. In this thought I am prompted by Bernard Williams's genealogies of ancient ethics. Williams writes of his own work on antiquity that "It is not a question of *reviving* anything. . . . What is alive from the Greek world is already alive and is helping (often in hidden ways) to keep us alive."[50] The point of turning toward ancient ethics on this view is not to refuse modern ethics in the name of a forgotten ethical utopia, but rather to bet-ter understand what our modern ethics are made of and how they might be made even better. The aim is to better understand the conditions of possibility of ethical action in the present. Exploring ancient ethics, in conversation with modern eth-ics, helps us clarify ethical possibilities that are still alive in the present, even if they are sometimes hidden from plain view. Williams helpfully makes explicit here a central desideratum of genealogical research that too often remained only implicit in Foucault's histories of ancient ethics.

Perhaps Foucault too did not intend a revival of a golden age of Greek eth-ics so much as an explication of ancient ethical practices still potential within our present.[51] Yet we still might find this project normatively deficient in certain important respects.[52] What needs to be shown is how a fuller understanding of these ancient aspects of ourselves enables us to respond to our present moral problematizations with any serious normative claim such that we could begin to recognize any given response as better or worse than others. Foucault, along with Williams after him and Nietzsche before both, helps us see our ancient Greek possibilities, but this does not go all that far toward helping us see our way toward their actualization in the modern West. If the question of revival is dodged, then some other similar question about application or manifestation will need to take its place. Until such time as we clarify how it is that these practices can be disarticulated from some of the resolutely pre-modern features of their original enactment, and at the same time joined to at least some of the core features constitutive of our modern or contemporary practices, we will not be able to invite these practices into our ethical living in the fullest way possible. And a fullest possible ethics is exactly what we should expect of ourselves.

If the developments in Foucaultian ethics I hope to help provoke are to take place, then they are likely to do so as guided by an orientation of self-transformative freedom. The point of describing Foucaultian ethics in terms of self-transformative freedom is to emphasize the dynamic quality of Foucault's conception of freedom such that practices of freedom might be made to travel better. This dynamic freedom can be put in contrast to more static conceptions of freedom as a normative commitment. My emphasis on freedom's dynamic and transformative qualities is unfortunately missed in much of the recent revisionist scholarship on Foucaultian freedom, where Foucault is read as returning us to Enlightenment-style conceptions of freedom as a commitment to autonomy. My sense is that a Foucaultian ethics of autonomy would veer toward a commitment-centered rather than an orientation-focused approach. To make my case for the latter, it will thus be useful to consider the best contemporary account of Foucaultian freedom drawn up in terms of a commitment to capacities of autonomy. My argument, contra this account, is that freedom in Foucault should not be seen as a commitment invested with normative authority to which we can appeal as a rule, but rather as an orientation we assume in developing whatever normative commitments we might experimentally take on in the face of the problems that bear down upon us. This is why, as I have been arguing, freedom in Foucault should not be theorized in terms of autonomy but rather in terms of transformation.

The compelling contrast case for Foucaultian freedom as autonomy is offered by Amy Allen in her reinterpretation of Foucault as a kind of Kantian in *The Politics of Our Selves*.[53] The difference at issue here can be put as follows: I fail to see that Foucault theorizes freedom as autonomy in the sense that Allen would need in order to adequately reply to the standard charge that Foucault lacks normative resources. Allen suggests that we can realize a viable normative project in Foucault's work by recognizing that he affirmed a seamless connection between power and autonomy. The view is that power and autonomy are always interlaced in Foucault such that there is no question of power so thoroughly dominating us as to extinguish our autonomy. I agree that this is the right way to approach the question of the normative purchase of Foucault's thought, but I am not sure that the concept of autonomy that Allen ascribes to Foucault actually does the job. I think the job is better performed by a conception of freedom not as autonomy (which would function as a substantive normative commitment) but rather as self-transformation (which would function as a procedural normative orientation).

Before turning to criticisms of Allen's view, it is worth speculating about the motivation behind her conception of Foucaultian freedom so as to make explicit how those motivations differ from my own. Allen's project is motivated in large part, I suspect, by worries in contemporary political philosophy and feminist theory about agency and subjectivity. No one doubts that the subject became an object of severe criticism in twentieth-century philosophy. The subject was, almost everywhere, desubstantiated, deconstructed, and derided. After successfully developing these radical criticisms of the subject from the 1960s through the 1990s, political theorists and feminist philosophers alike began in the 1990s and 2000s to face up to the difficult question of how resistance to power could be possible without a subject of resistance. This question becomes particularly acute in the context of theoretical discourses in direct contact with political practice, such as in feminist theory. It is not surprising that political theorists accepting the radical critique of the subject would look to reinvest the historicized subject with substantive capacities of autonomy in response to the charge that desubstantiated and historicized subjects cannot mount resistance. Allen's conception of freedom as autonomy in Foucault, in other words, is in part an attempt to shore up the subject against the familiar criticism that Foucault leaves subjects too thin to resist the powers that dominate them.[54] I confess that I am less impressed by this familiar criticism than is Allen. I find sufficient room for resistance to power in the deep complexity of the desubstantiated subjectivities we inhabit. Part of Foucault's importance, on my view, consists in showing just how difficult resistance is to achieve. There is no need to attempt to overcome this practical difficulty by offering a theoretical solution to the problem. My criticism of Foucault, accordingly, is different. If one prominent criticism of Foucault holds that he lacks a theory of the subject that could provide us with normative resources for resistance, my concern is rather that Foucault lacks a theory of normativity that we historicized subjects might put to use to develop the resistance we find ourselves in need of.

Since Allen is motivated at least in part by worries that historicizing the subject divests us of room for resistance, she argues that Foucault offers a conception of freedom that can be captured by a two-part notion of autonomy as "capacities for critical reflection and self-transformation."[55] I agree with Allen that Foucault understood freedom in terms of critical reflection and self-transformation, but I understand these two related notions as orientations of practice rather than as possessed capacities. A conception of freedom in terms of capacities is problematic in two ways: first, it resuscitates questions concerning the Kantian transcendental subject that we should not see Foucault as posing; second, it resuscitates a conception of freedom as something that we can possess but not exercise, such that our freedom can be now-oppressed and now-liberated, which is precisely the operative conception of freedom in the modern moralities that Foucault found problematic. Allow me to address each of these worries in turn.[56]

The first worry is that conceiving freedom in terms of capacities suggests that these capacities must inhere in or be possessed by something. This in turn invites the disposed transcendental (or even worse, substantial) subject in through the back door. My approach of conceptualizing freedom as what we do rather than as what we are shuts the door on transcendental critique and opens up vistas of immanent critique. I readily concede that Allen can draw from Foucault's writings to justify a description of his views in her terms of "capacities" for "autonomy." For example, in his 1983 course lectures at the Collège de France, Foucault describes his project as "a history of ontologies which would refer to a principle of freedom in which freedom is not defined as a right to be free, but as a capacity for free action."[57] Yet I might note that even here Foucault's primary emphasis is on freedom as an action rather than as a state. Such a reading, focusing on the process of enacting capacities, suggests the possibility of an interpretation of autonomy as both capacity and process.[58] If this is Allen's view, and I think it is, then it seems that her interpretation of Foucault's ethics in terms of autonomous freedom could be accommodated to the framework I propose, with the crucial prerequisite that the majority of the emphasis is placed on the process or practice of freedom. But why is this prerequisite crucial?

Answering this question brings me to the second of my two worries about a conception of freedom as autonomous capacity. Construing freedom in such terms suggests the possibility that we can be both free and unfree at once—we can both be in possession of a capacity for freedom and yet unable to exercise that capacity. My worry is not that this is paradoxical, for it is not. This is a rather sensible description of cases of oppression. In such cases, our inherent freedom is chained, and the exercise of freedom requires liberation from these chains, be they physical, psychological, or of any other form. The problem is just that oppression is not our problem as often as we take it to be—and this is an insight I adopt from Foucault, as argued in the previous chapter. My claim, Foucault's claim, is not that oppression does not exist in our world, nor that liberation is not sometimes called for. Rather, my claim, following Foucault, is that an account of freedom as liberation from oppression tends to over-saturate contemporary reflection on the form that freedom might take. Foucault taught us to learn to look at freedom otherwise. The oppressive force of sovereign power is not always our problem—and hence liberation is not always our answer. Sometimes the power that constricts us is disciplinary in nature—and the effective response to discipline is not liberation but rather self-transformation. A conception of freedom as autonomous capacity gives us something to appeal to when we are in chains. But it does not tell us what to *do,* how to *practice* our freedom, how to *enact* our self-transformations, when our constrictions are the self-imposed and imperceptible chains of our subjectivation. The ethical orientation of transformation provides better guidance here, though it offers only as much guidance as can be provided by a formal or procedural orientation capable of being instantiated through a variety of substantive commitments. To the extent that this much guidance is precisely what philosophical reflection should aim to provide, no more and no less, his conception of self-transformative activity is Foucault's greatest contribution to our contemporary reflections on and work with freedom.

Normative Strengths and Normative Confusions

Throughout this chapter my concern has been with whether Foucault's ethics can yield viable normative resources in the sense of an ethical equipment that enables us to distinguish better from worse courses of action in the present. I have been arguing that we should put this question to Foucault's orientation of ethical practice as self-transformative rather than to Foucault's ethical commitments to substantive ideas of, for instance, ethical autonomy. Insofar as these commitments can be of use to us today, it is under the primary guidance of a self-transformative orientation. It is this orientation in Foucault's ethics that brings us closest to realizing a viable normative program therein.

However, it is as yet not entirely clear that Foucault's ethics of self-transformation provides sufficient normative resources for our ethical present. There are many unresolved questions. Why is transformation a good thing? What makes a given transformation the right one? How can practices of self-transformation actually help us address the crucial problematizations we face in the modern moral present? Even on the most charitable reading, these questions, I think, are not clearly answered in Foucault's work. My own view is that the best way of responding to these queries, and thus of clarifying how the ethical orientation of self-transformation might be used to generate normative resources, is to interpret this orientation in light of other ethical orientations drawn from neighboring philosophical traditions. My argument is that genealogists should draw on neighboring traditions to specify how we might reinvest Foucault's suggestions about how to improve ourselves with a more normatively robust conception of self-transformative practice than what is featured on the surface of Foucault's late ethical writings.

Here is where pragmatism and critical theory can be of enormous help to genealogy (it is not difficult to envision productive engagements with other philosophical traditions as well). What Deweyan pragmatists and Habermasian critical theorists supply that we cannot clearly find in Foucault are fuller answers to core questions concerning when, why, and how self-transformation can be taken up with normative authority. Critics will point out that transformation, if it is but mere change, may after all lead to degradation and decline, which too are species of change. Dewey and Habermas feature in their work ethical resources that are transformative in orientation but also carefully qualified as, to employ technical terminology, reconstructive. Reconstruction, especially in Dewey's work, can be understood as a species of transformation in which transformation functions to meliorate the problematic features characteristic of a problematization. Transformation can get you out of a bad situation, but perhaps by putting you into one that is even worse. Reconstruction is a species of transformation in which you make a bad situation better.

I am not claiming that Foucault's work could not be revisited in such a way as to produce the normative yield already developed by moral philosophers like Dewey and Habermas. I only want to take note that one really has to torture Foucault's texts to get them to produce such a yield. If that is the case, then those of us working in the genealogical tradition stand to gain much by refocusing attention on neighboring traditions such as pragmatism and critical theory. We genealogists can refocus in this way with a good conscience because, as I have shown, Foucault offered genealogy as a practice of problematization that functions as a first moment of inviting the work of ameliorative response as a second moment. If Foucault himself did not make good on his own promise of ethical responsiveness, then we can and should turn to others to fill in this second moment of critical inquiry as Foucault sought to develop it.

When turning to traditions other than genealogy for the purposes of conceptualizing a form of normative inquiry that might be compatible with genealogy, it is absolutely crucial to realize that there is no principled opposition to critical theory and pragmatism stemming from Foucault's work, neither from his genealogical problematizations nor from his own inchoate attempt to develop an ethical response to his problematizations. That this is so can be seen by noting that the deficits in Foucault's ethics are not rooted in a principled objection on his part to the kinds of substantive normative content featured in certain other ethical theories. Consistent with his core idea of self-transformative response is the thought that different moral problematizations do in fact require different normative content in order to successfully navigate these transformations. There is, therefore, no principled objection in Foucault's ethics to the possibility that normative commitments tailored from Deweyan or Habermasian cloth may be just what we need in certain moral situations. If there were to be a point of principled opposition between these different traditions of ethical theory, then it would have to be located on the level of what I have been calling orientation. But, as I will detail in the following chapter, there is a great deal of overlap between Foucault's conception of ethics as self-transformative and similar notions of moral reconstruction emphasized by the pragmatists and critical theorists.

If I am right that there is no principled reason why a good Foucaultian cannot turn to pragmatism and critical theory to enrich a Foucaultian ethics of self-transformation, it follows that most critics have been too harsh with Foucault's ethics even if they were nevertheless right to point out that there are definite normative tensions in his work. To show how, I would like to return again to a criticism I first addressed in Chapters 2 and 3, namely Nancy Fraser's forceful claim of a lack of normative resources in Foucault.[59] Recall that Fraser's argument concerns the "lack of an adequate normative perspective" to be found in Foucault's work.[60] This criticism remains the best touchstone for sorting out these issues in part because it mounts an argument against Foucault without taking that argument as a warrant for rejecting Foucault altogether. I shall here appropriate Fraser's argument for purposes she could not have anticipated when she forwarded her criticisms, but that she could perhaps endorse now.

My strategy requires that I appropriate, rather than merely reproduce, Fraser's argument in large part because I find her argument wanting with respect to its original target of criticism and yet insightful with respect to a slightly shifted target. Recall that in Chapter 3, I defended Foucault against one version of Fraser's criticism by arguing that his archaeological and genealogical work is simply not normatively ambitious in a sense that would be required for a particularly strong statement of her criticism to gain any traction. But in turning in the present chapter to Foucault's late work on ethics as a self-transformative response to the problematization of power and freedom in modernity, I have been arguing that this element in Foucault's work evinces a normative ambition. In claiming as much, I am prepared to concede to Fraser that this portion of Foucault's work evinces a normative deficit on its own terms. I thus find Fraser's diagnosis of Foucault accurate with respect to his late normatively ambitious ethics but misguided with respect to his earlier normatively cautious genealogies.

The irony in this appropriation of Fraser is that her criticisms were published in the early 1980s prior to the appearance of much of Foucault's later ethical work: as such her criticisms were explicitly addressed to Foucault's genealogies of the middle 1970s rather than to his later work on ethics. So, though I am more or less in agreement with Fraser, I am in agreement with her only in a sense that she could not have exactly anticipated at the time. By thus appropriating Fraser, but again for purposes I think she could and should endorse now, my strategy is to make good on the general diagnosis she offers by transposing it to an object of criticism that in fact did not exist when Fraser forwarded her argument, namely Foucault's late ethical writings. This transposition helps us see the lingering truth in Fraser's originally misguided criticisms. Foucault's earlier problematizational work was not really attempting the sort of normative project that Fraser accuses Foucault of falling short of. Of course he falls short in these respects. But that is a misleading way to make a point. If Fraser had instead pointed out that the genealogical aspects of Foucault's work do not attempt a normative reconstruction of the problematizations he diagnoses, and that he should take on board another form of inquiry that would enable him to do so, then I would be in full agreement. Had she made the criticism in this way, and I believe this is a plausible reading of the spirit (though not the letter, to be sure) of her arguments, she could have pointed to the normative deficiencies in genealogies without disparaging its diagnostic capacities. This strategy is in fact in keeping with Fraser's own ongoing relationship to Foucault, insofar as she continues to make use of his genealogical method as one part of her own broader efforts in critical inquiry.[61] It might thus appear that I conclude more or less just where Fraser left us over twenty-five years ago: Foucault provides "just the jolt we occasionally need to dereify our usual patterns of self-interpretation" and yet correctly responding to this jolt requires normative conceptions that Foucault himself cannot deliver.[62] With the qualifications already noted, this is exactly where I aim to conclude.

Foucault's defenders have, of course, been eager to suggest that Fraser's criticisms were entirely misguided because they were entirely off the mark. Such defenses of Foucault, however, concede too little to the force of arguments like Fraser's. These defenses require the strong claim that Fraser is demanding from Foucault a critical resource, namely normativity, that he never sought to provide, either in his work on power-knowledge or in his work on ethics(-power-knowledge). Such a claim is well too strong. For when Fraser asks of Foucault that he provide us with some amount of normative resources, I do not take her to be demanding normative commitments from Foucault in the sense of a coherent set of normative principles or a rigorous moral code. We need not see Fraser as demanding some infallible set of moral judgments from Foucault. We can rather read her as demanding from Foucault a fallibilistic orientation for transformative ethical practice. In other words, Fraser's worry as I take it and endorse it is not that Foucault does not tell us how to live, but rather that Foucault does not tell us enough about how we might set about the task of figuring out how to live for ourselves. Fraser's criticisms thus do not impose alien demands on Foucault, but are rather internal criticisms according to which Foucault lacks something he explicitly aimed to develop, namely an anticipatory analytic for ethical responsiveness. Foucaultians are too often far too wary of the concept of normativity.[63] Perhaps this is because the word connotes "normalization." But even here Foucault's point was never that normalization is always a bad thing. A demand for normativity need not be taken as an insistence upon the imposition of a rule if we can get by with a more modest concept of normativity as ethical equipment that enables us to develop better rather than worse courses of action.

In appropriating Fraser's criticism in this way, I want to issue a strong caution about using this line of criticism as a license for the inference that we should forget Foucault. Nothing could be further from my intention. The most unfortunate effect of the general critique of Foucault's normative utility for which Fraser is representative has been that a whole generation of critics, especially critics from within the traditions of pragmatism and critical theory, have tended to regard Foucault as a major philosophical opponent. Many of these critics have failed to successfully parse what we should take from Foucault and what we should leave behind, with the result being that a number of analytically distinct concerns about Foucault's work often pass together under the unified banner of a single argument. One way to frame my caution here is to distinguish two influential ways in which the criticism I have been considering has been forwarded over the past few decades. There are, in other words, distinct strong and weak forms of the general criticism for which I take Fraser's as representative. The stronger form

of the criticism is that Foucault was normatively confused in the sense of having snuck an implicit and illicit ethics into his genealogies through the back door.
The weaker form is that Foucault was normatively confused in the sense of having never achieved clarity on what sorts of ethical strategies we stand in need of
today. I endorse the criticism in the weaker sense while denying its stronger form.

Consider as an exemplar of the strong critique Habermas's criticisms of Foucault, according to which not only was Foucault normatively confused but also a
"crypto-normative" thinker whose work was haunted by a series of irresolvable
internal contradictions.[64] According to this criticism, Foucault's practice of genealogical critique relies on philosophical assumptions and methodological analytics that, for principled reasons, rule out the possibility that genealogical criticism
could account for agency and choice. I find Habermas's interpretations of Foucault needlessly uncharitable. Since it has generated a wealth of responses on behalf of Foucault, this is not the place to add yet another rebuttal. The best way of
rebutting Habermas's interpretations of Foucault is not to engage in the polemics
surrounding this interpretation but rather to simply paint a more attractive interpretation of Foucault's work. Much of this book has been an attempt to develop a
more usable interpretation of his work. According to the interpretation I am presenting, we can sensibly deny Habermas's strong criticism of Foucault and yet still
concede that Fraser's criticism has a point.

To see how, consider now Richard Rorty's stern but congenial criticisms of
Foucault.[65] Rorty agreed with Fraser and Habermas that we ought not to look to
Foucault if we are hoping to develop normative resources that might give us a clue
about what to do about the problems of power and freedom we moderns face today. But Rorty did not think this was a principled failing that followed as a necessary implication from some supposed attempt on Foucault's part to use genealogy to describe in dirty detail the dark underbelly of modernity. Rather, thought
Rorty, this normative project was just not Foucault's favored game, or was perhaps a game that Foucault did not think he was very good at. Either way, Rorty's
view is that Foucault did not play this game so well, but for no other reason than
that it did not quite capture his attention in the way that other games did. In a
1981 review essay on Foucault in the *London Review of Books*, Rorty lamented this:
"Foucault does not speculate about possible future utopias, either in connection
with sexuality or with anything else. His suggestions about reform remain hints.
But one wishes he would speculate. His obviously sincere attempt to make philosophical thinking be of some use, do some good, help people, is not going to get
anywhere until he condescends to do a bit of dreaming about the future, rather

than stopping dead after genealogising the present."[66] As I understand Rorty here, we should read Foucault as having been so fixated on critically demonstrating that practices formerly taken for granted were pernicious in unexpected ways that he never quite got around to considering how these very same practices might at the same time be quite valuable for certain political and ethical projects that no one should sensibly deny. This is indeed a real failing on Foucault's part, but it is a contingent failure of his work as a critic rather than an essential failing internal to his modality of criticism. Only the most ardent defenders would deny the truth in Rorty's claim to the effect that Foucault's work does not often yield the kinds of normative resources we need for responding to the problematic situations we confront amidst modern morality. And yet there is no deep and insightful reason why this is so, no big story that we can tell about this failure that could be used to refute a problematizing deployment of genealogy, no boogeyman in the closet that some clever wit who one day saunters along might call our attention to. So we can, with a good conscience, continue to make good use of Foucault.

It is worth noting in passing that, for his part, Foucault seemed to not see the great distance between his own work and the commitments of pragmatism and critical theory that Habermas and Rorty, albeit to different degrees, insisted upon. Frequently asked about his relation to Habermas's work, and the severe criticisms he had received, Foucault always refused to be baited into polemics. A characteristic remark is this: "I am quite interested in his [Habermas's] work, although I know he completely disagrees with my views."[67] Foucault also refrained from public criticism of Rorty. In a personal letter to Rorty in 1981, Foucault wrote (and in English, albeit not quite perfect, which I shall reproduce here exactly as written): "Forgive me not to have answered you since sent me your book [*Philosophy and the Mirror of Nature*]. I read it with most interest. It seems to me that it raises some of the basic questions that have been neglected those past years. I wish it to be translated into french. The reason why I did not answered sooner is that I would have liked to propose a translator to you. Unfortunately, french publishers are timid and conservative. There is no certainty at the moment."[68] Was Foucault serious about helping Rorty translate *Mirror*? It is probable, given that less than two years later Foucault would help launch the *Des Travaux* publishing series in an effort to offer a venue for books, explicitly inclusive of foreign works, that were rigorous and also different from what was then usual in France.[69] In any event, it is clear that Foucault saw in the work of both Rorty and Habermas much that was of interest. Perhaps Foucault did not engage in public criticism of Habermas and Rorty for precisely the reasons he suggests—because he found in their work companion travelers to his own self-understanding. Perhaps Habermas and Rorty were too often distracted by a certain reception of Foucault, and thus failed to see the proximity among genealogy, pragmatism, and critical theory.

Perhaps it is time to now finally admit what should have been obvious all along: many of the puffed-up criticisms of Foucault foisted on him over the past decade were simply overblown. Perhaps there is more to be gained than lost in putting genealogy into motion together with pragmatism and critical theory. The normative shortcomings in Foucault's work were not principled errors but rather more innocent weaknesses that flowed from nothing more profound than the shortness of sweet life itself.

Discriminating amongst these two versions of the standard criticism of Foucault is helpful just insofar as it enables us to see that his work is indeed entirely compatible with normatively robust work in pragmatist critical theory (but of course only if pragmatist critical theory is itself compatible with the jolt of genealogical problematization, as I think it is, or at least can be made to be in certain of its prominent instantiations). If we affirm the weaker criticism and deny the stronger criticism, we can accept that there is no principled reason why we could not now combine Foucaultian genealogical problematization with a Deweyan or Habermasian model of reconstruction in order to fashion a fuller apparatus for critical inquiry than is featured in either theory on its own.

My proposal for this is to regard genealogy and pragmatist critical theory as mutually reinforcing: *genealogy problematizes while pragmatist critical theory reconstructs.* We should delegate to genealogists the task of a diagnostic methodology for inquiry into problematizations, and to pragmatists and critical theorists we should delegate the task of deploying an anticipatory methodology for inquiry into the reconstruction of problematic situations. In doing so, we can and should regard the critical theorists and pragmatists as helping us specify in finer detail, and with greater justifiability, what is of value in the self-transformative ethical orientation only tentatively sketched by Foucault. Why should we think that one philosopher, or one philosophical tradition, has all the answers? We should draw freely from varying, even competing, philosophical traditions if it helps us achieve our goals. This might increase tensions or, even worse, implicate contradictions, but it need not do so if we are careful about what we take from each tradition.

7

Problematization plus Reconstruction

Genealogy, Pragmatism & Critical Theory

Reconciling Problematizers and Reconstructors

Throughout this book I have been working toward a conception of critical inquiry that brings together the methodological orientations of problematization and reconstruction. It is time to more tightly tie together these two elements of my proposed form of critical inquiry. In this concluding chapter I detail how what I have been calling problematization and reconstruction fit together quite naturally to form a broad-based conception of critique, in the capacious Kantian sense of critique I outlined in the introduction. Kant initiated a project in modern philosophical practice that remains of ineliminable value for the traditions of genealogy, pragmatism, and critical theory. I am not referring to Kant's projects of an architectonic of reason and a legislation of the moral will. That in Kant which lasts for us today is his project of critique—the severe work by which we inquire into second-order conditions of possibility of our first-order practical doings. In placing genealogy, pragmatism, and critical theory in the lineage of Kant, I aim to call attention to Kant's best achievements for us moderns. These achievements may not be dependent upon more textbook stories we are too often taught about Kant. Indeed, I can freely admit that Kant may not recognize himself in the critical methodologies I am discussing. But that is not my point. Rather my claim is that we can recognize enough of Kant in ourselves. What I seek, then, are connections on their own terms between Foucault's Kantian project of problematization on the one hand and the Kantian projects of reconstruction featured in the work of pragmatism and critical theory on the other.

One way of approaching this dual-aspect conception of critical inquiry is through Seyla Benhabib's description of the two dimensions of critical theory essential for any rigorous form of critique: "First is the *explanatory-diagnostic* aspect through which the findings and methods of the social sciences are appropriated in such a way as to develop an empirically fruitful analysis of the crisis potential of the present . . . The second dimension of critical theory is its *anticipatory-utopian* one; this constitutes the more properly normative aspect of critique. When explicating the dysfunctionalities of the present, a critical social theory should always do so in the name of a better future and a more humane society." At the core of Benhabib's two-dimensional model of critique is the idea that any successful practice of critical inquiry must work along both of these dimensions in reciprocal fashion: "Without an explanatory dimension, critical theory dissolves into mere normative philosophy; if it excludes the dimension of anticipatory-utopian critique, however, it cannot be distinguished from other mainstream social theories that attempt to gain value-free knowledge of the social world."[1] Benhabib's distinction between two necessary aspects of critical inquiry helps me specify the terms in which I want to hold together genealogy and pragmatist critical theory (for I here appropriate Benhabib's distinction for my own purposes moreso than I attempt to deliver on exactly what she aims for). My suggestion is that the need for what Benhabib calls "diagnosis" (I prefer to de-emphasize the "explanatory") can be supplied by genealogical problematization, while the need for what she calls "anticipation" (I prefer to de-emphasize the "utopian") can be filled in through pragmatic critical theoretic reconstruction.

Benhabib's model resonates surprisingly well with Foucault's sketch in "What is Enlightenment?" of the two aspects of a viable critical ethos for our present. Foucault there wrote, "the critique of what we are is at one and the same time the historical analysis of the limits imposed on us and an experiment with the possibility of going beyond them."[2] This two-dimensional project must, urged Foucault, give rise to "the labor of diverse inquiries" oriented by the genealogical and archaeological methodologies characteristic of his work. That Foucault's two dimensions of the "historico-critical" and "experimental" attitudes map well to Benhabib's "diagnostic" and "anticipatory" critique is confirmed earlier in his essay. The first dimension of Foucault's ethos consists of "a historical investigation into the events that have led us to constitute ourselves and to recognize ourselves as subjects of what we are doing, thinking, saying." In short, this is what Foucault practiced as genealogical and archaeological problematization: a historical diagnosis of the difficulties that motivate the continued elaboration of ourselves in the present. The second dimension of Foucault's ethos is an experimental attempt to "grasp the points where change is possible and desirable, and to determine the precise form this change should take." In short, this is Foucault's anticipatory project of self-transformation that he never brought to complete fruition. These two dimensions of critical theory constitute, says Foucault, a "historico-practical test of the limits we may go beyond." The historical dimension is diagnostic and problematizing. The practical-experimental dimension is anticipatory and, at least potentially, normatively reconstructive.

I have been describing Foucault's work in terms that enable us to perceive how he invoked both of these dimensions of critical inquiry. Foucault's genealogical practice of problematization is an exemplary model for how critical inquiry can be used to diagnose difficulties in our present situations that may have otherwise gone unnoticed or, if we had noticed them, may have been widely misperceived. Much of Foucault's work is best read as instantiating such critical problematizations of certain core practices, conceptions, and forms that are constitutive of our modernity. Foucault, however, did not only seek to unearth the problematizations in terms of which we moderns define ourselves. He also recognized the need for a positive and reconstructive response to the difficulties within which we labor. On the basis of his genealogies of the problematization of the reciprocal but incompatible forms of modern powers (discipline, biopower, governmentality) and freedoms (liberation, emancipation, autonomy), Foucault sought to elaborate possible ways of responding to the constitutive impasses of our modernity. Foucault's later work on ethics is a response to his previous work on power and knowledge—or, to put it otherwise, Foucault's work on the forms of power and knowledge constitutive of our modernity led him directly into his subsequent work on ways in which we might begin to ethically constitute alternative possibilities out of the very materials of modernity we have inherited and that we continue to elaborate.

Although Foucault's work clearly features resources that are both "explanatory-diagnostic" and "anticipatory-utopian" in Benhabib's sense, I have argued that he was far more successful in elaborating his diagnostic method of genealogy as problematization than he was in elaborating a reconstructive conception of ethics as an ongoing series of self-transformations. In differentially assessing these two aspects of Foucault's work in this way, it is crucial to note that genealogy as problematization does not in principle stand in the way of an experimentalist ethics of reconstruction. This means that we can legitimately appropriate Foucault's analytic of genealogical problematization for the purposes of elaborating our own conceptions of critical inquiry in the present without tying ourselves to Foucault's attempt at an analytic for transformative reconstruction. Genealogical problematization might then form one aspect of a viable practice of critical inquiry when paired with some other account of reconstructive response that is better worked out than Foucault's own account of an ethics of self-transformation. By employing such a procedure, we can affirm the importance of Foucault's work for contemporary critical inquiry and at the same time establish a more productive conception of the relationship between that work and other work that has proven valuable for contemporary critical inquiry.

To set the stage for this sort of combination, consider now one of the most vexed relations in contemporary philosophy, namely that between Foucault's genealogy and Jürgen Habermas's critical theory.[3] The massive engine of commentary constituting these debates has led to a number of obfuscating blockages. In only a few relatively rare cases (including most notably the works cited in the remainder of this section) has this debate led to more productive cross-fertilizations. In the past five to ten years the storm of these debates has somewhat subsided, due not so much to any resolution or victory as to mutual exhaustion on both sides. I would like to take advantage of this less tumultuous moment to propose that we now strike out in a new direction. Instead of traveling farther down those paths on which the oppositions between Foucault and Habermas are sharpened, I propose that we instead start developing a path toward their reconciliation.

To summarize the view I shall develop over the course of this chapter, my approach to reconciling Habermasian critical theory with Foucaultian genealogy involves preserving distinctive elements from each theoretical apparatus that the other theoretical apparatus does not feature. We preserve from Habermas, or at least from a certain pragmatized version of critical theory, a role that is not well played by genealogy as Foucault practiced it. And we preserve from Foucault a critical element not clearly featured in pragmatism and critical theory. If we fail to preserve distinctive elements of each tradition in this way, then we will end up courting reduction rather than reconciliation and combination. My proposal is that of carving a diagnostic of genealogical problematization out of Foucault and a normative apparatus of reconstructive inquiry out of a critical theoretical pragmatism based in Habermas, and also in the work of John Dewey. This approach enables us to focus on the true strengths of each tradition and at the same time relieves us of the burdens of the dead weight that drags on each. It frees us to dispense with Foucault's anticipatory sketches of an ethics of self-transformation where we find those sketches largely incomplete. It also frees us from having to take on board Habermas's knotted accounts of the core problems we moderns face today, accounts that (at least in the monumental *Theory of Communicative Action*) largely revolve around broad-brush Weberian claims for the colonization of life-world experiences by system processes that introduce distortions into communicative procedures. My approach, in short, is to focus on what is best in Foucault and what is best in Habermas to see if we might be able to nudge these pieces a little closer together. We need not, for these purposes, nudge their whole projects together by requiring a systematic assimilation of Habermasian theory and Foucaultian theory. We can rather pick and choose from Habermas and Foucault what we need to realize our vision of a form of critical inquiry that is effectively problematizing-diagnostic and effectively reconstructive-anticipatory.

The very idea of a reconciliation that stands behind my approach draws much of its inspiration from one of the most fruitful contributions to the Foucault-Habermas debates to appear in a long while. Amy Allen's recent work on Foucault and Habermas offers a breath of fresh air on debates that have come to seem increasingly stuffy.[4] A firm commitment to both traditions of genealogy and critical theory enables Allen to reach well beyond the impasses of many of the now stale arguments on behalf of either Foucault or Habermas to locate a middle ground where Foucaultians and Habermasians can more productively dialogue. Allen's procedure is to nudge Foucault and Habermas a little bit closer to one another by emphasizing the centrality of autonomy for Foucault's work and the need for contextualism prompted by Habermas's work: "Thus, by reading Foucault in a way that emphasizes his connection to the Kantian Enlightenment tradition and by interpreting Habermas in a more historicized, contextualist, and pragmatic direction, it is possible to stake out a productive and fertile middle ground."[5] An argument for bringing Foucault and Habermas nearer to one another in this way is crucially valuable because, as Allen rightly notes, "the Foucault/Habermas debate centers on a substantive tension that lies at the very heart of social and political theorizing," namely the tension "between rationality and power." Allen's contribution thus involves "integrating the insights of these two thinkers" for the purposes of addressing the deep tensions in political theory that otherwise remain in place if we fail to resolve the Foucault-Habermas debate itself.[6]

My project in this chapter follows, in its general orientation, Allen's approach. But I depart from her view on many of the finer details insofar as I resist some of the particular philosophical commitments she attributes to Foucault and Habermas in the project of "modifying or recasting their views."[7] Allen's strategy requires a fairly substantive rereading of both thinkers—the connection between Foucault and Kant focuses in many instances on "the peculiarly Kantian flavor of autonomy in Foucault's work," whereas for Habermas, Allen urges "scaling back the overly ambitious claims that [he] makes regarding the possibility of untangling validity from power, a possibility that he frames in terms of the context transcendence of validity claims."[8] These substantive rereadings are requisite for Allen because her aim is to bring both thinkers together at a more robust philosophical level. This strategy is, for my purposes, too ambitious. I propose to reconcile genealogy and critical theory at the level of methodology. For these purposes, I can recast both traditions in ways that does not require sacrificing some of the central insights of each. So in contrast to Allen's provocative wholesale-philosophical integration of Foucault and Habermas, I shall be aiming for a more modest retail-methodological combination of the two. This more modest strategy allows me, and this is the key point, to leave Foucault and Habermas as robust, or scaled-up, as we find them, provided we restrict each approach to the methodological domain to which it is delegated.

There is, to be sure, room enough in the realm of philosophical critique for both Allen's strategy and mine. But allow me nevertheless to explain my caution about Allen's strategy, with the caveat that this is more an expression of an unsettling worry than a justification of a settled conviction. A danger that faces any attempt at a wholesale assimilation of two philosophical traditions, such as Allen's, is that of reducing each theoretical apparatus to the other. This danger is clearly featured in earlier rounds of debates between defenders of Foucault and Habermas. The two camps proved themselves quite willing to reduce the theoretical apparatus offered by the other camp into their own terms. Habermasian validity claims became little more than effects of power in the hands of the Foucaultians, while Foucaultian freedom as resistance became little more than an empty strategic gesture in the hands of the Habermasians. Allen fares much better than this. Yet her project of a broad-based philosophical reconciliation amongst Foucault and Habermas could function to invite these polemics in through the back door even if she has kept them locked out up front. My view is that we need not aim for a wholesale philosophical synthesis of these two traditions. We can get all we need from a more modest retail combination of the methodological strengths featured in each tradition. I think a methodological combination via delegation is enough, in part because I think we best read genealogy and critical theory not as grand philosophical systems but rather as philosophical contributions to a critique of our present that would require a social scientific deployment of the methodological analytics and diagnostics they feature in their work.

My core worry is that a more wholesale approach potentially risks reducing critical theory and genealogy to a set of lowest common denominators. It is not that I detect philosophical errors in the set common to genealogy and critical

theory, but rather that I see no need for paring down the resources of both traditions in order to locate their compatibility with one another on the basis of such
commonalities.

To begin with this danger as it is expressed in Allen's rereading of critical
theory, her approach could be seen as courting the reduction of critical theory
into genealogical terms in advising that we should be "much more cautious than
Habermas has tended to be about claiming a strongly universalistic or context-
transcendent status for these commitments."[9] To the extent that universality and
context-transcendence are really at the core of Habermas's reconstructive normative project, we cannot, or at least should not, simply ask him to give up these features of his work. I thus go to greater lengths than Allen does to show that we can
in fact preserve an important sense of universalizability in critical inquiry without
contravening the equally strong emphasis on contingency featured in genealogy.
That said, I follow Allen, who is on this point following other contemporary critical theorists such as Thomas McCarthy, in emphasizing the importance of a conception of context-sensitive universality for Habermas's project. In thus offering a
contextualist reading of universalizability, I arrive in the end at a view that is quite
similar to Allen's, but with the crucial difference that my view is explicit in its unwillingness to sacrifice universality for contextual-sensitivity. My argument here
depends on showing the compatibility of universality and contextual contingency.
If I can show this, then I can show that Habermas expressly preserves universalizability through contextualism, and in a way that is compatible with Foucaultian
contextualist contingency. Not only does this enable us to repair to a more recog-
nizably Habermasian view, but it also enables us to develop the genealogical tradition in a direction that will make it increasingly fit for diagnostic projects that explicitly invite a reconstructive response.

I aim also to avoid the risk of reducing genealogy to critical theory that is
courted by Allen's strategy of emphasizing an overly strong conception of freedom
as autonomy in Foucault. Foucault's ethics, understood as a responsive practice
of self-transformation, can be ably inflected by the reconstructive ethical orientation made available by my reading of Habermas's critical theory. For the purposes
of this combination we do not require anything nearly so weighty, or controversial, as an idea of autonomy that would surreptitiously invite the companion ideas
of liberation and emancipation back into the debate. I developed this argument in
the previous chapter.

In the end, my worry is just that Allen too much emphasizes autonomy and
too much de-emphasizes universality. These are minor quibbles, to be sure, but
the fine-grained differences I focus herein enable me not so much to reject Allen's

views (for on the whole I do not) as to more finely feature the crucial philosophical matter that is at the heart of any attempt to think genealogy, pragmatism, and critical theory together.

This crucial philosophical matter concerns universality and contingency, and their relation. Why does this matter here? My methodological-delegational combination of genealogy and pragmatist critical theory must, of course, rigorously rule out any potential inconsistencies in underlying philosophical assumptions. We cannot delegate diagnosis to Foucault and reconstruction to Habermas if there are conceptual obstacles that divide these practices of diagnosis and reconstruction against one another. On this point, Allen is certainly most correct.[10] In the context of increasingly social scientific interpretations of genealogy and critical theory, there is a continuing role for philosophy that consists in interrogating social-science methodologies with respect to their core philosophical commitments. According to my measure, the greatest deal of anxiety in the Foucault-Habermas debates have been provoked around the compatibility of two core philosophical commitments to universality (in Habermas) and contingency (in Foucault). The Foucault-Habermas debates have thus invoked a great deal of heavy weather concerning a supposed opposition between universality and contingency. But, as I will show in the following section, these concepts need not be seen as opposed at all. Properly speaking, contingency picks out a modality, and universality picks out a scope. There is, therefore, no obvious (no necessary) contradiction in their being deployed together. The simultaneous presence of contingency and universality could lead in practice to the intensification of tensions, but there is no reason why these tensions cannot be productive for ever more fruitful projects of critique and inquiry.

The core of my strategy involves the idea that we do not need not to push Habermas and Foucault too far toward one another philosophically in order to achieve a methodological combination of their projects. I prefer a more modest delegation strategy. We should assign methodological tasks to each tradition, according to their strengths, in such a way as to continue to affirm their persisting differences: genealogy serves a diagnostic function, and critical theory an anticipatory function. Delegation obviates a need, perhaps unattainable, for deeper integration.

A strategy of delegation has the further advantages of facilitating the use of Foucault and Habermas to criticize one another in a way that reveals the strengths and weaknesses of each theoretical apparatus. This enables us to affirm the strong points of each approach so as to compensate for the weaknesses in the other. To further specify, consider that paradigmatic statement of the Foucault-Habermas debate offered by David Hoy and Thomas McCarthy in their co-authored book *Critical Theory*. In this exchange Hoy argues on behalf of one side: "[a] Foucaultian approach to the history of the human sciences would seem effectively to show that Habermas's paradigm of problem-solving is too narrow. Genealogy asks the prior question of how the problems that are supposedly to be solved come to be perceived as problems in the first place."[11] Hoy is right that Foucault helps us recognize the blindness of a narrowly reconstructive enterprise. Genealogy as such can be used to enrich critical theory. But it must also be noted that we can, on the other hand, use Habermas to recognize the blindness of the narrow problem-generating focus featured by Foucault. This point is developed by McCarthy on behalf of the other side in his contribution to the dialogue: "whereas the genealogist resolutely brackets the validity claims embedded in practices, the better to objectify them, the critical theorist tries to reconstruct and critically engage those claims."[12] In short, Hoy and McCarthy both ably argue that Foucault and Habermas can be used to reveal weaknesses in one another's approach. But rather than seeing these revelations as grounds for recognizing a divide that need always separate genealogy from critical theory, I draw a different set of conclusions.[13]

My alternative is to affirm the distinctive values of both the apparatuses of diagnosis yielded by genealogical problematization and those normative apparatuses yielded by critical theory such as reconstruction. We can, in other words, regard diagnostic problematization and normative problem solving as complements to one another. Developing a full-scale practice of critical inquiry that includes both of these apparatuses would require picking and choosing the best elements from each of Foucault and Habermas with an eye toward developing a way of integrating those elements. This approach results in a more attentive comparison of the work of Foucault and Habermas than has thus far been achieved in the existing literature. Habermasians have too often assumed at the outset that Foucault needed to provide a reconstructive-anticipatory account of normative practice if his project was to be of any use at all. Foucaultians have too often assumed that Habermas needed to get clear on the depth of the problem of power in the modern realities for which he was sketching normative criteria. But this sort of cross-engagement is staged on unnecessarily uneven terrain. My alternate approach to comparing these two bodies of work is to see if the critical-diagnostic aspects of one can be fit together with the critical-anticipatory aspects of the other. In the context of Foucault's work, this does not require that we find in his work an actually viable concept of normative reconstruction, but rather that we find in his apparatus of genealogical problematization a practice of inquiry that is not in principle incompatible with a broadly critical-theoretical account of normative reconstruction. In the context of Habermas's work, the correlative requirement is only for an apparatus of reconstructive problem solving that is not in principle incompatible with a broadly genealogical account of problematization.

What I am thus seeking is a revised frame of reference for assessing the relations between Foucaultian genealogy on the one hand and Habermasian critical theory on the other. For too long the possibility of a productive Foucault-Habermas dialogue has been blocked by the inappropriate terms that have been used to stage such a conversation. "The Foucault/Habermas debate was a non-event," Allen forcefully notes.[14] Her point is that this non-debate was largely a product of the secondary literature. The prevailing interpretations of these thinkers with which the secondary literature operates is that of Foucault as a subversive intellectual and of Habermas as a vindicatory theorist. But to frame our interpretations of these thinkers in these ways is to ensure that the conversation between them cannot even get going. I am offering different interpretations of genealogy and critical theory so as to stage much-needed methodological collaborations. Foucault is not practicing subversion—he is philosophizing in the manner of problematization. Habermas is not practicing vindication—he is, like Dewey, focusing the work of thought as reconstruction. In the older frame of subversion and vindication, it is practically inevitable that Foucault and Habermas will fail to meet just insofar as they represent opposed intellectual tendencies. In the newer frame of problematization and reconstruction, by contrast, they cannot but fail to meet just insofar as the logic of question and response is not one of contradiction but rather one of reciprocal rhythm.

This sort of rhythm, and the commitment to historicity implied therein, raises important questions about how the differing methodological tools I am discussing can be deployed. My emphasis on historicity throughout may lead to a potential misinterpretation according to which problematization is in every instance a methodology for backward-facing historians while reconstruction is always a methodology for forward-facing anthropologists or sociologists. Problematization and reconstruction need not be parsed along temporal lines, even if that is one useful way of parsing genealogy and pragmatism, and the way that I most persistently pursue here. Despite my pursuits, other options are possible, and so worth mentioning. Problematization can take the historical form as specified by the genealogist, but it can also assume a more future-oriented form as in, for example, Paul Rabinow's anthropology of the contemporary and George Marcus's anthropology as cultural critique.[15] Reconstruction can take forward-facing form as specified by pragmatists or anthropologists of the contemporary, but it might in other instances involve rearguard projects calling for the excavation of past reconstructions as in R. G. Collingwood's histories of question and answer.[16] The diagnosis involved in problematization in some instances need not concern itself with genesis, as is the case with diagnosing a broken bone in an emergency surgery, where questions of how the bone came to be broken need not be asked. The work involved in reconstruction similarly need not always look forward to the future if a reversion to a prior state is all that is called for, as in restoring a computer backup after a system crash.

Problematization should be seen as diagnostic and reconstruction as responsive, such that genealogy and pragmatism can be seen as just one of many possible models of how each might be practiced. Having affirmed the wide potential variance in our deployment of problematization and reconstruction, I shall here focus on problematization in its genealogical form and reconstruction in its pragmatist and critical theoretic forms. I find these deployments of problematization and reconstruction particularly effective insofar as they can happily commingle in the present, where the backward-facing genealogist hands off material to the forward-facing pragmatist. There are other ways of diagnosis and responding to our situations, but for me none is quite so invigorating as pragmatist reconstruction and genealogical problematization. I thus persistently parse problematization and reconstruction temporally in terms of their respective objects of inquiry, the one focusing mostly on the historical past and the other mostly on the future of the present.

Before developing this argument in the sequel of this chapter, let me contextualize my contribution here within the book as a whole, and also provide a map of the terrains I am traversing. In the preceding chapters I have sought to show, first, how an interpretation of genealogy focused as a methodological project of problematization enables us to route around the familiar criticism that Foucault's work is strictly incompatible with normative critical theory, and second, what Foucault's conceptualizations of modernity look like when construed in terms of such a rereading of his methodology. In the next section of this chapter, I will address a philosophical issue concerning the compatibility of universality and contingency that has consistently chilled the reception of Foucault amongst audiences where his methodological contributions might otherwise make a valuable difference. In the section following that, I will apply this philosophical insight to my foregoing interpretation of genealogy. In the following two sections, I will then take up the project of featuring a pragmatist critical-theoretical methodology of normative reconstruction that I propose to pair with genealogical problematization. This pairing is needful insofar as Foucault's ethical writings fail to supply a sufficient set of normative equipment, although not for the reason that his project in genealogical critique blocks a path to normativity (as argued in the previous chapter). In order to develop a conception of normative reconstruction that can be compatible with genealogical problematization, I will turn to the pragmatist philosophy of Dewey and the critical-theoretical program mapped out by Habermas. I will begin with Dewey's pragmatism, which I find rooted in many of the very same Kantian aspirations that inform Foucault's genealogy and Habermas's critical theory. On the face of things, Deweyan pragmatism is more obviously compatible with Foucaultian genealogy than is Habermasian critical theory, even if only because pragmatism has traditionally been more friendly than critical theory to the themes of complexity, contingency, and critique at the heart of genealogy. After using Dewey to pave the way to a rapprochement between Habermas and Foucault, I will then turn to critical theory proper to show that there is no principled reason why a strongly Habermasian variant of critical theory replete with its attendant emphasis on universality cannot be reinterpreted in such a way as to fully integrate the contingency at the heart of both genealogy and pragmatism. The crucial load-bearing piece of the philosophical presuppositions of my argument is this: the compatibility of processes-of-contingency and universalization-in-action. This compatibility, I shall show in the next section, is best expressed in terms of a differential between two characteristic qualities of the two dimensions of critical inquiry that I am calling "problematizing diagnosis" and "reconstructive anticipation."

The Compatibility of Contingency and Universality

At the outset, the major philosophical obstacle to my proposed combination-via-delegation of pragmatist critical theory and genealogy concerns a worry about the possibility that Foucaultian genealogy is informed by philosophical commitments to contingency that are contradictory to philosophical commitments to processes of universalization central to critical-theoretical pragmatism. Foucaultians will sensibly suggest that the strong requirement for universalizability that forms the core of the Habermasian and Deweyan normative-utopian wing of my conception of critical inquiry is straightforwardly inconsistent with Foucault's rejection of universalism.[17] Such worries can be answered by a two-step procedure involving a re-examination of, first, Foucault's genealogical insistence on historical contingency and, second, Habermas's and Dewey's defenses of universality. I shall show how for each, contingency and universality can be (though need not be) held together, at least with respect to philosophical methodology.

To set the stage for these interpretations of genealogy, pragmatism, and critical theory, I first need to situate the ensuing discussion of contingent universality in its theoretical context in order to clarify the import of my argument in more general philosophical terms. In his contribution to the Foucault-Habermas debates, James Tully writes of these debates as invoking an issue that "runs throughout the humanities and social sciences in the tension between general and universal approaches."[18] Against the common wisdom for which Tully is here merely a best representative, I submit that for both Foucault and Habermas the core issue is not whether we work with generals or universals (though clearly there are respective tendencies toward one or the other in the work of both) so much as it is whether we inflect both generality and universality with contingency or with necessity. The contingency-versus-necessity contrast is by far the more crucial one for contemporary philosophy. This more-important contrast need not implicate that other contrast between generality and universality. It is often thought that universality implicates necessity while generality implicates contingency. The core of this thought revolves around a supposed opposition between contingency and universality that too easily passes as unspoken wisdom in contemporary critical discussions. I fail to see the opposition. What follows is an effort in explaining why.

My key point is this: contingency specifies a modality and universality specifies a scope, and there need be no opposition between modalities of any value and scopes of any scale. There is, of course, a straightforward modal opposition between necessity and contingency. And this, I am urging, is a distinction important for both Foucaultians on the one hand and Habermasians and Deweyans on the other. A crucial step in my argument involves recognizing that all of the philosophical perspectives under examination here fall down on the same side of that important distinction. All are focused on contingency rather than necessity insofar as they are prepared to affirm what Thomas McCarthy calls, referring specifically to genealogy and critical theory, "the impurity of reason . . . its embeddedness in culture and society, its entanglement with power and interest, the historical variability of its categories and criteria, the embodied, sensuous and practically engaged character of its bearers." Inflecting generals and universals with necessity yields classical transcendental philosophy such as that featured in Kant's first two *Critiques*. McCarthy's argument is that critical theory and genealogy together avoid this approach in favor of their shared "transformation cum radicalization of the Kantian approach to critique."[19] Inflecting generals and universals with contingency yields historicized forms of critical inquiry that the practice of critical inquiry can make ample use of even if for different purposes of reconstruction and problematization.

These two inflections lead to two radically different conceptions of universality. On the one hand is a classical ideal of universality as a *universalism* that carries necessity in its train. On the other hand is a more contemporary conception of universality as *universalizability* in the sense of a process of universalization that is always under way and yet never complete. Distinguishing these two conceptions of universality in this way helps us affirm the crucial theoretical category of contingent universals: these are the contingent processes of universalization in which we always already find ourselves caught up. This category is crucial insofar as it gives us a way of gaining analytical grip on those of our present practices that themselves have such a severe grip on us.

An attempt to think of contingency and universality together is not wholly new on the theoretical scene, even if it still grates against many ears. One prominent context in which it has been featured in recent years is in a set of debates between the influential post-Marxist Ernesto Laclau, the post-Lacanian Slavoj Žižek, and the post-Foucaultian Judith Butler.[20] I find Butler's quasi-genealogical interventions in these debates on the mark. However, the strategy through which contingent universality is affirmed by Laclau and Žižek is articulated on a decisively different register than what I pursue here. Their two arguments remain, in the end, formal. This is to say that their argument is of a form that would show *that* universality is always already a contingent construction. My view is that all of the action is with *how* contingent universals are composed. I do not seek to show that universality always *must* be contingent, something that I am not sure how one would go about showing. My more modest Foucaultian point is just that some universals are contingent, and that one crucial task for contemporary critical inquiry involves diagnostic genealogies and critical reconstructions of these contingent universals. Thus departing from Laclau's and Žižek's positions in these debates, my Foucaultian perspective is much closer to Butler's position in the trialogue on behalf of "a temporalized conception of universality."[21] Although in these debates Butler often develops arguments to the effect *that* universality must always be contingent,[22] her reflective position seems to be that one of our most urgent tasks today is that of the analysis of actual contingent universals.[23] In an interview given around the same time as her engagement with Laclau and Žižek was published, Butler notes that "the pragmatic dimension of the politics ends up particularizing the problem of universality in a very interesting way."[24] This perspective places *universalist* conceptions of universality to the side, and in so doing opens up a conception of universality as contingent and pragmatic *universalizability*. This Foucaultian perspective, it is my argument, is highly congenial to a Deweyan-Habermasian perspective on the same.

A perspective building on genealogy and pragmatist critical theory in this way offers a decisive new direction for philosophical methodologies looking to affirm contingency and universality together. Contemporary philosophy that begins in

Kant too often adopts, either uncritically or unwittingly, the core transcendental elements featured in Kant's theoretical and practical philosophy. This leads to an indefensible universalism in which universality and necessity proceed apace. These transcendental yearnings are at once the most antiquated and the most un- necessary elements of the Kantian project. They should be discarded rather than revived. The form of post-Kantian critical inquiry that we can develop on the plat- forms provided by Foucault, Habermas, and Dewey offers a break from this tran- scendental apparatus while at the same time carefully preserving the core of the Kantian project of critique: inquiry into conditions of possibility.

To preview the argument I will give with respect to Dewey and Habermas in later sections, my claim will be that universalizability captures the central sense in which the pragmatists and critical theorists are interested in universality. An idea of universality as a process is not a far stretch for most pragmatists, especially those like Dewey who are impressed with the range and portability of scientific achievement—universality for a pragmatist is paradigmatically represented in the fact that scientists worlds apart can get the same results in carefully specified and cautiously constructed laboratories. That a conception of universality as a process is more of a stretch in the critical-theory tradition seems obvious, but I will locate it in Habermas by offering an interpretation of his work that explicitly emphasizes his more pragmatist themes, or what Richard J. Bernstein discerns as "the prag- matic turn" in Habermas's work.[25] Tracking this pragmatic turn in Habermas's work, McCarthy ably captures the core of the interpretation of immanent social critique that I shall offer: "communicative rationality may be understood tempo- rally (it is an ongoing accomplishment), pragmatically (which is never absolute but always only for all practical purposes), and contextually (in ever changing cir- cumstances), *without surrendering* transcendence (it turns on validity claims that go beyond the particular contexts in which they are raised) or idealization (and rests on pragmatic presuppositions that function as regulative ideals)."[26] Before developing the plausibility of an idea of universalizability in the work of Dewey and Habermas in later sections, allow me to first address the seemingly more pro- vocative idea that Foucaultian genealogy can comfortably make use of the same category.

Genealogy's Contingent Universals

Genealogy is not an anti-universalist project so much as it is a historicizing and temporalizing project. As such, genealogy can conceivably be construed as com- patible with the historicization and temporalization of universality. Though it is clearly not one of the dominant themes of his writings, Foucault himself did in

232 Genealogy as Critique

fact emphasize universality on more than one occasion. In a short topical piece on the role of intellectuals in political life, Foucault describes his "theoretical ethic" as one that is unafraid to oppose power with "inviolable laws and unrestricted rights" insofar as his aim is to "be respectful when a singularity revolts, intransigent as soon as power violates the universal."[27] Foucault is not here advising the model of what he elsewhere called the "universal intellectual" but is rather noting the crucial idea that his contrasting model of the "specific intellectual" can invoke universalizable ideals within the specificity of their singular domain.[28] In another of his more methodological writings, Foucault describes a form of "criticism" that simultaneously pursues the universal and the historical: "Singular forms of experience may perfectly well harbor universal structures; they may well not be independent of the concrete determinations of social existence. . . . That [thought] should have this historicity does not mean it is deprived of all universal form, but instead that the putting into play of these universal forms is itself historical."[29]

Foucault in the quotations above, particularly in the final one, seems to want to leave room for universality within his problematizations just insofar as universality can be construed as shot through with temporality and historicity. According to such a construal, universality is a dynamic process of universalizability rather than a static property theorized under universalism. That such a category is consistent with Foucault's genealogy is far from obvious. It is thus unsurprising that Foucault's commentators have almost universally decried universalism.

As a paradigmatic example, consider the interpretation of Foucault offered by Giorgio Agamben. I earlier expressed severe reservations about Agamben's ontologization of some of Foucault's key concepts, such as his ontologization of biopower in *Homo Sacer*.[30] I regard the ontologization of genealogy's historical categories to be exemplary of a problematic but prominent tendency in contemporary theory to deploy Foucaultian concepts without attention to Foucaultian methodology as a guide for that deployment.[31] If Agamben sees biopower everywhere, Foucault rigorously discerned it in precisely specified contexts examined through patient genealogical inquiry.[32] But admittedly, the work in question is an appropriation of Foucault for Agamben's own purposes, rather than a commentary on Foucault for scholarly purposes, and one philosopher can appropriate another for whatever purposes they see fit. What I find most puzzling, however, is the interpretation of Foucault forwarded by Agamben in his essay "What Is an Apparatus?" The essay is concerned with Foucault's analytic idea of *dispositif* (a term that is usually translated as "apparatus" but in the current English edition of *The Will to Know* is translated, I think rather usefully in fact, as "deployment").[33] Agamben provides an engaging description of the analytical category of *dispositif* in terms that closely resemble my previous descriptions of Foucault's analytic idea of problematization: "It is a heterogeneous set that includes virtually anything, linguistic and nonlinguistic, under the same heading . . . The apparatus itself is the network that is established between these elements."[34] Agamben quotes Foucault's own description of a *dispositif:* "a thoroughly heterogeneous ensemble . . . [that] itself is the system of relations that can be established between these elements."[35] Agamben claims that this analytic category, which he rightly regards as central to Foucault's method, functions to specify objects of inquiry that play the role that traditional universals have for other philosophers: "Apparatuses are, in point of fact, what take the place of the universals in the Foucaultian strategy."[36] Now, as Agamben points out, Foucault of course refused to interpret the objects of his analyses through the grid of invariant or universal concepts, as if Reason or Sexuality always existed the same everywhere and could be used as a categorical grid through which to read any and every historical formation.[37] But Foucault's explicit rejection of the universality of methodological *categories* and *concepts* (a rejection that Agamben himself implicitly rejects in his ontologization of biopower) does not entail a rejection of the idea that the *objects* of these inquiries are themselves universalizable.

Against the standard anti-universality interpretation of Foucault, the beginnings of an alternate approach are developed in recent work by David Hoy, who calls attention to the possibility that Foucault's work features an idea of "the temporality of universals." Hoy argues that "Although Foucault may be suspicious of particular claims to universality, he need not deny the applicability of all universal structures or values."[38] In other words, the genealogist can undertake a commitment to the process of universalization. Or to put it yet another way, the genealogist need not be wary of the context-transcendent capacity of many of the most remarkable forms of human practice. In his previous work (as in his dialogue with McCarthy I referred to previously), Hoy remained much closer to a more traditional reading of Foucault in his severe suspicions of the applicability of this notion of universality.[39] And yet even in that earlier work, Hoy was already suggesting that Habermasian context-transcendence and Foucaultian context-boundedness may in fact come to the same thing in practice.[40] I find this sort of thought worth developing along the lines suggested in Hoy's more recent work, especially his shrewd suggestion that "Foucault's thought must be that the universal is not the sole provenance of the universalist."[41]

Hoy's idea of the temporality of universals may be taken in two senses. In a first sense it might be seen as the view that a timeless but virtual universality emerges into reality within specific historical contexts. In a second sense it might be seen as the view that universality is itself a temporally conditioned process such that universality is contingently achieved over time. Though these two inflections of Hoy's idea may be related, I take the second interpretation to be the more crucial consequence of his proposal, at least for my purposes here. In this second sense, the idea of the temporality of universality gains its initial bearings from the observation that Foucault was like Habermas in that he was struck by the stability and resiliency of certain particular forms of human practice in remarkably different conditions. While different contexts institute different constraints, it is a remarkable fact truly in need of explanation to observe the singular consistency of the problematization of disciplinary power across an incredible diversity of institutional contexts: "Is it surprising that prisons resemble factories, schools, barracks, hospitals, which all resemble prisons?"[42] Yes, in fact, it is surprising. It is one of the central aims of *Discipline and Punish* to help us explain this remarkable cross-context conjunction of strategies, techniques, and practices. Indeed all of his books are most profitably read as developing conceptualizations that allow explanations of such surprising stabilities. *The Will to Know,* to take another case, is an inquiry into the process of the proliferation of heteronormative sexuality in the nineteenth century. Although it is clear that part of Foucault's concern in that book is to emphasize how heteronormativity is in fact not universal across all of human history, it is helpful to understand the book as also attempting to show how heteronormativity has come to increasingly assume near-universal appeal in the present. Foucault's genealogies could be profitably seen as attempts to come to terms with past processes of universalization-in-action or what we might somewhat less heroically call context-transcending-in-action.

This brings me back to the crucial conception of universality for my argument, which could be called *universalization-in-action* or, just as well, *universalizability without universalism.* Taking this conception seriously helps us see that contingency and complexity contrast respectively to necessity and simplicity, but neither need contrast to universality. We must be rigorous on this score. For a universalist interpretation of universality implicates necessity. Foucault would reject that, in part because he rejects necessity and in part because it yields a simplifying conception of universals. Foucault did not teach us to reject universals so much as he taught us to reject our urge to simplify universals. Think Freud. Think Marx. Think Descartes. Think Plato. Think of all those brilliant stories by philosophers who have promised that they could bundle up the entirety of human joy and suffering into a single lustrous idea. Foucault taught us to be wary of anyone who would perpetrate a singular spiffy answer to a maddeningly complex problem. Avoiding such reductivisms, a conception of universality as universalizability attaches contingency rather than necessity. In so doing it inspires complexity rather than simplicity. Foucault, I think, can be profitably read as focusing much of his energy on universals in precisely these aspects of their contingency and complexity. Foucault's genealogies are in part a commitment to explicating the complex and contingent conditions of possibility of some of our most constraining universals. Of course, that is not all they are, for they are also a commitment to explicating the conditions of possibility of practices that are best characterized as "almost universal" in the sense of being remarkably stable and enormously widespread. The narrow shade separating these "almost universal" practices from "never-universal but always-universalizing" practices seems hardly important.

This formulation, however, raises the specter of an objection that appears to seem crippling for my proposal. Some philosophers will reply that "full universality" is a far cry from what I am calling "near universality" and "tending toward universalization." Universality is a concept that does not admit of degrees, they will urge. Perhaps. But I respectfully disagree. My point is that we need to learn to understand universality as our achievement, and to do so we need to understand it as an ideal that guides processes that admit of degrees. If universality is interpreted according to the traditional requirements of philosophical universalism, we will be severely and rightly chastened in any search for universals that we might want to mount. The actual researches (social-scientific and philosophic) explicating our actuality can do much with a concept of universalizability but very little with a theory of universalism. All of the interest, in other words, goes with processes of universalization. To see why, consider some examples.

The history of science, the subfield in which Foucault himself got his start, offers an abundance of instructive examples of processes of contingent universalization. Paul Rabinow astutely notes that "Science is universal, but human beings do it so that means it's historical, and it could have been otherwise, and it's contingent."[43] The best way to glean the good sense of Rabinow's general point about science as a contingent universal is by way of particular examples of contingent universals in science. To feature a few such examples, allow me to dig a few more treasures out of Ian Hacking's work. Hacking's *The Emergence of Probability* and *The Taming of Chance* are philosophical histories that tell the story of the process of the universalization of our sciences of probability.[44] That story culminates, for now at least, in what Hacking calls "the imperialism of probabilities," which he convincingly describes in terms of the ubiquitous presence of statistics in our lives.[45] Hacking's achievement consists in showing how the processes resulting in this universality, ubiquity, or empire (pick your favorite term) of numbers was much more complex and contingent than we have been taught to think. And yet the end result is no less an instance of achieved universality than any other scientific endeavor with equal portability and success—one is hard-pressed to find sciences that travel further and faster than these sciences of numbers. In describing the contingent construction of the statistical world in which we live, Hacking helps us realize that an explication of the achievement of universality need not invoke a realist ontology according to which the universals of science are part of the fabric of an independent nature. We can affirm the achievement of universality as the culmination of long historical processes whose outcome is a portable and successful scientific procedure that no one is prepared to doubt. Probability works everywhere. That it does so is an achievement. It is something we humans have struggled to enact. That struggle was complex and full of contingencies. There is nothing that necessitated that it had to work.

Another memorable example found in Hacking's more recent work involves a brief but fecund reference to the proliferation of standard weights and measures. Everyone can agree that a meter is a meter, no matter where you go. The meter presents us with an instance of universality that is seemingly so indisputable as to be trivial. But it turns out that actual practices of measuring are more complex and that their universalization is anything but trivial. Hacking writes: "Transport is seldom emphasized in philosophical talk about measurement. But it is the essence of measurement, and continues into the work of modern national bureaux of standards. . . . We think of the volt as a standard unit of electric potential, but people who do standards need to construct apparatus that provides the transportable volt, that is, a standard unit of electric potential that can be taken or transmitted to any laboratory or electrical plant in the land."[46] Hacking's point is deceptively simple, and as such it bears remembering: universalizable standards have to be designed, developed, distributed, and deployed. Any electrician knows that you cannot measure volts just by thinking about them. You have to use one of those little plastic machines. You can buy a cheap one at the hardware store for as little as a dollar, or you can procure an expensive precision model that will cost you thousands. Either way, some group of people made (designed, developed, distributed) that little tool you hold in your hand (and are ready to deploy). And some other group of people made previous iterations of slightly different instruments. This goes all the way back to the very first devices. From clunky first-generation proto-tools (which, in the case of the voltmeter, were hardly portable) we eventually get to pocket devices that enable us to measure anywhere we (with our machines) can go.

Still not convinced that these are universals? Of course they are. The very point of standard measures and sciences of numbers is that we can take them anywhere. The universalization of such matters may be a process that requires both time and energy, but it yields no less sturdy a universal for that reason. Think of the ubiquitous presence of the standard meter in our built environments: there is practically nothing in our surroundings that has not been parsed out in milli-meters or kilometers. If you want to leave the city and get away from all these measurements, you will have to go a long way off the beaten path indeed. Even your favorite nature reserve has been measured out time and time again, as your collection of trail maps attests. If you do manage to find some remote corner where cartographers have not yet roamed with their GPS devices or botanists with their pocket rulers, you can always bring along your own. The universalization of measures is a process, and it counts as an impressive achievement, as has long been recognized, for instance by John Quincy Adams in 1821: "Weights and mea-sures may be ranked among the necessaries of life to every individual of human society. The knowledge of them, as in established use, is among the first elements of education, and is often learned by those who learn nothing else, not even to read and write."[47] The history of this extraordinary achievement is full of com-plexities and contingencies. Genealogy is well-suited to its description.

In tracing histories of such processes of universalization, genealogy provides a useful counterweight to our mistaken tendency to associate universality with necessity. Genealogy helps us attend to the conflicts, contests, and competitions buried within every contingent process of universalization. Genealogy helps us see that even universalizable practices as seemingly trivial as standards of weights and measures have a history in which are buried complex sequencings of contin-gent selections. The consequences of these histories are often anything but trivial. This is made poignant by considering standards in the process of their formation. One way to see this point is to attend to other kinds of standards that are today just now emerging, such as organic agriculture standards, green building stan-dards, and certain technological communications protocols. Witnessing the un-folding formation of standards in our midst helps us excavate conditions all too commonly sealed away in practices that have achieved universalization. But uni-versalization is always achieved through a historical process. These processes do not have to unfold as they do. There are untold numbers of conditioning con-straints on the future being developed today by bodies such as the International Standards Organization, the American National Standards Institute, the Internet Engineering Task Force, and the International Social and Environmental Accredi-tation and Labeling Alliance. Looking back from the future we shall witness in the annals of these institutions a rich history filled with all manner of contingencies. Their decisions of today, whose contingency is plain to anyone who knows how to look, shall condition the future of tomorrow.

Shift now to yet another kind of standards, such as those familiar to us from Foucault's work, namely standards of social measure, or social metrics, or what are more familiarly called social statistics. The history of social measurement is not only a chapter in the history of the statistical style of scientific thinking, as Hacking tells it, but also a chapter in the history of the political rationality of the modern nation-state, as Foucault tells it when he describes the importance of statistical normalization and normation for the emergence of disciplinary and biopolitical technologies of power.[48] The universalization of these standards of social measure, which are now so ubiquitous as to be recited daily on the front page of every website and newspaper with unquestioning innocence, is a long story replete with all kinds of contingent detours. Within these normalizing standards of social measure (ranging from average life expectancies and genetic proclivities for diseases to gross domestic products and rates of unemployment to grade-point averages and entrance-examination scores) are buried long-running processes of emergence whose histories helps us maintain cognizance of the dangers that are always carried along by what would otherwise pass as natural, innocent, pure, and unadulterated. These stories should not be taken as showing that social measures are tools for oppression, nor as demonstrating that on average they do more harm than good. They should rather be offered as ways of showing how social measures are constitutive components of widespread political problematizations whose dangers are always lurking.

Shift again, now away from scientific standards altogether to instances of contingent universalization in the context of political and social theory. Consider the contested case of human rights universalism. If human rights ever do get universalized, it will not be due to the dawning of the light of some universal truth in all rational creatures. It will be due to the difficult labor of proliferating across a diversity of contexts the practices, institutions and strategies that sustain human rights. Such a process of proliferation would undoubtedly begin with practices first conceived in the eighteenth century, then instantiated over the course of the twentieth century, and (potentially) transformed over the course of the next century into a remarkably stable apparatus protecting a complete suite of basic rights for every human being. If such a universalization can be achieved, future genealogists will be able to tell its story in a way that sacrifices none of the contingency and complexity of the process on the altar of necessity and parsimony. The story of the universalization of human rights, if we are ever able to tell it, will not be a heroic and monumental epic but will rather be a compendium of humble ephemera, wayward errands, and long struggles. It will be a story filled with county courthouses and countless bureaucrats, just as the story of the voltmeter is filled with all kinds of rather unassuming little phenomena like rubber gloves, electronics manufacturing entrepreneurs, and lots and lots of wire. In considering such instrumentalities as human-rights norms, genealogy will have a role to play in the retroactive gaze into the past that will help us gain grip on that which conditions our forward-looking projects of properly orienting ourselves within universalization processes as they continue to unfold.

The value of Foucault's genealogy for the process of the universalization of human rights can be gleaned by considering Benhabib's recent contribution to the discourse of universal human-rights norms. Benhabib argues for regarding universal human-rights norms as aspirations whose universalization must be achieved by specific and localized application-cum-transformation. In this view the universalization of the instrumentalities of human-rights norms is set to take place by way of contextual application through other local instrumentalities such as those courtrooms and lawyers just noted. Benhabib develops this idea in terms of a notion of "democratic iteration" that she develops through Jacques Derrida's conceptualization of "iterability," according to which every repetition of a word or concept functions necessarily to reapply that word or concept with a difference.[49] This turn to deconstruction helpfully supplements Benhabib's own reconstructive critical theory to an extent, but a fuller engagement requires more than the mere philosophical points that every application of a concept transforms that concept, and that every repetition of a practice transforms that practice. What Benhabib's critical-theoretical reconstruction of the localizing application of universalizing norms requires is a critical orientation that would enable us to inquire into the contextual conditions in which these norms must be differentially applied as we universalize them. What we need, in other words, is not the mere fact that difference is implicit in application but rather a rigorous inquiry into the different conditions of application through which application will become both possible and then actual. Foucaultian genealogy as I have been describing it (and not Derridean deconstruction, at least as I understand it) is exactly what Benhabib's project requires. Genealogy enables us to grasp what might be called the actual historical conditions of democratic iteration. Genealogy plus pragmatic critical theory can in this way take us beyond stale rehearsals of the fact that human rights instruments are both contingent and universal in order to reveal the detailed processes that show us how human rights instruments get contingently universalized. Understanding the actual details of these contingent universalizations helps us better assess their value and validity, which too often takes place under the sign of inflated generalizations failing to attend to universalization-in-motion.

A final example of contingent universalization helps further illuminate the process of inquiry (genealogical or otherwise) into contingent universals. Throughout my discussions of genealogy I have drawn freely from the work of anthropologists. Allow me to do so one last time, noting that I find anthropology so fecund for my purposes here because that discipline (or at least those portions I tend to read) is all about inquiry in the form of immersion in the details: anthropology revels in the contingencies and complexities that philosophy too often wants to wish away by way of unhelpful generalization. In thinking about universalization in motion, my sense is that anthropology (and history, and sociology) is essential for philosophy. Consider one of the most discussed contingent universals of our times (also no doubt a large part of almost any story we hear about human rights). Globalization is no doubt a central concern for us today. But too often the term is bandied about without detail to what it might mean. Anthropologists have been among the most sensitive to the stricture to avoid abstractions about globalization in order to descend into the details of globalizations in action; that is, into sites and styles of statist politics, capitalist economics, and modern science as they go universal.[50] A particularly instructive case for my purposes is offered by Anna Lowenhaput Tsing's *Friction: An Ethnography of Global Connection.*[51]

Friction opens with a frank confrontation with universals, thereby refusing to shy away from the contested terrain they take us into: "This book is about aspirations for global connection and how they come to life in 'friction,' the grip of worldly encounter. Capitalism, science, and politics all depend on global connections. Each spreads through aspirations to fulfill *universal* dreams and schemes. Yet this is a particular kind of universality: It can only be charged and enacted in the sticky materiality of practical encounters." Understanding the universality of capital, science, and state involves gaining sight of these universals in action, as they gain grip through global connections, and thereby disseminate. Tsing is clear and forceful about the gains her methodology funds: "Abstract claims about the globe can be studied as they operate in the world. We might thus ask about universals not as truths or lies but as sticky engagements. . . . Neither those who place their ideas inside the universal nor those who discredit it as false pause to consider how universals work in a practical sense." Facility with the practical work of universals is, I am urging, one of the tasks for which genealogy (like pragmatism and critical theory) is well-suited. But to do this work, philosophers in all three traditions would benefit by spending time learning from recent anthropology. What would we learn from Tsing? In one chapter, she tracks capitalist formations as they hop from Indonesian frontier jungles to Canadian stock markets to worldwide networks of precious-metals investment. Her goal is decidedly not to show *that* capitalism now has a (strangle-)hold everywhere. Rather, her inquiry demonstrates *how* capitalist finance gains friction in localities, and in so doing leverages itself to friction in other localities, such that pretty soon it is leveraged across a remarkable diversity of sites. But this self-leveraging of global capital should not be construed as monolithic, precisely because its globalization depends on the varied frictions induced by its localizations. As Tsing reports: "My point is to show the heterogeneity of capitalism at every moment in time. Capitalist forms and processes are continually made and unmade; if we offer singular predictions we allow ourselves to be caught by them as ideologies."[52] Finding out how a universal operates involves finding out how it flows through multitudinous localities to arrayed globalities, how it hops and bounds from site to site to site. Finding out *how* requires inquiry. The injunction to inquire is one stricture that genealogy shares with contemporary anthropology.

Now, these and other examples notwithstanding, some critics will surely object that my favored sense of universality in terms of practical universalization processes is a far cry from a stricter sense of principled universalism. There may remain, in other words, the worry that my sense of universality is mere descriptive generalization in a way that falls too far short of a more robust principled universalism. My reply to this objection is just the pragmatic one of pointing out that all the emphasis *should* go with actual processes of universalizing practical assemblages rather than with purported universal principles. What matters to us is not the formal universality of a principle of human rights. What matters, rather, is the practical universalization of the assemblages in virtue of which standards, rights, and whatnot are instantiated in an ever-expanding set of contexts. These universals may be contestable, and we may want to unseat or entrench them, as the case may be. But the point is that we will lack practical grip on how these universals work if we treat them as abstract principles only, losing sight thereby of the apparatus through which they function. Voltage without a voltmeter is unmeasurable just as human rights without a lawyer and a court are an empty abstraction that will never on their own save a single sufferer. Fuller assemblages of practices and their apparatus offer a view of a sense of universality that genealogists can readily endorse. So too can, as I shall now argue, pragmatists and critical theorists.

Pragmatism's Reconstructive Project

Pragmatism situates critique in a philosophical terrain emphasizing contingency and complexity in a way that is remarkably resonant with Foucaultian genealogy. Despite this philosophical overlap, there are methodological divergences that can prove valuable if situated in these broader philosophical compatibilities.

On the one hand, pragmatists are simply better than Foucault at explicating and defending the kinds of context-dependent normative resources that both pragmatism and genealogy explicitly call for. Despite the fact that there is no principled reason why Foucault could not offer ethical and political commitments, pragmatist critics like Richard Rorty were nonetheless right to complain that Foucault never really got around to offering the kinds of ethical and political commitments we would need to respond to the problematizations of our modernity. Foucault was simply too busy explicating and intensifying the problematization bits. We (I mean we genealogists or users of genealogy) need not deny that this was a real failure on Foucault's part. But neither should we refuse to see it as an accidental failure (he never got around to it, he died rather young, etc.) rather than an essential incoherence in his work (there are principled reasons why he did not do it, etc.).

On the other hand, Foucault was clearly quite better than pragmatists like Rorty and Dewey at clarifying and intensifying the problematic situations in which we find ourselves. Whatever the merits of pragmatism, it has clearly not been a strength of that tradition to root out and dig up some of the most intractable political and cultural problems of which we were scarcely aware prior to their analyses. Pragmatists like to begin with problems that are already there, taking whatever you give them, and start working with that. As for the difficult labor of actually coming to recognize something as problematic, pragmatism is actually not all that helpful. This tendency on the part of pragmatists has led to a number of unjustified, though certainly understandable, criticisms of pragmatism. The most prominent such criticism is that pragmatism is a paean to instrumental rationality or scientific method. A second related criticism is that pragmatism lacks a theory of power. A third related criticism is that pragmatism lacks a sense of the tragic. I find all three criticisms misguided, but I also find them entirely understandable as interpretations, just insofar as pragmatists have not done enough to shore up their tradition with respect to potential problems that certain of their critics have had a good nose for.[53]

To respond to the criticisms that continue to dog each tradition, pragmatism and genealogy can redress the deficiencies hindering each by combining their own resources with those resources furnished in the other. A conception of genealogical problematization serves to nicely counterbalance the instrumentalist tendencies of pragmatism. Similarly, pragmatist reconstruction works from the other side as a useful counterweight against the genealogical tendency to slip into sterile denunciation. This combination of pragmatism and genealogy is, in the first place, made possible by the fact that neither tradition requires a principled refusal of the work of the other tradition. Foucault may not have devoted his life to reconstruction, and Dewey may not have devoted his to problematization, but the work of each clearly invites the work of the other, and there were more than just a few occasions on which each thinker took up the other mode of inquiry. Insofar as both pragmatism and genealogy affirm the importance of both reconstruction and problematization, I am suggesting that we would do well to take Dewey as our model of the first and Foucault our model of the second.

Not only does my approach have the methodological and philosophical advantages that I have been urging, but it also has the additional benefit of working through some of the scholarly impasses that have functioned to block fuller engagements between contemporary practitioners of these two traditions (in both philosophy and the social sciences).[54] Influential pragmatists including Richard Rorty and Cornel West have expressed serious doubts about the possibility of a combination of pragmatism and genealogy.[55] But in recent years others have begun seriously exploring the possibility of a richer connection between these two traditions. These include, in the first place, intellectual historical studies of the shared concept of "history of the present" found in both Dewey and Foucault as well as broader intellectual histories of the important role played by pragmatism in the genesis of late–twentieth-century French thought.[56] A number of philosophical arguments have been offered by a handful of commentators.[57] Most notable for my purposes, Paul Rabinow has sketched out a pathway to mutual interaction between pragmatists and genealogists precisely on the terrain of the reconstructive and problematizing procedures featured by both.[58] Others have recently begun to implement combined forms of genealogical-pragmatist and Foucaultian-Deweyan inquiry.[59] Lastly, I have argued for this combination of pragmatism and genealogy in my own earlier work—whereas my first book came at these matters from the side of pragmatism, I have here come at them more from the side of genealogy.[60]

Having spent the majority of the foregoing chapters developing a description of genealogical problematization, I turn at this point to explicating the pragmatist procedure of reconstruction as it is featured in the work of Dewey. The first point to begin with in the present context is that reconstruction is comparable in many respects to the conception of transformation that Foucault began developing in his final years. For both involve the forward-looking work of freedom. Vincent Colapietro observes that "There is no deeper affinity between John Dewey and Michel Foucault than the patient and painstaking labor both devoted to the always justifiable impatience for freedom."[61] I discern two key points of overlap between Dewey's and Foucault's conceptions of freedom: first, the problem-solving or response-giving orientation of both, and second, the sense in which both are inflected by temporality and historicity, or what I like to call "transitionality." In the first place, both reconstruction and transformation are envisioned as responses to problematic situations. Foucault's ethics is a responsive ethics. So too is Dewey's in that it is aimed at the amelioration of extant problems and difficulties. Both Foucault and Dewey thus reject the classical philosophical ideal of a form of normativity that, as it were, generates itself for no reason other than to exist. For Foucault and Dewey, rather, normativity gets generated in the context of and for the sake of responding to, by transforming and reconstructing, problems. Normative ideals do not sustain themselves in the abstract. We construct them amongst ourselves in relation to our problematic environments. This relates to the second point of overlap, namely a sense of normativity as temporally and historically inflected. Insofar as normativity gets constructed in response to problems, it cannot be timeless. Rather, our normative conceptions, beliefs, and actions must be indexed to the historical situations in which they arise and the temporal flow in which they do the work that they perform for us. These two points of overlap mark Foucault's ethics and Dewey's ethics as substantial departures from prevailing modern ethical traditions first instituted in the late eighteenth century by Kant and Bentham, but also from recently revived ancient ethical traditions rooted in the thought of Aristotle. This is not to say that Foucault and Dewey depart completely from the quintessential triumvirate of right, good, and virtue. It is rather to suggest that they depart from crucial assumptions typically associated with that triumvirate. And, importantly, the precise points at which they depart from the tradition are more or less the same for each thinker.

Despite these overlaps, there remains at least one crucial difference that seems to separate Foucault's and Dewey's conceptions of ethical responsiveness. Reconstruction contains a robust normative inflection that often goes lacking in Foucault's conception of ethics as transformation. Reconstruction aims at something like transformations that we can affirm as good or worthwhile. In this sense, reconstruction connotes an aiming toward improvement, whereas transformation connotes only an aiming toward change. In short, the difference between reconstructive improvement and transformative change is the difference between changes that possess some kind of normative validity and changes that pull very little normative weight. That difference goes a long way if we are thinking about how to best develop responses to the problematic situations in which we find ourselves. It is one thing to merely transform these situations so that they might be otherwise. It is quite another thing, and a far more demanding labor, to reconstruct these situations in a way that actually meliorates their deficits.

And that, melioration, is the key to what pragmatism is all about.[62] At the very heart of the pragmatist spirit is a meliorist sensibility that consists in training

our efforts and energies toward progressive improvement. This sensibility constitutes the core of the pragmatist tradition running all the way back to Emerson and
all the way forward to Rorty. At the center of this tradition stands the classical triumvirate of Peirce, James, and Dewey. Dewey's are among the best reflections on
pragmatist meliorism where he frames them through the process of inquiry that
realizes growth. Nearly every facet of Dewey's philosophical project can be focused in terms of his devotion to explicating the process of growth, or education,
or learning, or any of the other varied synonyms for these in the Dewey lexicon.
In each instance, Dewey described this process as a temporally inflected and historically located affair.[63] Dewey's most consistent label for that process of inquiry
central to his philosophic vision was "reconstruction."

The book in which reconstruction is most clearly featured is his 1920 *Reconstruction in Philosophy*. He there described melioristic reconstruction as follows:
"Meliorism is the belief that the specific conditions which exist at one moment,
be they comparatively bad or comparatively good, in any event may be bettered."
The essential thing about melioration for Dewey is the process of growth rather
than the outcome of having grown: "The process of growth, of improvement
and progress, rather than the static outcome and result, becomes the significant
thing. . . . Not perfection as a final goal, but the ever-enduring process of perfect-
ing, maturing, refining is the aim in living." Whereas Foucault seemed rather ambiguous concerning the normative value of self-transformation, Dewey is positively unabashed. Growth is both good and right: the process of reconstruction
is in fact constitutive of the good and the right themselves: "Growth itself is the
only moral 'end.'"[64] In subsequent years Dewey would with increasing precision
explicate the reconstructive process in terms of progressive responses to problematic situations. This is a conception of inquiry that would come to imbue every aspect of Dewey's thought from his ethical vision of democracy to his work in
epistemology, from his aesthetics to his logic to his theory of education. The last
sentence of Dewey's *Reconstruction* states well the reconstructive, meliorative, and
educative impulse imbuing every aspect of his philosophical practice of cultural
critique: "To further this articulation and reveletation of the meanings of the current course of events is the task and problem of philosophy in days of transition."[65]

The great importance of education for Dewey's formation of reconstructive
inquiry is worth taking special note of here insofar as it anticipates Habermas's
later conceptualization of the reconstructive sciences (which draw in large part on
the developmental psychology of Lawrence Kohlberg, who himself drew on Dewey).
Dewey in one of his bolder moments once wrote that "philosophy may even be

defined as the general theory of education."[66] Dewey's explication of melioristic transformation in reconstructive terms was amply informed by his firsthand research in educational theory and developmental psychology at the University of Chicago Laboratory School, which he set up and ran from 1896 to 1904. The Laboratory School was an experimental educational institution at which Dewey developed and tested many of the methods of learning that he would later formalize in his years at Columbia University Teachers College. In his work at Chicago and Columbia, Dewey developed a philosophy of education that radically transformed America's school system. He is to this day still widely recognized as one of the most important educational theorists of the twentieth century.[67]

At the heart of Dewey's educational theory and methodology is his pragmatist conception of reconstruction. This is described in his 1916 book, *Democracy and Education,* where he outlines a sequential series of five features of "reflective experience": doubt, anticipation, survey, elaboration, and testing. One of Dewey's primary aims in the book is to encourage a vision of education that does not reduce this process of experiential reflection, or what he simply calls thinking, to the knowledge in which it results. Education must be a pedagogy of experience, not a reproduction of knowledge. The aim should be to learn how to know rather than to learn what is already known: "for we live not in a settled and finished world, but in one which is going on, and where our main task is prospective."[68]

Dewey devoted enormous philosophical energies to both practically engaging and reflectively explicating reconstructive inquiry. This was a lifelong commitment on his part that culminated in his most rigorous account of the reconstructive "pattern of inquiry" in his 1938 book *Logic: The Theory of Inquiry.* He there offered the following "definition" of inquiry: "the controlled or directed transformation of an indeterminate situation into one that is so determinate in its constituent distinctions and relations as to convert the elements of the original situation into a unified whole."[69] Dewey's is a conception of reconstruction as a process of transformation with an additional component of remediation that can pull more normative weight than can the rather more threadbare ethical concepts that Foucault had developed by the end of his life. That, in large part, is why Deweyan self-reconstruction provides a more useful way of following up on Foucaultian self-problematization than does Foucault's own conception of self-transformation.

Deweyan self-reconstruction also stands in need of Foucaultian self-problematization as its methodological counterpart.[70] This need is signaled by a crucial deficit in Dewey's pragmatist account of reconstruction as problem solving. Dewey follows Peirce in placing an enormous explanatory weight on the problematic or doubtful features of the situations in which we find ourselves: "What determines the selection of operations to be performed? There is but one answer:—the nature of the problem to be dealt with."[71] But that is hardly an answer. Imagine this dialogue with the pragmatist: "What motivates the work of reconstruction you talk about? —Problems do. –Oh good, and what then explains our need for the work of reconstruction? —Problems do. –Oh yes, of course, but one last question: Where do problems come from?" To this crucial question Dewey has no real answer, even if the diehard pragmatist will still try to work up a few vague gestures on his behalf. In virtue of what is a situation problematic? How do we come to appropriately perceive problems in terms that might enable us to undertake the work of reconstruction? And, most important of all, what enables us to transform a situation that is generally regarded as acceptable or legitimate into one that comes to be recognized as unacceptable or illegitimate? For the purposes of political and ethical critique, this last question is crucial. At the social level it marks the difference between a self-satisfied group that is unable to problematize itself and a self-aware group that is able to dynamically doubt even its most cherished ways. At the individual level it marks the difference between the person who cannot be brought to recognize their failings and the person with a capacity for confident irony.

If pragmatism generally lacks a conception of problematization, then genealogy is well prepared to fill in the deficit. Genealogy presents itself as a viable candidate for this job in part because, as I have shown, the genealogical practice of problematization aims precisely to excavate the materials with which we have contingently constructed ourselves so that we might take up these materials and reconstruct them in a way that improves our situations. Genealogy, understood as a project of problematization and not a project of subversion, invites the reconstructive reformism characteristic of the pragmatist attitude. Just as pragmatist reconstruction requires critical problematization to supply it with a material to work on, problematization requires critical reconstruction to take up its material and transform it into something better.

Genealogy agitates and pragmatism meliorates. I envision their dual deployment as follows: genealogical problematization is used to specify the details of a problematic situation in which we find ourselves; pragmatist reconstruction is then used to clarify and augment the practical responses to this problematic situation that are already being elaborated in practice. This can be developed as a reciprocal process such that the two forms of critical inquiry inform one another in mutually enriching fashion. We may begin with a small-scale problematization of a certain element in a situation. On the basis of this small-scale endeavor we may be able to fashion a small-scale reconstruction of that situation. Perhaps the small-scale reconstruction enables us to perceive additional difficulties. At that point, we can turn back to problematization to further excavate materials that give us insight into this difficulty and its conditions of possibility. This further genealogy can then act as a basis for a further pragmatist response. In this manner, genealogy and pragmatism inform one another in reciprocal fashion. We might envision the whole process as circular—not, of course, as viciously circular, but as circular in an expansive manner that enables us to improve our cultural condition along its edges by experimentally diagnosing and reconstructing what we take to be the limits of our present: picture not a static circle but rather a process of cyclical expansion like a spiral.

Dewey was like Foucault in that his work was primarily oriented around the actual process of doing inquiry. Dewey is a much less interesting thinker if we abstract from his philosophy his concrete working inquiries in education undertaken at the Laboratory School and elsewhere. Foucault is simply unimaginable without all of the historical scholarship. Already in terms of their commitment to and undertaking of practices of inquiry that are simultaneously philosophical and social-scientific do we have grounds for pulling together the work of Dewey and Foucault. But there are further reasons for thinking that problematization and reconstruction are a natural fit. Just as Foucault undertook to clarify and intensify the nominal problematizations that were already under development in practice, Dewey undertook to clarify and augment the nominal reconstructions that are the province not of theory but of theoretically informed practice. It is in this sense that pragmatism is not a claim on behalf of a systematic philosophy that can solve practical problems from the armchair, but is rather a claim for philosophy as an inquiry into existing practical processes. Dewey rightly and respectfully obeyed William James's insightful, if often misunderstood, claim that pragmatism is a method. Indeed, for James, "it is a method only."[72] Pragmatism is methodological in the same sense in which genealogy is methodological. Neither is a method in that pernicious sense of aprioristic theory that can determine practice in advance by mere acts of thought. Both are instead methods in the productive sense of a way of orienting critical inquiry into extant practices for the purposes of theoretically enriching these practices. Both problematization and reconstruction embody that curious but productive tension between practical transformation and theoretical explication whereby the philosopher does not make problems or solve problems all by themselves so much as they offer methodological orientations for inquiring into actual processes of problem-production and problem-resolution that are already under way in practice.

This helps explain why in addition to their shared commitment to first-order inquiry and practice (e.g., Dewey's hands-on work at the Lab Schools and Foucault's in the context of prisons), Dewey and Foucault were most heavily invested in explicating a second-order account of their first-order inquiries. Just as Foucault's second-order problematizations help us understand that this form of inquiry is aimed at explicating the conditions of possibility of the present, Dewey's second-order reconstructions clarify that he envisions inquiry as in part an explication of the conditions of possibility of the melioration of the present, or the conditions of possibility of a better future.

In mentioning conditions of possibility in this context I intend to draw attention to the Kantian inheritance that informs both genealogy and pragmatism. For both pragmatism and genealogy take from Kant the core idea of critique as an inquiry into limiting conditions of possibility but dispense with the transcendental trappings with which Kant himself associated this idea. Recall my distinction between critique and transcendental critique in Chapter 3. This is the distinction between inquiry into limiting conditions of possibility and just one form that such critical inquiry might take where it is concerned to explicate the universal and necessary conditions of synthetic *a priori* cognition of objects. I take this distinction from Kant himself, whose major writings were rigorously committed to transcendental critique but whose lesser writings intimate the possibility of alternative forms of non-transcendental critique. The separation of Kantian critique from Kantian transcendental idealism is crucial for recognizing that pragmatism remains faithful to critique in Kant's sense. Although many pragmatists understand their philosophical tradition as an alternative to Kant, I think we ought to be a little more fine-grained in our comparative analysis. Pragmatism is surely an alternative to both transcendental and metaphysical philosophy. But it need not for that reason constitute an alternative to critical philosophy. And it is the project of critique, I have been urging, that is Kant's true legacy to contemporary philosophy. Allow me to defer a little longer my detour through pragmatism in order to show that it too, like genealogy, is an explicit contribution to this legacy.

The Kantian roots of pragmatism are worth explicit discussion given the long-standing antipathy toward Kant on the part of many pragmatists, perhaps most notably Rorty.[73] Such antipathy notwithstanding, recent scholarship has begun to make some headway in the direction of explicating the Kantian roots of pragmatism. A convincing background for these newer reinterpretations are offered by classic intellectual histories of pragmatism including books by H. S. Thayer and Bruce Kuklick, and an article by Murray Murphey dubbing the Cambridge Pragmatists "Kant's Children."[74] Against this backdrop, a more recent suite of

contemporary neopragmatists, including no less than Hilary Putnam, Richard Bernstein, Joseph Margolis, and Robert Brandom, have forwarded claims for the Kantian sensibility at the core of our pragmatism(s).[75] Focusing more directly on figures, there is now fairly wide recognition of Kant's decisive though by no means
unambiguous influence on Peirce,[76] and studies of Kantian themes in James and
Dewey have begun to appear in recent years.[77] Also of note is the recent tendency
on the part of some Kantian philosophers to lay a claim to some core parts of the
pragmatist tradition; most notable in this regard is Habermas, discussed in the following section.[78] We also now finally have a first-rate broad-based study explicitly
devoted to explicating pragmatism as a Kantian project, namely Sami Pihlström's
Naturalizing the Transcendental: A Pragmatic View. Pihlström's book shows how to
pragmatize Kant's project: "Kant's transcendental philosophy was concerned with
the conditions of our being able to represent and cognize a structured world of
empirical objects . . . The pragmatist trick is to treat these conditions as socially,
culturally, and historically (or, in a broad sense, 'practically') constrained, changing, and reinterpretable."[79] This is exactly that Hegalian radicalization of Kant I am
attributing to genealogy. Pihlström insists that this move keeps good company
with contemporary Kantians like Onora O'Neill in her "procedural, historicized,
and essentially anti-foundationalist" reading of Kant.[80] But to clarify, whereas
Pihlström describes this move as transforming the Kantian idea of *transcendental*
philosophy, I take it as a transformation of the Kantian idea of *critical* philosophy.[81]
Once the conditions of possibility that critique reveals are situated in the way that
Pihlström urges (historically, socially, and otherwise contextually), they need no
longer be transcendental (universally and necessarily *a priori*). And yet they do
still count as critical conditions of possibility for our practices. Despite this rather
small quibble, I can agree with the more general outline of Pihlström's book as
summarized in this claim: "The task of critical philosophy is to help us understand
our human situation by providing an account of such conditions 'from within' the
experiential field they make possible."[82]

   Since Dewey is my emblem for pragmatism in these pages, let me turn briefly
to some of his writings about Kant in order to plant a seed of discontent over the
all-too-common interpretation of Dewey as anti-Kantian.[83] First, it should be recognized that Dewey, like Foucault, had a lifelong interest in Kant. His 1884 disser-
tation was titled "The Psychology of Kant," and thereafter he continued to write
about Kant all his life. "The Copernican Revolution" is the title of the final chapter of Dewey's 1929 *The Quest for Certainty.* Dewey there explicates his pragmatism
with explicit reference to Kant by showing how pragmatism builds on Kant (in
its critical constructivism) and also goes well beyond him (in its abandonment of
transcendentalism). Dewey's claim in that chapter to a Kantian inheritance is fo-

cused in terms of Kant's revolutionary change of perspective from the old project of explaining how our thought is adequate to reality to the new project of explicating the conditions of possibility for thought as such. According to this Kantian proposal our thought is conditioned such that we shall never need an independent account of reality shorn of its engagement with what we think. All we need is a precise delineation of the conditions of thinking itself. Dewey goes this far with Kant, and then starts egging him even further to go beyond transcendentalism in favor of experimentalism. Dewey summarizes this as the view that "an idea in experiment is tentative, conditional, not fixed and rigorously determinative" and explicitly contrasts this to transcendental critique: "There is nothing hypothetical or conditional about Kant's forms of perception and conception. They work uniformly and triumphantly; they need no differential testing by consequences. The reason Kant postulates them is to secure universality and necessity instead of the hypothetical and the probable."[84] Despite his refusal of Kantian transcendentalism, Dewey's project ever remained one of Kantian critique, insofar as it was an inquiry into the conditions that make possible the correct uses of thought, or what Dewey called intelligence. There is a deeply Kantian resonance in the central problematic structuring Dewey's attempt to understand how, in a philosophic universe that can no longer brook the eternal, we can maintain a grip on normativity or correctness. This problematic was concisely stated by Dewey at the outset of his 1938 *Logic: The Theory of Inquiry* when he wrote: "How, it will be asked, can inquiry which has to be evaluated by reference to a standard be itself the source of the standard? How can inquiry originate logical forms (as it has been stated that it does) and yet be subject to the requirements of these forms?"[85] These, I submit, are deeply Kantian questions.

Dewey's Kantianism is best seen as follows. Kant enabled the constructivist breakthrough according to which the conditions of human cognition are constructed by us rather than the unknowable divine. But he still construed cognition as subject to universal and necessary constraints. This raises an insoluble problem concerning whether these invariant constraints are also constructs of our thought—a new variation on an old scholastic debate about whether divine reason is constrained by eternal requirements of reason itself. Kant held that the operations of human thought could not construct its own invariants insofar as finite thought cannot construct universality and necessity out of itself. But he recognized that he still needed to give an account of these constraints if he was going to posit them, and so he invented the notion of transcendental critique to account for how we might nevertheless account for these constraints. According to this account, we cannot have access to realities independent of cognition because the very process of cognizing involves a mediation of the noumenal behind our own backs, as it were. Kant, in short, was willing to dispense with the idea of a reality in itself independent of cognition but then realized that he had to save a transcendentalized version of this idea if he was to account for the universal and necessary constraints on cognizing as such. Hegel caught on to Kant's trick right away, and insisted against Kant that universality and necessity were the yield of a cunning of reason that is in the process of historically unfolding. But why, Dewey wondered, should we continue to hold that cognition is constrained with the force of necessity? For Dewey, there is nothing either outside (no divine or metaphysical force) or inside (no transcendental idea or history) thinking necessitating its course.

In rejecting the necessity that Kant sought Dewey nevertheless retained a modest conception of universality as a kind of practical ideal, but he reconceptualized the project of critique by detaching universality from necessity. For Dewey, universality is a quality of methods, which are universalized through practical procedures of contingent dissemination. Dewey thus writes of "the inherent universality of scientific method."[86] Dewey explains his conception at one point in terms of what he called "relational universality": "The *universality* that belongs to scientific theories is not that of inherent content fixed by God or Nature, but of range of applicability—of capacity to take events out of their apparent isolation so as to order them into systems."[87] Universality, for Dewey, involves applicability, and in this way universality and contextuality are always interwoven.

Dewey's revision of Kant in these terms is strikingly resonant with a similar move in Habermas, as I shall show in the following section. Both pragmatism (in Dewey) and critical theory (in Habermas) inherit from Kant the key idea of constructivism. Thought conjures its own conditions of possibility out of itself. Thought is as a bottomless contingency from out of which we pull ourselves up. Thought is our achievement, and it shall ever be as fragile or as sturdy as we manage to make it.

Critical Theory's Reconstructive Project

Turning now to Habermas, there is considerably amplified resistance in proposing a connection to Foucault along the lines of that which connects pragmatism to genealogy. I have already suggested some of the ways in which the dialogue between Foucault and Habermas has been remarkably strained. But I discern important methodological connections that, in turn, lead to the promise of interesting new philosophical points of contact.

In what ways does Habermas help us in developing the work of critique in its normative dimension? How do the resources he provides resonate with similar such resources as made available by Deweyan pragmatism as well as Foucaultian genealogy? To begin answering these questions, I want to emphasize the strong Kantian overtones of Habermas's project. Though Dewey was like Foucault in inheriting a Kantian sensibility, neither was ever as explicitly Kantian as Habermas. In Habermas's hands, normative philosophy works empirically and philosophically to specify the conditions of possibility of those of our competencies that can rightly be seen as achievements rather than endowments. The normative center of Habermas's philosophy can be seen in these terms as a Kantian project of critique. Habermas has given a variety of expressions to this center throughout his career. I here read Habermas as I read Foucault, namely as developing so many non-identical attempts to reconfigure the Kantian project of critique. A standard sequencing of Habermas's works runs as follows: he first outlined a more social-scientific program of critique in *Knowledge and Human Interests* (1968), only to turn to a more theoretical and massively monumental outline in the two-volume *The Theory of Communicative Action* (1981), which he then turned back on again in his later work in an explicitly political-theoretical vein in *Between Facts and Norms* (1992). Although I draw in what follows on works from across Habermas's career, it should be noted that his major books are not all cut from the same cloth. My discussions of Habermas do not account in the main for fine distinctions of detail that are contingent upon an exhaustive engagement with the development of his thought over time. This is because my attempt involves the more humble and simple task of discerning a Kantian project of normative critique at the heart of Habermas's philosophy that can be shown to be compatible with both genealogical diagnosis and pragmatist normative philosophy as described above.

I begin with a useful homonym. In early work Habermas offers a conception of "reconstructive" sciences that bears more than just a linguistic affinity with Dewey's pragmatist conception of "reconstruction." The two uses of the same term are, to be clear, by no means identical. While reconstruction for pragmatists like Dewey invokes the future-facing work of articulating the resolution of problems, reconstruction for critical theorists like Habermas more often has to do with the backward-looking work of understanding how past resolutions of problems have been achieved. Despite this crucial difference, the shared orientation I shall here exploit concerns the point that reconstruction for both Dewey and Habermas refers to what both write about in terms of processes of learning and of problem solving. In this respect, there is more than just a shared spirit in the work that these conceptions of reconstruction are being asked to do, even if that spirit is clearly not identical.

The best key to Habermas's use of the idea of reconstructive methodology is offered in a set of essays from the 1970s published in English as a little book titled *Communication and the Evolution of Society*. Both Axel Honneth and Thomas

McCarthy have described these essays as indicative of a deep and important shift in Habermas's work.[88] For it is in these essays that Habermas first gains full clarity about his crucial idea of reconstructive learning processes. Habermas develops this philosophical conception in conversation with pragmatists, logical positivists, and analytic language philosophers, but above all with the pragmatist-inspired developmental psychologies of Jean Piaget and especially Lawrence Kohlberg. Habermas's essays develop a conception of reconstruction that resonates on many levels with Dewey's conception of pragmatic reconstruction as a learning process. For Dewey, reconstruction involves melioration or problem solving: we reconstruct a situation by developing novel means for rectifying problems or difficulties implicit in the situation. While Habermas's conception of reconstruction is certainly not identical with the pragmatist notion, there is an important and instructive analogy that I want to here elucidate.[89] Habermas offers us the following definition: *"reconstruction signifies taking a theory apart and putting it back together again in a new form in order to attain more fully the goal it has set for itself."*[90] Borrowing explicitly from Piaget, but also implicitly echoing Dewey and Mead, Habermas describes patterns of reconstruction as "rules for possible problem solving" and as individual and social "learning mechanisms."[91]

In more recent work these themes remain at the core of Habermas's approach to normative critical theory. For instance, in an essay on Mead in his 1988 *Postmetaphysical Thinking,* Habermas explicates the process of individuation-through-socialization by reference to intersubjective processes of problem solving that Mead theorized in symbolic-interactionist terms.[92] And in his 1999 *Truth and Justification,* Habermas offers a self-titled "Kantian pragmatist" view, according to which "epistemology must explain the deeply complex learning processes that sets in when the expectations that guide our actions are problematized."[93] Reconstruction for Habermas, as for Dewey, is more like a philosophical clarification of practical problem solving than it is like the philosophical solving of practical problems. The role of the philosopher is not to come up with clever solutions to practical difficulties. Rather the role of the philosopher is to develop a methodological orientation for critical inquiry by virtue of which we can clarify and augment reconstructive processes that are already under way in practice. Reconstructive methodology is thus second-order for Habermas as for Dewey. Further, the dual sense of critical theoretical reconstruction as the verbal activity of the philosopher plus the nominal object of philosophical inquiry corresponds well to the dual sense of verbal and nominal problematization described previously in my discussion of Foucault. Indeed, in just the ways that pragmatism and genealogy belong together, as discussed in the previous section, a similar case can be made for a combination of critical theory and genealogy.

The most persistent problem, rooted in a perceived philosophical incompatibility, that has proven a stumbling block for those seeking to develop connections among critical theory on the one hand and contextualist traditions such as pragmatism and genealogy on the other concerns the strong requirement for universalizability generated in Habermas's second-order explication of the rules for problem solving. This requirement, of course, has much to do with Habermas's normatively ambitious conception of reconstruction. In Habermas's early work this took the form of an unabashed transcendentalism in which universality and necessity were entrained: "If we want to subject processes of reaching understanding (speech) to a reconstructive analysis oriented to general and unavoidable presuppositions in the same way as has been done for cognitive processes, then the model of transcendental philosophy undeniably suggests itself."[94] Here we confront a commitment to universality that seems flatly incompatible with the emphases on contingency and complexity coloring the more contextualist historicisms of Dewey and Foucault. Habermas is unequivocal in his claim that reconstructive sciences aim to elucidate the underlying presuppositions of universalizability as a condition of possibility of any communicative interaction whatsoever. This is most perspicuous in his principle of universalization, according to which norms are valid only if *"All* affected can accept the consequences and the side effects its *general* observance can be anticipated to have for the satisfaction of *everyone's* interests."[95] Clearly this is a revision of Kant's universalizability test for moral maxims. So, we might ask, is it really consistent with pragmatism and genealogy?

The impasse here concerns the supposed opposition between universalism and contextualism. Foucaultian genealogy is like Deweyan pragmatism in its firm commitment to contextualist complexity and contingency. There is on the other hand a clear impulse in Habermasian critical theory toward universalist parsimony and necessity. This opposition between the contextual and the universal has been sharpened time and time again in recent decades. Indeed it forms a kind of leitmotif through which we can read many of the most central debates over theory in recent decades: identity versus difference, essentialism versus constructionism, foundations versus practices, objectivity versus relativity, cosmopolitanism versus particularism, and yes, also Habermas versus Foucault. One of the most fruitful handles for picking up these issues is provided by the disagreements between critical theorists like Habermas and pragmatists like Rorty. Canvassing these disagreements will motivate my broader argument here that we can find means of connecting the critical theoretical emphasis on universality with the pragmatist and genealogical emphasis on contingency.

Rorty has tirelessly criticized Habermas for endorsing an ideal of universality that he finds in principled competition to the pragmatist endorsement of an ideal of context-sensitivity. Rorty interprets Habermas's demand for universal validity in terms of a distinction between unconditional truth and conditioned justification. Habermas, says Rorty, makes too much of the idea of a "transcendent moment" that, "seems to me to run together a commendable willingness to try something new with an empty boast."[96] Rorty's pragmatism allows him to affirm the importance of transporting our achievements from context to context. Yet it also often prevents him from allowing that our context-bound achievements have any context-transcending implications. Rorty offers a memorable image that nicely condenses his concerns about Habermas's conflation between "making an assertion" and "implicitly claiming to be able to justify it to all audiences, actual and possible": the latter claim, says Rorty, would be "like the village champion, swollen with victory, predicting that he can defeat any challenger, anytime, anywhere."[97] At the core of Rorty's concern there evidently lies a very strong interpretation of transcendentality according to which Habermas's "transcendent movement" implies something like timeless properties of universality and necessity.[98]

But I am not so sure that Habermas wants to hold himself to such a high standard. Certainly he does not need to. Indeed, in work produced right on the heels of the strong universalism articulated in *The Theory of Communicative Action*, Habermas began to back off, in large part as a response to cautions concerning a strong transcendentalism raised by a number of sympathetic critics (most notably Axel Honneth, Thomas McCarthy, Seyla Benhabib, and Richard Bernstein). Habermas explicitly dropped the emphasis on strong forms of transcendentality: "What earlier was relegated to transcendental philosophy . . . now gets adapted to the circle of reconstructive sciences."[99] Habermas has, ever since, been migrating toward a more relaxed standard of universality according to which universalization proves to be nothing higher than the project of extending our achievements to every possible context in which they might work. Surely we can do that without assuming the swollen pride of the village champion. Perhaps the confidence implicit in Habermas's conception of universality is nothing much more grand than the forward-looking gaze that often accompanies a job well done. What village champion does not seek out newer and greater challenges on the heels of their latest victory? Perhaps, in other words, the impulse for universalization defended by Habermas is nothing grander than the impulse for growth defended by Dewey. If this is transcendence, it is horizontal and temporal, not vertical and eternal.

The prospective orientation of the horizontal look out into the future is precisely where critical theory and pragmatism come together. In their enterprises of looking forward they share much, including hopes for the universalization of the best achievements we moderns have mustered out of ourselves: democracy, human rights, liberty, equality, and more humble accomplishments like potable water, penicillin, and pneumonia vaccines. These are not the kind of universals that come stitched into the metaphysical fabric of reality. Yet why should we not hope that they may yet be universalized? The universality involved here is a universalization of practices rather than a universalism of principles. What matters with human rights, just as with penicillin, is not so much the portability of the principle as it is the transportation of the assemblages by which the principle is made to function in contexts where it is needed. This is precisely the sense in which Dewey, as I showed previously, endorses exactly the ideal of universality that I detect in Habermas. Dewey shows pragmatists how to accept an idea of universality freely and without the over-anxious worry that Rorty always felt when facing that concept.[100]

Rorty's overly cautious view is characteristic of an overreaction on the part of a wide number of critics who insist that Habermas relies on a universalism that is clearly incompatible with contingency. It is easy enough to see why readers of Habermas have felt the need to push back so strongly against this universalism. For Habermas is prone to making old-fashioned-sounding philosophical noises about universals that would—and should—prick the ears of any contextualist or historicist. Despite such noises, the signal-to-noise ratio in Habermas is usually in his favor. So we should try harder to sort out the signal. Doing so would involve picking out those elements of Habermas's work that are more markedly pragmatist in orientation and using them as a basis for weaning Habermasian critical theory off of the errors implicit in its more universalistic and transcendental moments. I am suggesting that Deweyans and Foucaultians can be comfortable with Habermas's strong emphasis on universalizability if we can find ways of reinterpreting this emphasis in terms of contingent rather than necessary universalization—and I am suggesting that this is made possible by interpreting universalizability through the lens of the kind of pragmatism that I have already argued is compatible with genealogy.

I propose a relatively simple, if not controversial, distinction between two strategies for reading Habermas. The first strategy will take most of its cues from Habermas's monumental 1981 *The Theory of Communicative Action*. This remains by far the dominant interpretive strategy in the contemporary literature, in part because many of Habermas's most influential ideas are worked out in that text. The second strategy adopts a different course in taking most of its cues from some of Habermas's work since then, including his 1992 *Between Facts and Norms* and 1999's *Truth and Justification*, where he overtly returns to the pragmatist roots evident in his much earlier work, such as his 1968 *Knowledge and Human Interests*. The trajectory of Habermas's philosophic career suggests that the second reading is truer to his overall intentions. In the wake of criticisms of the strong universalism laid out in the *Theory of Communicative Action*, Habermas moved toward a weaker conception of universality in his later works that many commentators have found compatible with the core pragmatist commitments of contextualism and fallibilism. In many ways, the project of *Between Facts and Norms* is a return to the pragmatism central to *Knowledge and Human Interests* as interpreted through central doubts in *The Theory of Communicative Action* about metaphysical-sounding appeals to supposedly real interests.

We would do better to look to Habermas for what we can positively gain from his writings rather than to what we should negatively reject. This involves taking Habermas at his word when he calls himself a "Kantian" who nevertheless "detranscendentalizes" reason. Rortyan pragmatists may have justifiable beefs with the Kantian vision of transcendental philosophy and the flat universalism it invokes. But we can get these beefs off of our chest without chastising post-Kantians like Habermas who invoke transcendence and universality in a far less puffed-up sense as something like processes of transcending specific contexts and of universalizing validity claims. Do pragmatists and genealogists really need to make bones with these ideas? Do we really want to deny that some of our practices transcend the contexts in which they emerge, perhaps even in some cases achieving universal validity across all contexts? Those with nagging worries about such thoughts are probably skeptically focusing on rather demanding practices that do not easily admit of context-transcending universalization: they perhaps focus too much on controversial moral content. But if we shift our initial frame of focus to more humble cases, we can begin to glimpse the sense of the idea: think again of standards of measurement, which work just about everywhere, or perhaps a little more challenging, our hopes for the universalization of basic human rights. The trick is to not get too carried away. Reconceiving universality as a process helps us stay humble so that we do not get so excited that we start beating one another over the head with our supposedly already-universal ideals.

Rorty was surely right that the most difficult point to accept in Habermas's critical theory, especially as articulated in the works of the *Theory of Communicative Action* period, concerns his claims for the context-transcendent universality of our validity claims. This core aspect of Habermas's work does indeed seem to run counter to my proposed redescription of his views. This is why I follow others in pushing recent critical theory toward a kind of pragmatist contextualism in emphasizing the value of genealogy for understanding the problematic features of situated context. My claim here is just that critical theory can be nudged far enough toward pragmatism in this direction without forcing an abandonment of a commitment to universality. We can reinterpret universality in such a way as to explicate its intimate connections with contextualism rather than its reliance on a defunct philosophical universalism. Indeed I take it as one of the singular contributions of Habermas's work to clear the way toward a conception of critical inquiry that integrates both context-transcendence and context-boundedness. Too many pragmatists and genealogists neglect to emphasize this aspect of his critical theory. So, in the remainder of this section, I would like to emphasize this theme.

The crucial point for my argument is this: context-transcendence surely cannot involve transcending those features of our problematic contexts that are relevant to the application of normative reconstructions in the first place.[101] Universalizable norms, unless they are to remain purely formal, have to apply to something. Eschewing extremist formalism requires interpreting context-transcendence as the transcendence of only those context-dependent features of situations that are not relevant to the application of the universalizable practical normativity in virtue of which we reconstruct the problematic features of those situations. If context-transcendence required transcending those situational features necessary for the specification of the problem that our norms are meant to reconstruct, then we would have no terms in which to assess the situation as now normatively reconstructed or still normatively problematic once it gets invested with norms. In short, context-transcendence is intelligible only if it does not require us to transcend context-relevant features of situations that are necessary for the assessment of those situations as either problematic or reconstructed.

Consider that Habermas's emphasis on universality is ambiguous between two interpretations, each of which is motivated by one of my two reading strategies. On the one hand we might (if we are only reading *The Theory of Communicative Action*) interpret it as an emphasis on a *universalism* that is already instantiated in each and every issuance of a reconstructive claim (be it cognitive or normative). On the other hand we might (if we focus more on *Between Facts and Norms*) interpret it as a yearning for *universalizability* such that each and every issuance of a reconstructive claim is seen as positing its validity in a way that requires actually transcending the context in which the claim is issued. To this distinction between universalism and universalizability corresponds a further distinction between what might be called "context-transcendentalism" and "context-transcending" as a distinction between a theoretical principle on the one hand and a practical process on the other. I think the latter interpretation of the two paired distinctions makes better sense of Habermas's overall project. An ideal of universalizability is better suited than one of universalism to the crucial switch from monological to dialogical rationality that Habermas stresses throughout many of his writings.

Rereading Habermas through this distinction is supported by interpretations of his work offered by three of his best commentators who also take themselves to be furthering his project. Start with the interpretation offered by Axel Honneth: "the universalization test . . . must now be conceived of as a procedure that can find appropriate application only in a discussion among all those potentially affected . . . not just in the light of his or her own particular arguments, but also against the background of the arguments of all those affected."[102] On this reading, Habermas's view is that universality must be instantiated by means of extending (i.e., applying) reconstructive validity claims to the actual contexts for which they seek to be valid. We cannot simply posit universality monologically according to the old philosophical foundation of universalism. Rather we must implement universality dialogically, within actual practices of universalizing our validity claims. Explicating Habermas's stress on universality in terms of the process of universalizing validity claims across contexts in a way that does not require a universalist assertion of validity as already warranted in every context before being interpreted into the constraints of those contexts also enables us to recognize a synergy of context-transcendence and context-boundedness in Habermas's critical theory. The idea of a universalizing process of context-transcending better captures this synergy than does the idea of a philosophical universalism already transcendental to each and every context. This is a point that Thomas McCarthy has also emphasized: "we cannot help but have it both ways, that is, agree upon *some* decontextualized—abstract, general, formal—norms, values, principles, rights, procedures, and the like, which must then be ongoingly contextualized—interpreted, elaborated, applied—in particular situations."[103] Universality requires reinterpreting our validity claims against the backgrounds supplied by the contexts to which these claims are extended. The idea is that of universalization as ongoing reinterpretation across varying contextual backgrounds. This point has also been ably developed by Seyla Benhabib, who notes that the "reconstructive sciences replace transcendental philosophy today" because they link up the call for universalizability with the orientation toward contingency appropriate to historically situated critical theory. Benhabib turns Hegel's riposte to Kant into her own reply to Habermas: "There is also a dialectic of form and content in the program of communicative ethics insofar as the principle of universalizability does not result from the formal and minimal premises of theory alone, but can only be justified with reference to additional assumptions." These additional assumptions must be fleshed out as we move from context to context. Benhabib's insight is to draw out the strengths of this slow drift from Kantian toward Hegelian thought in terms of a more situated conception of critical theory to help us recognize the need for integrating "contextualization" with "universalizability."[104] Here precisely is where Habermas can be productively melded with the thought of contextualists like Foucault and Dewey.

The interpretation I am advocating is one that has not only been stressed by many of Habermas's best interpreters in the tradition of critical theory, but also by Habermas himself, who has frequently noted that reconstructive inquiries mark a decisive break from the core of Kantian transcendentalism without sacrificing the Kantian impulse toward universalization. In light of such a change in the conception of how critical theory might best do its work, Habermas calls his a "Kantian pragmatist" view.[105] Habermas in recent work has also explicitly committed himself to the "detranscendentalization" of the Kantian project.[106] He quotes Hilary Putnam to elucidate his own position: "Reason is . . . both immanent (not to be found outside of concrete language games and institutions) and transcendent (a regulative idea that we use to criticize the conduct of all activities and institutions)."[107] As Habermas interprets both Putnam and himself, the upshot of detranscendentalization is a relocation of the classical tension between empirical and transcendental into the worldly tension between processes of context-bound and context-transcending validity. This shift from transcendental universalism to reconstructive universalizability is most fully elaborated in *Between Facts and Norms* where it is described as a persisting tension between context-transcending validity and context-bounded validity. Here is a representative, and also heavily quoted, passage from Habermas's book: "validity claims are Janus-faced: as claims, they overshoot every context; at the same time, they must be both raised and accepted here and now if they are to support an agreement effective for coordination. . . . The universalistic meaning of the claimed validity exceeds all contexts, but only the local, binding act of acceptance enables validity claims to bear the burden of social integration for context-bound everyday practice." Habermas's description of this tension in the first sections of the book borrows heavily from the pragmatism of Charles Santiago Peirce who teaches us, says Habermas, that "it is within time that the learning processes of the unlimited communication community build the bridges that span all local and temporal distances."[108] We can, Habermas seems to be urging, learn to recognize a value in the relation between contingency and universality precisely by understanding the relation as a tension rather than a contradiction. The tension, in short, is between the yearning for context-transcending universality posited by validity claims on the one hand and the context-bound application of these validity claims on the other. Since universality must be actual-ized through real dialogical encounters, Habermas's theory generates a tension according to which validity claims must both strive for universality and at the same time never attain fully universality. But this tension is not debilitating. It is in fact enormously productive when seen from the vantage of dynamic universalizability processes rather than the vantage of a static property of universality.[109]

Contextualists, then, need not worry. Habermas should be seen as doing nothing more threatening than pushing the pragmatist insight that universalization, where it holds, is a historically mediated and temporally inflected process, as exampled by Dewey's conception of "relational universality" not as a universalism of "inherent content" but as a universalizability specified by "range of applicability."[110] Contextualists and universalists need not disagree over the basic idea that our practices, insofar as they express normative achievements (which all practices do), are always conditioned by a tension between context-bound past successes and context-transcending appeals for further future successes. Claims for universalizability must be experimentally tested in actual practical processes rather than asserted by fiat as properties inherent in the nature of things. We may make bets about the future, but we should all be prepared to acknowledge that the bets should not pay until the race has actually been run. A great deal of work—that is, experimental testing—is involved in specifying which features of contexts are and are not relevant. Therein lies the productive tension between contingent facticity and universalizing validity about which pragmatists, critical theorists, and genealogists can all agree. All of these forms of immanent critical inquiry today must work with contingent universals rather than assuming that there need be an opposition between context and transcendence. I discern here a productive interdigitation, the productivity of which is a function more of practical experimentation than of theoretical argumentation.

To locate this general point in the context of two other recent contributions to critical theory: I agree with both the emphasis on context-boundedness offered by Amy Allen and the emphasis on context-transcendence defended by Maeve Cooke while disagreeing with Allen's caution about universality and Cooke's caution about context-boundedness.[111] I propose to have it both ways because I think all of the action is at the level of the practical work of determining the contextual features of the situations we find ourselves in to which our context-transcending norms would apply. Norms need be both bound to their contexts and capable of transcending those contexts. Anything that works must work here and now and also be capable of working somewhere else too, though that "somewhere else too" must become a new "here and now" to make good on what is otherwise a merely empty capability. In the abstract, where everything remains indeterminate, norms cannot do the work by virtue of which they are valuable—normativity in that sense is but a promise of virtue such that it pays to remember the pragmatist point that a promise never saved a life or stopped an injustice. It is only by being rendered practical in implementation that norms can work—promises do all of their work when they are cashed out in deeds. Norms can be rendered practical, can be cashed out, only insofar as we are able to determine features of contexts in which they are to be applied. Genealogy is crucial for the work of such implementation insofar as it gives us grip on our contexts with respect to problems that are expressly in need of normative resources for their repair. Thus, the further the critical theory tradition travels down the path of pragmatist sensitivity to context without sacrificing its commitment to universality, the closer it comes to recognizing the uses of genealogy for its purposes. Genealogy has an indispensible role to play within the program of pragmatist critical theory precisely insofar as it helps us grasp those features of problematic situations that form the basis of our ongoing assessment of those situations once we begin to experimentally reconstruct them.

To see how this could work, consider again the tension between the complexity of contexts and the relative parsimony of universalizable norms. What this tension suggests is that our norms must be continually reapplied and reinterpreted in the situations in which they function. Habermas is explicit about this in an essay which, it is worth noting in passing, is titled "A Genealogical Analysis": "A moral obligation cannot follow from the so to speak transcendental constraint of unavoidable presuppositions of argumentation alone; rather it attaches to the specific objects of practical discourse, namely, to the norms *introduced* into discourse to which the reasons mobilized in deliberation refer."[112] The process of reapplication and reinterpretation requires thick specifications of the problematic features of the various contexts to which our validity claims get extended. This is precisely where genealogy can play a crucial role for critical theoretical reconstruction. For genealogy helps us articulate those of our situations that are problematizations in need of normative reconstruction.

Genealogy, and not something else, is just what is needed here insofar as existing programs of reconstructive critical theory remain insufficient for the purposes of problematization. Normative reconstruction is oriented toward explicating the conditions of possibility of the positive learning embodied in normative and cognitive processes. But this orientation is not particularly helpful if we need to explicate the conditions of possibility of the dangers or problems inherent in these very processes. Critical theorists, recognizing this, have not been blind to the need for diagnosis as a component of their work. But critical theory does not facilitate as rich a diagnostic as does genealogy. There are a great many more such relevant contextual features (expressing a great deal more contingency and complexity) constitutive of the problematic situation than critical theorists have tended to emphasize. To the extent that critical theory does approximate such a conception of problematization, it too often relies on a conception of ideology critique out of tune with the post-foundational urge of contemporary critical theory itself.[113] It is thus notable that in recent decades critical theorists have increasingly distanced themselves from the classical conception of ideology to the point where today the concept is hardly featured in the best recent work within the tradition. In doing so, the critical theorists have gained an edge against the foundationalism of previous iterations of their tradition, but they have also decidedly reoriented their work toward normative reconstruction and away from critical problematization. This points to a lacuna in contemporary critical theory that genealogy can ably fill in.

The strengths of critical theory today lie in its anticipatory-utopian capacities rather than in its diagnostic-critical attempts at a problematization of our present. Thus we can affirm the value of critical theory for anticipatory reconstruction while delegating the tasks of diagnostic problematization to genealogy, which is much better prepared for those purposes. Indeed genealogy is tailored exactly for the kinds of problematizing functions that critical theory today is so much in need of. Like critical theory, genealogy is also articulated in a post-foundational key that forestalls all the familiar criticisms that have been leveled against classical forms of ideology critique rooted as they are in overarching theoretical apparatuses implementing overblown conceptual generalizations. This points the way toward how apparatuses of diagnostic problematization and normative reconstruction may yet fit together in complementary fashion: genealogy explicates the background problematizations against which our normative reconstructions get reapplied and reinterpreted. Benhabib has articulated a synergistic relation between problem and response that resonates well with the stepwise procedure of circular expansion that I envision: "every new stage of learning brings with it new problems and a new awareness of problems which in turn require new solutions."[114] Agreeing with Benhabib on this point, I leave off where she argues that critical theory is better-equipped than genealogy for the work of diagnostic problematization.

Despite decades of missed dialogue, I find critical theory particularly well-positioned today to appreciate the advantages of a genealogical specification of the relevant contextual features of the problematic situations in which we find ourselves. I take part of my confidence from the shared interdisciplinary nature of both critical theory and genealogy. The genealogist draws amply on work by historians, anthropologists, and sociologists in their attempt to problematize the history of the present. This is not unlike the work of Habermas and the Frankfurt School more generally insofar as their work is clearly both philosophical and social-scientific in its orientation.[115] Genealogy represents a particularly valuable model for orienting the same sort of combined philosophic and social-scientific inquiry. In considering this model we should think not only of Foucault's own histories but also of the enormous wealth of historical, anthropological, and sociological research of a Foucaultian orientation that has been produced in his wake. There is no need for Habermasians to deny the value of all this work undertaken in a Foucaultian vein. Indeed, many prominent contemporary critical theorists have already suggested that they find these sorts of Foucaultian inquiries invaluable for their own work in critical theory. My proposal is to suggest, then, that we ought to take very seriously indeed McCarthy's claim that, "Foucault's powerful insights and techniques . . . can be developed more fruitfully as a continuation of, rather than as an alternative to, critical social theory."[116]

One final consideration in favor of a combination of genealogy and critical theory in these terms is Habermas's own positive appeals to what he calls "genealogy" albeit without explicit reference to Foucault.[117] It is not clear if Habermas is here backpedaling on his former harsh response to Foucault or if he is intensifying that criticism by means of co-opting the conceptual constellation that forms the core of Foucault's methodological contribution. I prefer the first option, because it seems to me the best way to make sense of Habermas's own positive claims on behalf of genealogy, which are as follows: Habermas argues that his "justification strategy" for universalizability (namely the idea that norms of discourse must be really and actually introduced into dialogue by participants themselves) is one that "must be supplemented with genealogical arguments drawing on premises of modernization theory if [universalizability] is to be rendered plausible." The universalizing impulse of context-transcending validity, Habermas explicates elsewhere in this essay, finds a home in the idea that "issues of justice result from an idealizing extension of the ethical problematic" in which we find ourselves located.[118] While processes of reconstruction are crucial for manifesting such context-transcending "idealizing extensions," I am urging that genealogical processes of problematization must supplement this process in the form of articulating the context-bound "ethical problematics" that can be extended only in actual practical endeavors.

There is a great deal more that goes into genealogical projects of problematization in specifying the kinds of problems that we work to normatively reconstruct than has usually been acknowledged. In specifying the problematic situations where our context-transcending moral norms apply, a great deal more contingency and complexity informs our understanding that has traditionally been thought by those who have occupied the anticipatory-reconstructive wings of critical inquiry. Foucault's critical project of genealogical problematization is extremely well-positioned, resting as it does within the explanatory-diagnostic wings of critical inquiry, to take up this task of specifying the problematic situations to which our normative reconstructions ought to be contextually applied. If this is so, then Foucaultian genealogy has a clear role to play *within* contemporary critical theory. Genealogy is not just a tangential project nor a mere afterthought. Genealogy is crucial for explicating the full complexity and contingency of the problematic situations in which we find ourselves such that we can fully grasp the relevant features of these situations in applying and reapplying the universalizable normative commitments that help us reconstruct these situations such that we do not become buried by their problematicity.

Aspectival Differences in the Critique of Contingent Universals

Despite the common ground between genealogy and pragmatist critical theory that my arguments have established, it will be obvious to the astute observer that important differences continue to separate the philosophical perspectives considered herein. It simply cannot be denied that Foucault emphasizes contingency and complexity almost always without reference to universality. Habermas, from the opposite angle, emphasizes universalizability in a way that very often occludes the role of contingency and complexity. (Dewey, like Rorty, is generally perched, not often comfortably, somewhere between.)

These lingering differences do not pose insuperable obstacles to the conception of critical inquiry I am arguing for—in fact, they are the source of much of its value. The philosophical compatibility I require for my project of combination-via-delegation does not amount, after all, to identity, or even yet to synergy. But perhaps synergies between genealogy and critical theory are precisely what we need for a truly effective form of critical inquiry that picks and chooses the best elements from both theorists. Such synergies, I am suggesting, will be a result of actual deployments of diagnostic problematization and normative reconstruction alongside one another. As for identities, I explicitly resist these. Synergies presuppose differences. We ought not, and only in part because we cannot, identify the traditions of genealogy and pragmatist critical theory. The distinctions are real, and also, fortunately, productive.

But if I want to preserve differences, I owe an account of them. So what, then, accounts for the remaining differences separating Foucault (and others like Nietzsche and Deleuze) from Habermas and Dewey (and others like Mead, Rorty, and Fraser)?

I propose the following explanation: that aspectival differential between the backward gaze of the genealogist and the forward thrust of the critical theorist. Looking backward into the past that is constitutive of our present, the genealogist tends to see a welter of enormous complexity whose contingency is laid quite bare. Looking backward into the past, then, the genealogist is eager to critically feature the processes by which we have become who we are. For these purposes one need not, and indeed perhaps should not, have high normative ambitions. By contrast, the critical theorist is like the pragmatist in that they more often face the other way. Looking forward to better futures, they are more likely to hope for the universalization of all that is best in the present. Anyone who values democracy, human rights, liberty, or equality is likely to understand the yearning for universalizability that often accompanies these ideals. Looking forward into the future sponsors our search for normative validity, that is, for specifically moral conceptions of that which may yet be universal. It is to be expected that we should hope that some shimmering future may yet offer the universal fulfillment of those few fragile achievements in which we recognize our best work. This difference, then, helps us locate the distinction between, without denying the compatibility of, the Habermasian-Deweyan impulse toward reconstructive validity (in a normative sense) and the Foucaultian impulse toward genealogical problematization (in a more descriptive sense).

Not only are these perspectives compatible, but they can also be understood as reciprocally informing one another. One way of seeing this is by way of the Kantian perspective common to all three traditions at the heart of my argument. That Kant is a common focal point for all of these traditions takes us far in seeking out the retail methodological reconciliation I am arguing for. Consider Onora O'Neill's description of the project of Kantian critique as involving reason's construction of itself such that it might achieve a grasp of both the past and the future: "History looks backward, politics forward. Temporalized beings can understand reasoning only under the form of time; but they can look ahead as well as backward."[119] And indeed we do well to look in both directions. Doing so enables us to engage the tensions between universality and contingency. Allow me to explain.

There is no reason why the forward-facing work of reconstruction cannot affirm the contingency and complexity that is likely to accompany the long and arduous universalization of our best practices. A pragmatist vision of reconstruction that affirms the possibility of the process of universalizability across contexts is here in order. This is precisely the common meeting point of Deweyan pragmatism and Habermasian critical theory. It is also the general direction in which both recent pragmatism and recent critical theory have drifted. This is the direction of context-sensitive universalizability. There is furthermore no reason why the forward-facing work of reconstruction must concern itself with universality. It might—and in many cases quite successfully does—offer a more limited orientation in aiming for extensive generality or even local specificity. Sometimes the work of reconstruction does not require changing the world, but rather changing something much smaller, such as oneself. It bears remembering that such changes may amount to achievements worthy of our highest praise.

There is also no reason why the backward-facing work of problematization could not engage more fully with processes of universalizability. I am of course prepared to admit that Foucault is perhaps not our only good guide in these matters. Foucault always seemed to prefer extensive and widespread practices that have come to constrain us enormously but never down to every detail. His histories of heteronormativity, discipline, and the like are stories of the emergence of remarkably stable and increasingly crucial practices. They may be stories of tending-toward-universality, but they are not quite stories of universality-achieved. And yet there is nothing preventing the genealogist from investigating problematizations that condition the achievement of universality. Historical processes culminating in universality may be few and far between, but they are not nonexistent.

Thus, I conclude, the truly massive difference of emphasis distinguishing the perspectives of genealogy and pragmatist critical theory are not expressions of underlying principled differences of the sort that should encourage us to make heavy weather out of supposed philosophical incompatibilities. While searching our pasts for the conditions of possibility of our present, Foucault was wont to emphasize contingency and complexity. While focusing on the future conditions of possibility for what is best in the present, Habermas, like Dewey, has tended to emphasize universalizability. But these differences of emphasis fit well with my proposal for delegating to genealogy the project of historical problematization and to pragmatist critical theory the project of future reconstruction. We will not often find universality in the past in part because we do not often find it in the present. Where we do find it, we may find it necessary to problematize it. Where we do descry universality in political, social, or cultural matters we may want to rudely interrupt it. This is in part because we will also hope that what is very best in our present may yet dawn across every context suffering the absence of its light.

Reconstructing the present often involves developing and deploying ideals that we cannot but help believe might be successfully proliferated to ever more contexts. The universalizing impulses of reconstruction are nicely balanced against the differentiating impulses of problematization.

It is as such that reconstruction and problematization can work in tandem as two complementary methodological orientations for critical inquiry. The genealogical element will emphasize the ongoing problematizations to which these practices are a response. The critical theoretical pragmatist element will emphasize the reconstructive successes involved in the practical responses. To the extent that we want to understand the deficiencies of such practices, we should turn to genealogy, and where we want to understand their strengths, we should turn to critical theory and pragmatism. We post-foundational thinkers ought to be prepared to affirm the fallibilism central to both. Doing so enables us to recognize the need for the contributions of both taken together. Problematization requires reconstruction to complete its work just as reconstruction stands in need of problematization to propel it. A critique that performs only one of these operations will find itself very quickly exhausted and defused and, then, finally, ignored.

Concluding Remark

Problematization and reconstruction each have their own distinctive contribution to make to contemporary critical inquiry. These distinctive contributions can be developed in such a way as to enable dynamic synergies between the two. Such synergies are worth developing precisely insofar as they facilitate forms of critical inquiry that are of decisive importance for problematizing and reconstructing our contemporary realities. The philosophical contributions of genealogy, pragmatism, and critical theory represent a rigorous yet supple alternative to the overstated speculation, or what might be called the inflexible dreaminess, instantiated in more fashionable critical enterprises that have recently captured too much attention. It is by way of a reworking of the Kantian critical project that Foucault, Habermas, and Dewey (and others I have drawn on here) were able to depart not only from the failed universalisms of Marx and Freud, but also from the failed transcendental universalism of Kant. Against all Metaphysical and Foundational universalisms, the traditions of genealogy, pragmatism, and critical theory offer sufficient methodological facilities for seeing how philosophy can move forward with a more modest grip on universalization processes. Each of these three philosophies offers methodologies for retaining universality by detaching it from necessity and attaching it to contingency. Each thus holds open a promise for new practices of the work that philosophy may become. After the collapse of First Philosophy, we are in desperate need of a reorientation concerning the work of philosophy. My proposal is that genealogy, pragmatism, and critical theory offer a turning of philosophy toward the severe work of cultural critique. Turned, or perhaps returned, in this way, philosophy can mount forms of cultural critique that facilitate gaining grip on the contingently universalizing conditions of the possibility of our practices of modernity. To thusly renew philosophy, and to preserve therein the work of severest thought, we will have to muster the courage to confront a set of entrenched assumptions about ourselves as philosophers and as critical inquirers. We must let our selves become discomposed, and find our way to becoming recomposed once again. Some share of what philosophy has become may now wither away, so that new philosophies and new philosophers may yet brightly bloom again.

Notes

Introduction

1. Foucault 1976a, 78, 79
2. Foucault 1976a, 103
3. Foucault 1976a, 33
4. Foucault 1976a, 105–6. Foucault's term "dispositif" translated into English here as "construct" and elsewhere in the text as "deployment" has been the subject of much critical interrogation; one standard translation is "apparatus."
5. Foucault 1977a, 194
6. Here, as a kind of parlor game, is an alphabetized list of books or articles beginning with the words *A Genealogy of . . .* (or some such formulation): Anti-Americanism, Black Female Sexuality, Control Structures, Dignity as the Absence of the Bestial, Economic Science, Foucault, Girlhood, Hysteria in Modern France, Islamic Radicalism, Jihadism, Knowledge Management, Literary Multiculturalism, Modernism, New Sensibility Cinema in Israel, Orientalism, Private Life in Soviet Russia, Queer Theory, Ritual, Sovereignty, Taboo on Chemical Weapons, Urban Schoolteachers, Violence, Women's Madness. (Strangely, I could not find, despite much searching, any genealogies beginning with X, Y, or Z.) Some will recognize my parlor game as mimicking Ian Hacking's opening gambit in his fine book *The Social Construction of What?* (1999a, 1).
7. This work includes, most notably for my purposes, that of Ian Hacking, Paul Rabinow, Arnold Davidson, and Ladelle McWhorter. From these four I have learned much about what genealogy does, and how to *do* a genealogy, following (though never exactly) Foucault. Others, most especially David Hoy, Amy Allen, Barry Allen, and Nikolas Rose have helped me understand much *about* Foucault and genealogy.

8. For detailed discussion and defense of the distinction between *method* (or *analytic*) and *concept* in Foucault, see Koopman and Matza (2013/forthcoming); we also distinguish these two elements from the *categories* (e.g., power/knowledge, discourse) through which an analytic is operationalized and the *doctrines* (e.g., nominalism) of a philosophical nature and *conclusions* (e.g., the central place of the prison in the swarming of the disciplines) of a historical nature that these inquiries yield. In a companion piece, I use this distinction to parse two uses of Foucault, one building on his methodology (as represented by Hacking) and the other deploying his concepts without due methodological rigor (as represented by Agamben); see Koopman (2013c/forthcoming). In another context, I have pressed this distinction to work in a discussion of pragmatist methodology; see Koopman (2011). This distinction figures crucially in projects on which I am now at work concerning what positive work philosophy can expect of itself in our post-foundational and post-metaphysical context.

9. For background on Foucault's reception in America, see Cusset (2003) and for background on Foucault's quite different reception in France, see Dosse (1992).

10. See Hacking (1975, 1990), Rabinow and Dreyfus (1982), and Rabinow (2003). Two other representatives of this second way of approaching Foucault include Arnold Davidson (2001a) and Ladelle McWhorter (2009). This list is by no means exhaustive.

11. Foucault 1978a, 1–2. Foucault pleads elsewhere, "I in no way construct a theory of power. . . . Thus I am far from being a theoretician of power. At the limit, I would say that power, as an autonomous question, does not interest me" (1983b, 451–2).

12. On deconstructive genealogy, see Derrida (1988, 1991).

13. Cusset 2003, 280

14. See Koopman (2009a). Both books argue for a genealogical pragmatism. In the first book I show how pragmatism gains much by this combination. Here I show how genealogy can gain equally much. These two books are meant to express the same underlying philosophical sensibility—the books are born of the same period of thought, inquiry, and study.

15. Foucault 1984g, 314. According to the notations in DE.IV.631, the first portion of this sentence—that which refers to the critical tradition of thought—was written by Ewald, though Foucault himself must have thought this appropriate enough as to not stand in need of revision. It must be admitted, nonetheless, that this feature renders the textual evidence imperfect, hence the need for the fuller textual elaboration in the pages to follow.

16. Foucault 1964, 20

17. Foucault 1966a, 342

18. Foucault 1972b, 98

19. Foucault 1978e, 50

20. Foucault 1984c, 315

21. See Norris (1994) for a useful summary of the standard view. For early revisionist work emphasizing the importance of Kant for Foucault, see Hacking (1981, 1984, 2002b), Deleuze (1986a), and Rajchman (1989); among more recent revisionist work, see Cutrofello (1994), Dean (1994), Schmidt and Wartenberg (1994), Hutchings (1996), Han-Pile (1998, 2005), Taylor (2003), Allen (2003, 2008), Hengehold (2007), McGushin (2007), and Djaballah (2008). These revisionist works give expression to a wide variety of strategies for connecting Foucault to Kant. I further engage this literature in Chapter 3 where I follow Hacking and Allen in particular in an attempt to counterbalance the undeservedly influential revisionist strategies of those who reclaim Foucault's Kantianism in the form of a transcendental history.

22. See work by Sluga (2002, 2005, 2010) and Babich (2009) for excellent recent treatments of both Nietzsche and Heidegger in Foucault. I regard the link to Nietzsche as important but often misinterpreted (in Chapter 2 I am careful to show what Foucault does *not* get from Nietzsche). I take the link to Heidegger as largely tenuous, following the example of Veyne's (2008, Chapter 6) cautions about claims for Heidegger's influence.

23. Foucault 1984c, 315

24. See Koselleck 1959, 103–15

25. Foucault 1984c, 319

26. Foucault 1978/1982d, 336; though quoted with notable frequency, it is not often remarked that this line is located in the midst of a few short paragraphs on Kant in one of Foucault's most important essays, "The Subject and Power."

27. Foucault 1981a, 457

28. See Foucault 1984c, 309

29. Foucault 1984d, 257

30. Foucault 1978/1982d, 335–6

31. Foucault 1984j, 382–3

1. Critical Historiography

1. Nietzsche 1874, Preface, 8

2. See Williams, 2002, 18–19

3. See Williams 2002, Chapter 4

4. Williams 2002, 1

5. Williams 2002, 3

6. Hacking 2002b, 24–5

7. Foucault 1969b, 53

8. Foucault 1975a, 30–1

9. Foucault 1978d, 101

10. Foucault 1983a, 286

11. See Koopman (2009a, Chapter 1) explicating cultural critical philosophy as manifest in the tradition of philosophical pragmatism. Indeed much more can be said on these matters, in Foucault and others, than I can here muster in a few pages—in a future project I hope to take up these themes in greater detail by exploring the varieties of cultural critical philosophy as central to the history of what we now call philosophy.

12. Further discussions by Foucault of the connection between politics and philosophy, or the political role of intellectuals, can be found in Foucault (1977b, 126–33; 1978b, 288–90; 1979a, 33–7; and 1981a, 456–8); see also Deleuze (1985, 269–70) and Kritzman (2006, 270ff.) for further perspectives on Foucault's role as an engaged critic in the late 1960s and early 1970s.

13. Foucault 1983a, 21

14. Foucault 1983a, 262

15. Foucault 1983a, 289

16. Foucault 1983a, 288

17. Foucault 1983a, 351

18. Foucault 1967a, 293; see also Poster (1992).

19. For a fuller discussion of the relation between archaeology and genealogy, see Koopman (2008).

20. See most famously Habermas (1985) and most recently Paras (2006).

21. See Gutting (1989), Bernauer (1990), Han-Pile (1998), Flynn (2005), and my criticisms in Koopman (2008).

22. Rabinow and Dreyfus argue that Foucault's archaeology left him stranded with "the strange notion of regularities which regulate themselves." Foucault's archaeology is not sufficient to explain historical transition, and so "the archaeologist must attribute causal efficiency to the very rules which describe these practices' systematicity" (Rabinow and Dreyfus 1982, 84). This is linked by Rabinow and Dreyfus to the political concerns that for Foucault became increasingly important in the late 1960s. If archaeology cannot help bring into focus that which motivates, substantiates, and perpetuates the rules and regularities that are in place, then it cannot even begin to critically examine these rules and regularities. Thus Rabinow and Dreyfus conclude that "there is no place in archaeology for a discourse with social significance" (Rabinow and Dreyfus 1982, 89). This is not exactly a refutation of archaeology. But it is a clear statement of

the limits of a narrow practice of archaeology. To surpass these limits, Foucault needed to fashion a critical apparatus that included something else in addition to archaeology. As further explained in the following paragraph, I pursue the lead of Rabinow and Dreyfus's two-part explanation given in terms of an internal lack of explanatory capacity and an external lack of political efficacy. My explanation is internal in that I focus on the inner philosophical limitations of archaeology in terms of its incapacities to account for the motion of historical time, and also external in that I give a considerably larger role to the political limitations of archaeology in terms of its critical incapacities. While my explanation is in this way largely consistent with that given by Rabinow and Dreyfus, it is worth noting some of the ways in which I diverge from their approach. For example, I do not attempt to explain the vicissitudes of Foucault's thought in terms of his relation to other analytical models prominent in the philosophical and social scientific contexts in which he traveled intellectually (notably, the structuralism informing the work of Claude Levi-Strauss, Jacques Lacan, and Louis Althusser or the hermeneutics developed in the work of Charles Taylor, Clifford Geertz, or Martin Heidegger).

23. Davidson 1986, 227

24. Foucault 1969a, 208

25. Foucault 1969a, 174, 172

26. Foucault 1969a, 183, 192

27. See Foucault's "The Order of Discourse" (1970a) and "Nietzsche, Genealogy, History" (1971) for the most canonical statements concerning Foucault's methodological expansion of archaeology into genealogy. But more telling for my purposes, aside from *The Archaeology of Knowledge* itself, are Foucault's 1972 essay "Return to History" (1972a) and his 1973 Rio lectures titled "Truth and Juridical Forms." First, "Return to History" marks an early, if not halting, shift concerning the continuity-versus-discontinuity issue in historiography. In this essay, Foucault evinces explicit interest in the study of historical transformation, whereas previously he had been content to study history under the sign of discontinuity alone. At the very end of the essay he reiterates the point that structural and serial history "are theoretical instruments by means of which one can—contrary to the old idea of continuity—really grasp both the discontinuity of events and the transformation of societies" (1972a, 431). It is not at all clear that Foucault here provided any historiographical techniques that would gain insight into the how and why of cultural transformation. But what is clear is that Foucault is here explicitly claiming interest in processes of social and cultural change and that this is an interest that Foucault had not at all claimed in his earlier archaeological work. Similarly, his 1973 Rio lectures provide evidence of a shift concerning

the archaeological privilege given to knowledge as the primary plane or vector for critical attention. The key claim here is that knowledge cannot be analyzed in isolation: "Knowledge is simply the outcome of the interplay, the encounter, the junction, the struggle, and the compromise between the instincts" (1973, 8). Herein is an important shift toward genealogy, in which it would be made explicit that knowledge and power cannot be fruitfully studied apart from one another. Knowledge is invented, it descends and develops, as the outcome of complex relays between knowledge and power: "Through Nietzsche's text, one can restore, not a general theory of knowledge but a model that enables us to tackle the object of these lectures: the problem of the formation of a certain number of domains of knowledge on the basis of the relations of force and the political relations in society" (1973, 15). Though relatively unsophisticated in comparison to later elaborations, there is already a clear methodological upshot in this awkward formulation. One need only replace "on the basis of" with "in their intersection with" in the passage just cited in order to arrive at a rather precise conception of what Foucault would later offer under the banner of genealogy in the form of an inquiry into relations amongst pathways of knowledge and power.

28. Foucault 1983b, 446; cf. Foucault 1978d, 107. It is notable that these are precisely the questions concerning truth that would prompt Bernard Williams (2002) to take up genealogy for the purposes of an inquiry into the historical conditions of the virtues of truthfulness. Nietzsche's texts from around the period referenced by Foucault include *The Dawn: Reflections on Moral Prejudices* (1881) and *Human, All Too Human* (1878) along with the two works published as its sequels, *Mixed Opinions and Aphorisms* (1879) and *The Wanderer and His Shadow* (1880). Foucault, apparently, did not consider more typically "primary" texts such as *Beyond Good and Evil* (1886) and *On the Genealogy of Morals* (1887) to be central influences.

29. Mitchell Dean notes: "The historical-theoretical project Foucault's writings on Kant imply and which the rest of his work can be shown to exemplify [is directed toward] the political and ethical issues raised by *our* insertion in a particular present, and by the problem of action under the limits establishing the present" (Dean 1994, 51).

30. Foucault 1967b, 606; cited via Huffer 2010, 89 and also reprinted in Carrette (1999).

31. Foucault 1984c 304, 309; cf. 1983a, 13

32. Nietzsche 1887a, Preface, §6

33. Deleuze (1962); see also Clark (1990) and Hill (2003).

34. On the wide influence of Deleuze's book on his contemporaries, see Hoy 2004, 21.

35. Deleuze 1962, 52, 88

36. Deleuze 1962, 91

37. Rabinow and Dreyfus 1982, 114; an instructive contrast is offered by Barry Allen (1999), who presents an effective case that Foucault here only reproduces many of the usual biases of traditional epistemology.

38. Foucault 1975, 27a

39. See Foucault 1975a, 1975b, 1976b, 1978a and for a concise exemplar 1974a, 63–73 describing disciplinary practices in religious, military, and labor contexts.

40. Allen 1998, 174; for further useful commentary on the power-knowledge relation, see Allen 1998, 176 and Oksala 2005, 97.

41. Foucault 1969a, 190

42. Foucault 1969a, 192

43. Foucault 1970a, 232–34

44. Foucault 1983b, 455

45. Foucault 1970b, 71

46. Foucault 1983a, 42; cf. 1978a, 1, 1978/1982d, 340, and 1983b 451–52. In her discussion of these matters Han-Pile (1998, 142–44) argues that Foucault hopelessly vacillates between contradictory "metaphysical" and "nominalist" accounts of the power-knowledge relation, but this criticism seems to ignore the possibility of a critical inquiry into power that is neither strictly metaphysical nor exclusively nominalist because it is instead robustly philosophical and empirical at the same time.

47. Foucault 1984h, 9

48. Rabinow and Marcus 2008, 64; on emergence see further Rabinow 2008, 24, Rabinow and Dan-Cohen 2005, 1 and Rabinow 1996, 2.

49. For earlier uses of the concept of emergence, but without such fully explicit self-conscious thematization, see Foucault 1966a, 250ff., 344ff. and 1969a, 41ff., 62ff..

50. Foucault 1971, 377, 378, 380

51. Foucault 1969a, 21–30 and 1968; see also the helpful discussion by O'Farrell (1989, 57ff.).

52. Sartre 1966, 87; see discussions of these exchanges by Eribon (1991, 163ff.) and Flynn (2005, 240ff.).

53. See articles by Le Bon (1967) and Amiot (1967) against Foucault and for rejoinders on Foucault's behalf see Daix (1967) and Canguilhem (1967).

54. On Foucault's reception by the discipline of professional historians see Megill (1987), many of the essays collected in Goldstein (1994), and the more recent summary in Han-Pile (2005).

55. See Eribon 1991, 238ff. on Sartre's and Foucault's mutual political engagements.

56. Foucault 1969a, 166, 172

57. Foucault 1971

58. Michon 2002, 173

59. Foucault 1976a, 99; cf. 1978e, 60

60. Foucault 1978c, 226. Also in 1978, in his course lectures, Foucault returned for a few brief moments to the problems of the great ruptures he had charted in *The Order of Things*. Now, armed with genealogy, Foucault confidently and deftly describes the transition from the episteme of representation to that of the human sciences: "I think that if we look for the operator of transformation for the transition from natural history to biology, from the analysis of wealth to political economy, and from general grammar to historical philology, if we look for the operator that upset all these systems of knowledge, and directed knowledge to the sciences of life, of labor and production, and of language, then we should look to population" (Foucault 1978a, 78). We can safely ignore the reference to population for the time being, because the important point for the question at hand is that Foucault here implicitly acknowledges that in his earlier work he had failed to specify the crucial "operator of transformation." It had taken the subtle shift from archaeological studies of being to genealogical studies of emergence in order to locate the problematics operating as the motives for historical transformation.

61. LaCapra 2000, 148

62. Foucault 1972a, 430

63. Foucault 1978f, 581

64. Flynn 2005, xii

65. Hoy 2009b, 10; see also Hoy 2009a, 204ff. and, on this point in Deleuze, Hoy 2009, 214ff.

66. Foucault 1984d, 257

67. See Gutting (1989), O'Farrell (1989), and Bernauer (1990) for three undeniably excellent early books on Foucault that are also representative of the scholarship on the whole in that they do not feature the word "problematization" at all in their rather exhaustive indices.

68. See Han-Pile (1998, 1), Flynn (2005, xi), and May (2006, 107); by contrast, Castel (1994) acknowledges the centrality of problematization throughout all of Foucault's work but is unfortunately rather critical of its methodological function.

69. The review of Foucault's work offered in this paragraph reproduces ideas in Koopman (2013a).

70. See Foucault 1978a, 9ff., 65, 78, 88, 89, 230, 323 and the classic statement in 1984a, 1–32.

71. Foucault 1975a, 227; 1975b, 134, 139 (cf. 124, 129 of the French edition), and 1976f, 274. Two scholars, Flynn (2005, 325, note 61) and Kelly (2009, 167, note 224), have recently traced the concept back to the 1976 article but did not locate its earlier antecedents.

72. Foucault 1966a, 76

73. Foucault 1961, 381, 419, 458

74. Foucault 1954, 79

75. See Deleuze (1966, 1968, 1969) and the discussion of other possible sources in Chapter 4.

76. Foucault 1984a, 12

77. Rabinow and Dreyfus 1982, 89, 125

78. The metaphor first occurred to me in conversation on these matters with Arnold Davidson in Chicago at a Foucault Circle meeting—my thanks for the fecund suggestion of the idea of methodological "neutralization" as helping to make sense of the relevant shifts in Foucault's procedures.

79. Foucault 1973, 409 as quoted in Davidson 2001c, 204.

80. Davidson 2001c, 205. Similar interpretations are offered by Rabinow and Dreyfus (1982, 9), O'Farrell (1989, 69), Kusch (1991, 111), Flynn (2005, 153), and Huffer (2010, xiv). Despite finding myself in such good company here, it is undeniable that misleading interpretations still dominate much of the literature.

81. Huffer (2010) excellently demonstrates the thematic resonance between *The Will to Know* and *History of Madness*. I find even stronger connections to the themes of *Discipline and Punish*. Good evidence for the latter connection is provided by Foucault himself (1974a, 12–16 and 1984g, 316).

82. See Foucault 1984g

83. Foucault 1978b, 267

84. Canguilhem 1992, 32

2. Three Uses of Genealogy

1. See MacIntyre 1981, 222

2. Craig 2007, 182

3. See Nietzsche (1887a), Darwin (1871), and Hume (1757).

4. See Williams (2002), Skinner (1998, 2009), Craig (1991), and Hobbes (1651).

5. Allen (2004, 2008)

6. Craig 2007, 184

7. My argument here borrows from and develops my earlier work in Koopman (2009b).

8. Williams 2002, 20

9. Nietzsche 1887, Pref. §6, 7

10. Williams 2002, 31ff.

11. Nietzsche 1887, Pref. §7, 8

12. Foucault 1984b, 11

13. I want to enter an important caveat at this point. For the purposes of my project in differentiating normatively ambitious from normatively modest genealogy, I need not assert that the readings of Nietzsche and Williams offered below are the most useful interpretations of their rich bodies of work. I do, of course, think that my interpretations offer a very good way of making sense of *most,* if not quite *all,* of what Nietzsche and Williams were up to. But I can concede that there are other ways of reading Nietzsche and Williams that, though not more textually accurate, are perhaps more philosophically productive. I can also freely admit that Foucault himself probably read Nietzsche in this more productive sense, as suggested by my references in later chapters to certain Nietzschean themes in Foucault. I can make these concessions because my goal here is not to offer definitive interpretations of Nietzsche and Williams. I aim only to put forward intelligent interpretations of their work that help emphasize the deficiencies in certain uses of genealogy that I believe their work clearly exhibits in numerous places (which I shall, of course, be citing). My argument primarily concerns Foucault's third sense of genealogy in contrast from the first two senses—I am only secondarily concerned with Nietzsche and Williams. The primary argument thus does not depend on my subsidiary interpretations of Nietzsche and Williams so much as it depends on my effectively contrasting these interpretations and the interpretation of Foucault I shall begin forwarding later in this chapter but more fully in the next. My primary point is that Foucault is neither "subverter" nor "vindicator," but rather "problematizer." I use Nietzsche and Williams as emblems for the first two uses of genealogy. But it is the uses themselves that matter to my arguments, and not the emblems I pin them to. This concession might, however, seem to imply the unfortunate possibility that my argument attacks a straw man.

14. Klement 2002, 384; see also Cohen and Nagel (1934), which may be the first rigorous elaboration of the genetic fallacy as such.

15. For recent probing of the genetic fallacy, see Crouch (1993), Rosenbaum (2002) and Klement (2002). For early critical responses by pragmatists to the analytic charge that historicist philosophy always commits the genetic fallacy, see Wiener (1946) and Lavine (1962).

16. Williams 2002, 6

17. See Williams 2002, 1–7

18. Williams 2002, 63

19. See Rorty (1995a)

20. Williams 2002, 66. Barry Allen offers a similar observation in his review of Williams: "Where Rorty enlists Davidson in a neo-positivist project of over-coming philosophy, Williams enlists him for the Nietzschean project of reframing philosophical problems about truth in ethical and genealogical terms" (2003a, 373–74).

21. Williams 2002, 12

22. Williams 1981, 17

23. Clark 2001, 120n3

24. Williams 2002, 61

25. Williams 2002, 61

26. Williams 2002, 7

27. Williams 2002, 36, 263

28. See Chapters 7, 8, and 9, respectively, of Williams (2002); note that the genealogy of liberal social critique (Chapter 9) is the least developed in the book, but a much fuller account is offered in Williams (2005). In truth, Williams's book is actually more complex. In Chapter 3 he also offers an entirely different gene-alogy of the origins of truthfulness itself. Unlike the later historical genealogies, Williams offers this early account as an explicitly fictional genealogy. It is not at all clear that these armchair thought experiments are really genealogies at all, so I leave this chapter to the side for the purposes of my exposition.

29. Rorty 2002, online; Barry Allen similarly writes, "What more is there to value in truth, given due value to the ethical and discursive practices of truthful-ness?" (2003a, 375).

30. Williams 2002, 38, 58, 92

31. Williams 2002, 7

32. Williams 2002, 11

33. Peirce to James, June 12, 1902 in Perry 1935, 286

34. Williams 2000, 192; for further discussion of Williams's use of history in philosophy, see Koopman (2010a).

35. Williams 2002, 93

36. Williams 2002, 93

37. See Rorty (2002), Allen (2003a), and Hacking (2004) for arguments as to why.

38. I thus agree, although in a rather roundabout way, with Hilary Putnam, who chides Williams for seeing only two possible positions, namely relativism or scientism such that "what is missing in this dichotomy is precisely the idea that characterized my pragmatist 'enlightenment'" (2001, 122).

39. Williams 2002, Chapter 3

40. Williams 2002, 92

41. Williams 2002, 92

42. Allen 2003a, 367

43. Hacking 2004, 147

44. Putnam 2004, 121; from his 2001 Spinoza lectures.

45. Rorty 2002

46. See Sleat (2007, 291) for further agreement with Allen and Hacking, but contrast also Craig (2007, 199) who urges that the specific advantage of genealogy is that it enables us to explicate the elusive connection instrumental and intrinsic value.

47. Nietzsche 1888, III, D, I; see the history of Nietzsche reception by Vattimo (1985).

48. Nietzsche 1878, IX, §517

49. Nietzsche 1887b, V, §344

50. See respectively Williams 2002, 12ff. and Foucault 1983b, 446. A valuable general study of Nietzsche's question and its implications is offered by Allen (1993, ch. 3).

51. Neitzsche 1887a, III, §27

52. MacIntyre 1990, 39 and Habermas 1985, 74. Both MacIntyre and Habermas attempt to lump Nietzsche and Foucault together under a unified banner of subversive genealogy—it should now be plain that I find this lumping deeply mistaken.

53. Foot 1994, 3 and Danto 1994, 39

54. MacIntyre 1990, 49

55. MacIntyre 1990, 205

56. MacIntyre 1990, 55

57. MacIntyre 1990, 215

58. Deleuze 1962, 8

59. Deleuze 1962, 195

60. Deleuze 1962, 35

61. Deleuze 1962, 188

62. Deleuze 1962, 99

63. Deleuze 1962, 107

64. Deleuze 1962, 82 commenting on Nietzsche (1888, II, 9).

65. Deleuze 1962, 188

66. Descombes 1991, 73, 70, 71, 86, 90

67. See Blondel (1986) and Kofman (1972).

68. Roth 2006, 311

69. Nehemas 1985, 110. Also on the genetic fallacy in Nietzsche and Hume, see Hoy (1986), where the argument is that we cannot always use genealogy to undermine moralities because if genealogy is to be of any use it must have some potentially positive results too: if accounts of the development of a practice can only be used to show that a practice is unjustified, then such accounts have no bearing on the actual justification of a practice. Less convincingly, see Paul Loeb (1995), where it is argued that Nietzsche is better seen as holding a view in which the genetic fallacy itself begs the question against the revaluation of values that Nietzsche is proposing. To make this point, however, Loeb has to substantially play up Nietzsche's anti-democratic and pro-aristocratic bias. I take it that this is precisely the use of genealogy that Nehemas was attempting to help Nietzsche out of.

70. Nehemas 1985, 129, 133

71. Nehemas 1985, 137

72. Nehemas 1985, 223–30

73. See Rorty (1989)

74. Rorty often invoked Nietzsche as the best exemplar of his own conception of a romantic culture and is referred to often in the *Contingency* book and elsewhere in connection with the concerns just raised. Rorty is thanked in the Preface to Nehemas's book (1985, ix), and he knew well the portrait of Nietzsche as affirmative thinker developed by Nehemas and Deleuze.

75. See Hacking (1990, 1998a, 2002a) and Rabinow (2003, 2008) as discussed below. See also Davidson's *The Emergence of Sexuality* (2001a), McWhorter's *Racism and Sexual Oppression in Anglo-America: A Genealogy* (2009) as well as a number of works listed in the following note.

76. The following books and articles are all worth attention, though this is an incomplete list: Donzelot's *The Policing of Families* (1977), Asad's *Genealogies of Religion* (1993), Chauncey's *Gay New York* (1995), Poovey's *A History of the Modern Fact* (1998), Rose's *Powers of Freedom* (1999) and *The Politics of Life Itself* (2006), Dean's *Governmentality* (1999a), Joyce's *The Rule of Freedom* (2003), Reardon's *Race to the Finish* (2004), Mahmood's *Politics of Piety* (2005), and Feder's *Family Bonds* (2007). See also a variety of relatively early interventions by Foucault's students including Ewald (1990), Pasquino (1991), Gordon (1991), and Burchell (1991). See further work by Baker (1994), Fujitani (1996), Lemke (1998, 2001), Dean (1999b), Hunt (1999), and Clifford (2001).

77. See Hacking (1975, 1990)

78. See Hacking (1995, 1998a)

79. See Hacking (1983, 2007a)

80. See Hacking (1980, 1991b, 2009; the last represents an interim report on work in progress that presumably will come out at some future date in longer and more detailed form).

81. Hacking 2002b, 23

82. Hacking 1988, 70, cf. Hacking 2002b, 24–25

83. Rabinow and Rose 2006, 215. Rose writes elsewhere, "Where so many judge, however, I have tried to avoid judgment, merely to sketch out a preliminary cartography of an emergent form of life and the possible futures it embodies. And in doing so, not to judge, but I hope, to help make judgment possible. To open the possibility that, in part through thought itself, we might be able to intervene in that present, and so to shape something of the future we might inhabit" (2006, 258–59).

84. See Hacking (1991a, 2007b, forthcoming).

85. See Rabinow (1996, 1999, 2005, 2009)

3. What Problematization Is

1. See Fraser (1981)

2. Foucault 1982b, 358; I thank Amy Allen for calling my attention to this passage some years ago just as I was beginning work on this book in earnest.

3. Foucault 1983c

4. Foucault 1983d, 380

5. Foucault 1980a

6. My strategy contrasts to Amy Allen's (2010) recent defense of Foucault against Fraser. Allen accepts Fraser's second premise (that Foucault used genealogy in order to forward normative conclusions by way of genetic arguments) but refuses Fraser's first premise (that genetic reason is straightforwardly fallacious). Allen explicitly considers but then rejects the strategy I propose here (2010, 87).

7. Habermas 1985, 282

8. This final qualification is crucial. I here leave open the possibility that Foucault attempted to develop normative resources in other non-genealogical aspects of his work. I explicitly argue in Chapter 6 that in Foucault's ethical writings he did indeed aim to supply something quite like normative resources, but that to the extent that they are normative, these writings should not be read as genealogical. My point for the time being is simply that Foucault does not take genealogy by itself to have any particular claim on reconstructive validity. Genealogy, I will also later argue, is the best part of Foucault's intellectual legacy and should be retained even by those suspicious of his more normatively ambitious later work.

9. May 2007, 138, 136

10. Sawicki 2005, 393

11. Foucault 1983f, 171

12. Foucault 1983e, 256

13. May 2006, 103

14. See Takacs 2004, 880, and Schaff 2004, 67

15. Foucault 1983f, 74

16. Foucault 1984d, 312–13

17. Foucault 1979, 311

18. Foucault 1980, 288

19. Foucault 1984e, 114

20. Foucault 1984b, 10

21. Foucault 1978a, 118

22. Foucault 1978a, 65

23. Foucault 1984i, 394 (translation modified; cf. DE4.688)

24. Portions of the material in this section were developed in response to insightful comments and questions offered during and after a SPEP session in Pittsburgh in 2008, where I presented a paper on problematization in Foucault and Deleuze. My interlocutors at that session, all of whom deserve thanks for their interventions, were Paul Patton, Jana Sawicki, Edward McGushin, Zach Vanderveen, Jared Hibbard-Swanson, and Jeff Edmonds. The ideas were then further refined in light of helpful conversations with Paul Rabinow in Berkeley.

25. This dual-aspect character of history has been noted widely, for instance by De Certeau (1975, 21, 288). The dual-aspect character of Foucault's concept of problematization has been noted (though not in fully identical terms) by others including Castel (1994, 240), Deacon (2000, 140), and O'Leary (2002, 115).

26. I owe the idea that this tension between the nominal and verbal aspects of problematizations should be valued precisely for its capacity to generate and sustain what Foucault himself often called "thought" to discussions with Paul Rabinow, who recently expresses the related thought that "Foucault's own analysis, it is clear, was meant both as a diagnostic and as a means of making such problematizations more visible, available, and open to remediation" (2011a, 90).

27. Foucault 1984a, 11

28. Rose 1996, 42

29. Rose 1999, 18

30. See Hacking (1998a), Rabinow (1999), Rabinow and Bennett (2009), Rose (1999), and DeLanda (2006).

31. Hacking 1998a, 86, 13

32. See Foucault 1975b, 257 (the *Abnormal* course lectures); 1969a, 161, 169 (*The Archaeology of Knowledge*); and 1961, 51, 364 (*History of Madness*).

33. Foucault 1978a, 239

34. Foucault 1978e, 64

35. Rose 1999, 287

36. Foucault 1978a, 117

37. For another instructive view of social theory without reliance on ulti-mate micro- and macro-analyses, see DeLanda (2006), borrowing heavily from Deleuze in terms that Foucaultians can find helpful.

38. Hacking 1984, 238

39. Allen 2008, 24

40. As for the view that Foucault's debt to Kant is in terms of his implicit epistemology, see my discussion of Han-Pile (1998, 2005) below. For Foucault's Kantian ethics, see suggestions by Hacking (1984, 239), Allen (2008, 65), and Cutrofello (1994, 99). In departing from this aspect of these works I note that Allen, Cutrofello, and Hacking all situate Foucault's ethics as Kantian in very dif-ferent ways. See also Djaballah (2008) for an attempt, somewhat similar to my own, to resituate Foucault as Kantian in terms of the project of critique.

41. Foucault 1983g, 85

42. Foucault 1983d, 20–21

43. See Foucault (1984c) and Hacking (2002b).

44. Hacking 2002b, 23

45. Hacking 1981, 79

46. See Han-Pile (2005), Cutrofello (1994), Thompson (2008), Oksala (2005), and in a somewhat different vein, Visker (1999).

47. The authors cited in the previous note all hold that Foucault's archaeo-logical methodology offers a quintessentially phenomenological combination of "historicity" and "transcendentality." But they do not sufficiently consider the possibility that Foucault sought to detach critique as inquiry into conditions of possibility from transcendental critique as inquiry into universal and neces-sary such conditions. I engage these arguments with the phenomenological-transcendental interpretation of Foucault at greater length in Koopman (2010b), published with an instructive reply by Thompson (2010), and my re-reply (2010c).

48. Veyne 2008, 34

49. Foucault 1972b, 98

50. Foucault 1969, 203; cf. 13, 28, 54, 88, 109, 182, 192

51. See for just one example the first lecture of Foucault's 1983 Collège de France course (1983a) This lecture is glossed by Gros (2008, 379) in his "Course

Context" explicitly in my terms as separating "critical" and "transcendental" Kantian heritages; see similar distinctions by McGushin (2007, 246ff.) and Hutchings (1996, 102ff.).

52. Kant 1781, A11/B25

53. Kant 1790, Pref./3

54. Kant 1781, A11/B25, cf. A761/B789

55. Kant 1790, Intro./17

56. See O'Neill (1989) and Cutrofello (1994) on the importance for Kant of a "discipline" of reason.

57. Foucault 1984c, 315

58. Foucault 1969a, 15

59. Foucault 1966a, xxiii; see later anticipating problematization in writing of "the conditions that make a controversy or problem possible" (75).

60. Foucault 1963a, xix

61. Foucault 1979a, 36

62. A precedent for my proposed dual approach is offered in certain strains of the literature on Kant. The psychological overtones of Kantian constructivism were severely rebuked by Strawson (1966) whose important contribution was to show that Kant's critique of the bounds of experience did not require the incoherent faculty psychology on which he based it. Many commentators since, including O'Neill (1989) and Rockmore (2007), have emphasized the importance of reinterpreting constructivism as a culturally variable rather than a psychologically invariable process.

63. Kant 1785, 412

64. See Kant (1798a, 1798b); on Kant's later publications as definitively invested in his philosophical project see Wilson (2006) disputing the earlier views of Brandt (1999) and Jacobs and Kain (2003).

65. The discussion in this paragraph builds on Amy Allen's work on Foucault's Kantianism (2008, 24–39).

66. Foucault 1964, 66; consider also other remarks from this text: "The internal structure of the *Anthropology* and the question that secretly animates it take the same form as the interrogation of the *Critique;* there is an ambition to know the possibilities and the limits of knowledge" (from the online Bove translation; cf. 1964, 118 in the Nigro and Briggs translation).

67. Foucault 1964, 92

68. For a discussion of these historiographical matters with respect to some of my earlier claims about Foucault's Kantianism, see my reply in Koopman (2010d) to McQuillan (2010).

69. See Habermas (1999a, 2001b) and helpful commentary by Amy Allen (2011a).

70. Strawson 1966, 44. It is worth mentioning that, according to personal conversations with Foucault scholar Arnold Davidson, there is evidence that Foucault read some Strawson (among many other analytic philosophers) with great interest during his time in Tunisia in the late 1960s.

71. Rockmore 2007, 231–32

72. Han-Pile 1998, 141

73. Han-Pile 1998, 145. Gutting (2003, par. 10) effectively disputes Han-Pile's assertion, but see her reply (Undated). See also at greater length Todd May's (1993, 69–109) account of the epistemology of genealogy offered in terms of a pragmatist distinction between justification and truth. The arguments of both Gutting and May suit my purposes here quite fine, but I develop a different kind of argument against the attempt to inflict certain Kantian perplexities onto Foucault's work.

74. A contrast to this view is discernible in the widely endorsed views of Kripke (1972) to the effect that *a priori* epistemology does not always imply metaphysical necessity; see also Hacking (1998b, §5) differentiating necessary, a priori, and analytic. This pair of arguments notwithstanding, I prefer to leave matters terminological as Kant put them.

75. For a broader view on the vexed relation between history and objectivity from the angle of contemporary professional historiography, see Peter Novick (1988).

76. For one such reading of Kant see Barry Allen (2003) on the great distance between Kant and Darwin on the reality of contingency.

77. Kant 1790, §76.252 and 1785, 463

78. In Koopman (2010d) I describe this as "appropriationist" historiography. Foucault defended the same: "For myself, I prefer to utilize the writers I like. The only valid tribute to thought such as Nietzsche's is precisely to use it, to deform it, to make it groan and protest. And if commentators then say that I am being faithful or unfaithful to Nietzsche, that is of absolutely no interest" (1975c, 53–54).

79. Rabinow 1994, 14

80. See Daston and Galison (2007), Poovey (1999), Davidson (2001a). See Hacking (2002b, 8ff.) for his references to this and other work. See Kusch (2010) for a useful critical discussion of Hacking and historical epistemology. I would suggest that Poovey's work is perhaps even more Foucaultian in her explicit analytic focus on the category of problems for thought (1999, 21ff.), though she does not cite Foucault as a source of this focus—perhaps because she, like most, reads Foucault through a different lens than that of problematization.

81. For a good start, see Hacking (1999b).

82. Daston and Galison 2007, 19

83. Rabinow 1999, 4 and 1996, 2; Tobias Rees excellently captures the operative idea in stating that "the contemporary is a technical term that allows us to decompose emergent phenomena—for example, synthetic biology—into different elements that are assembled into one form constitutive of the phenomena in question" (Rees in Rabinow and Marcus, et. al., 2008, 58).

84. Rabinow 1989, 9

85. Rabinow 1999, 172

86. On the complex relation between Foucault and Bourdieu see De Certeau (1980, 61ff.) and Hoy (2004, 21ff.).

87. Bourdieu 1980, 87, 54

88. Bourdieu 1997, 109

89. See especially Hacking (2002b), and on the Kantian terms of what Hacking elsewhere calls his "constructionism," see Hacking (1999a, 40–53; cf. 165).

90. Hacking 1991b, 181

91. See Hacking (1980, 1991b, 2009), though my descriptions of Hacking's views here are largely based on a seminar he gave at the University of California, Santa Cruz in the winter of 2008. Hacking is clear that he borrows while transforming the idea of styles of reasoning from Crombie (1994) and the idea of kinds of truthfulness from Williams (2002).

92. See Hacking 2009, 46

93. Hacking 1991a, 32

94. Daston and Galison 2007, 205

95. Deleuze and Guattari 1991, 36

96. Deleuze and Guattari 1991, 47 and Deleuze 1995, 25

97. See for one instructive discussion Smith (2001).

98. Veyne 2008, 2

99. Veyne 1978, 156

100. Veyne 1978, 182. Veyne is of course not the only scholar to discern in Foucault an inspiring alternative to all the classical critical apparatuses suffused in Freud and Marx. Rabinow notes too that "If Foucault's work does indeed function in the future as a central organizer of social discourses, it will do so in a way radically different discursively, institutionally, politically, and—dare I say— psychologically from the work of Marx and Freud" (Rabinow 1984, 26). And Richard Rorty titled his 1981 review of Foucault's work "Beyond Nietzsche and Marx" (Rorty 1981a). For some of his own attempts to distance his work from Freud and Marx, see Foucault (1976g and 1967c).

101. Veyne 1978, 153

102. Veyne 1978, 167

103. Foucault 1981a, 456

104. Kant 1781, Axi (note)

4. What Problematization Does

1. Canguilhem 1968, 29; cf. Canguilhem (1977)

2. See Davidson (1994a, 1996), though my view is that the effect of these arguments is to align Foucault not with analytic philosophy so much as with pragmatist philosophy insofar as Davidson's version of Wittgenstein is much more of a pragmatist than a typical analyst in the positivist or post-positivist mold.

3. Braudel 1958, 27; I have corrected the translation by substituting "accepted" for "excepted" as given in the cited edition to translate the French "acceptée."

4. Dosse 1987, 92

5. Braudel 1958, 48

6. Dosse notes that Braudel still emphasized an overarching dialectical continuity between these different levels of time (Dosse 1987, 92; cf. Dosse [1992, 260ff.] and Braudel [1958, 48]) in such a way that Annales history could perhaps be seen as more of an influence on an archaeological Foucault as has been suggested by Martin Kusch (1991, 12ff.). Despite decomposing time into several temporal registers, Braudel yet remained faithful to the Annales paradigm of a "total" and "global" history that Foucault and others would sunder in taking the idea of pluralized time to its historiographical limits. And yet despite Foucault's departure from Braudel's extremely classical ideal of history as unifying the social sciences, we can nonetheless situate Foucault's own development of temporal pluralization in a lineage to which Braudel made definite contributions.

7. See Heidegger (1927). This suggestion opens up other interesting points of connection between Foucault and other thinkers, connections that, however, cannot rightly be described as influences or sources: consider Thomas Kuhn (1962) and his conception of the role of anomaly in theory change or R. G. Collingwood (1939) and his method of question-and-answer in historiography.

8. Le Goff, as quoted in Dosse 1987, 55

9. See Althusser (1962, 1968)

10. Canguilhem 1943, 35; see also Canguilhem 1968, 30.

11. The connection has been mentioned briefly in a short and cursory article by Colwell (1997), but the primary focus is on "series" and "event" rather than on "problematization."

12. Deleuze in Foucault and Deleuze 1972c, 208; this claim is attributed to Foucault with surprising frequency despite coming from the text of Deleuze's contribution to the exchange.

13. DeLanda 2002, 5 and Rajchman 2000, 8; cf. Boundas 1996, 88 and Patton 1996, 10. But as was the case with early commentaries on Foucault, most recent commentaries on Deleuze entirely ignore the role that this concept plays in his thought—see for example Hallward (2006) and Lampert (2006), which give this concept little emphasis.

14. Deleuze and Guattari 1991, 2, 16

15. Deleuze 1968, 212

16. See Deleuze 1966, 20ff. and 1963, 25

17. Deleuze 1966, 15

18. Deleuze 1966, 15

19. Deleuze 1966, 20

20. This point of connection between Deleuze and Foucault also provides a possible point in favor of one of my broader arguments here on behalf of a linkage between pragmatism and genealogy. Specifically, I discern in the post-structuralist conception of problematization as objective and practice a point of connection to the pragmatist conception of problems elaborated by John Dewey and Charles Santiago Peirce. Dewey, for example, similarly holds that problems are objective features of situations rather than mere subjective perceptions of failure (see Dewey 1916a, 70 and 1938a, 109). This point of connection has been previously noted by Rabinow (see Rabinow 2003, 15ff.). I consider the broader connection between pragmatism and genealogical philosophy in the final chapter.

21. Deleuze 1969, 54

22. Deleuze 1968, 169

23. Deleuze 1968, 158, 159, 163

24. Foucault 1984a, 11

25. Deleuze 1968, 161, 162

26. Deleuze 1969, 122

27. Deleuze 1968, 164; the parenthetical note to the previous sentence is in observation of Deleuze's claims in *Difference and Repetition* that problems are in fact dialectical, but not in the traditional sense of dialectical opposition (1968, 164, 179).

28. Deleuze often described the alternative to dialectical negation in terms of creative affirmation: "Practical struggle never proceeds by way of the negative but by way of difference and its power of affirmation" (1968, 208). On this point I detect a point of possible divergence from Foucault, for whom the alternative

292   Notes to pages 137–138

to negation did not involve affirmation so much as the rigor of remaining in the space of problematization.

29. Foucault 1970c, 358–59

30. See Deleuze 1962, 8ff.

31. Deleuze 1986a, 116

32. The intellectual history I have been tracing can be extended further back, namely into an inquiry into the intellectual genesis of Deleuze's concept of problematization, to help motivate the broader connections between genealogy and pragmatism (and certain pragmatized strands of critical theory) that I shall argue for in the final chapter. One could give an intellectual historical account of the genesis of this conception that helps us trace a line from Foucault through Deleuze and Bergson back to William James and forward from there to pragmatists such as John Dewey and Richard Rorty and even quasi-pragmatists such as Jürgen Habermas. If such an account can be given, we would have additional warrant for taking Foucault's practice of genealogical problematization as a natural ally of more reconstructive traditions in philosophy—it is also useful to note in this regard that Deleuze commentators Rajchman (2000) and DeLanda (2002) make much of his practice of problematization and are also explicit in affirming in his thought a kind of pragmatism. This, unfortunately, is not the occasion for me to recount that longer intellectual history in full. I can here but sketch the outlines of what this story would look like.

Those outlines might proceed as follows. Foucault developed his conception of problematization on the basis of Deleuze's work. Deleuze, in turn, developed the concept in conversation with Bergson. It should be noted in this regard that the general idea of philosophical problematization makes its first appearance in Deleuze's work not in the book on Nietzsche, but in the book on Bergson. Indeed, much of that book is focused on explicating the sense in which Bergsonism implies a shift from a solutions-only use of philosophy to a problems-and-solutions practice of philosophy. In Bergson, the idea of philosophy as focused on problems can, I think, be plausibly situated in relation to the work of James. The claim here is, of course, not that Bergson borrowed his conception of problematization from James. The claim is much more tenuous and involves remarking on the depth of the intellectual exchange between Bergson and James in the early 1900s. Both recognized a deep mutual affinity for one another's work. While they disagreed on much, I suggest that they found a great deal of common terrain in their shared respect for the sense in which philosophy can be used not only to solve problems, but also to get problems into proper view. In James this idea is fairly explicit, though in subsequent pragmatists such as Dewey and Rorty we do not always find it expressed with the lucidity it has in James's work.

Nonetheless, it is there in their work, and explicitly so, for it is a core aspect of the pragmatist way of thinking.

Each of the episodes in this intellectual history would need to be developed in greater detail before this account could be used to establish anything approaching definitiveness. Such a fuller account will have to wait for another occasion. For now, I merely want to suggest the story and take note of its plausibility. Should it turn out to be accurate, we have good reason for seeing in genealogy a close historical kinship with pragmatism. Until that accuracy can be verified, all I have is a good hunch. Sometimes it pays to run with our hunches. But prudence requires we work out the details.

33. For discussion on the terms of this divergence I would like to thank Thomas Nail and Nicolae Morar, though I likely still proffer here a position with which they would disagree.

34. Deleuze 1990, 170–71

35. Deleuze 1986b, 106; it is striking how similar are Deleuze's formulation in the 1986 Parnet interview and the 1990 Negri interview.

36. Rabinow 2009, 28

37. Hoy 2004, 72

38. Sawicki 1994, 288

39. Rabinow 1997, xix; cf. Rabinow and Dreyfus 1982, 109

40. Rose 1999, 59; cf. Rose 2006, 4ff.

41. Brown 2001, 113

42. Butler 1990, 138

43. Foucault 1969a, 26 and 1971, 371. For another example that is ambiguous between the two readings I propose, consider: "History serves to show how that-which-is has not always been, i.e., that the things which seem most evident to us are always formed in the confluence of encounters and chances, during the course of a precarious and fragile history . . . [S]ince these things have been made, they can be unmade, as long as know how it was that they were made" (Foucault 1983b, 450). The ambiguity is in the last clause: Foucault here surely emphasizes *that* present practices are historical and so not inevitable but he also just as surely points out that remaking our practices requires knowing *how* they have been made.

44. Brown 2001, 106

45. Brown 2001, 118

46. Brown 2001, 106

47. Butler 1990, 138

48. Butler 1990, 146, 147

49. For one recent account, see Ben-Menahem (2009).

50. Rabinow 2009, 31, quoting within from Foucault (1978c, 225; DE4.22)

51. Foucault 1984e, 117

52. Foucault 1984e, 117

53. Foucault 1984e, 118

54. Rabinow 1999, 12

55. Foucault 1984c, 316, 319

56. See Fraser (1981) and Habermas (1985)

57. Geuss 2002, 211

58. Geuss's article is published alongside a paper by Martin Saar as the proceedings of a panel that took place at a major Foucault symposium (other presenters at the conference included Axel Honneth, Judith Butler, Nancy Fraser, and Paul Veyne) held in Frankfurt only weeks after the World Trade Center bombings in September 2001. Saar's paper features the standard interpretation of Foucaultian genealogy as a subversive enterprise to which I am objecting: "Genealogies project delegitimizing, denaturalizing perspectives on the processes of subject constitution and construction" (2002, 236).

59. Lemke 2002, 50

60. The key published writings that fill in parts of this missing story include the "Omnes et Singulatim" lectures at Stanford in 1979 (1979b), the "About the Beginnings of the Hermeneutics of the Self" seminars at Berkeley and Dartmouth in 1980 (1980b), the "Political Technology of Individuals" lectures at Vermont in 1982 (1982c), and certain portions of Foucault's Collège de France course lectures during these years, especially the outline provided in the March 9, 1983 lectures in the *Government of Self and Others* course lecture series (1983a). As for the supposedly written but still-unpublished fourth volume, it remains an unfortunate mystery to too many of us, but the still-unpublished 1980 *On the Government of the Living* course lecture series may still shed some light on this aspect of Foucault's researches.

61. Deleuze 1986b, 110

62. Canguilhem 1992, 32

63. Lemke 2002, 50

64. Rose 1999, 62

65. See Hoy (2004)

66. Foucault 1978/1982d, 342. Concerning the date of composition of this passage, Arnold Davidson has argued, I think rightly, that the latter portions of the essay (presumably 340ff. in the cited edition) were probably written earlier than the 1982 date when it was first published as an appendix to Rabinow and Dreyfus (1982); evidence for this includes a close examination of certain key for-

mulations in those portions which are repeated almost word for word in other lectures and texts from 1978 (Davidson 2011, 39, note 4).

67. In addition, see: Rajchman's distinction between "practical" and "ideal" freedom in Foucault; he specified the former as "rooted not in autonomy or the capacity to determine actions according to rules all must rationally accept, but rather in the unwillingness to comply, the refusal to acquiesce, to fit ourselves in the practices through which we understand and rule ourselves and each other," and therefore "freedom not as the end of domination but as revolt within its practices" (1985, 92, 115); and Stone's distinction between "practices of freedom" and "processes of liberation" in response to a standard criticism of Foucault's ethics of freedom (2011, 102).

68. Rose 1999, 65

69. Hoy 2009a, 205

5. Foucault's Problematization of Modernity

1. Foucault 1967a, 293

2. I see Foucault's methodological grip on modernity as well approximated in contemporary critical thought by anthropologists; see for instance Rabinow (1999) on science as practices, Zaloom (2006) and Ho (2009) on capitalism as practices, and Tsing (2004) on globalization practices. All of these books explicitly refuse to engage in totalizing epochal analyses, working instead at the level of analyzing practices so as to fashion concepts adequate to what is emergent. This is notable given that their subject matters are in many instances paradigms of epochal analysis. I return to Tsing in Chapter 7 below. Stimulating thoughts on the stakes of "epochal" versus "topological" methodologies in Foucault are offered by another anthropologist in Collier (2009), who locates Foucault's shift a little differently than I do here.

3. Foucault 1984c, 309

4. I dutifully note that there are, of course, other readings of Weber that emphasize different, perhaps better, aspects of his work. Indeed I suspect that much of the recent revisionist scholarship, which I do not here employ, may indeed be more accurate to Weber. But fidelity to Weber is not my aim. The dominance of Weberian thinking (even if it may not be entirely true to Weber's own mind) is an effect of a theory of modernity established in Weber's classic terms of bureaucratic rationalization as made influential by prominent sociological interpretations of Weber, most notably that of Talcott Parsons, who was one of the most influential sociologists on the world scene during the mid-century fevers of academic professionalization. It is this Weber, the Parsonian Weber, who

has come to have a distorting influence on our understanding of Foucault's writings about modernity. See Parsons (1937) and also Löwith (1932) and Bendix (1966) for the standard influential readings. But see also Mommsen (1992), Scaff (1989), and Hennis (1987) for revisionist readings. Note that it is Parson's Weber with whom Habermas (1981a) wrestles in his equally influential work, as noted in a review essay by Giddens (1982). See Swedberg (2005, 226) on these and other divergence in recent Weber scholarship. See Koopman (2010e) for further discussion of competing conceptualizations of modernity in Weber, Foucault, and Dewey.

5. While most critics have not often explicitly connected Foucault's thought to Weber's, my claim is that they have explicated Foucault in terms of Weberian concepts that were not really his. The existing comparative literature that is explicit about Foucault and Weber almost unanimously affirms a tight connection between the two; see O'Neill (1986), Dews (1987), Gordon (1987), Turner (1987), Owen (1994), and especially Szakolczai (1998). In a similar vein, Fraser (1981) sees Foucault as arguing for Weberian conclusions but without being Weberian enough. An important exception that explicitly refuses to interpret Foucault in Weberian categories is Dean (1994). Also notable are those who claim a Foucault-Weber alliance but on the basis of an interpretation of Weber that abandons the influential sociological interpretation handed down by Parsons in favor of a more nuanced interpretation according to which Weber, like Foucault, attempted to fashion a critical apparatus for undertaking inquiry into the core problems of modernity, as argued by Rabinow (2003).

6. Rorty 1981a, 6

7. Bernauer 1990, 16

8. Weber 1905, 181. Note that the English resonance of Weber's term has been handed down through the influential Parsonian lineage of Weberian thought, while other interpretations are of course possible, as noted by Swedberg (2005, 132).

9. Agamben 1995, 20; for further criticisms of Agamben see Koopman (2013c).

10. Foucault 1975a, 169; see also Foucault 1983i, 0:30:23–0:39:31.

11. Gutting 1989 71, 74, 89, 109

12. In addition to the influential interpretations of Gutting and Derrida just discussed in the main passage, see De Certeau (1975, 40) and Gauchet and Swain (1980). The debates in France surrounding the publication of Foucault's book are excellently detailed in Roudinesco (2005, 65ff.) and Weymans (2009).

13. Derrida 1963, 31, 36, 59, 62

14. Foucault 1972e, 413

15. Derrida 2003, 151

16. Lentricchia 1988, 70

17. Habermas 1985, 293

18. Habermas (1981b, 1985) and Fraser (1981); see related criticisms by Walzer (1983), Taylor (1984), McCarthy (1990), and MacIntyre (1990).

19. For further discussion of the impasse between Derrida and Habermas, see helpful contributions by Bernstein (1991) and Hoy (1989).

20. For a response to Derrida, see Foucault (1972e), and for an indirect reply to Habermas, see Foucault (1984c).

21. Foucault 1961, 529 also quoted in Eribon 1989, 97; this passage can be found in the recently translated longer version of *Histoire de la Folie* but not the abridgement published in English as *Madness and Civilization.*

22. Foucault 1961, 29, 32, 459, 460

23. Foucault explicitly states this as a methodological dictum at the outset of his 1979 Collège de France course lectures (1979b, 3).

24. Foucault 1961, 488

25. Rajchman 1985, 117

26. O'Farrell 1989, 78

27. Foucault 1961, 536

28. Hacking 2011, 16

29. Foucault 1961, 145, 497

30. Foucault 1961, xxxiii and as quoted in Derrida 1963, 43; this passage can be found in the recently translated longer version of *Histoire de la Folie* but not in the abridged *Madness and Civilization* publication.

31. Hacking 2011, 19

32. Foucault 1961, xxviii

33. Gutting (1989, 89–91) helpfully registers this shifting emphasis through *History of Madness;* and see again the discussions in Hacking (2011, 19ff.).

34. Foucault 1961, 101, 82; cf. 431, 437

35. Foucault 1961, 343–52. Huffer (2010, 194–234) offers one of the few discussions of this section of *Madness,* and I am greatly indebted to her reading, which is of course much fuller than what I offer here. There are many points where my discussion resonates with Huffer's, indeed because the present discussion of *Rameau's Nephew* derives its inspiration almost entirely from Huffer's work.

36. Foucault 1961, 344

37. Foucault 1961, 352

38. Foucault 1963b, 80

39. Foucault 1961, 139

40. Nietzsche 1872, §21

41. See Nietzsche 1886, §2, §23, §24. Note that while Foucault sensibly restricted the theme of reciprocal incompatibility to histories of modernity, Nietzsche incautiously deployed it much more widely—I emphasize this point in Chapter 2; see also discussion by Sluga (2002, 2005, 2010).

42. Though clearly not identical to the concepts of freedom discussed by Foucault, I will in what follows often roll the concept of autonomy into this package. This is certainly not because I find autonomy everywhere equivalent to liberation, but rather because the high modern ideal of autonomy is in so many instances a philosophical bulwark for the practices of liberation that are Foucault's most steady target. A capacity of autonomy, as drawn up by modernity's most august philosophers, provides justification, support, and reinforcement for the liberties. For a counter view see work by Amy Allen (2008), which I discuss at length in Chapter 6.

43. Han-Pile 1998, 175, 185, 172. One is clearly reminded of the criticisms of Habermas (1985). While the Habermasian critique has certainly not gone unanswered, my response differs from those of most previous defenders of Foucault insofar as the tendency thus far has been to read Foucault's late work on ethics as an answer to the question about power posed by Habermas; see exemplary discussions by Kelly (1994b) and Osborne (1999). I insist, on the contrary, that we cannot answer Habermas with Foucault. This is because Habermas put his questions in a form that misinterprets Foucault's project. Rather than answering Habermas, my approach is to show that Foucault was setting up a different problem than the typical Weberian problems that Habermas addressed. As it turns out, I argue in the following chapter, Habermas can help us formulate rather decent answers to Foucault's problems.

44. Foucault 1975a, 199

45. Foucault 1975b, 48 essentially recapitulating Foucault 1975a, 194

46. Foucault 1975a, 184ff.

47. Foucault 1979b, 325; see helpful discussion by Colin Gordon (1991).

48. Foucault 1975, 222; cf. 1976a, 145. For the purposes of my argument here it presents no difficulties that Foucault subsequently revised the terms of this claim in his 1978 course lectures: "I was not completely wrong, of course, but, in short, it was not exactly this. . . . More precisely and particularly, freedom is nothing else but the correlative of the deployment of apparatuses of security" (1978a, 48). Whereas in 1975 Foucault's claim was that disciplinary power and liberationist freedom form the reciprocal and incompatible problematization of our modernity, in 1978 his claim was that powers of "security" and freedoms of "circulation" form this reciprocally incompatible problematization. This shift in nuanced detail does not undermine my overall argument here that the core point of Foucault's problematization of modernity takes the form of a re-

ciprocal but incompatible relationship between various apparatuses of modern power and various apparatuses of modern freedom. Though I speak most often of "disciplinary power" and "liberationist freedom," these terms should be taken as shorthand for "disciplinary-biopolitical-security powers" and "autonomy-liberation-circulation freedoms."

49. Hoy 2004, 100

50. Butler 2000, 740

51. Butler 1990, 10

52. Butler 2002, 218; on Butler's complicated relationship to Foucault, see Allen (1999) and on Butler's essay on Foucault, see Hoy (2004, 93–100).

53. Foucault 1982a, 252

54. Butler 2000, 741

55. See Foucault (1977c)

56. Foucault 1983h, audio recording, 1:06:05

57. Foucault 1984f, 282–83

58. I am thinking specifically of such works as "The Subject and Power" (1978/1982d), the *Security, Territory, Population* (1978a) course lectures, *The Birth of Biopolitics* (1979a) course lectures, and various other essays and interviews from this period. See the discussion of this ambiguity at the end of Chapter 4.

59. For an instructive approach to shifts in Foucault's works in these years that makes productive use of the more standard emphasis on the importance of governmentality as a bridge between politics and ethics, see Thompson (2003).

60. For these biographical details I of course owe much to the standard biographies by Eribon (1989), Macey (1993), and Miller (1993), though I owe much more to conversations with Paul Rabinow at Berkeley, whose work in Rabinow (2009) offers a better statement of what I am here only gesturing at.

61. Foucault 1978a, 201; on the relation between "counter-conduct" and "resistance" in these lectures see work by Davidson (2011).

62. Foucault 1978a, 201

63. Foucault 1979a, 67; translation modified from "freedoms" to "liberties" following the French usage of "libertés."

64. Among those who have argued that there is a basic incoherence between the so-called middle and late works are Dews (1989), McCarthy (1990), Han-Pile (1998), and Paras (2006). Among those who have argued for important continuities between the so-called middle works of the 1970s and late works of the 1980s are McWhorter (1999), O'Leary (2002), Oksala (2005), Hofmeyr (2006), Heyes (2007), Nealon (2008), Allen (2008), and Huffer (2010).

65. Paul Rabinow recently expresses these two moments of Foucault's work. Of the genealogical writings, Rabinow writes, "For Foucault the primary task of the analyst was not to proceed directly toward intervention so as to repair the

situation's discordancy, as one could imagine those in the pragmatist traditions advocating, but rather to pause, reflect, and put forth a diagnosis" (2011a, 92). Of the later ethical writings, and especially the work in the late course lectures, Rabinow describes a shift toward a project that "would seem to imply the necessity to move beyond the traditional forms of genealogy with their disruptive metric and their backward-facing positionality," in favor of "a critical and spiritual practice of transformation of the self and others" (2011a, 94).

My terminology of methodologies of problematization and reconstruction is meant to facilitate putting these two moments of Foucault's work into productive relation.

6. Foucault's Reconstruction of Modern Moralities

1. Foucault 1981b, 88
2. See Deleuze 1986b, 110 and Canguilhem 1992, 32; see the quotations above in the final section of Chapter 4.
3. Rajchman 1989, 220
4. McGushin 2007, 22, xv
5. Gilson (unpublished)
6. See the citations above in Chapter 4, note 60.
7. See Foucault 1983a, 69–70
8. Scott 1990, 57; but for a more recent, and more nuanced, view see Scott (2011).
9. As quoted by Miller (1990, 489, note 11), according to whom the back-cover blurb for the original French edition of *Surveiller et punir* was written by Foucault himself. See also Foucault 1975c, 53 (also cited by Miller).
10. Foucault 1972d, xiii, xiv
11. Foucault 1983e, 271
12. Bové 1988, xiii; see also Christoph Menke's (2003, 209) claim that Foucault's "opposition of aesthetic-existential [i.e., ethical] and disciplinary practices does not lie in the area of their content, procedure, or goals, but rather in what Foucault repeatedly referred to as their 'attitude,'" which I take to map to what I have been calling their "orientation."
13. See Foucault 1984a, 25–32 and 1984b, 240
14. See Williams 1985
15. Foucault 1983f, 166
16. Foucault 1980c, 152
17. Foucault 1979c, 444
18. Foucault 1980d, 323
19. Gros 2005, 697, 707

20. Rajchman 1991, 111; cf. Rajchman (1985, 1986).

21. Faubion 2001, 97

22. Huffer 2010, 243

23. Foucault 1984j, 284

24. Foucault 1982e, 245

25. Foucault 1982e, 245

26. Rabinow 1997, xxxii. Rabinow more recently writes of Foucault's late work as an attempt to "turn philosophy once again into a critical and spiritual practice of transformation of the self and others" (2011a, 94).

27. Foucault 1984c, 315, 312, 319

28. Foucault 1984e, 201

29. That Foucault was near upon the project of elaborating these connections in detail is suggested by the first lecture of his 1984 Collège de France lecture where he describes the past few years of his research on ethics in antiquity as a "several years long Greco-Latin 'trip'" from which he hopes to return that year "to some contemporary problems" (1984h, 2; cf. 5). He would not live to realize those hopes. See also Lectures 1, 2, and 9 of the 1983 Collège de France lecture series (1983a).

30. Foucault 1982a, 15

31. Foucault 1984j, 294

32. Foucault 1982a, 189, 190

33. Foucault 1982a, 251, 309

34. Greenblatt 1980, 257; cited by Foucault 1984a, 11

35. Foucault 1982a, 252

36. See Faubion (2011), Heyes (2007), Mahmood (2005), and McWhorter (1999).

37. Heyes 2007, 116

38. Mahmood 2005, 36

39. Faubion 2011, 121

40. Mahmood 2005, 195

41. Faubion 2011, 8

42. Mahmood 2005, 24

43. See McWhorter (1999, 2009).

44. McWhorter 1999, xvii, xix

45. An enlightening discussion of such possibilities is found in Rabinow and Marcus (2008); for an example of some of the work discussed therein, see the ongoing experiment in cross-disciplinary collaboration involving Rabinow, Faubion, and others at *The Anthropological Research on the Contemporary Collaboratory* (http://anthropos-lab.net).

46. In addition to those already cited who make a strong claim for self-transformation in Foucault's work, namely Rajchman (1991), Faubion (2001), Gros (2005), and Huffer (2010), others have emphasized, but without centralizing to the same degree, self-transformation in their interpretation of Foucault's ethics: see Rabinow (1997), McWhorter (1999), O'Leary (2002), Oksala (2005), Heyes (2007), Allen (2008), and Colapietro (2011). My aim is of course not to discount any of this work, but rather to invite these and other scholars to reorient their use of Foucault's ethics according to the idea of a self-transformation.

47. See Allen (2008) and Huffer (2010), with convincing arguments for this approach to Foucault.

48. For an attempt to take my own provocation seriously, see Koopman (2013b/forthcoming) discussing what I take to be the major ethical commitments or injunctions expressed in Foucault's writings: aesthetics, pleasure, parrhesia, and philosophy.

49. See Nussbaum (1986), MacIntyre (1981), Williams (1985), Anscombe (1958), and Foot (1958).

50. Williams 1993, 7

51. See Veyne 2008, 106

52. See Hadot 1989, 230; see the response to Hadot's worries by Davidson (1994b) as well as related criticisms in a different key by Wolin (1986).

53. See Allen (2008) and also the compelling cases made by Oksala (2005) and O'Leary (2002).

54. For criticisms of Foucault along these lines see Alcoff (1990, 2000); see also a different line of response to these worries in Bevir (1999).

55. Allen 2008, 2

56. I have aired the first worry in Koopman (2011a), to which Allen's response (2011b) offers fruitful terms for continued conversation, which conversation I aim to continue here with my second objection.

57. Foucault 1983a, 310; see also other passages cited by Allen (2011b, 133).

58. This is the fruitful suggestion offered by Allen (2011b, 134); see also Sawicki (2005, 388) commenting on Allen (2008).

59. Fraser (1981). For helpful insights on Fraser's criticisms I thank Amy Allen, though she may still not agree with my interpretations.

60. Fraser 1981, 33

61. See Fraser (1994, 2009).

62. Fraser 1983, 65; see also Fraser (1985).

63. For a recent example especially relevant to my later attempt to initiate more enriching dialogue between Foucault and Habermas, see Taylor (2009).

64. See Habermas (1985).

65. See Rorty (1981b). For another version of such a more congenial criticism, see Richard Bernstein (1989)—on a continuum, Bernstein's criticisms are the most measured, Rorty's in the middle, Fraser's a little more severe, and Habermas's by far the most severe. For a detailed discussion of Rorty's many and shifting criticisms of Foucault see Małecki (2011).

66. Rorty 1981a, 6

67. Foucault 1984f, 298

68. Foucault in Rorty (RRP, Box 23, Folder 2)

69. I thank Paul Rabinow for reminding me of the intention of the *Des Travaux* series in this connection.

7. Problematization plus Reconstruction

1. Benhabib 1986, 226, 142

2. Foucault 1984c, 319

3. See Hoy and McCarthy (1994) and the contributions to Kelly (1994a), and Ashenden and Owen (1999) for a representative sampling.

4. Allen (2008, 2009, 2010, 2011c)

5. Allen 2008, 177

6. Allen 2009, 3, 4; cf. 2008, 4–10.

7. Allen 2009, 4. For an earlier exchange on the issues discussed herein see Koopman (2011a) critiquing integration in favor of the delegation strategy and a response by Allen (2011b) defending the integration strategy. In many ways my approach here (though not the contents of my claims) tracks closely to Nancy Fraser's pragmatist contribution to the Foucault-Habermas and Butler-Benhabib debates in *Feminist Contentions,* especially where she suggests that "We should adopt the pragmatic view that there are a plurality of different angles from which sociocultural phenomena should be understood" (1995, 166).

8. Allen 2008, 65, 8

9. Allen 2009, 27–28

10. See especially Allen (2011b, 139–41) clarifying Allen (2008).

11. Hoy in Hoy and McCarthy 1994, 163

12. McCarthy in Hoy and McCarthy 1994, 226

13. Their more recent work suggests that both Hoy (2009a, 228ff.) and McCarthy (2004, 164ff.) would be amenable to the alternative peacemaking strategy I propose.

14. Allen 2009, 1

15. See Rabinow (2003, 2008), Marcus (1999), Marcus and Fischer (1986), and Rabinow and Marcus (2008).

16. See Collingwood (1946)

17. See Owen (2005) for a particularly informative example of the common anti-universalist refrain in the literature on Foucault.

18. Tully 1999, 108

19. McCarthy 1990, 43–44

20. See Butler, Laclau, and Žižek (2000).

21. Butler in Butler, Laclau, and Žižek 2000, 25

22. See Butler in Butler, Laclau, and Žižek 2000, 35.

23. See Butler in Butler, Laclau, and Žižek 2000, 169.

24. Butler 2000, 745

25. See Bernstein (2010)

26. McCarthy in Hoy and McCarthy 1994, 72

27. Foucault 1979d, 453

28. See Foucault 1977b, 127 on the "universal" versus "specific" intellectual contrast.

29. Foucault 1984e, 335; Foucault immediately goes on to connect these two "principles" (his word) of universality and historicity with a third principle of transformative critique that he explicates in explicitly Kantian terms.

30. See Agamben (1995)

31. For further discussion of this distinction between *concepts* and *methods* in Foucaultian philosophy, see Koopman and Matza (2013/forthcoming). For further criticisms of Agamben in terms of these methodological distinctions see Koopman (2013c/forthcoming).

32. In a related vein on Foucault and Agamben, see Oksala (2010).

33. See Agamben (2006)

34. Agamben 2006, 2, 3

35. Foucault 1977a, 194 (quoted in Agamben 2006, 2). Foucault himself goes on to describe the "major function" of these ensembles in their given historical moments as "responding to an *urgent need*" (Foucault 1977a, 195). This reference to an "urgent need" suggests to me that what Foucault was trying to pick out with the analytic category of a *dispositif* is what he would later bring into clearer focus through the analytic idea of a problematization.

36. Agamben 2006, 7

37. See Agamben 2006, 7 and Foucault 1979a, 3; cf. Hoy 2009a, 234

38. Hoy 2009b, 13; cf. Hoy 2009a, 234ff.

39. See Hoy 1994, 177ff.

40. See Hoy 1994, 268ff.

41. Hoy 2009b, 14

42. Foucault 1975, 228

43. Rabinow in Rabinow and Marcus 2008, 110

44. Hacking (1975, 1990)

45. Hacking 1990, 5

46. Hacking 2009, 96. The source cited is a report on work-in-progress regarding a larger project with which I became acquainted in presentations on these matters by Hacking at the University of California at Santa Cruz in the winter of 2008. For another approach to standards, complementary in many but not all respects, to my and Hacking's Foucaultian approach, see the collection by Star and Lampland (2008). For a readable history of measure, see Crease (2011).

47. Adams 1821

48. Foucault (1975a, 1976a, 1978a), Hacking (1990); cf. Ewald (1990) and Mader (2007) on social measure.

49. See Benhabib 2006, 47ff. and Benhabib forthcoming.

50. See Ong and Collier (2008) for a good starting point.

51. Tsing (2004)

52. Tsing 2004, 1, 6, 7, 76. Two recent anthropologies of finance capitalism also excellently capture the kind of picture of offered by Tsing of capitalism not as ideology but as practice-in-universalizing-motion. Karen Ho's (2009) ethnography of Wall Street investment banking and Caitlin Zaloom's (2006) study of Chicago and London commodities trading houses both deftly trade in hapless abstractions about hegemonic capitalist universalism in favor of inquiries that show just how capital gets differentiated as it gets universalized. This is useful because it gives our concepts of universal capital the frictional grip we would need from which to launch any kind of critique. This is valuable just now insofar as this kind of grip tends to go largely missing in fashionable gestural pronouncements about the failings of capitalism or neoliberalism or liberalism (as if these things are just one thing, and as if these terms tend to name anything at all when bandied about with the level of abstraction that is common in too much contemporary critical discourse). Ho and Zaloom help us see how to make good on Tsing's plea that "Rather than assume we know exactly what global capitalism is, even before it arrives, we need to find out how it operates in friction" (2004, 12). What these kinds of accounts help us see, I am arguing, is that all the action is to be found just where there is action. The action in universality is accordingly not in universalisms but rather in universalizations.

53. For influential statements of Dewey's pragmatism as lacking a sense of the tragic, see Royce (1891), Bourne (1917), Mumford (1926), Niebuhr (1932), Horkheimer (1947), Mills (1964), Diggins (1994), and for a defense of Dewey on this count, see Hickman (2001, 65–82 and 1990, 166–95). On Dewey's pragmatism as lacking a theory of power, see Mills (1969), discussion by Pratt (2011),

and a defense of Dewey by Rogers (2009, Chapter 5). On Dewey's pragmatism as blind to the tragic, see West (1993) and a defense of Dewey by Glaude (2008, Chapter 1). For a fuller discussion of all three critiques of pragmatism more generally, see Koopman (2009a, Chapter 7).

54. See my introduction in Koopman (2011b) for further reflection on these matters.

55. See Rorty (1981b) and West (1989).

56. See Auxier (2002) and Livingston (2001).

57. See, in addition to work discussed below arguments by Tejara (1980), Stuhr (1997, 2003), Colapietro (1998a, 1998b, 2011), and Reynolds (2004). See also a number of the papers collected (by me, I admit) in a recent special issue of *Foucault Studies* arguing the value of a connection between pragmatism and genealogy, particularly the contributions by Rabinow, Colapietro, May, Edmonds, Gayman, and Stone to the collection Koopman (2011b).

58. Rabinow (2003, 2008, 2011b, 2012/forthcoming)

59. See, for instance, forthcoming work by Nick Dorzweiler.

60. Koopman (2009a, Chapter 7)

61. Colapietro 2011, 37

62. See my discussions in Koopman (2006 and 2009a, Chapter 1).

63. On the temporal-historical rhythm of inquiry itself, see Dewey (1916a, 1/MW10.320, 18/MW10.331).

64. Dewey 1920, 178, 177/MW12.181

65. Dewey 1920, 213/MW12.201

66. Dewey 1916b, 328/MW9.338

67. On Dewey's influence on American educational theory and practice see Martin (2003).

68. Dewey 1916b, 150–151/MW9.158

69. Dewey 1938a, LW12.108

70. I can here only sketch this argument since my central purposes in this book concern not pragmatism but genealogy; I develop these criticisms of pragmatism in much greater detail in the final chapter of Koopman (2009a).

71. Dewey 1929, LW4.99

72. James 1907, 31. Much more could be said about the sense in which genealogy and pragmatism can be read as methodological. I expect this to be a central concern in my next project.

73. For one of his many expressions of antipathy see Rorty 1980, 160.

74. See Thayer (1968), Murphey (1968), and Kuklick (1977).

75. See Putnam (1995), Bernstein (2006), Brandom (2009), and Margolis (2010).

76. See Apel (1967), Christensen (1994), and Kaag (2005).

77. See Carlson (1997) and Seigfried (2001).

78. See Habermas (1999) and the discussion below.

79. Pihlström 2003, 34

80. Pihlström 2003, 74

81. See Pihlström 2003, 49n65 noting his possible conflation of these terms.

82. Pihlström 2003, 35

83. For the most recent statement of this common interpretation see Johnston (2006).

84. Dewey 1929, LW4.230, 231; see for a related account Dewey 1906, 206–13/MW3.

85. Dewey 1938a, LW12.13

86. Dewey 1938b, LW13.281

87. Dewey 1920 (1948), xv/MW12.262 (the quote is from the 1948 introduction to the 1920 volume).

88. See Honneth (1985, 257) and McCarthy (1978, 264).

89. In the tradition of pragmatism, most especially in Dewey, reconstruction is the very heart of normativity. In the tradition of critical theory, at least as represented in Habermas, normativity assumes a much wider valence such that reconstruction is just one form that normativity takes in a career of variations on this central theme. It is almost a truism to assert that critical theory, at least for Habermas, is much more normatively ambitious than pragmatism, at least for Dewey. This is one of the sources of the enduring philosophical friction that always kept separate the views of Rorty and Habermas. Despite this friction, however, it is clear that in both critical theory and pragmatism there is a common commitment to reconstructive conceptions of normativity. And it is these analogous conceptions of normativity that I seek to draw attention to, so as to suggest the need for supplementing critical practices of genealogical problematization with distinctive but complementary critical practices of reconstruction. In order to develop this analogy, I need not demonstrate full-scale philosophical identity between pragmatism and critical theory. All I need to show is an analogy of commitment as well as, of course, the nonpresence of any overt philosophical incompatibilities.

90. Habermas 1976b, 95

91. Habermas 1976b, 121

92. Habermas 1988, 173–78

93. Habermas 1999, 13

94. Habermas 1976a, 23

95. Habermas 1983, 65

96. Rorty 2000a, 6

97. Rorty 2000b, 56

98. This is not just Rorty's concern. Others who criticize Habermas's supposed universalism as inconsistent with pragmatism include Aboulafia (2002b), Margolis (2002), Rockmore (2002), and Bernstein (2010).

99. Habermas 1985, 297; contrast Habermas (1976a) where he was still explicitly holding on to the philosophy of "transcendentalism."

100. In addition to Rorty (2000a, 2000b) see also Rorty (1995b) for further expressions of this over-anxiousness.

101. See Forst (1994)

102. Honneth 1995, 296

103. McCarthy 1994, 81; cf. 228–30

104. Benhabib 1986, 264, 297, 74

105. See especially Habermas (1992, 1999a) and for further self-reflections on his work as pragmatist, see Habermas (1998, 1999b, 2000, 2002, 2008).

106. Habermas 1999a, 17

107. Habermas 1999a, 221 quoting Putnam; see also Habermas 1988, 137ff. on Putnam.

108. Habermas 1992, 16, 21, 15

109. My argument in this paragraph draws on Benhabib (1986, 72–76) and Chambers (1995, 233–35); I disagree with crucial elements of the discussion of these issues offered by Bookman (2002, 66–68).

110. Dewey 1920 (1948), xv/MW12.262 (the quote is from the 1948 introduction to the 1920 volume).

111. See Allen (2008) and Cooke (2006).

112. Habermas 1996, 45

113. For an analysis of the function of ideology in critical theory, see Geuss (1981).

114. Benhabib 1986, 271. Where I depart from Benhabib's analysis is in terms of her explication of diagnosis in terms that remain within the vocabulary of critical theory in appeals to "systemic" crisis and anticipation in terms of "lived" crisis (1986, 142, 226). In this I take my cues in part from Honneth's *Critique of Power* (1985, xvi–xvii, 268–69) insofar as one central claim in that book is that Habermas's critical theory stands at a crossroads between the Weberian diagnosis of rationalization at the heart of *The Theory of Communicative Action* and a quite different anticipatory vision of the social struggle for recognition offered in *Knowledge and Human Interests* (and subsequently taken up by Habermas again in *Between Facts and Norms*).

115. See Jay (1973) for a useful history of the Frankfurt School.

116. McCarthy in Hoy and McCarthy 1994, 230, following Fraser 1983, 65 and Bernstein 1989, 164.

117. For a different reading of Habermas's recent usage of genealogy, namely as both problematizing and vindicatory according to my typology in Chapter 2, see Allen (2011a).

118. Habermas 1996, 45, 28

119. O'Neill 1989, 22

Bibliography

Foucault References

References to Anthologies and Collections of Foucault's Works

Foucault, Michel. DE1, DE2, DE3, & DE4. *Dits et Ecrits, Tomes I–IV.* Daniel Defert and François Ewald (eds.). Paris: Gallimard, 1994.

Foucault, Michel. EW1. *Essential Works, Volume 1: Ethics, Subjectivity, and Truth.* Ed. Paul Rabinow. New York: New Press, 1997.

Foucault, Michel. EW2. *Essential Works, Volume 2: Aesthetics, Method, and Epistemology.* James Faubion and Paul Rabinow (eds.). New York: New Press, 1998.

Foucault, Michel. EW3. *Essential Works, Volume 3: Power.* James Faubion and Paul Rabinow (eds.). New York: New Press, 2000.

Foucault, Michel. FR. *The Foucault Reader.* Ed. Paul Rabinow. New York: Pantheon, 1984.

Foucault, Michel. PK. *Power/Knowledge.* Ed. Colin Gordon. New York: Pantheon Books, 1980.

Foucault, Michel. PPC. *Politics, Philosophy, Culture: Interviews and Other Writings, 1977–1984.* Ed. Lawrence Kritzman. New York: Routledge, 1988.

References to Foucault's Works

Foucault, Michel. 1954. "Introduction" to Binswanger's *Dream and Existence* in DE1.

Foucault, Michel. 1961 (2006). *History of Madness.* Jean Khalfa and Jonathan Murphy (trans.). New York: Routledge.

Foucault, Michel. 1963a (1973). *The Birth of the Clinic: An Archaeology of Medical Perception.* A. M. Sheridan Smith (trans.). New York: Vintage.

Foucault, Michel. 1963b (1998). "A Preface to Transgression" in Foucault, *Essential Works, Volume 3: Aesthetics, Method, and Epistemology.* Ed. James D. Faubion. New York: New Press.

Foucault, Michel. 1964. "Introduction to Kant's *Anthropology.*" Roberto Nigro and Kate Briggs (trans.). Los Angeles: Semiotext(e), 2008. Also available online as Foucault, "Introduction to Kant's *Anthropology from a pragmatic point of view,*" Arianna Bove (trans.), at http://www.generation-online.org/p /fpfoucault1.htm, Feb. 2008.

Foucault, Michel. 1966 (1970). *The Order of Things: An Archaeology of the Human Sciences.* New York: Vintage, 1970.

Foucault, Michel. 1967a. "On the Ways of Writing History" in EW2.

Foucault, Michel. 1967b. "Qui êtes-vois, professeur Foucault?" in DE1.

Foucault, Michel. 1967c. "Nietzsche, Freud, Marx" in EW2.

Foucault, Michel. 1968. "Réponse à une question" in DE1; also in *Esprit* 36, no. 5, May 1968: 850–74; also in English as "History, Discourse and Discontinuity ('Réponse à une question')," Anthony M. Nazzaro (trans.) in *Salmagundi* 20, Summer–Fall 1972: 225–48.

Foucault, Michel. 1969a (1972). *The Archaeology of Knowledge.* A. M. Sheridan Smith (trans.). New York: Pantheon.

Foucault, Michel. 1969b. "Foucault Responds to Sartre" radio interview by Jean-Pierre El Kabbach, trans. John Johnston, in Foucault, Sylviere Lotringer (ed.), *Foucault Live.* New York: Semiotext(e), 1989.

Foucault, Michel. 1970a. "The Order of Discourse" as appendix (under the title "The Discourse on Language") to Foucault 1969a.

Foucault, Michel. 1970b. "Le Piège de Vincennes" interview with P. Loriot in DE2.

Foucault, Michel. 1970c. "Theatrum Philosophicum" in EW2.

Foucault, Michel. 1971. "Nietzsche, Genealogy, History" in EW2.

Foucault, Michel. 1972a. "Return to History" in EW2.

Foucault, Michel. 1972b. "A Historian of Culture" debate with Giulio Preti in Foucault, Sylvère Lotringer (ed.), *Foucault Live: Collected Interviews, 1961–1984.* New York: Semiotext(e), 1996.

Foucault, Michel and Deleuze, Gilles. 1972c (1980). "Intellectuals and Power" conversation with Gilles Deleuze, in Foucault, Donald Bouchard (ed.), *Language, Counter-Memory, and Practice.* Ithaca, N.Y.: Cornell University Press.

Foucault, Michel. 1972d (1983). "Preface" to Gilles Deleuze and Félix Guattari, *Anti-Oedipus.* Robert Hurley, Mark Seem, and Helen R. Lane (trans.). Minneapolis: University of Minnesota Press.

Foucault, Michel. 1972e (1998). "My Body, This Paper, This Fire" in Foucault, *Essential Works, Volume 2: Aesthetics, Method, and Epistemology.* Ed. James D. Faubion. New York: New Press.

Foucault, Michel. 1973. "De l'archéologie à la dynastique" interview with S. Hasumi in DE2.

Foucault, Michel. 1974 (2006). *Psychiatric Power, Lectures at the Collège de France, 1973–4*. Arnold Davidson, Jacques Lagrange, François Ewald, and Alessandro Fontana (eds.), Graham Burchell (trans.). New York: Picador.

Foucault, Michel. 1975a (1997). *Discipline and Punish: The Birth of the Prison*. Alan Sheridan (trans.). New York: Vintage Books.

Foucault, Michel. 1975b (2003). *Abnormal, Lectures at the Collège de France, 1974–5*. Arnold Davidson, Valerio Marchetti, Antonella Salomoni, François Ewald, and Alessandro Fontana (eds.), Graham Burchell (trans.). New York: Picador.

Foucault, Michel. 1975c (1980). "Prison Talk" interview with J.-J. Brochier in Foucault, *Power/Knowledge*. Ed. Colin Gordon. New York: Pantheon.

Foucault, Michel. 1976a (1978). *The History of Sexuality, Volume 1: An Introduction* (*The Will to Know*). Robert Hurley (trans.). New York: Vintage Books.

Foucault, Michel. 1976b (2003). *Society Must be Defended, Lectures at the Collège de France, 1975–1976*. Arnold Davidson, Mauro Bertani, François Ewald, and Alessandro Fontana (eds.), David Macey (trans.). New York: Picador.

Foucault, Michel. 1976c. "The Politics of Health in the Eighteenth Century" in FR.

Foucault, Michel. 1976d. "Preface to *Anti-Oedipus*" (English-language edition) in EW3.

Foucault, Michel. 1977a. "The Confession of the Flesh" in PK.

Foucault, Michel. 1977b. "Truth and Power" in EW3.

Foucault, Michel. 1977c. "Lives of Infamous Men" in EW3.

Foucault, Michel. 1978a (2007). *Security, Territory, Population, Lectures at the Collège de France, 1977–1978*. Arnold Davidson, Michel Senellart, François Ewald, and Alessandro Fontana (eds.), Graham Burchell (trans.). New York: Palgrave Macmillan.

Foucault, Michel. 1978b. "Interview with Michel Foucault" by D. Trombadori in EW3.

Foucault, Michel. 1978c. "Questions of Method (Round Table of 20 May 1978)" in EW3.

Foucault, Michel. 1978d. "On Power" in PPC.

Foucault, Michel. 1978e. "What is Critique?" in Foucault, *The Politics of Truth*. Ed. Sylvère Lotringer. Los Angeles: Semiotext(e), 2007.

Foucault, Michel. 1978f. "La scène de la philosophie" interview with M. Watanabe in DE3.

Foucault, Michel. 1978g/1982d. "The Subject and Power" in EW3.

Foucault, Michel. 1979a (2008). *The Birth of Biopolitics, Lectures at the Collège de France, 1978–1979*. Arnold Davidson, Michel Senellart, François Ewald, and

Alessandro Fontana (eds.), Graham Burchell (trans.). New York: Palgrave Macmillan.

Foucault, Michel. 1979b. "Omnes et Singulatim" in EW3.

Foucault, Michel. 1979c. "For an Ethic of Discomfort" in EW3.

Foucault, Michel. 1979d. "Is It Useless to Revolt?" in EW3.

Foucault, Michel. 1980a. "Power, Moral Values, and the Intellectual" interview by Michael Bess in *History of the Present*, Spring, 1988: 1–2, 11–13. Available online at http://www.vanderbilt.edu/historydept/michaelbess/Foucault %20Interview.

Foucault, Michel. 1980b. "About the Beginnings of the Hermeneutics of the Self" in Foucault, *The Politics of Truth*. Ed. S. Lotringer. Los Angeles: Semiotext(e), 2007.

Foucault, Michel. 1980c. "Subjectivity and Truth (Howison Lecture at University of California at Berkeley, Oct., 1980)" in Foucault, *The Politics of Truth*. Ed. S. Lotringer. Los Angeles: Semiotext(e), 1997.

Foucault, Michel. 1980d. "The Masked Philosopher" interview with Christian Delacampagne in EW1.

Foucault, Michel. 1981a. "So Is It Important to Think?" interview with Didier Eribon in EW3. Also published under the title "Practicing Criticism" in Foucault, *Politics, Philosophy, Culture: Interviews and Other Writings, 1977–1984*. Ed. L. D. Kritzman. New York: Routledge, 1990.

Foucault, Michel. 1981b. "Subjectivity and Truth: Course Summary, 1980–1981" in EW1.

Foucaut, Michel. 1982a (2005). *The Hermeneutics of the Subject, Lectures at the Collège de France, 1981–1982*. Arnold Davidson, Frédéric Gros, François Ewald, and Alessandro Fontana (eds.), Graham Burchell (trans.). New York: Picador, 2005.

Foucault, Michel. 1982b. "Space, Knowledge, Power," in Foucault, *Essential Works of Michel Foucault: Power*, 358. Ed. James D. Faubion. New York: The New Press, 2000.

Foucault, Michel. 1982c. "The Political Technology of Individuals" in EW3.

Foucault, Michel. 1982d (also cited as 1978/1982a). "The Subject and Power" in EW3.

Foucault, Michel. 1982e. "Space, Knowledge, and Power" interview in Foucault, *The Foucault Reader*. Ed. Paul Rabinow. New York: Pantheon, 1984.

Foucault, Michel. 1983a (2010). *The Government of Self and Others, Lectures at the Collège de France, 1982–1983*. Arnold Davidson, Frédéric Gros, François Ewald, and Alessandro Fontana (eds.), Graham Burchell (trans.). New York: Palgrave Macmillan.

Foucault, Michel. 1983b. "Structuralism and Post-Structuralism" in EW2.

Foucault, Michel. 1983c. "Ethics and Politics" unedited and unpublished full interview with Paul Rabinow, Richard Rorty, Martin Jay, Leo Lowenthal, and Charles Taylor at the University of California at Berkeley in April 1983 (portions of this interview were later edited and republished as Foucault 1983d). Bancroft Library Special Collections, University of California at Berkeley, MSS 90/136 z, Box 1, File 1:4.

Foucault, Michel. 1983d. "Politics and Ethics: An Interview" in Foucault, *The Foucault Reader.* Ed. Paul Rabinow. New York: Pantheon, 1984.

Foucault, Michel. 1983e. "On the Genealogy of Ethics: An Overview of Work in Progress" interview with Paul Rabinow and Hubert Dreyfus, Berkeley, April 1983 in EW1.

Foucault, Michel. 1983f. *Fearless Speech.* Ed. Joseph Pearson. Los Angeles: Semiotext(e), 2001.

Foucault, Michel. 1983g. "What is Revolution?" in Foucault, *The Politics of Truth.* Ed. Sylvère Lotringer. Lysa Hochroth and Catherine Porter (trans.). Los Angeles: Semiotext(e), 2007.

Foucault, Michel. 1983h. "The Culture of the Self," Regent's Lecture, Part I, April 12, 1983 at UC Berkeley. UC Berkeley online archive http://dpg.lib .berkeley.edu/.

Foucault, Michel. 1983i. "The Culture of the Self," Regent's Lecture, Part II, April 12, 1983 at UC Berkeley. UC Berkeley online archive http://dpg.lib .berkeley.edu/.

Foucault, Michel. 1984a (1990). *The Use of Pleasure: The History of Sexuality, Volume 2.* Robert Hurley (trans.). New York: Vintage Books.

Foucault, Michel. 1984b (1990). *The Care of the Self: The History of Sexuality, Volume 3.* Robert Hurley (trans.). New York: Vintage Books.

Foucault, Michel. 1984c. "What is Enlightenment?" in EW1.

Foucault, Michel. 1984d. "The Concern for Truth" interview with François Ewald in PPC.

Foucault, Michel. 1984e. "Draft Preface to *The History of Sexuality, Volume Two*" in EW1.

Foucault, Michel. 1984f. "The Ethics of the Concern for Self as a Practice of Freedom" in EW1.

Foucault, Michel. 1984g. "Foucault, Michel, 1926–" published under the pseudonym Maurice Florence, reprinted in Gutting, 1994.

Foucault, Michel. 1984h (2011). *The Courage of Truth, Lectures at the Collège de France, 1983–1984.* Arnold Davidson, Frédéric Gros, François Ewald, and Alessandro Fontana (eds.), Graham Burchell (trans.). New York: Palgrave Macmillan.

Foucault, Michel. 1984i. "Interview with *Actes*" by Catherine Baker, June 1984 in EW3.

Foucault, Michel. 1984j. "What is Called 'Punishing'?" interview with F. Ringelheim in EW3.

All Other References

Aboulafia, Mitchell, ed. 2002a. *Habermas and Pragmatism*. New York: Routledge.

Aboulafia, Mitchell. 2002b "Introduction" to Aboulafia (2002a).

Adams, John Quincy. 1821. "Report to The Congress" as quoted in "A Brief History of Measurement Systems." Available online at http://standards.nasa.gov /history_metric.pdf.

Agamben, Giorgio. 1995 (1998). *Homo Sacer: Sovereign Power and Bare Life*. Daniel Heller Roazen (trans.). Stanford, Calif.: Stanford University.

Agamben, Giorgio. 2006. "What is an Apparatus?" in Agamben, *What is an Apparatus? and Other Essays*. David Kishik and Stefan Pedatella (trans.). Stanford, Calif.: Stanford University Press, 2009.

Alcoff, Linda Martín. 1990. "Feminist Politics and Foucault: The Limits to a Collaboration" in Arlene Dallery and Charles Scott (eds.), *Crises in Continental Philosophy*. Albany: SUNY Press.

Alcoff, Linda Martín. 2000. "Who's Afraid of Identity Politics?" in Paula Moya and Michael Hames-Garcia (eds.), *Reclaiming Identity: Realist Theory and the Predicament of Postmodernism*. Berkeley: Univ. of California.

Allen, Amy. 1999. *The Power of Feminist Theory: Domination, Resistance, Solidarity*. Boulder, Colo.: Westview.

Allen, Amy. 2003. "Foucault and Enlightenment: A Critical Reappraisal" in *Constellations* 10, no. 2: 180–98.

Allen, Amy. 2008. *The Politics of Our Selves: Power, Autonomy, and Gender in Contemporary Critical Theory*. New York: Columbia University Press.

Allen, Amy. 2009. "Discourse, Power, and Subjectivation: The Foucault/Habermas Debate Reconsidered" in *The Philosophical Forum* 40, no. 1, Spring: 1–28.

Allen, Amy. 2010. "The Entanglement of Power and Validity: Foucault and Critical Theory" in Timothy O'Leary and Christopher Falzon (eds.), *Foucault and Philosophy*, 78–98. Cambridge: Blackwell.

Allen, Amy. 2011a. "'Having One's Cake and Eating It Too': Habermas's Genealogy of Post-Secular Reason" in Craig Calhoun, Eduardo Mendieta, and Jonathan VanAntwerpen (eds.), *Habermas and Religion*. Cambridge: Polity Press.

Allen, Amy. 2011b. "Power, Autonomy and Gender: Reply to Critics" in *Current Perspectives in Social Theory* 29: 131–44.

Allen, Amy. 2011c. "Foucault and the Politics of Our Selves" in Koopman (ed.), "Foucault Across the Disciplines" special issue of *History of the Human Sciences* 24, no. 4, Oct.: 43–60.

Allen, Barry. 1993 (1995). *Truth in Philosophy.* Cambridge, Mass.: Harvard University Press.

Allen, Barry. 1998. "Foucault and Modern Political Philosophy" in Jeremy Moss (ed.), *The Later Foucault: Philosophy and Politics.* London: Sage.

Allen, Barry. 1999. "Power/Knowledge" in Karlis Racevskis (ed.), *Critical Essays on Michel Foucault.* New York: G. K. Hall.

Allen, Barry. 2003a. "Another New Nietzsche" in *History and Theory* 42, Oct.: 363–77.

Allen, Barry. 2003b. "The Abyss of Contingency: Purposiveness and Contingency in Darwin and Kant" in *History of Philosophy Quarterly* 20, no. 4, Oct.: 373–91.

Allen, Barry. 2004. *Knowledge and Civilization.* Boulder, Colo.: Westview Press.

Allen, Barry. 2008. *Artifice and Design: Art and Technology in Human Experience.* Ithaca, N.Y.: Cornell University Press.

Althusser, Louis. 1962 (2005). *For Marx.* Ben Brewster (trans.). New York: Verso.

Althusser, Louis. 1968 (1970). *Reading Capital.* Ben Brewster (trans.). London: NLB.

Amiot, Michel. 1967. "Le Relativisme culturaliste de Michel Foucault" in *Les Temps modernes,* no. 248, Jan.

Anscombe, G.E.M. 1958. "Modern Moral Philosophy" in *Philosophy* 33, no. 124, Jan: 1–19.

Apel, Karl-Otto. 1967 (1995). *Charles S. Peirce: From Pragmatism to Pragmaticism.* John Michael Krois (trans.). Atlantic Highlands, N.J.: Humanities Press.

Asad, Talal. 1993. *Genealogies of Religion: Discipline and Reasons of Power in Christianity and Islam.* Baltimore, Md.: Johns Hopkins University Press.

Ashenden, Samantha, and David Owen, eds. 1999. *Foucault contra Habermas: Recasting the Dialogue between Genealogy and Critical Theory.* London: Sage.

Auxier, Randall. 2002. "Foucault, Dewey, and the History of the Present" in *The Journal of Speculative Philosophy* 16, no. 2, Summer: 75–102.

Babich, Babette. 2009. "A Philosophical Shock: Foucault Reading Nietzsche, Reading Heidegger" in Prado (ed.), *Foucault's Legacy.* New York: Continuum.

Baker, Keith Michael. 1994. "A Foucauldian French Revolution" in Jan Goldstein (ed.), *Foucault and the Writing of History.* Oxford: Blackwell.

Bendix, Reinhard. 1966. *Max Weber: An Intellectual Portrait.* London: Methuen.

Benhabib, Seyla. 1986. *Critique, Norm, and Utopia: A Study of the Foundations of Critical Theory.* New York: Columbia University Press.

Benhabib, Seyla. 2006. *Another Cosmopolitanism: Hospitality, Sovereignty, and Democratic Iterations.* Oxford: Oxford University Press.

Benhabib, Seyla. Forthcoming. "Cosmopolitan Norms, Human Rights and Democratic Iterations" delivered as a Presidential Lecture at the Stanford University Center for the Humanities, October 27, 2008.

Ben-Menahem, Yemima. 2009. "Historical Necessity and Contingency" in Aviezer Tucker (ed.), *A Companion to the Philosophy of History and Historiography.* Malden: Blackwell.

Bernauer, James. 1990. *Michel Foucault's Force of Flight.* Atlantic Highlands, N.J.: Humanities Press.

Bernstein, Richard J. 1989. "Foucault: Critique as a Philosophical *Ethos*" in Bernstein, *The New Constellation.* Cambridge, Mass.: MIT Press, 1992.

Bernstein, Richard J. 1991. "An Allegory of Modernity/Postmodernity: Habermas and Derrida" in Bernstein, *The New Constellation.* Cambridge, Mass.: MIT Press, 1992.

Bernstein, Richard J. 2006. "The Pragmatic Century" in Sheila Greeve Davaney and Warren G. Frisina (eds.), *The Pragmatic Century.* Albany: SUNY.

Bernstein, Richard J. 2010. "Jürgen Habermas's Kantian Pragmatism" in Bernstein, *The Pragmatic Turn.* Cambridge: Polity.

Bevir, Mark. 1999. "Foucault and Critique: Deploying Agency against Autonomy" in *Political Theory* 27, no. 1, Feb.: 65–84.

Blondel, Eric. 1986 (1991). *Nietzsche: The Body and Culture.* Seán Hand (trans.). Stanford, Calif.: Stanford University Press.

Bookman, Myra. 2002. "Forming Competence: Habermas on Reconstructing Worlds and Context-Transcendent Reason" in Aboulafia, 2002a.

Boundas, Constantin. 1996. "Deleuze-Bergson: An Ontology of the Virtual" in Patton (ed.), *Deleuze: A Critical Reader.* Oxford: Blackwell.

Bourdieu, Pierre. 1980 (1990). *The Logic of Practice.* Richard Nice (trans.). Stanford, Calif.: Stanford University Press.

Bourdieu, Pierre. 1997 (2000). *Pascalian Meditations.* Richard Nice (trans.). Stanford, Calif.: Stanford University Press.

Bourne, Randolph. 1917. "Twilight of Idols" in Bourne, Olaf Hansen (ed.). *The Radical Will.* New York: Urizen Books, 1977.

Bové, Paul. 1988. "The Foucault Phenomenon: The Problematics of Style" as foreword to Gilles Deleuze, *Foucault.* Minneapolis: University of Minnesota Press.

Brandom, Robert. 2009. *Reason in Philosophy: Animating Ideas.* Cambridge, Mass.: Belknap.

Brandt, Reinhard. 1999. *Kommentar zu Kants Anthropologie.* Hamburg: Felix Meiner.

Braudel, Fernand. 1958. "History and the Social Sciences: The Long *Durée*" in Braudel, *On History*. Chicago: University of Chicago Press, 1980.

Brown, Wendy. 2001. *Politics Out of History*. Princeton, N.J.: Princeton University Press.

Burchell, Graham, Colin Gordon, and Peter Miller. 1991. *The Foucault Effect*. Chicago: University of Chicago Press.

Burchell, Graham. 1991. "Peculiar Interests: Civil Society and Governing 'The System of Natural Liberty'" in Burchell, Gordon, and Miller, 1991.

Butler, Judith, Ernesto Laclau, and Slavoj Žižek. 2000. *Contingency, Hegenomy, Universality: Contemporary Dialogues on the Left*. New York: Verso.

Butler, Judith. 1990. *Gender Trouble*. New York: Routledge.

Butler, Judith. 2000. "Changing the Subject: Judith Butler's Politics of Radical Resignification" interview with Gary A. Olson and Lynn Worsham in *JAC* 20, no. 4: 727–65.

Butler, Judith. 2002. "What is Critique? An Essay on Foucault's Virtue" in David Ingram (ed.), *The Political*. Oxford: Blackwell.

Canguilhem, Georges. 1943 (1991). *The Normal and the Pathological*. Carolyn R. Fawcett (trans.). New York: Zone Books.

Canguilhem, Georges. 1967. "The Death of Man, or Exhaustion of the Cogito?" Catherine Porter (trans.) in Gutting 1994 (translated from the French in *Critique*, 24, July 1967: 599–618).

Canguilhem, Georges. 1968. "The History of Science" in Canguilhem, *A Vital Rationalist*. Ed. François Delaporte. New York: Zone, 1994.

Canguilhem, Georges. 1977 (1988). *Ideology and Rationality in the History of the Life Sciences*. Arthur Goldhammer (trans.). Cambridge, Mass.: MIT Press.

Canguilhem, Georges. 1992 (1997). "On *Histoire de la folie* as an Event" in Arnold Davidson (ed.), *Foucault and His Interlocutors*. Chicago: University of Chicago Press.

Carlson, Thomas. 1997. "James and the Kantian Tradition" in Ruth Anna Putnam (ed.), *The Cambridge Companion to William James*. Cambridge: Cambridge University Press.

Carrette, J. R., ed. 1999. *Religion and Culture*. Manchester: Manchester University Press.

Castel, Robert. 1994. "'Problematization' as a Mode of Reading History" in Jan Goldstein (ed.), *Foucault and the Writing of History*. Cambridge: Blackwell.

Chauncey, George. 1995. *Gay New York*. New York: Basic Books.

Christensen, C. B. 1994. "Peirce's Transformation of Kant" in *Review of Metaphysics* 48: 91–120.

Clark, Maudemarie. 1990. *Nietzsche on Truth and Philosophy*. Cambridge: Cambridge University Press.

Clark, Maudemarie. 2001. "On the Rejection of Morality: Bernard Williams's Debt to Nietzsche" in Richard Schacht (ed.), *Nietzsche's Postmoralism*. Cambridge: Cambridge University Press.

Clifford, Michael. 2001. *Political Genealogy After Foucault: Savage Identities*. New York: Routledge.

Cohen, Morris, and Ernest Nagel. 1934. *An Introduction to Logic and Scientific Method*. New York: Harcourt, 1934.

Colapietro, Vincent. 1998a. "American Evasions of Foucault" in *Southern Journal of Philosophy* 36, no. 3, Fall: 329–51.

Colapietro, Vincent. 1998b. "Entangling Alliances and Critical Traditions: Reclaiming the Possibilities of Critique" in *The Journal of Speculative Philosophy* 12, no. 2, Summer: 114–33.

Colapietro, Vincent. 2011. "Situation, Meaning, and Improvisation: An Aesthetics of Existence in Dewey and Foucault" in Koopman (ed.), "Foucault and Pragmatism," special issue of *Foucault Studies*, no. 11, Feb.: 20–40.

Collier, Stephen J. 2009. "Topologies of Power: Foucault's Analysis of Political Government beyond 'Governmentality'," in *Theory, Culture, and Society* 26, no. 6, 78–108.

Collingwood, R. G. 1939. *An Autobiography*. Oxford: Oxford University Press, 1939.

Collingwood, R. G. 1946 (1994). *The Idea of History*. Oxford: Oxford University Press.

Colwell, C. 1997. "Deleuze and Foucault: Series, Event, Genealogy" in *Theory & Event* 1, no. 2.

Cooke, Maeve. 2006. *Re-Presenting the Good Society*. Cambridge, Mass.: MIT Press.

Craig, Edward. 1991. *Knowledge and the State of Nature: An Essay in Conceptual Synthesis*. Oxford: Oxford University Press.

Craig, Edward. 2007. "Genealogies and the State of Nature" in Alan Thomas (ed.), *Bernard Williams*. Cambridge: Cambridge University Press.

Crease, Robert P. 2011. *World in the Balance: The Historic Quest for an Absolute System of Measurement*. New York: W. W. Norton.

Crombie, Alistair C. 1994. *Styles of Scientific Thinking in the European Tradition*. 3 vols. London: Duckworth.

Crouch, Margaret. 1993. "A 'Limited' Defense of the Genetic Fallacy," in *Metaphilosophy* 24, no. 3, July: 227–40.

Cusset, François. 2003 (2008). *French Theory: How Foucault, Derrida, Deleuze, & Co. Transformed the Intellectual Life of the United States*. Jeff Fort (trans.). Minneapolis: University of Minnesota Press.

Cutrofello, Andrew. 1994. *Discipline and Critique: Kant, Poststructuralism, and the Problem of Resistance*. Albany: SUNY Press.

Daix, Pierre. 1967. "Sartre est-il dépassé?" in *Les Lettres françaises*, no. 1168–69, Feb.: 1–10.

Danto, Arthur C. 1994. "Morality and Moral Psychology: Some Remarks on *The Genealogy of Morals*," in Richard Schacht (ed.), *Nietzsche, Genealogy, Morality*. Berkeley: University of California Press.

Darwin, Charles. 1871. *The Descent of Man, and Selection in Relation to Sex*. New York: D. Appleton.

Daston, Lorraine, and Peter Galison. 2007. *Objectivity*. New York: Zone.

Davidson, Arnold. 1986. "Archaeology, Genealogy, Ethics," in Hoy, 1986a.

Davidson, Arnold. 1994a. "Foucault and the Analysis of Concepts," in Davidson, 2001a.

Davidson, Arnold. 1994b. "Ethics as Ascetics: Foucault, the History of Ethics, and Ancient Thought," in Gutting, 1994.

Davidson, Arnold. 1996. "Structures and Strategies of Discourse: Remarks Towards a History of Foucault's Philosophy of Language," in Davidson (ed.), *Foucault and His Interlocutors*. Chicago: University of Chicago Press.

Davidson, Arnold. 2001a. *The Emergence of Sexuality: Historical Epistemology and the Formation of Concepts*. Cambridge, Mass.: Harvard University Press.

Davidson, Arnold. 2001c. "On Epistemology and Archeology: From Canguilhem to Foucault," in Davidson, 2001a.

Davidson, Arnold. 2011. "In Praise of Counter-Conduct," in Koopman (ed.), "Foucault Across the Disciplines" special issue of *History of the Human Sciences* 24, no. 4: 25–41.

De Certeau, Michel. 1975 (1988). *The Writing of History*. Tom Conley (trans.). New York: Columbia University Press.

De Certeau, Michel. 1980 (2002). *The Practice of Everyday Life*. Steven Rendall (trans.). Berkeley: University of California Press.

Deacon, Roger. 2000. "Theory as Practice: Foucault's Concept of Problematization" in *Telos* 118: 127–42.

Dean, Mitchell. 1994. *Critical and Effective Histories: Foucault's Methods and Historical Sociology*. New York: Routledge.

Dean, Mitchell. 1999a. *Governmentality: Foucault, Power, and Social Structure*. London: Sage.

Dean, Mitchell. 1999b. "Normalising Democracy: Foucault and Habermas on Democracy, Liberalism, and Law," in Ashenden and Owen, 1999.

DeLanda, Manuel. 2002. *Intensive Science and Virtual Philosophy*. New York: Continuum.

DeLanda, Manuel. 2006. *A New Philosophy of Society: Assemblage Theory and Social Complexity*. New York: Continuum.

Deleuze, Gilles, and Felix Guattari. 1991 (1994). *What is Philosophy?* Hugh Tomlinson and Graham Burchell (trans.). New York: Columbia University Press.

Deleuze, Gilles, 1962 (2006). *Nietzsche and Philosophy.* Hugh Tomlinson (trans.). New York: Columbia University Press.

Deleuze, Gilles. 1963 (1983). *Kant's Critical Philosophy.* Hugh Tomlinson and Barbara Habberjam (trans.). London: Althone Press.

Deleuze, Gilles. 1966 (1991). *Bergsonism.* Hugh Tomlinson and Barbara Habberjam (trans.). New York: Zone Books.

Deleuze, Gilles. 1968 (1994). *Difference and Repetition.* Paul Patton (trans). New York: Columbia University Press.

Deleuze, Gilles. 1969 (1990). *The Logic of Sense.* Mark Lester and Charles Stivale (trans.). New York: Columbia University Press.

Deleuze, Gilles. 1985. "Foucault and The Prison" interview by Paul Rabinow and Keith Gandal in Barry Smart (ed.), *Critical Assessments of Michel Foucault, Volume 3.* London: Routledge, 1994.

Deleuze, Gilles. 1986a (1988). *Foucault.* Seán Hand (trans.). Minneapolis: University of Minnesota Press.

Deleuze, Gilles. 1986b (1995). "A Portrait of Foucault" conversation with Claire Parnet in Deleuze, *Negotiations,* Martin Joughin (trans.). New York: Columbia University Press.

Deleuze, Gilles. 1990. "Control and Becoming" in Deleuze, *Negotiations.* New York: Columbia University Press, 1995.

Deleuze, Gilles. 1995 (2001). "Immanence: A Life," in Deleuze, *Pure Immanence: Essays on A Life.* Anne Boyman (trans.). New York: Zone Books.

Derrida, Jacques. 1963 (1978). "Cogito and the History of Madness" in Derrida, *Writing and Difference.* Alan Bass (trans.). Chicago: University of Chicago Press.

Derrida, Jacques. 1988 (1993). *Aporias.* Thomas Dutoit (trans.). Stanford, Calif.: Stanford University Press.

Derrida, Jacques. 1991 (1992). *The Other Heading.* Pascale-Anne Brault and Michael B. Nass (trans.). Bloomington: Indiana University Press.

Derrida, Jacques. 2003 (2005). "The 'World' of the Enlightenment to Come (Exception, Calculation, Sovereignty)" in Derrida, *Rogues: Two Essays on Reason.* Pascale-Anne Brault and Michael Naas (trans.). Stanford, Calif.: Stanford University Press.

Descbomes, Vincent. 1991 (1997). "Nietzsche's French Moment," in Luc Ferry and Alain Renaut (eds.), *Why We Are Not Nietzscheans,* Robert De Loaiza (trans.). Chicago: University of Chicago Press.

Dewey, John. 1906. "Experience and Objective Idealism" in Dewey, *The Influ-*

ence of Darwin On Philosophy. Bloomington: Indiana University Press, 1965. Reprinted in Dewey, MW3.

Dewey, John. 1916a. *Essays in Experimental Logic.* New York: Dover Press, 1958. Reprinted in Dewey MW10.

Dewey, John. 1916b. *Democracy and Education.* New York: Free Press, 1966. Reprinted in Dewey MW9.

Dewey, John. 1920. *Reconstruction in Philosophy,* enlarged edition. Boston: Beacon, 1948. Reprinted in Dewey MW12.

Dewey, John. 1929. *The Quest for Certainty,* in Dewey LW4.

Dewey, John. 1938a. *Logic: The Theory of Inquiry,* in Dewey LW12.

Dewey, John. 1938b. "Unity of Science as a Social Problem," in Dewey LW13.

Dewey, John. EW, MW, & LW. *The Complete Works of John Dewey* including *The Early Works* (EW1–5), *The Middle Works* (MW1–15), *and The Later Works* (LW1–17). Jo Ann Boydston et al. (eds.). Southern Illinois University, 1969–90. [*Dewey references are cited as follows: page numbers given for the earlier editions of the work before the slash and page numbers for the complete works edition after the slash; if only one page is cited, it is from the complete works.*]

Dews, Peter. 1987. *Logics of Disintegration: Post-Structuralist Thought and the Claims of Critical Theory.* London: Verso.

Dews, Peter. 1989. "The Return of the Subject in Late Foucault," in *Radical Philosophy,* 51, Spring: 37–41.

Diggins, John Patrick. 1994. *The Promise of Pragmatism.* Chicago: University of Chicago Press.

Djaballah, Marc. 2008. *Kant, Foucault, and Forms of Experience.* New York: Routledge.

Donzelot, Jacques. 1977 (1997). *The Policing of Families.* Robert Hurley (trans.). Baltimore, Md.: Johns Hopkins University Press.

Dosse, François. 1987 (1994). *New History in France.* Peter V. Conroy, Jr. (trans.). Chicago: University of Illinois Press.

Dosse, François. 1992 (1997). *History of Structuralism, Volume 2: The Sign Sets, 1967–present,* Deborah Glassman (trans.). Minneapolis: University of Minnesota Press.

Eribon, Didier. 1989. *Michel Foucault.* Betsy Wing (trans.). Cambridge, Mass.: Harvard University Press, 1991.

Ewald, François. 1990. "Norms, Discipline, and Law," Marjorie Beale (trans.), in *Representations* 30, Spring: 138–61.

Faubion, James D. 2001. "Toward an Anthropology of Ethics: Foucault and the Pedagogies of Autopoiesis" in *Representations* 74, Spring: 83–104.

Faubion, James D. 2011. *An Anthropology of Ethics*. Cambridge: Cambridge University Press.

Feder, Ellen. 2007. *Family Bonds: Genealogies of Race and Gender*. Oxford: Oxford University Press.

Flynn, Thomas. 2005. *Sartre, Foucault, and Historical Reason, Volume Two: A Poststructuralist Mapping of History*. Chicago: University of Chicago Press.

Foot, Philippa. 1958. "Moral Beliefs," in *Proceedings of the Aristotelian Society* 59: 83–104.

Foot, Philippa. 1994. "Nietzsche's Immoralism," in Richard Schacht (ed.), *Nietzsche, Genealogy, Morality*. Berkeley: University of California Press.

Forst, Rainer. 1994 (2002). *Contexts of Justice: Political Philosophy Beyond Liberalism and Communitarianism*. John M. M. Farrell (trans.). Berkeley: University of California Press.

Fraser, Nancy, and Linda Gordon. 1994 (1997). "A Genealogy of 'Dependency': Tracing a Keyword of the U.S. Welfare State," in Fraser, *Justice Interruptus: Critical Reflections on the 'Postsocialist' Condition*. New York: Routledge.

Fraser, Nancy. 1981 (1989). "Foucault on Modern Power: Empirical Insights and Normative Confusions" in Fraser, *Unruly Practices: Power, Discourse and Gender in Contemporary Social Theory*. Minneapolis: University of Minnesota Press.

Fraser, Nancy. 1983 (1989). "Foucault's Body Language: A Posthumanist Political Rhetoric?" in Fraser, *Unruly Practices*. Minneapolis: University of Minnesota Press.

Fraser, Nancy. 1985 (1989). "Michel Foucault: A Young Conservative?" in Fraser, *Unruly Practices: Power, Discourse and Gender in Contemporary Social Theory*. Minneapolis: University of Minnesota Press.

Fraser, Nancy. 1995. "Pragmatism, Feminism, and the Linguistic Turn," in Linda Nicholson et al., *Feminist Contentions: A Philosophical Exchange*. New York: Routledge.

Fraser, Nancy. 2009. "From Discipline to Flexibilization? Rereading Foucault in the Shadow of Globalization," in Fraser, *Scales of Justice: Reimagining Political Space in a Globalizing World*. New York: Columbia University Press.

Fujitani, Takashi. 1996. *Splendid Monarchy*. Berkeley: University of California Press.

Gauchet, Marcel, and Gladys Swain. 1980 (1999). *Madness and Democracy: The Modern Psychiatric Universe*. Catherine Porter (trans.). Princeton, N.J.: Princeton University Press.

Geuss, Raymond. 1981. *The Idea of a Critical Theory*. Cambridge: Cambridge University Press.

Geuss, Raymond. 2002. "Genealogy as Critique," in *European Journal of Philosophy* 10, no. 2: 209–15.

Giddens, Anthony. 1982. "Reason without Revolution? Habermas's *Theorie des Kommunikativen Handelns*," in *Praxis International* 3: 318–38.

Gilson, Erinn. Unpublished. "Elaborating an Ethic of Problem and Response through Foucault and Deleuze," presented at *The Foucault Circle Annual Meeting*, Earlham College, Feb. 2008. Ms. on file with the author.

Goldstein, Jan, ed. 1994. *Foucault and the Writing of History*. London: Blackwell.

Gordon, Colin. 1987. "The Soul of the Citizen: Max Weber and Michel Foucault on Rationality and Government," in S. Whimster and S. Lash (eds.), *Max Weber, Rationality and Modernity*. London: Allen and Unwin.

Gordon, Colin. 1991. "Governmental Rationality: An Introduction," in Burchell, Gordon, and Miller, 1991.

Greenblatt, Stephen. 1980. *Renaissance Self-Fashioning*. Chicago: University of Chicago Press.

Gros, Frédéric. 2005. "Le souci de soi chez Michel Foucault," in *Philosophy & Social Criticism* 31, nos. 5–6: 697–708.

Gros, Frédéric. 2008. "Course Context," in Foucault, *The Government of Self and Others*. Ed. François Ewald, Alessandro Fontana, and Frédéric Gros. New York: Palgrave Macmillan, 2010.

Gutting, Gary. 1989. *Michel Foucault's Archaeology of Scientific Reason*. Cambridge: Cambridge University Press.

Gutting, Gary. 2003. "Review of Béatrice Han's *Foucault's Critical Project*," in *Notre Dame Philosophical Reviews*, May 2003, available online at http://ndpr.nd.edu /review.cfm?id=1262.

Gutting, Gary, ed. 1994. *The Cambridge Companion to Foucault*, first edition. Cambridge: Cambridge University Press.

Gutting, Gary, ed. 2005. *The Cambridge Companion to Foucault*, second edition. Cambridge: Cambridge University Press.

Habermas, Jürgen. 1968 (1971). *Knowledge and Human Interests*. Jeremy J. Shapiro (trans.). Boston: Beacon Press.

Habermas, Jürgen. 1976a. "What is Universal Pragmatics?" in Habermas, 1979.

Habermas, Jürgen. 1976b. *Zur Rekonstruktion des Historischen Materialismus*, in Habermas, 1979.

Habermas, Jürgen. 1979. *Communication and the Evolution of Society*. Thomas McCarthy (trans.). Boston: Beacon Press.

Habermas, Jürgen. 1981a (1985). *The Theory of Communicative Action*, two volumes. Thomas McCarthy (trans.). Boston: Beacon.

Habermas, Jürgen. 1981b. "Modernity versus Postmodernity," Seyla Benhabib (trans.), in *New German Critique* 22, Winter.

Habermas, Jürgen. 1983. "Discourse Ethics: Notes on a Program of Philosophical Justification" in Habermas, *Moral Consciousness and Communicative Action*. Christian Lenhardt (trans.). Cambridge, Mass.: MIT Press, 1990.

Habermas, Jürgen. 1985. *The Philosophical Discourse of Modernity*. Frederick Lawrence (trans.). Cambridge, Mass.: MIT Press, 1987.

Habermas, Jürgen. 1988 (1993). *Postmetaphysical Thinking*. William Mark Hohengarten (trans.). Cambridge, Mass.: MIT Press.

Habermas, Jürgen. 1992 (1996). *Between Facts and Norms*. William Rehg (trans.). Cambridge, Mass.: MIT Press.

Habermas, Jürgen. 1996 (1998). "A Genealogical Analysis of the Cognitive Content of Morality," in Habermas, *The Inclusion of the Other: Studies in Political Theory*. Ciaran Cronin (trans.). Cambridge, Mass.: MIT Press.

Habermas, Jürgen. 1998. "John Dewey, *The Quest for Certainty*," in Habermas, 2001a.

Habermas, Jürgen. 1999a (2003). *Truth and Justification*. Barbara Fultner (trans.). Cambridge: MIT Press.

Habermas, Jürgen. 1999b. "Richard Rorty, *Achieving Our Country*," in Habermas, 2001a.

Habermas, Jürgen. 2000. "Robert Brandom, *Making it Explicit*," in Habermas, 2001a.

Habermas, Jürgen. 2001a. *Time of Transitions*. Cambridge: Polity Press, 2006.

Habermas, Jürgen. 2001b. "From Kant's 'Ideas' of Pure Reason to the 'Idealizing' Presuppositions of Communicative Action: Reflections on the Detranscendentalized 'Use of Reason'," in Thomas McCarthy, William Rehg, and James Bohman (eds.), *Pluralism and the Pragmatic Turn: The Transformation of Critical Theory*. Cambridge, Mass.: MIT.

Habermas, Jürgen. 2002. "Postscript: Some Concluding Remarks," in Aboulafia, 2002a.

Habermas, Jürgen. 2008. " '. . . And to define America, her athletic democracy.' The Philosopher and the Language Shaper: In Memory of Richard Rorty," in *New Literary History* 39, no. 1, Winter: 3–12.

Hacking, Ian. 1975 (2006). *The Emergence of Probability*, second edition. Cambridge: Cambridge University Press.

Hacking, Ian. 1980. "Language, Truth, and Reason," in Hacking, 2002a.

Hacking, Ian. 1981. "The Archaeology of Michel Foucault," in Hacking, 2002a.

Hacking, Ian. 1983. "Making Up People," in Hacking, 2002a.

Hacking, Ian. 1984. "Self-Improvement," in Hoy, 1986a.

Hacking, Ian. 1988. "Two Kinds of New Historicism," in Hacking, 2002a.

Hacking, Ian. 1990 (2006). *The Taming of Chance.* Cambridge: Cambridge University Press.

Hacking, Ian. 1991a. "The Self-Vindication of the Laboratory Sciences," in A. Pickering (ed.), *Science as Practice and Culture,* 29–64. Chicago: University of Chicago Press.

Hacking, Ian. 1991b. "'Style' for Historians and Philosophers," in Hacking, 2002a.

Hacking, Ian. 1995. *Rewriting the Soul.* Princeton, N.J.: Princeton University Press.

Hacking, Ian. 1998a. *Mad Travelers.* Cambridge, Mass.: Harvard University Press.

Hacking, Ian. 1998b. "What mathematics has done to some and only some philosophers," in T. J. Smiley (ed.), *Mathematics and Necessity.* London: British Academy, 2000.

Hacking, Ian. 1999a. *The Social Construction of What?* Cambridge, Mass.: Harvard University Press.

Hacking, Ian. 1999b. "Historical Meta-Epistemology," in W. Carl and L. Daston (eds.), *Wahrheit und Geschichte.* Gottingen: Valdenhoeck and Ruprecht.

Hacking, Ian. 2002a. *Historical Ontology.* Cambridge, Mass.: Harvard University Press.

Hacking, Ian. 2002b. "Historical Ontology," in Hacking, 2002a.

Hacking, Ian. 2004. "Critical Notice of *Truth and Truthfulness,*" in *Canadian Journal of Philosophy* 34, no. 1, Mar.: 137–48.

Hacking, Ian. 2007a. "Kinds of People: Moving Targets," in *Proceedings of the British Academy* 151: 285–318.

Hacking, Ian. 2007b. "Natural Kinds: Rosy Dawn, Scholastic Twilight" in Anthony O'Hear (ed.), *Philosophy of Science, Royal Institute of Philosophy Supplements* 61: 203–39.

Hacking, Ian. 2009. *Scientific Reason.* Der-Lan yeh and Jeu-Jenq Yuann (eds.). Taipei: National Taiwan University Press.

Hacking, Ian. 2011. "Déraison," in Koopman (ed.), "Foucault Across the Disciplines," special issue of *History of the Human Sciences* 24, no. 4: 13–23.

Hadot, Pierre. 1989. "Reflections on the Notion of 'The Cultivation of the Self'," in Armstrong (ed.), *Michel Foucault: Philosopher.* Hempstead: Harvester Wheatsheaf, 1992.

Hallward, Peter. 2006. *Out of This World: Deleuze and the Philosophy of Creation.* New York: Verso.

Han[-Pile], Béatrice. 1998 (2002). *Foucault's Critical Project.* Edward Pile (trans.). Stanford, Calif.: Stanford University Press.

Han-Pile, Béatrice. 2005. "Is Early Foucault a Historian? History, history, and the Analytic of Finitude," in *Philosophy & Social Criticism* 31, nos. 5–6: 585–608.

Han-Pile, Béatrice. Undated. "Reply to Gary Gutting's Review of *Foucault's Critical Project*," available online at http://privatewww.essex.ac.uk/~beatrice/

Heidegger, Martin. 1927 (1996). *Being and Time*. Joan Stambaugh (trans.). Albany: SUNY Press.

Hengehold, Laura. 2007. *The Body Problematic: Political Imagination in Kant and Foucault*. University Park: Pennsylvania State University Press.

Hennis, Wilhelm. 1987 (1988). *Max Weber: Essays in Reconstruction*. Keith Tribe (trans.). London: Allen & Unwin.

Heyes, Cressida. 2007. *Self-Transformations: Foucault, Ethics, and Normalized Bodies*. Oxford: Oxford University Press.

Hickman, Larry. 1990 (1992). *John Dewey's Pragmatic Technology*. Bloomington: Indiana University Press.

Hickman, Larry. 2001. *Philosophical Tools for Technological Culture*. Bloomington: Indiana University Press.

Hill, R. Kevin. 2003. *Nietzsche's Critiques: The Kantian Foundations of his Thought*. Oxford: Oxford University Press.

Ho, Karen. 2009. *Liquidated: An Ethnography of Wall Street*. Durham, N.C.: Duke University Press.

Hobbes, Thomas. 1651 (1991). *Leviathan*. Ed. Richard Tuck. Cambridge: Cambridge University Press.

Hofmeyr, Benda. 2006. "The Power Not to Be (What We Are): The Politics and Ethics of Self-Creation in Foucault," in *Journal of Moral Philosophy* 3, no. 2, July: 215–30.

Honneth, Axel. 1985 (1991). *Critique of Power: Reflective Stages in a Critical Social Theory*. Kenneth Baynes (trans.). Cambridge, Mass.: MIT Press.

Honneth, Axel. 1995. "The Other of Justice: Habermas and the Ethical Challenge of Postmodernism," in Stephen K. White (ed.), *The Cambridge Companion to Habermas*. Cambridge: Cambridge University Press.

Horkheimer, Max. 1947 (1974). *The Eclipse of Reason*. New York: Seabury Press.

Hoy, David Couzens, and Thomas McCarthy. 1994. *Critical Theory*. Cambridge: Blackwell.

Hoy, David Couzens. 1986a (1991). *Foucault: A Critical Reader*. Malden: Blackwell.

Hoy, David Couzens. 1986b. "Nietzsche, Hume, and the Genealogical Method," in Y. Yovel (ed.), *Nietzsche as Affirmative Thinker*. Dordrecht: Martinus Nijhoff.

Hoy, David Couzens. 1989. "Splitting the Difference: Habermas's Critique of Derrida," in G. B. Madison (ed.), *Working Through Derrida*. Evanston, Ill.: Northwestern University Press.

Hoy, David Couzens. 2004. *Critical Resistance: From Poststructuralism to Post-Critique*. Cambridge, Mass.: MIT Press.

Hoy, David Couzens. 2009a. *The Time of Our Lives: A Critical History of the Phenomenology of Temporality.* Cambridge, Mass.: MIT Press.

Hoy, David Couzens. 2009b. "The Temporality of Power," in Carlos Prado (ed.), *Foucault's Legacy.* New York: Continuum.

Huffer, Lynn. 2010. *Mad for Foucault: Rethinking the Foundations of Queer Theory.* New York: Columbia University Press.

Hume, David. 1757 (1993). *The Natural History of Religion.* Ed. J. A. C. Gaskin. Oxford: Oxford University Press.

Hunt, Alan. 1999. *Governing Morals: A Social History of Moral Revolution.* Cambridge: Cambridge University.

Hutchings, Kimberly. 1996. *Kant, Critique, and Politics.* New York: Routledge.

Jacobs, Brian, and Patrick Kain. 2003. "Introduction" to Essays on Kant's Anthropology. Cambridge: Cambridge University Press.

James, William. 1907 (1975). *Pragmatism: A New Name for Some Old Ways of Thinking* in James, *Pragmatism and The Meaning of Truth.* Ed. Frederick Burkhardt. Cambridge, Mass.: Harvard University Press.

Jay, Martin. 1973. *The Dialectical Imagination.* Little, Brown.

Johnston, James Scott. 2006. "Dewey's Critique of Kant," in *Transactions of the Charles S. Peirce Society* 42, no. 4, Fall: 518–51.

Joyce, Patrick. 2003. *The Rule of Freedom: Liberalism and the Modern City.* New York: Verso.

Kaag, John. 2005. "Continuity and Inheritance: Kant's *Critique of Judgment* and the Work of C. S. Peirce," in *Transactions of the Charles S. Peirce Society* 41, no. 3, Summer: 515–40.

Kant, Immanuel. 1781 (1965). *Critique of Pure Reason.* Norman Kemp Smith (trans.). New York: Macmillan.

Kant, Immanuel. 1785 (1985). *Groundwork for the Metaphysics of Morals.* James W. Ellington (trans.). Indianapolis: Hackett.

Kant, Immanuel. 1790 (1951). *Critique of Judgment.* J. H. Bernard (trans.). New York: Hafner. [References are to Section.Page.]

Kant, Immanuel. 1798a (1970). *The Contest of Faculties,* in Kant, *Kant's Political Writings.* Ed. H. S. Reiss, H. B. Nisbet (trans.). Cambridge: Cambridge University.

Kant, Immanuel. 1798b (2006). *Anthropology from a Pragmatic Point of View.* Robert Louden (trans.). Cambridge: Cambridge University.

Kelly, Mark G. E. 2009. *The Political Philosophy of Michel Foucault.* New York: Routledge.

Kelly, Michael, ed. 1994a. *Critique and Power: Recasting the Foucault/Habermas Debate.* Cambridge, Mass.: MIT Press.

Kelly, Michael. 1994b. "Foucault, Habermas, and the Self-Referentiality of Critique," in Kelly, 1994a.

Klement, Kevin C. 2002. "When Is Genetic Reasoning Not Fallacious?" in *Argumentation* 16, no. 4, Dec.: 383–400.

Kofman, Sarah. 1972 (1993). *Nietzsche and Metaphor.* Duncan Large (trans.). Stanford, Calif.: Stanford University Press.

Koopman, Colin, and Tomas Matza. 2013/forthcoming. "Putting Foucault to Work: Analytic and Concept in Foucaultian Inquiry." Forthcoming in *Critical Inquiry.*

Koopman, Colin. 2006. "Pragmatism as a Philosophy of Hope: Emerson, James, Dewey, and Rorty," in *The Journal of Speculative Philosophy* 20, no. 2, Summer: 106–16.

Koopman, Colin. 2008. "Foucault's Historiographical Expansion: Adding Genealogy to Archaeology," in *Journal of the Philosophy of History* 2, no. 3, Fall: 338–62.

Koopman, Colin. 2009a. *Pragmatism as Transition: Historicity and Hope in James, Dewey, and Rorty.* New York: Columbia University Press.

Koopman, Colin. 2009b. "Two Uses of Genealogy: Michel Foucault and Bernard Williams," in Carlos Prado (ed.), *Foucault's Legacy,* 90–108. New York: Continuum Books.

Koopman, Colin. 2010a. "Bernard Williams on Philosophy's Need for History" in *The Review of Metaphysics* 64, no. 1, Sept.: 3–30.

Koopman, Colin. 2010b. "Historical Critique or Transcendental Critique in Foucault: Two Kantian Lineages" in *Foucault Studies,* no. 8, February: 100–21.

Koopman, Colin. 2010c. "Historical Conditions or Transcendental Conditions: Response to Kevin Thompson's Response," in *Foucault Studies,* no. 8, February: 129–35.

Koopman, Colin. 2010d. "Appropriation and Permission in the History of Philosophy: Response to McQuillan" in *Foucault Studies,* no. 9, September: 156–64.

Koopman, Colin. 2010e. "The History and Critique of Modernity: Dewey, Foucault, and Weber," in Paul Fairfield (ed.), *Dewey and Continental Philosophy,* 194–218. Carbondale: Southern Illinois University Press.

Koopman, Colin. 2011a. "The Direction of Contemporary Critical Theory: A Response to Amy Allen's *The Politics of Our Selves,*" in *Current Perspectives in Social Theory* 29: 91–104.

Koopman, Colin. 2011b. "Foucault and Pragmatism: Introductory Notes on Metaphilosophical Methodology," in *Foucault Studies,* no. 11, March: 3–10.

Koopman, Colin. 2011c. "Pragmatist Interpretations of Obama: On Two Ways of Being a Pragmatist," in *Contemporary Pragmatism* 8, no. 2, Dec.: 99–112.

Koopman, Colin. 2013a/forthcoming. "Problematization," in Leonard Lawlor and John Nale (eds.), *The Foucault Lexicon*. Cambridge: Cambridge University Press.

Koopman, Colin. 2013b/forthcoming. "The Formation and Self-Transformation of the Subject in Foucault's Ethics," in Chris Falzon, Timothy O'Leary, and Jana Sawicki (eds.), *A Companion to Foucault*. Malden: Wiley-Blackwell, 2013.

Koopman, Colin. 2013c/forthcoming. "Two Uses of Foucault in Hacking and Agamben." Forthcoming in *Constellations*.

Koselleck, Reinhart. 1959 (1988). *Critique and Crisis: Enlightenment and the Pathogenesis of Modern Society*. Cambridge, Mass.: MIT Press.

Kripke, Saul. 1972 (1980). *Naming and Necessity*. Cambridge, Mass.: Harvard University Press.

Kritzman, Lawrence. 2006. "The Intellectual" in Kritzman, *The Columbia History of Twentieth-Century French Thought*. New York: Columbia University Press.

Kuhn, Thomas. 1962. *The Structure of Scientific Revolutions*. Chicago: University of Chicago Press.

Kuklick, Bruce. 1977. *The Rise of American Philosophy*. New Haven, Conn.: Yale University Press.

Kusch, Martin. 1991. *Foucault's Strata and Fields*. Boston: Kluwer Academic.

Kusch, Martin. 2010. "Hacking's Historical Epistemology: A Critique of Styles of Reasoning," in *Studies in History and Philosophy of Science Part A* 41, no. 2: 158–73.

LaCapra, Dominick. 2000. *History and Reading: Tocqueville, Foucault, French Studies*. Toronto: University of Toronto Press.

Lampert, Jay. 2006. *Deleuze and Guattari's Philosophy of History*. New York: Continuum.

Lavine, Thelma Z. 1962. "Reflections on the Genetic Fallacy," in *Social Research* 29, Autumn: 321–36.

Le Bon, Sylvie. 1967. "Un Positivist désespéré: Michel Foucault," in *Les Temps modernes*, no. 248, Jan.

Lemke, Thomas. 1998. *Aspects of Enlightenment: Social Theory and the Ethics of Truth*. Lanham, Md.: Rowman and Littlefield.

Lemke, Thomas. 2001. "'The birth of bio-politics': Michel Foucault's lecture at the Collège de France on neo-liberal governmentality," in *Economy and Society* 30, no. 2, May: 190–207.

Lemke, Thomas. 2002. "Foucault, Governmentality, and Critique," in *Rethinking Marxism* 14, no. 3, Sept.: 49–64.

Lentricchia, Frank. 1988. *Ariel and the Police: Michel Foucault, William James, Wallace Stevens*. Madison: University of Wisconsin Press.

Livingston, James. 2001. *Pragmatism, Feminism, and Democracy: Rethinking the Politics of American History.* New York: Routledge.

Loeb, Paul. 1995. "Is There a Genetic Fallacy in Nietzsche's Genealogy of Morals?" in *International Studies in Philosophy* 27, no. 3: 125–41.

Löwith, Karl, 1932 (1982). *Max Weber and Karl Marx.* H. Fantel (trans.). London: Allen & Unwin.

Macey, David. 1993 (1995). *The Lives of Michel Foucault: A Biography.* New York: Vintage Books.

MacIntyre, Alasdair. 1981. *After Virtue: A Study in Moral Theory.* Notre Dame, Ind.: Notre Dame University Press.

MacIntyre, Alasdair. 1990. *Three Rival Versions of Moral Enquiry: Encyclopedia, Genealogy, and Tradition.* Notre Dame: Notre Dame University Press.

Mader, Mary Beth. 2007. "Foucault and Social Measure," in *Journal of French Philosophy* 17, no. 1, Spring: 1–25.

Mahmood, Saba. 2005. *Politics of Piety: The Islamic Revival and the Feminist Subject.* Princeton, N.J.: Princeton University Press.

Małecki, Wojciech. 2011. "'If happiness is not the aim of politics, then what is?': Rorty versus Foucault," in Colin Koopman (ed.), "Foucault and Pragmatism," special issue of *Foucault Studies*, no. 11, Feb.: 106–25.

Marcus, George, and Michael Fischer. 1986. *Anthropology as Cultural Critique,* second edition. Chicago: University of Chicago Press.

Marcus, George. 1999. "Critical Anthropology Now: An Introduction" in Marcus (ed.), *Critical Anthropology Now.* Santa Fe, N.M.: School of American Research.

Margolis, Joseph. 2002. "Vicissitudes of Transcendental Reason," in Aboulafia, 2002a.

Margolis, Joseph. 2010. *Pragmatism's Advantage.* Stanford, Calif.: Stanford University Press.

Martin, Jay. 2003. *The Education of John Dewey: A Biography.* New York: Columbia University Press.

May, Todd. 1993. *Between Genealogy and Epistemology.* University Park: Pennsylvania State University Press.

May, Todd. 2006. *The Philosophy of Foucault.* Chesham: Acumen.

May, Todd. 2007. "Equality as a Foucaultian Value: The Relevance of Rancière," in *Philosophy Today* 51, Supplement: 133–39.

McCarthy, Thomas. 1978 (1981). *The Critical Theory of Jürgen Habermas.* Cambridge, Mass.: MIT Press.

McCarthy, Thomas. 1990 (1991). "The Critique of Impure Reason: Foucault and the Frankfurt School," in McCarthy, *Ideals and Illusions*. Cambridge, Mass.: MIT Press.

McCarthy, Thomas. 2004. "Political Philosophy and Racial Injustice: From Normative to Critical Theory," in Seyla Benhabib and Nancy Fraser (eds.), *Pragmatism, Critique, Judgment: Essays for Richard J. Bernstein*, 147–68. Cambridge, Mass.: MIT Press.

McGushin, Edward F. 2007. *Foucault's Askesis: An Introduction to the Philosophical Life*. Evanston, Ill.: Northwestern University Press.

McQuillan, Colin. 2010. "Transcendental Philosophy and Critical Philosophy in Kant and Foucault: Response to Colin Koopman," in *Foucault Studies*, no. 9, Sept.: 145–55.

McWhorter, Ladelle. 1999. *Bodies and Pleasures: Foucault and the Politics of Sexual Normalization*. Bloomington: Indiana University Press.

McWhorter, Ladelle. 2009. *Racism and Sexual Oppression in Anglo-America: A Genealogy*. Bloomington: Indiana University Press.

Megill, Alan. 1987. "The Reception of Foucault by Historians," in *Journal of the History of Ideas* 48, no. 1, Jan.: 117–41.

Menke, Christoph. 2003. "Two Kinds of Practice: On the Relation between Social Discipline and the Aesthetics of Existence," James Ingram (trans.), in *Constellations* 10, no. 2: 199–210.

Michon, Pascal. 2002. "Strata, Blocks, Pieces, Spirals, Elastics and Verticals: Six Figures of Time in Michel Foucault," in *Time & Society* 11, no. 2/3: 163–92.

Miller, James. 1990. "Carnivals of Atrocity: Foucault, Nietzsche, Cruelty," in *Political Theory* 18, no. 3, Aug.: 470–91.

Miller, James. 1993. *The Passion of Michel Foucault*. New York: Anchor Books.

Mills, C. Wright. 1964. *Sociology and Pragmatism*. New York: Oxford University Press.

Mommsen, Wolfgang J. 1992. *The Political and Social Theory of Max Weber: Collected Essays*. Cambridge: Cambridge University Press.

Mumford, Lewis. 1926 (1983). *The Golden Day: A Study in American Literature and Culture*. Westport, Conn.: Greenwood.

Murphey, Murray. 1968. "Kant's Children: The Cambridge Pragmatists," in *Transactions of the Charles Peirce Society* 4: 3–33.

Nealon, Jeffrey T. 2008. *Foucault Beyond Foucault: Power and Its Intensification Since 1984*. Stanford, Calif.: Stanford University Press.

Nehemas, Alexander. 1985. *Nietzsche: Life as Literature*. Cambridge: Harvard University Press.

Niebuhr, Reinhold. 1932. *Moral Man and Immoral Society*. New York: Scribner's.

Nietzsche, Friedrich. 1872 (1967). *The Birth of Tragedy.* Walter Kaufmann (trans.). New York: Vintage.

Nietzsche, Friedrich. 1874 (1980). *On the Advantage and Disadvantage of History for Life (Untimely Meditations).* Peter Preuss (trans.). Indianapolis: Hackett.

Nietzsche, Friedrich. 1878 (1995). *Human, All Too Human.* Gary Handwerk (trans.). Stanford, Calif.: Stanford University Press.

Nietzsche, Friedrich. 1886 (1989). *Beyond Good and Evil.* Walter Kaufmann (trans.). New York: Vintage.

Nietzsche, Friedrich. 1887a (1994). *On the Genealogy of Morals.* Carol Diethe (trans.). Cambridge: Cambridge University Press.

Nietzsche, Friedrich. 1887b/1882 (1974). *The Gay Science* (first and second editions). Walter Kaufmann (trans.). New York: Vintage.

Nietzsche. Friedrich. 1888 (1967). *Ecce Homo.* Ed. and trans. Walter Kaufmann. New York: Vintage.

Norris, Christopher. 1994. "'What is Enlightenment?': Kant and Foucault," in Gutting, 1994.

Novick, Peter. 1988. *That Noble Dream: The 'Objectivity Question' and the American Historical Profession.* Cambridge: Cambridge University Press.

Nussbaum, Martha. 1986. *The Fragility of Goodness: Luck and Ethics in Greek Tragedy and Philosophy.* Cambridge: Cambridge University Press.

O'Farell, Clare. 1989. *Michel Foucault: Historian or Philosopher?* London: Macmillan.

O'Leary, Timothy. 2002. *Foucault and the Art of Ethics.* New York: Continuum.

O'Neill, John. 1986. "The Disciplinary Society: from Weber to Foucault" in *The British Journal of Sociology* 37, no. 1, March: 42–60.

O'Neill, Onora. 1989. *Constructions of Reason: Explorations of Kant's Practical Philosophy.* Cambridge: Cambridge University Press.

Oksala, Johanna. 2005. *Foucault on Freedom.* Cambridge: Cambridge University Press.

Oksala, Johanna. 2010. "Violence and the Biopolitics of Modernity," in *Foucault Studies* no. 10, Nov.: 23–43.

Ong, Aiwha, and Stephen J. Collier, eds. 2005. *Global Assemblages: Technology, Politics, and Ethics as Anthropological Problems.* Malden: Blackwell.

Osborne, Thomas. 1999. "Critical Spirituality: On Ethics and Politics in the Later Foucault," in David Owen and Samantha Ashenden, *Foucault contra Habermas.* London: Sage.

Owen, David. 1994. *Maturity and Modernity: Nietzsche, Weber, Foucault and the Ambivalence of Reason.* New York: Routledge.

Owen, David. 2005. "On Genealogy and Political Theory," in *Political Theory* 33, no. 1, Feb.: 110–20.

Paras, Eric. 2006. *Foucault 2.0: Beyond Power and Knowledge.* New York: Other Press.

Parsons, Talcott. 1937 (1968). *The Structure of Social Action.* New York: Free Press.

Pasquino, Pasquale. 1991. "Theatrum Politicum: The Genealogy of Capital— Police and the State of Prosperity," in Burchell, Gordon, and Miller, 1991.

Patton, Paul. 1996. "Introduction" to Patton (ed.), *Deleuze: A Critical Reader.* Oxford: Blackwell.

Perry, Ralph Barton. 1935 (1996). *The Thought and Character of William James* (abridged one-volume edition). Nashville, Tenn.: Vanderbilt University Press.

Pihlström, Sami. 2003. *Naturalizing the Transcendental: A Pragmatic View.* Amherst, Mass.: Humanity Books.

Poovey, Mary. 1999. *A History of the Modern Fact: Problems of Knowledge in the Sciences of Wealth and Society.* Chicago: University of Chicago Press.

Poster, Mark. 1992. "Foucault, the Present, and History," in *Michel Foucault: Philosopher,* T. Armstrong (trans.). London: Harvester Wheatsheaf.

Putnam, Hilary. 1995. *Pragmatism: An Open Question.* Cambridge: Blackwell.

Putnam, Hilary. 2001 (2004). "Enlightenment and Pragmatism," in Putnam, *Ethics without Ontology.* Cambridge, Mass.: Harvard University Press.

Putnam, Hilary. 2004. *Ethics without Ontology.* Cambridge, Mass.: Harvard University Press.

Pratt, Scott. 2011. "American Power: Mary Parker Follett and Michel Foucault," in Colin Koopman (ed.), "Foucault and Pragmatism" special issue of *Foucault Studies,* no. 11, Feb.: 92–105.

Rabinow, Paul, and Gaymon Bennett. 2009. "Synthetic Biology: Ethical Ramifications 2009," in *Systems and Synthetic Biology* 3, no. 1, Oct.: 99–108.

Rabinow, Paul, and Talia Dan-Cohen. 2005. *A Machine to Make a Future: Biotech Chronicles.* Princeton, N.J.: Princeton University Press.

Rabinow, Paul, and Hubert Dreyfus. 1982 (1983). *Michel Foucault: Beyond Structuralism and Hermeneutics,* second edition. Chicago: University of Chicago Press.

Rabinow, Paul, and George Marcus, et al. 2008. *Designs for an Anthropology of the Contemporary.* Durham, N.C.: Duke University Press.

Rabinow, Paul, and Nikolas Rose. 2006. "Biopower Today," in *BioSocieties* 1: 195–217.

Rabinow, Paul. 1984. "Introduction" to Foucault, *The Foucault Reader.* Ed. P. Rabinow. New York: Pantheon.

Rabinow, Paul. 1989. *French Modern: Norms and Forms of the Social Environment.* Cambridge, Mass.: MIT Press.

Rabinow, Paul. 1994 (2000). "Introduction: A Vital Rationalist" to Canguilhem, *A Vital Rationalist.* Ed. François Delaporte. New York: Zone Books.

Rabinow, Paul. 1996. *Making PCR: A Story of Biotechnology.* Chicago: University of Chicago Press.

Rabinow, Paul. 1997. "Introduction" to EW1.

Rabinow, Paul. 1999. *French DNA: Trouble in Purgatory.* Chicago: University of Chicago Press.

Rabinow, Paul. 2003. *Anthropos Today: Reflections on Modern Equipment.* Princeton, N.J.: Princeton University Press.

Rabinow, Paul. 2008. *Marking Time: On the Anthropology of the Contemporary.* Princeton, N.J.: Princeton University Press.

Rabinow, Paul. 2009. "Foucault's Untimely Struggle: Toward a Form of Spirituality," in *Theory, Culture, & Society* 26, no. 6: 25–44. Also reprinted in Rabinow, 2011.

Rabinow, Paul. 2011a. *The Accompaniment: Assembling the Contemporary.* Chicago: University of Chicago Press.

Rabinow, Paul. 2011b. "Dewey and Foucault: What's the Problem?" in Koopman (ed.), "Foucault and Pragmatism," special issue of *Foucault Studies*, no. 11, Feb.: 11–19.

Rabinow, Paul. 2012/forthcoming. "The Problem: Contemporary Inquiry," forthcoming in *The Pluralist*, 2012.

Rajchman, John. 1985. *Michel Foucault: The Freedom of Philosophy.* New York: Columbia University Press.

Rajchman, John. 1986. "Ethics after Foucault," in *Social Text* 13/14, Winter/Spring: 165–83.

Rajchman, John. 1989. "Foucault: The Ethic and the Work," in Armstrong (ed.), *Michel Foucault: Philosopher.* Hempstead: Harvester Wheatsheaf, 1992.

Rajchman, John. 1991. *Truth and Eros: Foucault, Lacan, and the Question of Ethics.* New York: Routledge.

Rajchman, John. 2000. *The Deleuze Connections.* Cambridge, Mass.: MIT Press.

Reardon, Jenny. 2004. *Race to the Finish.* Princeton, N.J.: Princeton University Press.

Reynolds, Joan. 2004. "Pragmatic Humanism in Foucault's Later Work," in *Canadian Journal of Political Science* 37: 951–77.

Rockmore, Tom. 2002. "The Epistemological Promise of Pragmatism," in Aboulafia, 2002a.

Rockmore, Tom. 2007. *Kant and Idealism.* New Haven, Conn.: Yale University Press.

Rorty, Richard. 1979. *Philosophy and the Mirror of Nature*. Princeton, N.J.: Princeton University Press.

Rorty, Richard. 1980 (1982). "Pragmatism, Relativism, and Irrationalism," in Rorty, *Consequences of Pragmatism*. Minneapolis: University of Minnesota Press.

Rorty, Richard. 1981a. "Beyond Nietzsche and Marx," in *London Review of Books* 3, no. 3, Feb. 19: 5–6.

Rorty, Richard. 1981b (1982). "Method, Social Science, and Social Hope," in Rorty, *Consequences of Pragmatism*. Minneapolis: University of Minnesota Press.

Rorty, Richard. 1989. *Contingency, Irony, and Solidarity*. Cambridge: Cambridge University Press.

Rorty, Richard. 1995a (1998). "Is Truth a Goal of Inquiry? Davidson vs. Wright," in Rorty, *Truth and Progress: Philosophical Papers, Volume 3*. Cambridge: Cambridge University Press.

Rorty, Richard. 1995b (1998). "Habermas, Derrida, and the Functions of Philosophy," in Rorty, *Truth and Progress: Philosophical Papers, Volume 3*. Cambridge: Cambridge University Press.

Rorty, Richard. 2000a. "Universality and Truth," in Robert Brandom (ed.), *Rorty and His Critics*. Cambridge: Blackwell.

Rorty, Richard. 2000b. "Response to Jürgen Habermas," in Robert Brandom (ed.), *Rorty and His Critics*. Cambridge: Blackwell.

Rorty, Richard. 2002. "To the Sunlit Uplands," in *London Review of Books* 24, no. 31, 31 Oct., available online at http://www.lrb.co.uk/v24/n21/print/rort01_.html.

Rorty, Richard. RRP. Richard Rorty Papers, MS-C017, Special Collections and Archives, the UC Irvine Libraries, Irvine, California.

Rose, Nikolas. 1996. "Governing 'Advanced' Liberal Democracies," in Andrew Barry, Thomas Osborne, and Nikolas Rose (eds.), *Foucault and Political Reason: Liberalism, Neo-liberalism, and Rationalities of Government*. Chicago: University of Chicago Press.

Rose, Nikolas. 1999. *Powers of Freedom: Reframing Political Thought*. Cambridge: Cambridge University Press.

Rose, Nikolas. 2006. *The Politics of Life Itself: Biomedicine, Power, and Subjectivity in the Twenty-First Century*. Princeton, N.J.: Princeton University Press.

Rosenbaum, Stuart. 2002. "Sustaining Pragmatism's Critique of Epistemology," in Paul Bube (ed.), *Conversations with Pragmatism*. New York: Rodopi.

Roth, Michael S. 2006. "Nietzsche in France," in Lawrence Kritzman, *The Columbia History of Twentieth-Century French Thought*. New York: Columbia University Press.

Roudinesco, Elizabeth. 2005 (2008). *Philosophy in Turbulent Times: Canguilhem, Sartre, Foucault, Althusser, Deleuze, Derrida*. Wiliam McCuaig (trans.). New York: Columbia University Press.

Royce, Josiah. 1891. "Review of Dewey's *Outlines of a Critical Theory of Ethics*," in *International Journal of Ethics* 1, 1891.

Saar, Martin. 2002. "Genealogy and Subjectivity," in *European Journal of Philosophy* 10, no. 2: 231–45.

Sartre, Jean-Paul. 1966. "Jean-Paul Sartre répond," in *L'Arc* 30: 87–96.

Sawicki, Jana. 1994. "Foucault, Feminism, and Questions of Identity," in Gutting, 1994.

Sawicki, Jana. 2005. "Queering Foucault and the Subject of Feminism," in Gutting, 2005.

Scaff, Lawrence A. 1989 (1991). *Fleeing the Iron Cage: Culture, Politics, and Modernity in the Thought of Max Weber.* Berkeley: University of California Press.

Schaff, Kory P. 2004. "Agency and Institutional Rationality: Foucault's Critique of Normativity," in *Philosophy and Social Criticism* 30, no. 1, Jan.: 51–71.

Schmidt, James, and Thomas Wartenberg. 1994. "Foucault's Enlightenment: Critique, Revolution, and Fashioning the Self," in Kelly, 1994a.

Scott, Charles. 1990. *The Question of Ethics: Nietzsche, Foucault, Heidegger.* Bloomington: Indiana University Press.

Scott, Charles. 2011. "Ethics at the Boundary: Beginning with Foucault" in *Journal of Speculative Philosophy* 25, no. 2: 203–12.

Seigfried, Hans. 2001. "Kants transzendental Wahrheit pragmatisch überholt," in Volker Gerhardt et al. (eds.), *Kant und die Berliner Aufklärung: Akten des IX. International Kant-Kongresses.* Berlin: Walter de Gruyter.

Skinner, Quentin. 1998. *Liberty Before Liberalism.* Cambridge: Cambridge University Press.

Skinner, Quentin. 2009. "A Genealogy of the Modern State," in *Proceedings of the British Academy* 162: 325–70.

Sleat, Matthew. 2007. "On the Relationship between Truth and Liberal Politics," in *Inquiry* 50, no. 3, June: 288–305.

Sluga, Hans. 2002. "Foucault Rethinks the Genealogy of Morals," in Gertraud Diem-Wille et al. (eds.), *Weltanschauungen des Wiener Fin de Siècle.* Frankfurt: Peter Lang.

Sluga, Hans. 2005. "Foucault's Encounter with Heidegger and Nietzsche," in Gutting, 2005.

Sluga, Hans. 2010. "'I am Simply a Nietzschean'" in Timothy O'Leary and Christopher Falzon (eds.), *Foucault and Philosophy,* 36–59. Cambridge: Blackwell.

Smith, Daniel W. 2001. "The Doctrine of Univocity: Deleuze's Ontology of Immanence," in Mary Bryden (ed.), *Deleuze and Religion.* New York: Routledge.

Star, Susan Leigh, and Martha Lampland, eds. 2008. *Standards and Their Stories:*

How Quantifying, Classifying, and Formalizing Practices Shape Everyday Life. Ithaca, N.Y.: Cornell University Press.

Stone, Brad. 2011. "Prophetic Pragmatism and the Practices of Freedom: On Cornel West's Foucauldian Methodology," in Colin Koopman (ed.), "Foucault and Pragmatism," special issue of *Foucault Studies*, no. 11, Feb.: 92–105.

Strawson, P. F. 1966. *The Bounds of Sense.* London: Metheun.

Stuhr, John. 1997. *Genealogical Pragmatism: Philosophy, Experience, and Community.* Albana: SUNY.

Stuhr, John. 2003. *Pragmatism, Postmodernism, and the Future of Philosophy.* New York: Routledge.

Swedberg, Richard. 2005. *The Max Weber Dictionary.* Stanford, Calif.: Stanford University Press.

Szakolaczai, Arpad. 1998. *Max Weber and Michel Foucault: Parallel Life-Works.* New York: Routledge.

Takacs, Adam. 2004. "Between Theory and History: On the Interdisciplinary Practice in Michel Foucault's Work," in *MLN* 119: 869–84.

Taylor, Charles. 1984. "Foucault on Freedom and Truth," in Hoy, 1986a.

Taylor, Dianna. 2003. "Practicing Politics with Foucault and Kant: Toward a Critical Life," in *Philosophy and Social Criticism* 29, no. 3: 259–80.

Taylor, Dianna. 2009. "Normativity and Normalization," in *Foucault Studies*, no. 7, Sept.: 45–63.

Tejera, V. 1980. "The Human Sciences in Dewey, Foucault and Buchler," in *Southern Journal of Philosophy* 18: 221–35.

Thayer, H. S. 1968 (1991). *Meaning and Action: A Critical History of Pragmatism,* second edition. Indianapolis: Hackett.

Thompson, Kevin. 2003. "Forms of Resistance: Foucault on Tactical Reversal and Self-Formation," in *Continental Philosophy Review* 36: 113–38.

Thompson, Kevin. 2008. "Historicity and Transcendentality: Foucault, Cavaillès, and the Phenomenology of the Concept," in *History & Theory* 47, Feb.: 1–18.

Thompson, Kevin. 2010. "Response to Colin Koopman's 'Historical Critique of Transcendental Critique in Foucault: Two Kantian Lineages'," in *Foucault Studies*, no. 8, Feb.: 122–28.

Tsing, Anna Lowenhaupt. 2004. *Friction: An Ethnography of Global Connection.* Princeton, N.J.: Princeton University Press.

Tully, James. 1999. "To Think and Act Differently: Foucault's Four Reciprocal Objections to Habermas' Theory," in Ashenden and Owen, 1999.

Turner, Bryan. 1987. "The Rationalisation of the Body: Reflections on Modernity and Discipline," in S. Whimster and S. Lash (eds.), *Max Weber, Rationality and Modernity.* London: Allen and Unwin.

Vattimo, Gianni. 1985 (2002). *Nietzsche: An Introduction.* Nicholas Martin (trans.). London: Athlone.

Veyne, Paul. 1978 (1997). "Foucault Revolutionizes History," Catherine Porter (trans.), in Arnold Davidson (ed.), *Foucault and His Interlocutors.* Chicago: University of Chicago Press.

Veyne, Paul. 2008 (2010). *Foucault: His Thought, His Character.* Janet Lloyd (trans.). Cambridge: Polity.

Visker, Rudi. 1999. *Truth and Singularity: Taking Foucault into Phenomenology.* Dordrecht: Kluwer.

Walzer, Michael. 1983. "The Politics of Michel Foucault," in Hoy, 1986a.

Weber, Max. 1905 (2003). *The Protestant Ethic and the Spirit of Capitalism.* Talcott Parsons (trans.). Mineola, N.Y.: Dover.

West, Cornel. 1989. *The American Evasion of Philosophy.* Madison: University of Wisconsin Press.

Weymans, Wim. 2009. "Revising Foucault's Model of Modernity and Exclusion: Gauchet and Swain on Madness and Democracy," in *Thesis Eleven* 98, no. 1, Aug.: 33–51.

Wiener, Philip P. 1946. "Logical Significance of the History of Thought," in *Journal of the History of Ideas* 7, no. 3, June: 366–73.

Williams, Bernard. 1981. "Nietzsche's Centaur," in *London Review of Books,* 17 June: 17.

Williams, Bernard. 1985. *Ethics and the Limits of Philosophy.* Cambridge, Mass.: Harvard University Press.

Williams, Bernard. 1993 (1994). *Shame and Necessity.* Berkeley: University of California Press.

Williams, Bernard. 2000 (2006). "Philosophy as a Humanistic Discipline," in Williams, *Philosophy as a Humanistic Discipline.* Princeton, N.J.: Princeton University Press.

Williams, Bernard. 2002. *Truth and Truthfulness: An Essay in Genealogy.* Princeton, N.J.: Princeton University Press.

Williams, Bernard. 2005. *In the Beginning Was the Deed: Realism and Moralism in Political Argument.* Princeton, N.J.: Princeton University Press.

Wilson, Holly. 2006. *Kant's Pragmatic Anthropology: Its Origin, Meaning, And Critical Significance.* Albany: SUNY.

Wolin, Richard. 1986. "Foucault's Aesthetic Decisionism," in *Telos,* no. 67, Spring: 71–86.

Zaloom, Caitlin. 2006. *Out of the Pits: Traders and Technology from Chicago to London.* Chicago: University of Chicago Press.

Index

Adams, John Quincy, 237
Agamben, Giorgio, 10, 159, 232–33, 272n8
Allen, Amy, 206–208, 262, 284n6, 303n6; on Foucault-Habermas debates, 221–24, 226
Allen, Barry, 72, 277n37, 281n20
Althusser, Louis, 14, 21, 47, 132
anthropology, 8, 115, 199, 226, 239–41; of the contemporary, 122, 126, 226
appropriationist historiography. *See* historiography, appropriationist
archaeology, 6, 13–20, 29, 30–55, 85, 93, 101, 110, 148; expansion into genealogy, 30–44, 131–33, 274n19, 274n22, 275n27, 278n60; as problematizational, 44–48; proposed alternative forms of, 36; and transcendentality, 110–12, 286n47
articulation, 1–4, 24, 26, 27, 39, 45, 50, 92, 151, 179, 245, 253, 263
assemblage, 4, 102–103, 107–108, 156, 241, 257. *See also* complexity
autonomy. *See* freedom, as autonomy

Benhabib, Seyla, 218–19, 239, 256, 260, 264

Bernauer, James, 158
Bernstein, Richard J., 231, 250, 256
biopolitics and biopower, 6–7, 37, 89–90, 101–102, 148, 152, 157, 167, 171, 173, 178, 183, 219, 232–33, 238, 298n48

bodies and pleasures. *See* pleasure
Bourdieu, Pierre, 123, 126
Braudel, Fernand, 21, 132
Brown, Wendy, 141–42, 145
Butler, Judith, 141–42, 172–73, 230

Canguilhem, Georges, 14, 21, 47, 56, 122–23, 131–33, 150
care of the self. *See* self, self-care
Collingwood, R. G., 227, 290n7
complexity, 12, 18, 19, 21, 23, 35–39, 47–48, 98–109, 128, 143, 156, 200, 207, 228, 255, 263, 266, 275n27; Bourdieu's use of, 123; exemplified, 234–41; Foucault's genealogical use of, 19, 98–109; Hacking's use of, 123–25; Rabinow's use of, 122–23
conditions of possibility, 1, 15, 17, 19, 21, 24, 26, 29, 33–34, 45, 93, 105,

110, 123, 124, 127, 161, 162, 189,
231, 249–52, 253–55, 270; historicity
versus transcendentality of, 21, 34, 85,
110–21, 250, 286n47; philosophical
problem of 'conditioned conditioners,'
103, 109–28
contextualism, 221, 223, 231, 239; compatibility with universality, 252, 255,
261; Habermasian notion of, 258–66
contingency, 4, 12, 19, 23, 98–109, 156,
223; anti-inevitability thesis, 5, 140;
Bourdieu's use of, 123; Foucault's
genealogical use of, 19, 21, 37, 43–
44, 48, 98–109, 128; Hacking's use of,
123–25; necessity and, 16, 120–21,
129 (see also necessity); Rabinow's use
of, 122–23; 'the that' versus 'the how'
(i.e., the fact of contingency versus
the history of contingencies), 44, 129–
30, 140–48 (see also anti-inevitability
thesis); universality and, see contingent universals; Williams's use of,
69–70
contingent universals, 19, 223–24, 228–
41, 252, 261–62, 266–69
contradiction (as a critical operation,
overvalued), 76–83, 137, 168, 184
counter-conduct, 152, 177–78, 299n61
critical inquiry, 5, 12, 17, 19, 23, 44,
99, 230, 266, 269; two dimensions
or tasks of (problematizing and reconstructing), 184–85, 216, 217–21,
228, 267
critical theory (Frankfurt School), 11,
19, 23, 90, 140, 155, 180, 181, 190,
210–16, 217–19, 229–31, 239, 252–
66, 266–69; compatibility with genealogical critique, 11–12, 19, 23, 130,
140, 180–81, 210–16, 220–28, 262–69
critique, 2, 5, 7, 14–19, 21, 85, 195, 217,
249–51, 253, 267; historical varieties
of, 121–28; Kant's notion of, 15; mo-

dernity as an object of, see modernity;
Nietzsche's notion, 32–34; as problematization, see problematization;
transcendental versus historical, 111–
21; without judgment, 93–98. See also
conditions of possibility; critical inquiry
crypto-normativity, 90, 185, 214
cultural critical philosophy, 12, 23, 26–
27, 274n11
Cusset, François, 10
Cutrofello, Andrew, 110

Darwin, Charles, 69, 120
Daston, Lorraine, 122, 125, 126
Davidson, Arnold, 30, 54, 84, 131,
271n7, 272n10, 279n78, 288n70,
290n2, 294n66, 299n61
DeLanda, Manuel, 133, 286n37
delegation strategy (for genealogy and
critical theoretical pragmatism), 181,
216, 222–24, 264, 266–69, 303n6
Deleuze, Gilles, 14, 21, 31, 33, 43, 47,
103, 126, 130, 187, 267, 292n32; on
Foucault, 150, 183; on Nietzschean
affirmativism, 75–80, 82; on Nietzschean critique, 33–34; on problematization, 132–40
Derrida, Jacques, 10, 169; criticisms of
Foucault, 155, 158, 160–63
desire, 174, 187, 203
Dewey, John, 11–12, 38, 181, 198, 210,
220, 226, 228, 231, 253, 254, 255,
256, 257, 261, 266, 268, 269, 291n20,
292n32; Kantian inheritance, 250–52;
reconstructive methodology, 241–52,
307n89
dialectics, 42, 76–83, 135–37
discipline and disciplinary power, 6–7,
22–23, 37, 89–90, 92, 94, 96–97, 105–
106, 148, 178, 179, 204, 209, 234; in
Foucault's genealogy of modern pow-

ers and freedoms, 159–60, 169–75,
182, 185–88 (*see also* liberation)
discursive formation, 31, 36, 41, 50, 54
dispositif, 4, 45, 53, 175, 232, 233,
271n4, 304n35
Dreyfus, Hubert, 9, 30, 35, 48, 94, 274n22
Duchamp, Marcel, 103–104

emergence, 2, 24, 39–44, 122, 147
empiricism, 62, 110, 113, 118, 126–27,
138; Foucault's empiricism, 110
episteme, 31, 32, 36, 38, 39, 40, 44, 53
ethics, 23, 55–56, 182–216; commitments in Foucault's, 202–209; Foucault's statuary of ethical antiquity
(metaphor), 202; orientations and
commitments distinguished, 189–90;
reconstructive ethics, 181, 223, 241–
66; in relation to politics in Foucault,
see politics; responsive ethics, 182–85;
self-transformative ethics, *see* self, self-
transformation. *See also* morality
exclusion. *See* modernity, exclusion, as
the logic of
experimentalism, 16, 137–39, 152, 165,
174–78, 194–95, 201–202, 218–19,
262 (*see also* self, self-transformation);
Dewey's account of, 246–51

Faubion, James, 193, 200, 301n45
Flynn, Thomas, 43
Foucault, Michel
CdF course lectures: *Security, Territory,*
Population (1978 CdF course lectures), 177; *The Birth of Biopolitics*
(1979 CdF course lectures), 112,
177; *The Hermeneutics of the Subject*
(1982 CdF course lectures), 196–
97; *The Government of Self and Oth-*
ers (1983 CdF course lectures), 27–
28; *The Courage of Truth* (1984 CdF
course lectures), 38

discussion of major works [note that
indexed references to Foucault's
major publications are only to explicit discussion of the texts and do
not include all citations and refer-
ences]: *History of Madness* (1961),
17, 22, 45, 46, 51, 52, 54, 132, 157–
63, 165–69, 182, 279n81; *The Birth*
of the Clinic (1963), 51, 54, 112, 165;
The Order of Things (1966), 13, 39,
40, 46, 50–54, 112; *The Archaeology*
of Knowledge (1969), 31, 34, 36, 41,
50, 51, 53–55, 111, 112; *Discipline*
and Punish (1975), 21, 22, 26, 35,
39, 43, 45, 46, 51, 53, 54, 55, 96,
105–106, 149–51, 156, 160, 161–
62, 165, 167, 169–74, 182, 185–89,
234, 279n81; *The Will to Know: The*
History of Sexuality, volume 1 (1976),
2–4, 53, 54, 149, 151, 165, 167,
171, 185–89, 232, 234, 279n81; *The*
Use of Pleasure: The History of Sexu-
ality, volume 2 (1984), 55, 95, 149,
151, 191, 196; *The Care of the Self:*
The History of Sexuality, volume 3
(1984), 52, 55, 149, 151, 196
discussion of themes, methods, concepts, and arguments: compatibility with critical theory and pragmatism via delegation strategy,
217–28; compatibility with critical theory and pragmatism via
the idea of contingent universals,
228–41; contingency and complexity in problematization, 109–
21; ethical commitments, 202–209;
ethical contributions as responsive, 182–85; ethics as oriented by
self-transformation, 189–202; history of modern discipline and liberation, 169–74; history of modern
madness and reason, 165–69; his-

tory of modern moralities, 185–89; history of modernity, through category of reciprocal incompatibility, 163–65; influence of Deleuze, 133–40; influence of Kant, 13–16; influence of Nietzsche and Kant, 32–34; influences proximate in contemporary French context, 130–33; method as critical in Kant's sense, 126–28; method as critical problematization, 16–19; method as political and philosophical, 26–30; method in *The Will to Know*, 2–4; method of problematization, 44–48; method of problematization as aiming toward reconstruction, 140–48; methods of archaeology and genealogy, their relation specified, 30–44, 49–51; normative deficits of ethical and reconstructive work, 209–16; normative modesty of genealogical-historical work, 87–98; periodization of work in ethics and politics, 148–53, 175–78; periodization of works via hourglass of threads metaphor, 51–56; reception of work, in North America via the "French Theory" combine, 8–13; reception of work as facilitated by critiques from Habermas and Derrida, 154–56. *See also* archaeology; biopolitics and biopower; discipline and disciplinary power; ethics; genealogy; politics; problematization

Fraser, Nancy, 267; criticisms of Foucault, 88–91, 95, 212–14

freedom, 23, 94–96, 148–53, 157–65, 169–81, 185–87, 191–202, 214, 243, 295n67, 298n42, 298n48; as autonomy, 152, 169, 171–75, 194, 206–208, 221–23, 298n42; as liberation, *see* liberation; as a practice, 194, 295n67; as a process (rather than a capacity),
206–209; as resistance, 4, 152–53, 171–73, 177, 178, 197, 207–208, 299n61; as self-transformation, *see* self, self-transformation

French theory, 10, 11, 79, 137, 154. *See also* Foucault, discussion of themes, methods, concepts, and arguments, reception of work, in North America via the "French Theory" combine

Galison, Peter, 122, 125, 126

genealogy: aims of, 129–30, 140–48; archaeology and, 30–44, 49–51; critical (i.e., Kantian), 16–19, 33–34, 109–21; Foucault's use of, 44–48, 98–121; methodological role, 5; of modernity, *see* modernity; Nietzsche's use of, 73–83; normative valences of, 62–64, 87–98, 209–16; parlor game demonstration of the current fashionability of, 271n6; problematization and, *see* problematization; reconstruction and, *see* reconstruction and reconstructive methodology; revising the received (and misleading) view of, 6–13; specification of, 1–7, 24–30, 44–48, 98–121; temporality and spatiality in, 43; three modes of (subversion, vindication, and problematization), 58–62; tradition of, 24–26, 58–62; Williams's use of, 65–73

genetic fallacy (and genetic argumentation), 62–64, 71, 74, 79, 80, 87–91

Geuss, Raymond, 147–48

governmentality, 149–52

Gros, Frédéric, 193, 286n51

Gutting, Gary, 160, 288n73, 297n33

Habermas, Jürgen, 11, 12, 169, 180, 181, 198, 210, 231, 234, 252–66; compatibility with Foucault, 215, 263–69; criticisms of Foucault, 74, 90–91, 95, 155, 158, 160–63, 214; Foucault-

Habermas debates, 220–28; genealogical history, adoption of, 265–66; self-avowed pragmatism of, 250, 253, 261–62; reconstructive methodology of, 253–54; universality and, 229, 257–60

Hacking, Ian, 9, 103, 104, 235, 272n8; discussions of Foucault, 109, 110, 166; discussions of Williams, 73; as genealogist, 25, 84–86; historical ontology, 85–86, 109–10; on standards of measure, 236–37; on styles of reasoning, 124–25

Han-Pile, Beatrice, 110, 117, 169–70, 277n46

Heidegger, Martin, 14, 47, 117, 273n22

Heyes, Cressida, 199, 200

historical epistemology, 122, 126, 288n80

historical ontology, 25, 85–86, 109–10, 122, 124–26

historicity, 19, 28, 29, 39, 41, 115, 226, 232

historiography: appropriationist, 17, 79, 115, 121, 122, 147, 212, 288n78; critical, 24–30, 97, 111–28. See also genealogy; history; history of the present

history, 1, 2–5, 18–19, 24–30, 39–44, 44–48, 59, 61, 70, 82, 85, 88, 118, 122–27, 140, 144–46, 267; as act (verb) and object (noun), 99. See also genealogy

history of the present, 20, 24–30, 44–48, 98

Honneth, Axel, 181, 253, 256, 260, 267

hourglass of threads (metaphor), 48–52

Hoy, David, 43, 140, 145, 152–53, 172, 233, 283n69; on Foucault-Habermas debates, 225

Huffer, Lynne, 193, 279n81, 297n35

human rights, 238–39, 241

Hume, David, 69, 115, 283n69

ideology critique, 97, 135, 264

inquiry. See critical inquiry

integration strategy (for genealogy and critical theoretical pragmatism), 221–24, 303n6

intensification, 27, 48

James, William, 11, 69–70, 73, 198, 245, 250, 292n32; pragmatism as a method only, 248

Kant, Immanuel, 7, 85, 109–21, 124, 127, 134, 194–95, 217, 221, 231, 244, 267, 269; critique in, 15, 17, 20, 21, 111–17, 128; influence on critical theory, 252; influence on pragmatism, 249–52; source for Foucault, 13–16, 32–34

knowledge, 4, 29, 31, 32, 52, 196–97; depth savoir, 33. See also power-knowledge

Laclau, Ernesto, 230

liberalism, 67, 82–83, 106–107, 178, 305n52; and neoliberalism, 177–78

liberation, 23, 94–96, 152–53, 157, 159, 162, 163–65, 169–75, 176–80, 186, 187–88, 208–209, 219, 223. See also freedom

MacIntyre, Alasdair, 74–76, 82, 204

madness, 46, 155–69; the mad philosopher, 168–69; and reason, 160–61, 166–69; and unreason, see unreason

Mahmood, Saba, 199, 200

McCarthy, Thomas, 223, 229, 231, 233, 254, 256, 260; on Foucault-Habermas debates, 225

McWhorter, Ladelle, 84, 201, 272n10

measurement, standards of. See standards of measure

metaphysics, recent attempts at a fashionable revival of an unworkable proposal for contemporary philosophy, 269 method and methodology, 4, 10, 20–23, 25, 29, 88–90, 97, 110, 233, 248, 252; method (or analytic) versus concept distinction, 6–7, 272n8, 304n31; potentiality for providing contemporary philosophy a forward motion and momentum, 269–70. *See also* genealogy, archaeology and; problematization; reconstruction and reconstructive methodology

modernity, 4, 17–18, 22–23; exclusion, as the logic of, 157–63; Foucault's accounts of, 154–75, 185–89; as practices rather than as epoch or era, 156–57; purification (or reciprocal incompatibility), as the logic of, 157, 163–65 (*see also* reciprocal incompatibility); Weberian accounts of, 157–63, 180–81, 221

morality, 33, 93–94, 191–92, 194–215, 245, 255; fascist (or control morality), 187; freespirit (or liberation morality), 187; genealogy of modern morality in Foucault, 185–89; Nietzsche on, 73–82; Williams on, 66–71. *See also* ethics

necessity, 39, 43, 103, 118, 119–21, 251–52, 255–56, 269; and contingency, 5, 16, 19, 144, 229 (*see also* contingency); and universality, 111–14, 119, 229–31, 234, 237–38

Nehemas, Alexander, 80–82

niches, 103–105. *See also* vectors

Nietzsche, Friedrich, 2, 5, 6, 7, 17, 18, 20, 21, 24–25, 60, 120, 129, 137, 160, 165, 167, 197, 206, 267, 273n22, 280n13, 283n69; affirmativism in, 76–83; critique in, 32–34; Foucault on, 32, 39, 168, 275n27, 288n78; genealogy in, 73–83; Kant and, 33; normative ambition of, 61, 64, 73–76, 82–83, 87; source for Foucault, 14, 32–34, 55, 131, 132; source for Williams, 66

normativity, 61–64, 189–90, 218, 267; compatible with genealogy, 140–48, 209–16, 220, 225–28; in critical theory, 252–66; Foucault's genealogy not ambitious about, 88–98; in pragmatism, 241–52

O'Farrell, Clare, 165

Oksala, Johanna, 110

O'Neill, Onora, 250

panopticon, 162, 187

parrhesia, 190, 203

Peirce, Charles Santiago, 69–70, 73, 245, 246, 250, 261, 291n20

phenomenology, 110–11, 117, 286n47

philosophy, 1, 12, 19, 23; cultural critical, *see* cultural critical philosophy; in relation to politics in Foucault, 26–31, 43–48, 274n22; way of life, as a, 190, 193, 203. *See also* thought, the severe work of

pleasure, 165, 177, 190, 203

politics, 142–46, 173, 184, 207–208, 267; in relation to ethics in Foucault, 55–56, 148–53, 175–81; in relation to philosophy in Foucault, *see* philosophy. *See also* power

Poovey, Mary, 122

postmodernism (although usually not a helpful term), 10–11, 73, 140, 154–56

power, 4, 9, 23, 29, 31, 32, 185–87, 221–22, 242; as an analytical category, 9, 272n8; depth *pouvoir*, 33; and freedom, 148–53, 157–63, 169–81; no "theory" of, in Foucault, 9, 37–38, 272n11. *See also* biopolitics and biopower; discipline and disciplinary power; power-knowledge

power-knowledge, 29, 34–38, 48, 102, 105–106, 150, 170, 219, 275n27; coproduction of, 36–37; multiplicity of vectors, 31, 34–39, 41–44, 131. *See also* biopolitics and biopower; discipline and disciplinary power; knowledge practices, and problematizations, 98–109

pragmatism, 241–52; compatible with genealogy, 11–12, 19, 23, 130, 140, 180–81, 210–16, 220–28, 266–69; as critical (i.e., Kantian), 217, 249–52; as reconstructive method, 243–47

present, the, 1, 2, 24–30; the history of, *see* history of the present

problem, as analytical category. *See* problematization

problematization, 1, 2, 16–19, 60–62; as act (verb) and object (noun), 98–102; centrality for Foucault's genealogy, 44–48; clarifying and intensifying, 98–101; enabling and disabling of practices, 100; expressed throughout Foucault's work, 46–47; fraught or dangerous, 92, 94; mode of critique, 16–19, 109–21; mode of distinctive genealogy, 83–86; of modernity, *see* modernity; normativity not a goal of, 87–98 (*see also* normativity); practices and, 103–109; reconstruction and, 140–48, 209–16, 217–28, 266–70; specification of, 98–103

punishment, 6, 26, 45, 93, 95, 97, 106, 164, 167; prison and, 8, 22, 35, 39, 56, 88, 96, 98, 113, 119, 143, 144, 159–60, 162, 169, 180, 234, 249

purification. *See* modernity, purification, as the logic of

Rabinow, Paul, 9, 30, 35, 39, 84–86, 89, 94, 95, 103, 122–23, 126, 139, 141, 145–47, 194–95, 235, 243, 274n22, 301n45; anthropology of the contemporary, 122–23

Rajchman, John, 133, 165, 183, 193

reason, 155–69; and madness, *see* madness, and reason

reciprocal incompatibility, 163–65. *See also* modernity, purification, as the logic of

reconstruction and reconstructive methodology, 12, 21, 22, 23, 182–85; in critical theory, 252–66; genealogy's invitation to, 140–48; in pragmatism, 243–47

regulation. *See* biopolitics and biopower

resistance, 4, 152–53, 172–73, 177–78, 207–208

Rorty, Richard, 11, 73, 89, 180, 181, 243, 245, 249, 257, 266, 292n32; criticisms of Foucault, 214–15, 242; criticisms of Habermas, 255–56; criticisms of Williams, 68–70; liberalism in, 82–83

Rose, Nikolas, 84, 85, 102, 103, 107, 141, 145, 152, 153, 176, 284n83

Sartre, Jean-Paul, 14, 31; criticisms of Foucault, 40–41

Sawicki, Jana, 93, 140, 145

self: self-care, 150, 151, 184, 203; self-transformation, 23, 93, 142, 153, 191–202, 206–209, 210–12, 219–20, 245–46. *See also* subject, the

sexuality, 2–4, 6, 36, 50, 56, 93, 119, 129–30, 145, 174, 234

singularity, 3, 4, 24, 50–53, 105–108, 142, 195

speculative realism, 269

standards of measure, 104, 236–38, 258; universalizability of, 119, 236–38

strategies, 3, 4, 47, 92, 96, 98, 101, 106–107, 131, 143, 189, 191, 205, 234, 238. *See also* practices, and problematizations

Strawson, P. F., 116, 288n70

subject, the, 52, 56, 148–53, 169–70, 173, 183, 196–97, 207–208; as a transformative practice, 192–93 (*see also* self, self-transformation). *See also* self subversion (mode of genealogy), 18, 20, 21, 59–60, 62, 64, 73–85, 87, 93, 95, 148, 226, 309n117

techniques, 98, 101, 102, 103, 131, 182, 189, 191, 234. *See also* practices, and problematizations
temporality, 19, 28–29, 43, 230, 231–35, 244–45, 261–62, 267; multiplicity of temporalities, 31–32, 39–44, 131–32
Thompson, Kevin, 286n47
thought, the severe work of, 1, 6, 9, 27, 31, 100, 138, 142, 146, 193, 217, 226, 270
transcendental critique. *See* critique
truth: in Foucault, 3, 13–14, 28, 32, 109, 196–97; in Hacking, 124; in Nietzsche, 74–76, 78, 80, 276n28; in Williams, 65–73
Tsing, Anna Lowenhaupt, 240–41, 295n2

universality: contingency and, *see* contingent universals; necessity and, *see* necessity; temporality of, 231–35;

universalizing versus universalism, 19, 228–41, 249–52, 255–63, 266–69
unreason, 51, 158, 166–69

vectors, 31, 34–39, 41–44, 51, 101, 103–108, 125, 131, 179. *See also* niches
Veyne, Paul, 14, 110, 273n22; iceberg metaphor for Foucault's historical method, 126–28
vindication (mode of genealogy), 18, 20, 21, 59–60, 62, 64, 65–73, 83–85, 87, 93, 95, 226, 309n117

Weber, Max, 295n4; Weberian theories of modernity, 157–63, 180–81, 221
West, Cornel, 243
Williams, Bernard, 2, 6, 7, 18, 20, 25, 60, 62, 129, 204, 205, 206, 280n13; genealogy in, 65–73; limits of modern moral philosophy, 191; normative ambition of, 61, 64, 67–68, 71, 87; truth and truthfulness according to, 65–73, 276n28

Žižek, Slavoj, 230

COLIN KOOPMAN is Assistant Professor of Philosophy
at the University of Oregon.

His first book is titled *Pragmatism as Transition: Historicity
and Hope in James, Dewey, and Rorty.*

He has written articles on various strands of genealogy
for *Critical Inquiry, Constellations, The Review of Metaphysics,
Journal of the Philosophy of History, History of the Human
Sciences, Foucault Studies,* and elsewhere.

CPSIA information can be obtained
at www.ICGtesting.com
Printed in the USA
JSHW022001030322
23563JS00001B/33